Francis Bacon

Human Presence

National Portrait Gallery, London

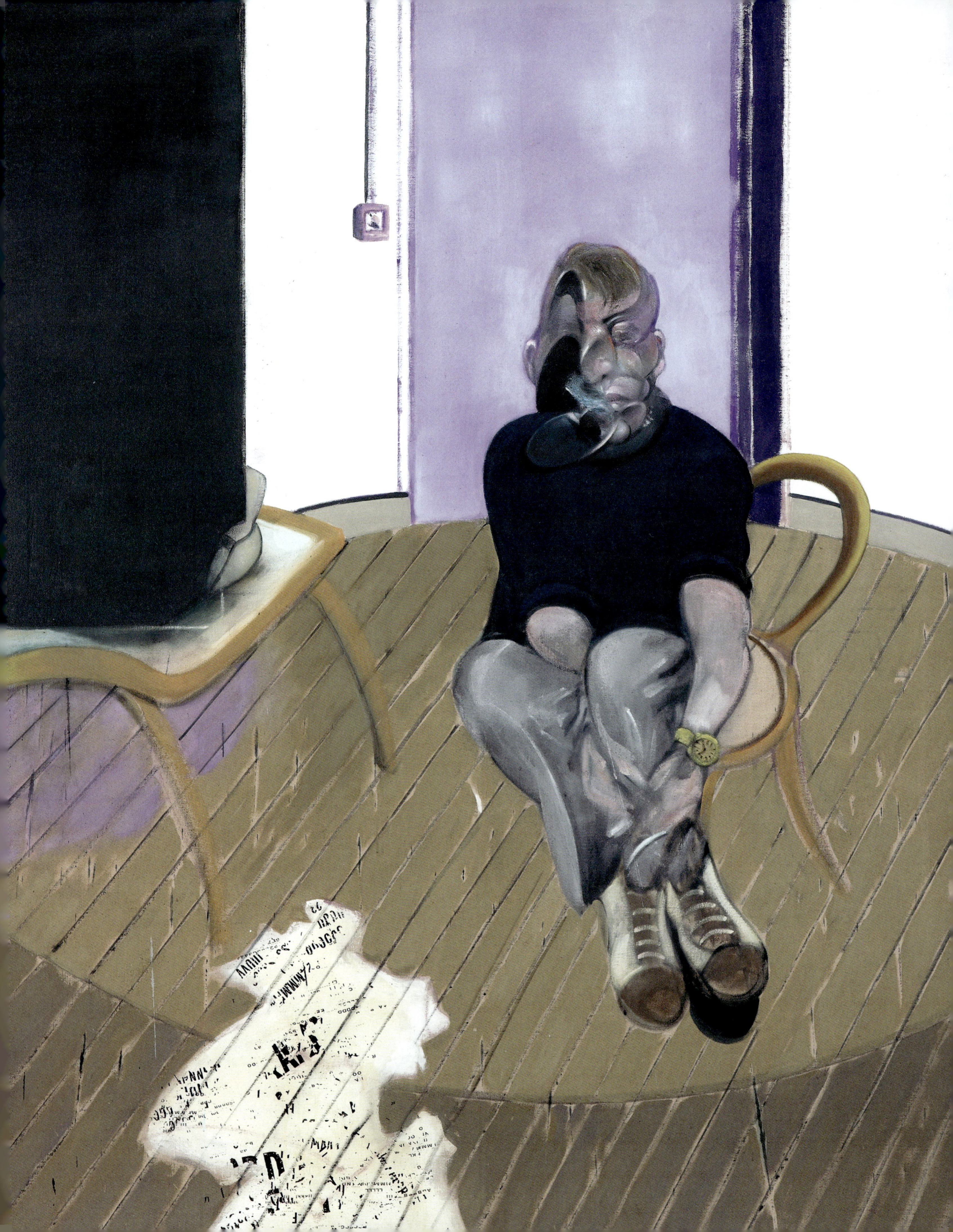

Francis Bacon

Human Presence

Rosie Broadley

With contributions by Georgia Atienza,
Tanya Bentley, Richard Calvocoressi,
James Hall, Martin Harrison,
Carol Jacobi, John Maybury,
Sophie Pretorius and Gregory Salter

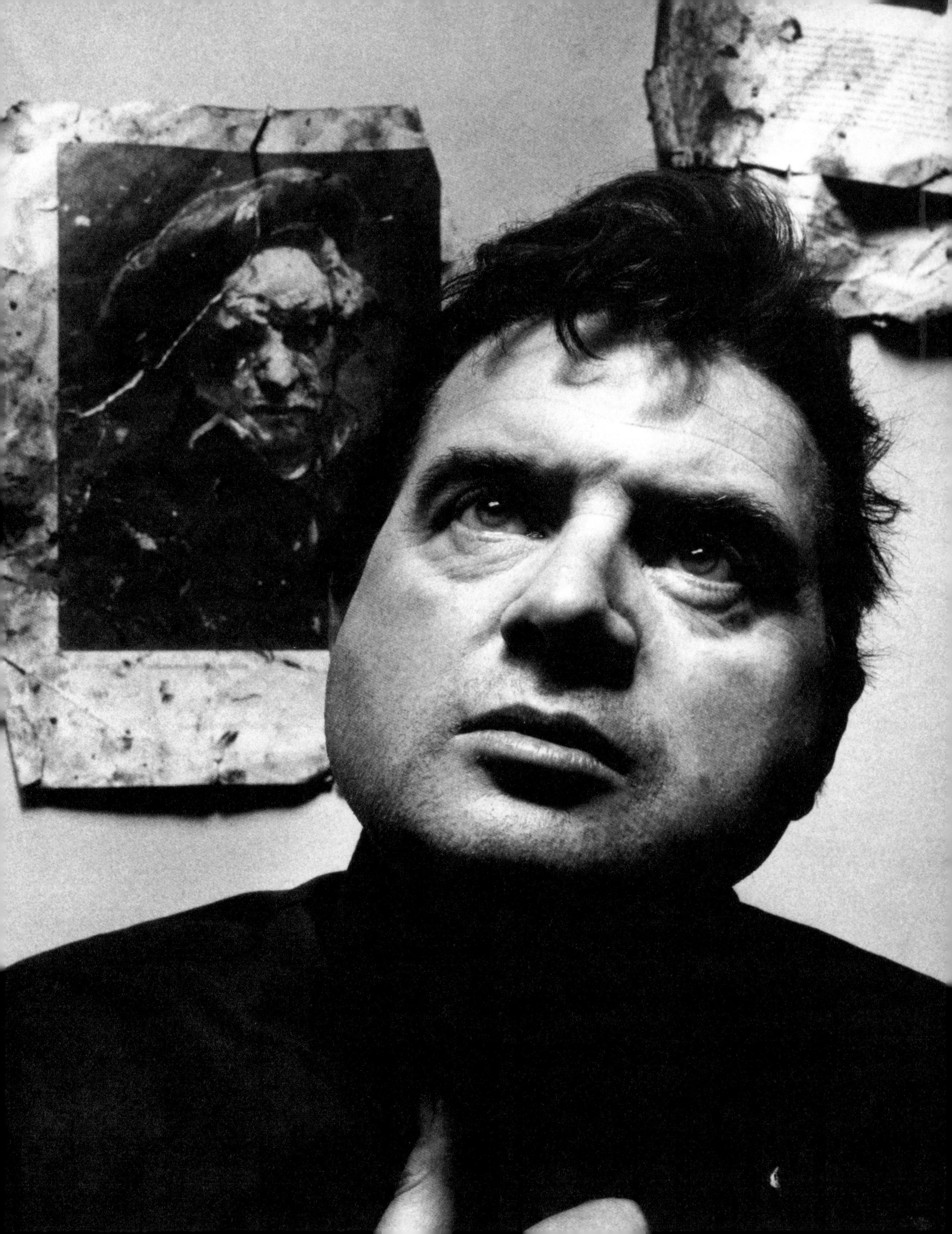

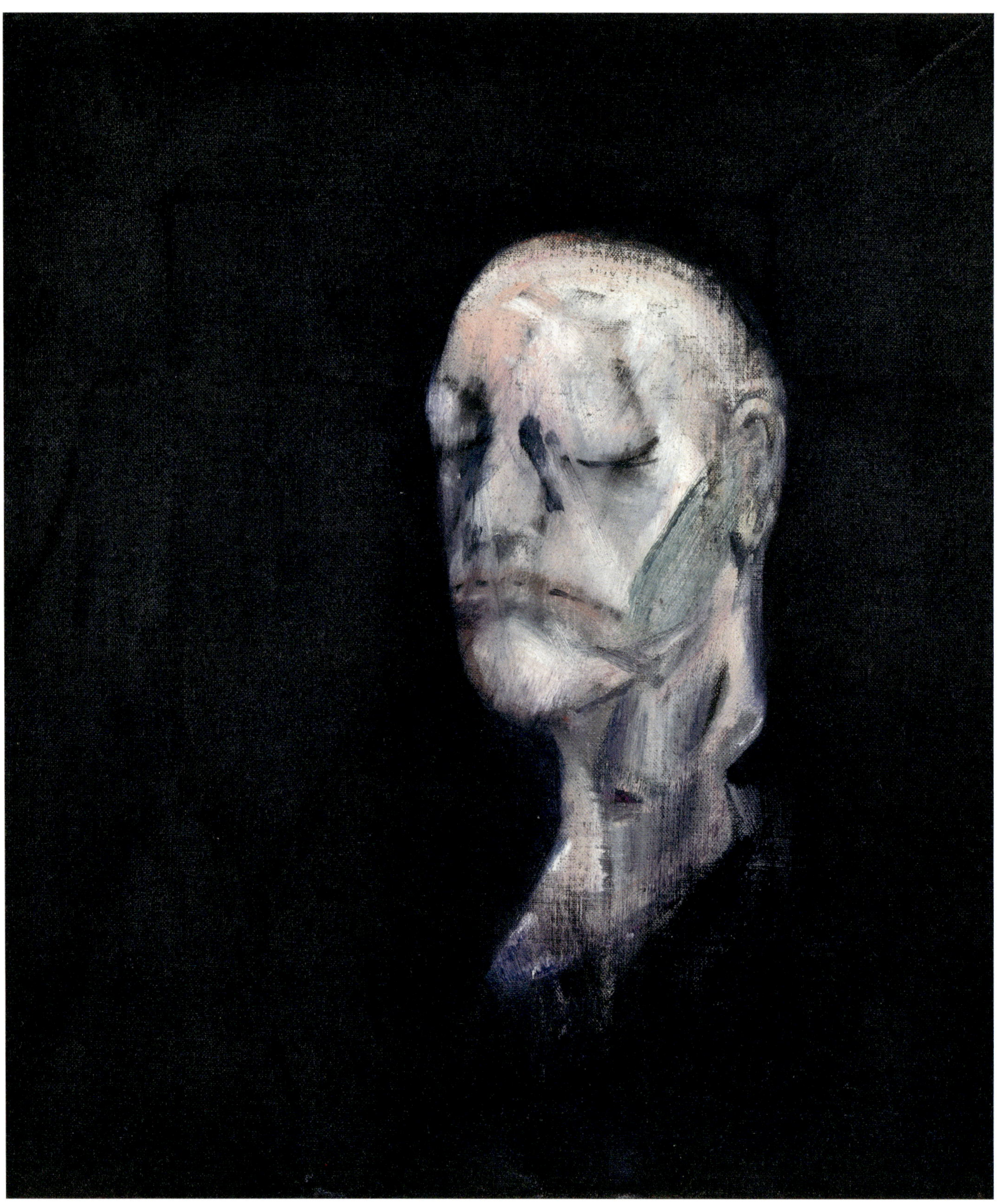

Francis Bacon *Study for Portrait II (after the Life Mask of William Blake)* 1955 Oil on canvas 610 × 508mm

Foreword

Francis Bacon, one of the greatest painters of the last century, was deeply engaged with portraiture. *Francis Bacon: Human Presence* is the first exhibition in nearly twenty years to focus on his portraits, and is consequently long overdue. This exhibition offers the opportunity to see this extraordinary body of work in the context of the Gallery's Collection, which extends back to the sixteenth century, and to reflect on Bacon's place within this lineage of figurative painters.

For much of his adult life, Bacon lived in London and spent his evenings in Soho, an area just a stone's throw from the Gallery. During the post-war era, the National Portrait Gallery was a staid institution: a pantheon of British royals, empire builders and industrialists. Bacon's relationship with it was, unsurprisingly, equivocal; there was little to inspire a forward-thinking artist who wore his own national identities – both British and Irish – lightly. He would visit the Gallery, but was generally dismissive of the British portrait tradition that is the cornerstone of our historic collection. Bacon was seeking a new way to depict the human figure, and to find a new truth in the genre of portraiture. It is therefore intriguing to learn that during the 1940s and 1950s, he lived and worked in studios previously owned by some of the most successful British portrait painters of the nineteenth and early twentieth centuries; artists whose works were staples of the National Portrait Gallery. In the 1940s, he leased 7 Cromwell Place, South Kensington, once home to the Victorian painter Sir John Everett Millais, whose portrayals of eminent men cemented his status as the leading artist of his day. By 1955, Bacon had moved to 28 Mallord Street, Chelsea, a draughty studio purpose-built for the artist Augustus John,

who began his career as a bohemian firebrand of modern art but later focused on commissions, portraying distinguished contemporaries. It was at this time that Bacon made a portrait based on a work from the National Portrait Gallery, albeit of one of our more unusual objects: the life mask of the poet and artist William Blake made by James Deville in 1823, which was the model for Bacon's *Study for a Portrait II* (opposite). A plaster replica of the mask, purchased in the Gallery shop for Bacon by a friend, the composer Gerard Schurmann, remained a striking feature of his studio, and can be seen in a photograph by Peter Stark (overleaf).

Portraiture is by its nature biographical, and through a close examination of its presence in Bacon's work, an intimate picture of the great artist emerges. The exhibition charts the development of portraiture through Bacon's career – including the series of 'screaming heads' and his obsession with Velázquez's portrayal of Pope Innocent X – but at its heart are his paintings of friends and lovers, those who inspired Bacon throughout his life. Some of these sitters were often living on the margins of polite society, surviving on their charm and wit, and had little in common with the high-society figures who sat for the formal portraits commonly found on the walls of public institutions. Bacon's self-portraits focus on the face he said he 'loathed'. In one of the many interviews with the artist recorded by critic David Sylvester, Bacon characteristically explained away self-portraits as something of a last resort, stating, 'people have been dying around me like flies and I've had nobody else left to paint but myself'. Bacon's own face fascinated photographers, and the Gallery is fortunate to hold some outstanding examples of photographic portraits of the artist.

In making this publication, we are delighted
to include contributions from writers working
in different disciplines to deepen our understanding of Bacon's practice, his relationships
and his legacy, and I extend my gratitude for
their expertise and insight. Our exhibitions are
not possible without the generosity of lenders,
and I am very grateful to those, both public and
private, who have supported this project and
shared so many incredible works. I am grateful
to all those involved in making this exhibition
and publication possible, in particular to
the exhibition curator Rosie Broadley, Senior
Curator of 20th-Century Collections at the
National Portrait Gallery, for her hard work,
dedication and continued oversight. We
are enormously grateful to Elizabeth Beatty,
Ben Harrison and Sophie Pretorius of The
Estate of Francis Bacon for their unstinting
support and invaluable guidance in putting
together this exhibition, to Martin Harrison
whose work on Bacon, including the *Catalogue
Raisonné*, has transformed Bacon studies, and to
Richard Calvocoressi, Melanie Clore, Francis
Outred and Per Skarstedt for their advice and
support in securing major loans for the
exhibition. We are delighted that we will have
the opportunity to share the exhibition with our
international touring partner, the Fondation
Pierre Gianadda in Martigny, Switzerland. I
would also like to extend my warmest thanks to
the Huo Family Foundation, who have
generously supported the exhibition.

**Dr Nicholas Cullinan OBE
Director, National Portrait Gallery**

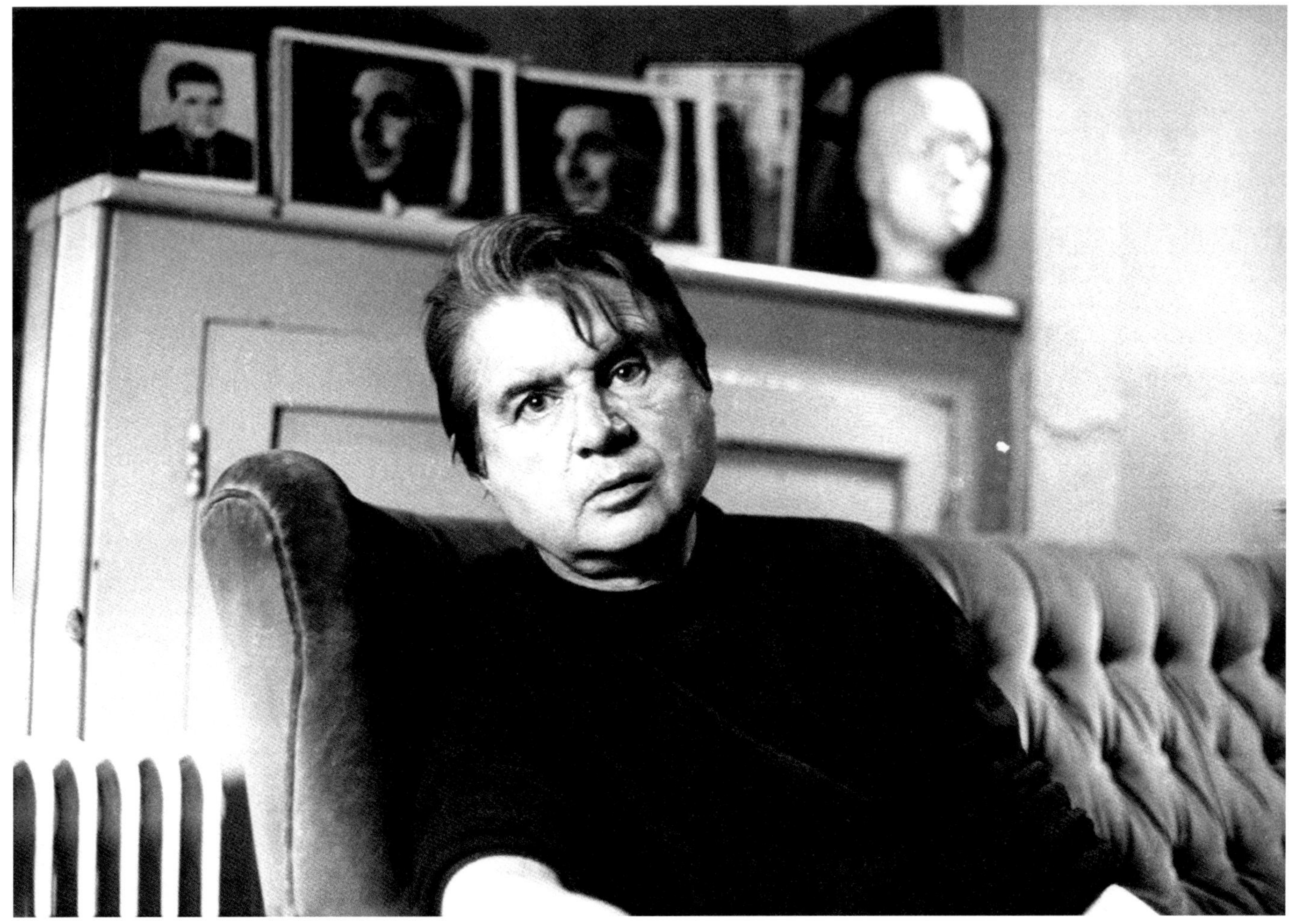

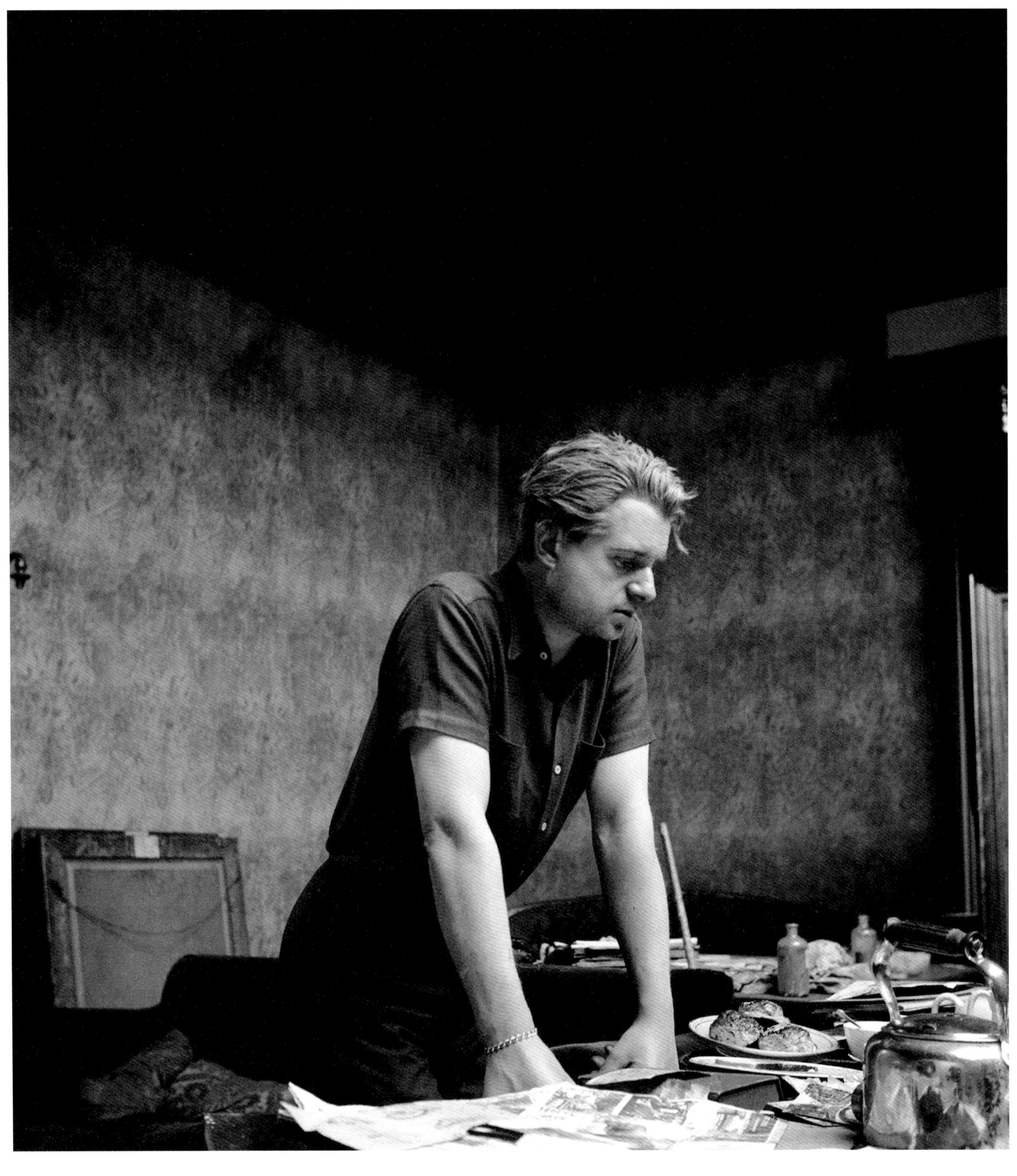

Fig.1 **Sam Hunter** *Francis Bacon at Cromwell Place* 1950 Archival inkjet print 381 × 381mm

Francis Bacon: Human Presence

Rosie Broadley

*'To me the mystery of painting today is how can appearance be made.
I know it can be illustrated; I know it can be photographed.
But how can this thing be made so that you catch the mystery
of appearance within the mystery of making?'*[1]

Francis Bacon's portraits are among the most potent and poignant of the twentieth century. He fused image and paint in a way that communicated 'directly onto the nervous system'.[2] For Bacon, portraiture was the pre-eminent painting genre, capable of expressing what it means to be human: 'I think art is an obsession with life and, after all, as we are human beings, our greatest obsession is with ourselves.'[3] Like other artists working in the post-war period, he rejected long-established expectations of what a portrait should entail – such as mimesis and flattery – but was nevertheless deeply committed to the genre, and held certain historic portraits and their artists in high regard.

Bacon emerged as an artist of note in 1946 and turned his attention to portraiture soon after. The paintings he made of anonymous male subjects in the late 1940s and early 1950s assumed the format of traditional portraits – smartly dressed individuals seated against dark backgrounds – but an unknown terror had been introduced, and his sitters appear trapped and screaming (cats 1–3). As Bacon's work evolved in the 1960s it became more personal and focused on a select coterie of sitters – Peter Lacy, Lucian Freud, Muriel Belcher, Henrietta Moraes, Isabel Rawsthorne, George Dyer and later John Edwards – many of whom were his drinking companions in the bars and clubs of London's Soho. Over subsequent decades Bacon painted other friends and acquaintances, but this core group provided the foundation and inspiration for his exhilarating reinvention of portraiture.

The artist's self-portraits, painted across four decades, convey his acute awareness of the fragility of existence: 'perhaps I have a feeling of mortality all the time ... I'm always surprised when I wake up in the morning.'[4] They not only track Bacon's relationship with his own appearance and his artistic and sexual identities, but also trace his changing technique and innovations in this format. One such innovation was the way in which he blurred the usual distinction between artist and sitter, occasionally merging his own image with those of his subjects, including Lucian Freud (cats 41 and 43) and George Dyer (cats 51–4), indicative of that fact that, for Bacon, identity was mutable and profoundly influenced by personal relationships.

The artist's life story has long fascinated art historians and admirers of his work, and numerous written biographies, documentaries and films have cemented Bacon in the popular imagination as a troubled genius, a high-living bon viveur and a queer icon. During his life, he engaged in numerous interviews, and these conversations provide an extraordinary insight into his unique approach to portraiture. Nevertheless, he carefully controlled the narrative about his life and work, causing the curator Henry Geldzahler to remark in 1975 that Bacon's words 'can often mask deep feelings, and they can veil privacies'.[5] Bacon's portraits and self-portraits offer an alternative form of biography that can be revelatory but also as enigmatic as his words.

This publication presents Bacon's portraits thematically, but also within a broader chronological structure and informed by recent research into Bacon's life that has penetrated some of the 'layers of obfuscation'[6] which the artist perpetuated. Biographies are provided for the individual sitters represented, some of whom figured so largely on his canvases, but who, in the literature, rarely emerge from the artist's shadow. The biographical lens of this exhibition is enhanced by the inclusion of portraits of Bacon himself, taken by some of the leading photographers of the twentieth century.

In addition, several contemporary perspectives, in the form of short essays by writers and art historians, shed light on his life, his practice, his subjects, and the impact that his portraits have had on audiences both during Bacon's life and beyond.

Backdrop

'I'm greedy for life; and I'm greedy as an artist ... And it's partly my greed that has made me what's called live by chance – greed for food, for drink, for being with the people one likes, for the excitement of things happening.'[7]

Francis Bacon was born in Dublin in 1909 to English parents. His father, Edward Bacon, a former major in the army, was of aristocratic descent, though his forebears had fallen on hard times. Bacon's mother, Winifred, came from

Fig.2   Francis Julian Gutmann (later Goodman)
Francis Bacon   1933   Gelatin silver print   225 × 203mm

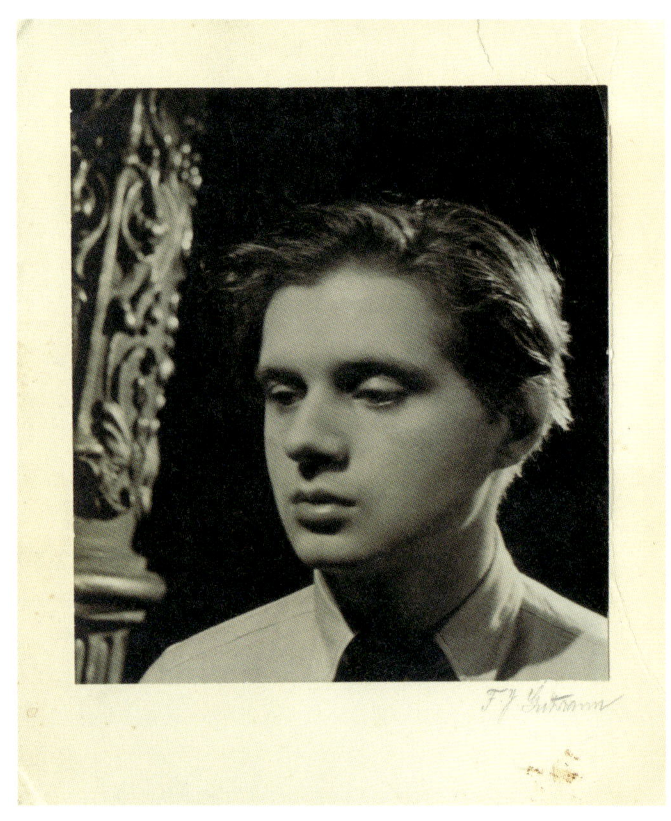

a wealthy family who had made their money
in the steel industry. The family were peripatetic,
living in various large houses in Ireland and
London. They socialised with the upper-class,
Anglo-Irish community, where life revolved
around horses and hunting. One of four siblings,
Bacon nevertheless felt isolated and unhappy;
he disliked riding, and animals brought on his
asthma. The children were primarily cared for
by their nanny, Jessie Lightfoot, with whom
Bacon remained extremely close until her death
in 1951. Throughout his childhood the spectre
of war was ever-present. The First World War
was followed by years of conflict in Ireland
in response to centuries of British rule and
whose colonial dominance was personified
by Anglo-Irish and English families like
the Bacons. He recalled: 'I grew up in an
atmosphere of threat for a long time.'[8]

Bacon had only a brief spell at school, but
a private tutor encouraged his love of classical
literature, Shakespeare and poetry. His
interest in art was cultivated by his maternal
grandmother. Bacon's growing awareness
of his homosexuality compounded his sense
of isolation and confused his already strained
relationship with his domineering father: 'He
didn't love me, and I didn't love him either …
It was very ambiguous though, because I was
sexually attracted to him. At the time, I didn't
know how to explain my feelings'.[9] Bacon's most
recent biographers identify his nascent sexuality
as profoundly formative for his art: 'What was
certain was that some volatile sexual compound
– father, groom, animal, discipline – gave
Francis a physical jolt that helped make him
into the painter Francis Bacon.'[10]

Bacon left home for London in 1925 and over
the next four years spent time in Berlin and
Paris, absorbing the cultures of both cities and
embracing their decadence. The art, avant-
garde cinema, photography, books and journals
to which Bacon had access in these modern
cities made an important impression on him.

This period, and its impact on his later
portraits, is explored by Richard Calvocoressi
(p.32). Bacon's first encounter with the work
of Pablo Picasso at the Galerie Paul Rosenberg
in Paris was a moment of epiphany that sparked
his decision to become a painter. His early
painting was encouraged by the Australian
artist Roy de Maistre, but he struggled to find
a consistent style during the 1930s, until his
focus began to shift to figuration and portraiture.

Portraits emerge

*'When I was young, I didn't, in a sense,
have a real subject. It's through my life and knowing
other people that a subject has really grown.'*[11]

Bacon spent the Second World War in London,
followed by several years in Monaco. There
he developed an obsession with one of the great
portraits of the seventeenth century, Velázquez's
depiction of *Pope Innocent X* (1649–50; fig.3),
a masterful representation of a supremely
powerful man, which became a presiding
theme in Bacon's work for several years.
At the time it was known to him only through
black and white reproductions, but this did
not inhibit his practice in any way. He described
how he 'became obsessed by this painting
and I bought photograph after photograph
of it. I think really that was my first subject.'[12]

By 1948 Bacon had returned to London where
he made a series of paintings culminating in
Head VI (cat.1), a reimagining of Velázquez's
Pope, in which he is seated on a throne
screaming, seemingly trapped in a transparent
box. In making this work, Bacon referred
to a still from the film *Battleship Potemkin*
and to found images including photographs
of dictators (fig.4). This radical appropriation
of diverse source material to make portraits
disrupted European cultural traditions
in a way that dissolved 'past into present',
and which projected modern anxieties.[13]

Bacon transformed the subject of the Pope, stripping away almost all vestiges of dignity and piety. He was acutely aware of the artifice involved in conventional portraiture and in public life, observing: 'We nearly always live through screens ... I sometimes think, when people say my work looks violent, that perhaps I have from time to time been able to clear away one or two of the veils or screens.'[14]

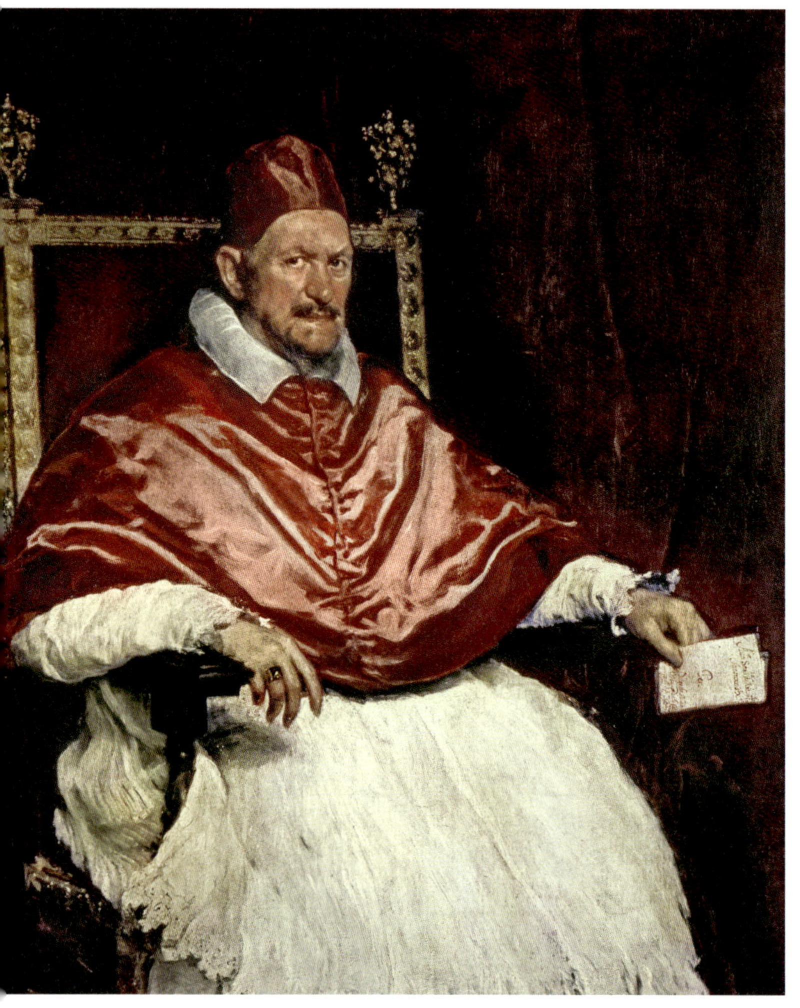

Fig.3   **Diego Velázquez**   *Pope Innocent X*   1649–50
Oil on canvas   1190 × 1140mm

Human presence

'I would like my pictures to look as if a human had passed between them, like a snail, leaving a trail of the human presence and memory trace of past events as the snail leaves its slime.'[15]

The 'human presence' to which Bacon referred in the early 1950s became more distinct after he embarked on a new relationship with Peter Lacy, whom Bacon described as the love of his life. The heightened drama of anonymous screaming heads made way for portraits that were more individualised, increasingly intimate and emotionally charged (cats 34–8). The earliest depictions of Lacy are ghostly, painted in a muted, tonal palette, including the most explicit representation of their intimacy, *Two Figures* (1953; p.50), which fuses hazy likenesses of both the artist and Lacy, with wrestling figures drawn from the photographs of Eadweard Muybridge. This is a painting that has had important resonances for queer audiences, both in the 1950s and today, as explored by Gregory Salter (p.48). The spectre of Lacy also haunts the series *Man in Blue I–VII* (cat.6), representing an isolated male figure, apparently located in a hotel bar. According to Bacon, Lacy was 'very neurotic and almost hysterical, this may possibly have come across in the paintings'.[16]

Bacon was also able to infuse human presence into the depiction of a lifeless object. He was commissioned by his friend the composer Gerard Schurmann to make a painting of the life-cast plaster head of the Romantic poet and painter William Blake (cat.8). Bacon had seen the original 1823 mask in the National Portrait Gallery, London, and Schurmann had even bought him a copy from the museum shop, which can be seen in photographs of Bacon's Reece Mews studio (p.9), although Bacon preferred to work from a photographic reproduction. The ghostly, monochrome palette used was common to Bacon's works at this time, but here, the pale paint is infused with blush

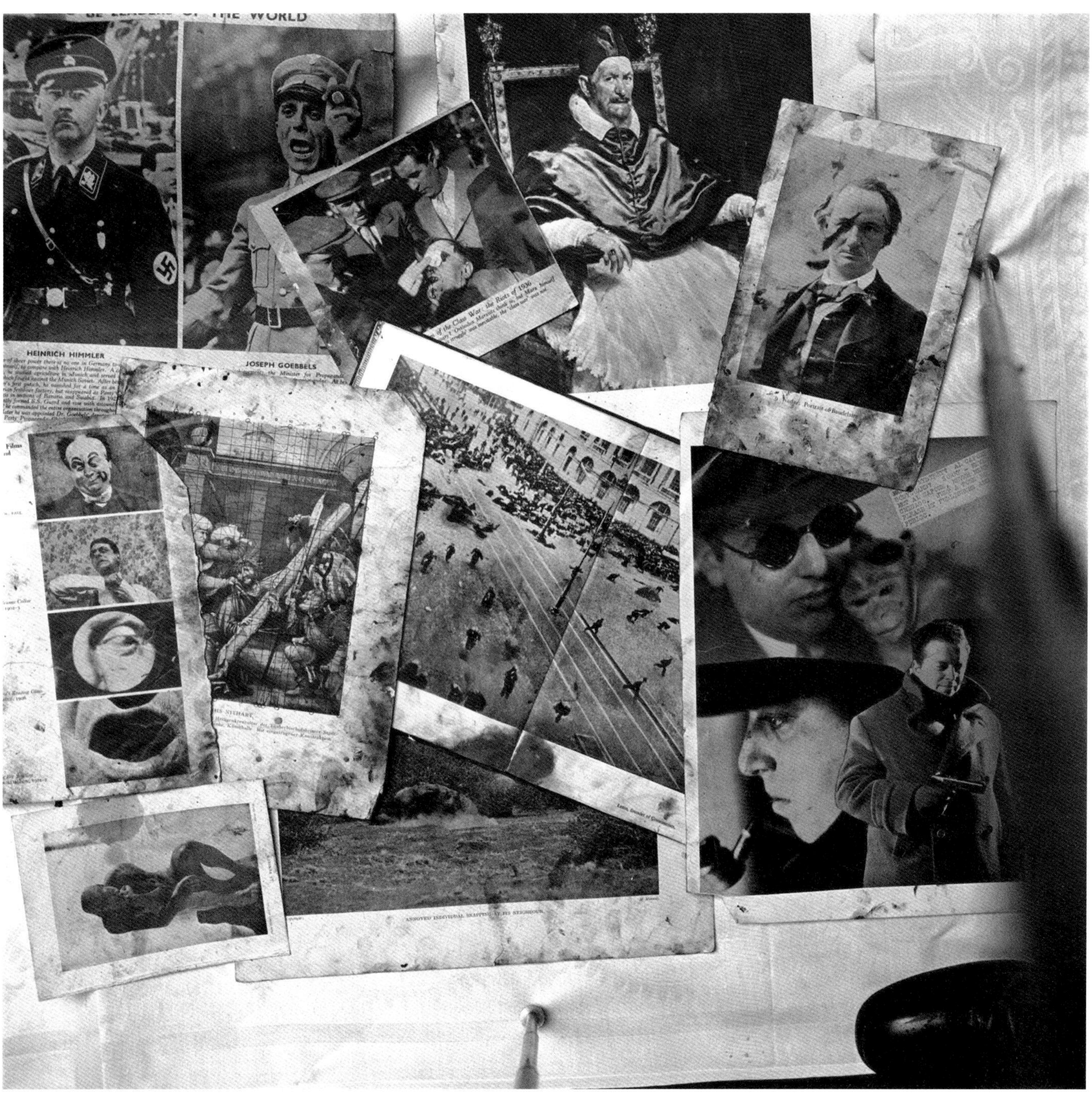

Fig.4 **Sam Hunter** Montage of material from Francis Bacon's Cromwell Place studio 1950
Archival inkjet print 381 × 381mm

pink, and the subject's expression suggests an active interior world. This small painting set an important precedent for the small heads and triptych head portraits that Bacon produced in the 1960s.

During this exploratory period, it is unsurprising that Bacon attempted painting directly from life, which had been the practice for portrait painters for centuries. However, while the paintings were mostly successful, he found life sittings inhibiting. He invited fellow painter Lucian Freud – whose close friendship with Bacon is explored by Tanya Bentley (p.52) – as well as patrons Sir Robert and Lady Sainsbury to sit for him in his studio (cat.32). Commissions were the bread-and-butter of the conventional portrait painter but were often fraught with prescriptive demands from the sitter or patron. Fortunately for Bacon, the Sainsburys 'did not expect to be flattered'.[17] The austere quality of the portraits of Lisa belie the fact that she found sittings with Bacon 'great fun', 'because he was so interested in everything'.[18]

Bacon was equally charming when painting the photographer Cecil Beaton, who described the artist as 'wise and effervescent and an inspired conversationalist'.[19] Beaton relished the idea of himself as a 'sort of Sainsbury floating in stygian gloom', but by the time he came to sit, Bacon's painting style had moved on and Beaton was shocked by what he saw: 'The face was hardly recognisable as a face for it was disintegrating before your eyes ... a swollen mass of raw meat and fatty tissues.'[20] Beaton was 'crushed' and 'staggered' by the piece; Bacon discreetly

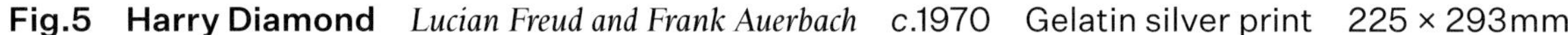

Fig.5   Harry Diamond   *Lucian Freud and Frank Auerbach*   c.1970   Gelatin silver print   225 × 293mm

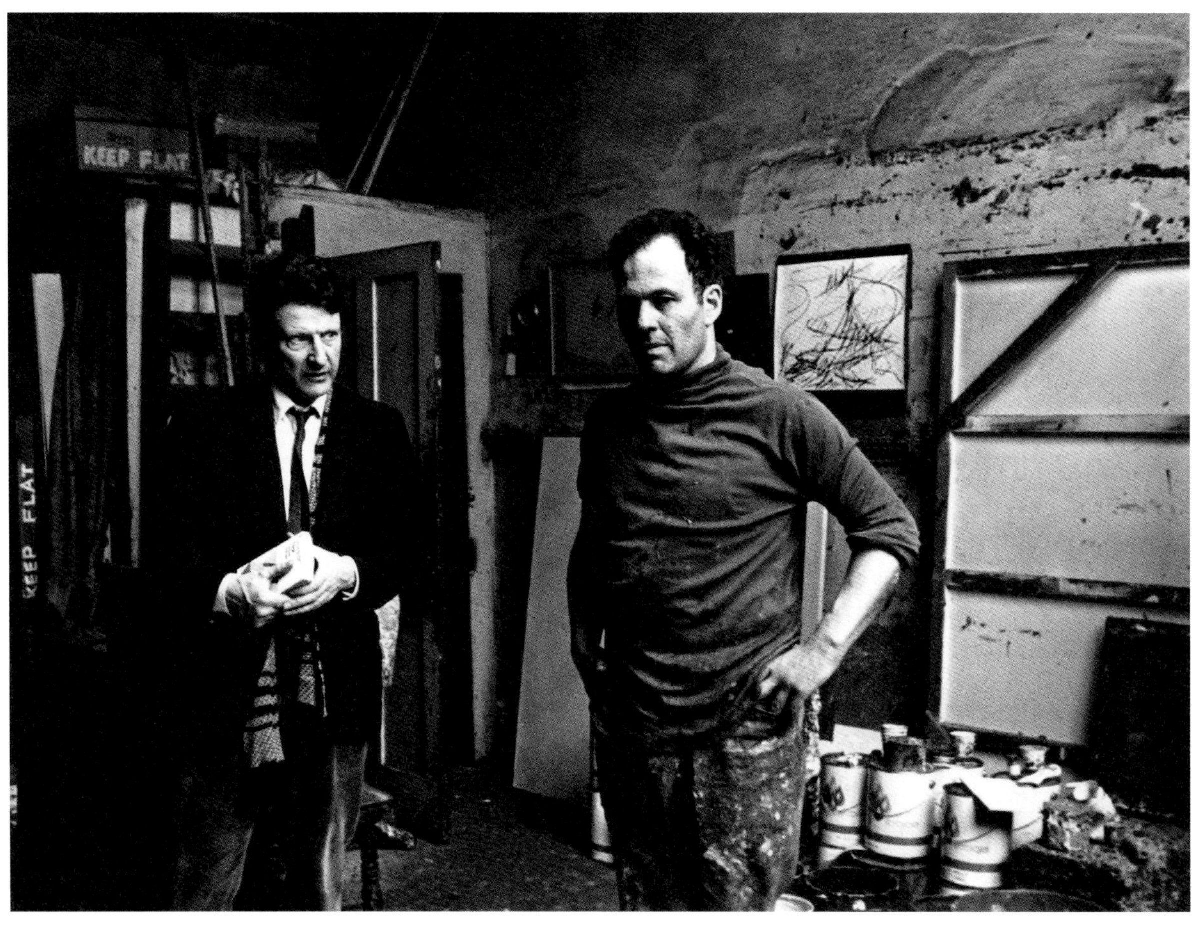

destroyed it.[21] This incident may have caused Bacon to draw a line under life sittings and he doubtless had it in mind when he attempted to explain to David Sylvester in 1966 why he preferred to work from photographs: 'I am not able to drift so freely as I am able to through the photographic image ... I find it less inhibiting to work from them through memory and their photographs than actually having them seated there before me.'[22]

Bacon's rejection of life sittings is a critical aspect of his portrait practice, and one that set him apart from contemporary figurative painters, such as Freud and Frank Auerbach (fig.5), who themselves appeared in Bacon's portraits (cat.42). Painting from life has long been considered the most 'authentic' approach to portraiture, representing a collaborative exchange between artist and sitter resulting in a more vivid representation. Freud demanded commitment from his sitters to pose daily over many months, and Auerbach allowed his sitter's presence to influence the way he painted a portrait. Authenticity was nevertheless important to Bacon, who talked about 'recording the fact' of his subject, whilst being mindful to protect them: 'If I like them, I don't want to practise before them the injury that I do to them in my work. I would rather practise the injury in private.'[23]

Art and artists

'Van Gogh got very close to the real thing about art when he said ... "What I do may be a lie ... but it conveys reality more accurately".'[24]

Bacon's first portraits were made in the aftermath of the destruction and suffering witnessed during the Second World War and the Holocaust. For many artists, the conventional presentation of man as a dignified and secure human being, exemplified by formal portraiture, seemed exhausted and irrelevant, and they turned to other forms of expression, including abstraction. For artists like Bacon and Alberto Giacometti, whom Bacon particularly admired, the question was how to remake figurative art for more uncertain and increasingly godless times. In this context, Bacon's use of the word 'study' in the titles of many of his portraits is particularly apposite. A study suggests something incomplete or unresolved and may refer as much to the humanity represented in any of his paintings as to the status of the portrait itself. During this period he also looked back to works by artists of the past, not only Velázquez, but also Edgar Degas and Vincent van Gogh. Van Gogh's painting, *The Painter on the Road to Tarascon* (1888; fig.6) was deconstructed by Bacon through a series of works made in 1957 (cats 13–4). These mark an important moment of transition in Bacon's use of colour. The ghostly monochromes of the early 1950s made way for brilliant reds, yellows and greens, which he also incorporated

Fig.6   Vincent van Gogh
The Painter on the Road to Tarascon   1888 (destroyed 1945)
Oil on canvas   480 × 440mm

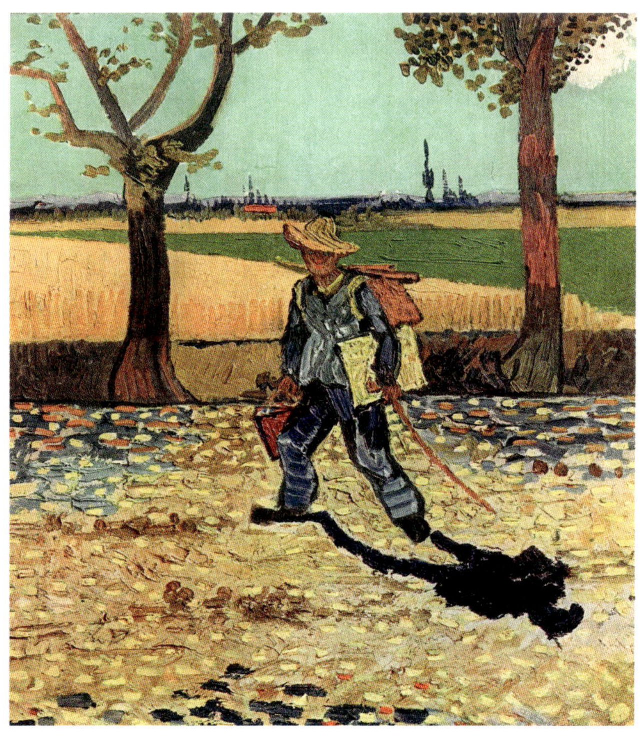

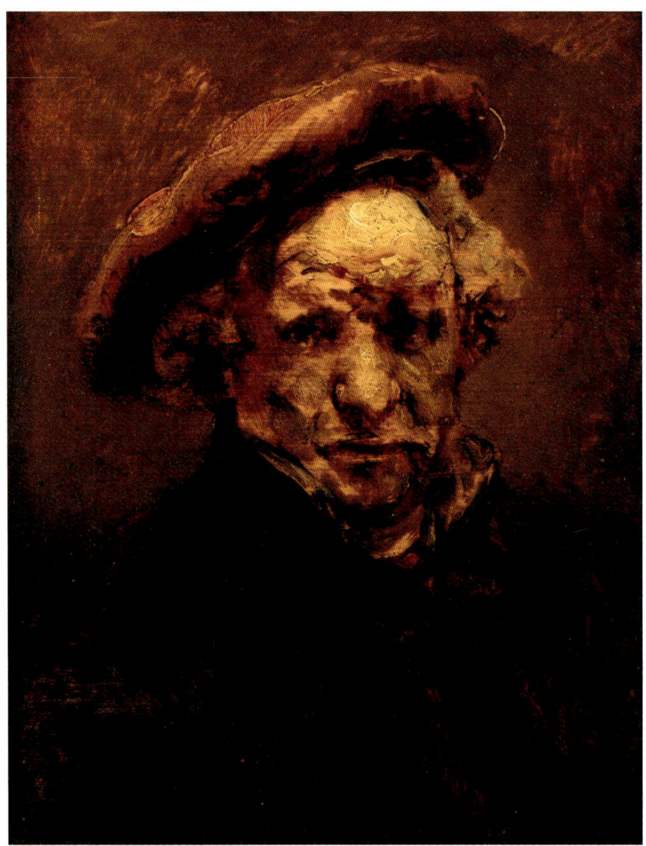

into portraits such as *Miss Muriel Belcher* (1959), where the viridian green background recalls the walls of the Colony Room club that she ran.

Rembrandt was arguably the most important touchstone artist for Bacon, who emulated the Old Master's extensive project of self-scrutiny across numerous self-portraits. Bacon was profoundly influenced by the way in which likeness emerged from Rembrandt's portraits through the apparently abstract application of paint. He described Rembrandt's *Self-Portrait with Beret* (*c*.1659; fig.7) as 'almost completely anti-illustrational'.[25] Bacon was somewhat dismissive of the British tradition of portrait painting exemplified by Sir Joshua Reynolds and Sir Thomas Lawrence, although he did admire certain near-contemporaries, including Graham Sutherland and Sir Matthew Smith. Smith achieved what Bacon described as 'a compete interlocking of image and paint', something that he aspired to and would achieve in his portraits from the 1960s. He explained, 'Every movement of the brush on the canvas alters the shape and the implications of the image. That is why real painting is a mysterious and continuous struggle with chance – mysterious because the very substance of paint ... can make such a direct assault on the nervous system.'[26]

All the pulsations of a person

'The living quality is what you have to get. In painting a portrait the problem is to find a technique by which you can give over all the pulsations of a person ... The sitter is someone of flesh and blood and what has to be caught is their emanation.'[27]

Until the late nineteenth century, the measure of the success of a portrait had been the strength of its resemblance to the person depicted. The advent of photography liberated artists from the need to replicate appearance. Bacon wanted to make more stimulating representations of people: 'to make an image and keep the likeness ... To combine the two is what creates tension and excitement.'[28] To this end, in the 1960s he began to sweep and drag his brush across the canvas in such a way that distorted and exaggerated the features of his subjects. His brushstrokes, and the movement and energy invested in them, evoked a palpable living presence in what was 'an attempt to bring the figurative thing up onto the nervous system more violently and more poignantly'.[29] While Bacon used paint to disrupt what was traditionally meant by the word 'likeness', in the midst of swirling paint he took care to retain certain visual signifiers of identity – George Dyer's distinctive profile, for example, or Isabel Rawsthorne's delicately arched eyebrows. Ciphers such as these would be repeated across Bacon's canvases.

From the early 1960s, photography would play an even more decisive role in Bacon's portraiture, as explored by Martin Harrison (p.28). He commissioned new images, asking his friend, the photographer John Deakin (fig.8), to take pictures of his lovers and friends to given specifications. By commissioning these photographs, rather than taking them himself, Bacon remained at one step removed from the sitter. Spared the distractions of social interaction that a live sitting would require, he could work more freely and efficiently. In John Deakin, Bacon recognised a kindred spirit whose vision for portraiture echoed Bacon's own, and which was similarly unforgiving. Of his own work, Deakin wrote: 'Being fatally drawn to the human race, what I want to do when I photograph it is to make a revelation about it. So my sitters turn into my victims.'[30] A heavy drinker with a caustic tongue, Deakin was the only photographer to have been hired and fired twice by British *Vogue*, where he frequently reduced models to tears. This was the type of tension Bacon was no doubt looking for. In the first published biography of Bacon, its author Daniel Farson described Deakin's work in striking terms that are usually reserved only for Bacon's portraits: 'They were photographs to recoil from, brutal portraits – intimate close-ups of the face – emphasising every blemish.'[31] Deakin photographed Bacon several times (pp.105 and 182) and described the artist as 'wonderfully tender and generous by nature, yet with curious streaks of cruelty, especially to his friends'.[32] Even with Deakin's photographs to hand, it was critical to the success of his portraits that Bacon knew his subjects well: 'The photographs are only used to make me remember their features, to revise my memory of them, as one would use a dictionary, really.'[33] For Bacon, Deakin's images were documents waiting to be transformed at the service of his own art. Sometimes this transformation was physical, the photographs being crushed, folded and daubed with paint in the studio so that they resembled the found images he continued to work from.

Bacon's most frequent subject besides himself was his lover George Dyer, whom he had met in late 1963. Dyer appears in some of Bacon's most ambitious and complex paintings, including *Portrait of George Dyer Riding a Bicycle* (cat.51), in which Bacon's own face can be seen within Dyer's profile silhouette. While male lovers featured prominently in his portraits, Bacon also painted numerous portraits of women, including one of his closest friends, the artist Isabel Rawsthorne. He had met Rawsthorne in Paris in the late 1940s and she was an important influence, as explored by Carol Jacobi (p.168). Bacon did not paint all his friends but tended to prefer to depict those who, like him, had led unconventional lives. In friendship, as in portraiture, Bacon required resilience: 'I've always thought of friendships

Fig.8   **Luke Kelly**   *John Deakin*   *c*.1970
Gelatin silver print   246 × 164 mm

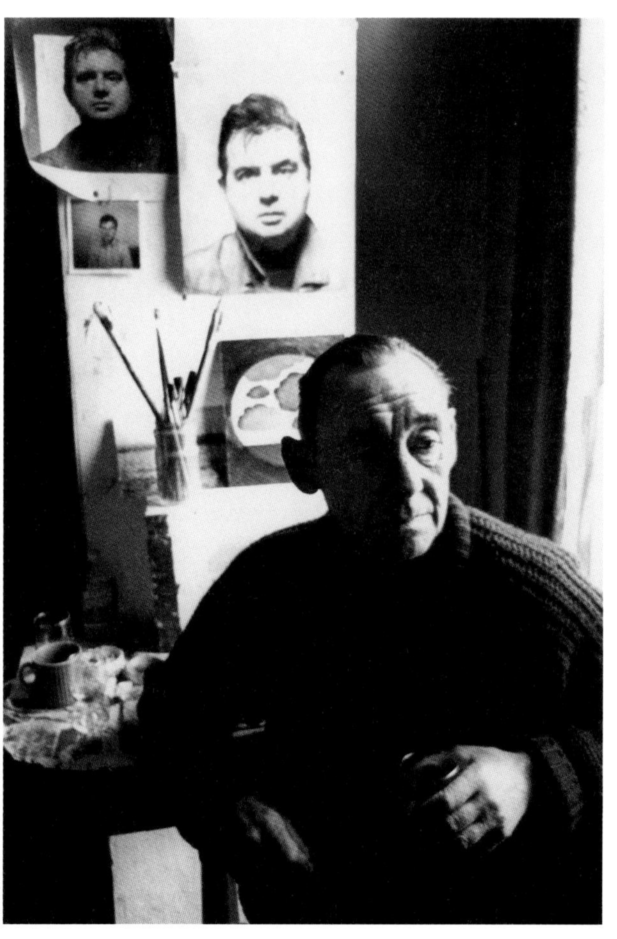

as where two people really tear one another apart and perhaps in that way learn something from one another.'[34] Bacon also admired physical beauty, telling Henrietta Moraes, who was cautious about posing nude: 'You're beautiful darling, and you always will be, you mustn't worry about that.'[35]

Bacon's paintings of his friends and lovers resonate with the artist's feelings for his sitters, and associated memories. The most moving examples are the commemorative portraits he made after Dyer's death in 1971. These include the so-called black triptychs (fig.9), a series of monumental portraits that document Dyer's final moments and that partly derive from photographs Deakin took of Dyer in Reece Mews (p.154). Dyer took his own life on the eve of Bacon's major retrospective at the Grand Palais in Paris, in the hotel suite that he shared with the artist. Bacon had assigned John Deakin to stay with Dyer while he was working, but Deakin had gone out for an evening in Paris, leaving Dyer alone.[36] Despite this egregious breach of trust, in life and in death, Bacon demonstrated extraordinary loyalty to the photographer, whose work had enabled some of his greatest portraits. Deakin, already ill, died shortly after Dyer and he named Bacon as his next of kin. Bacon identified his body and paid his funeral expenses. He wryly observed that Deakin's death was 'the last dirty trick he played on me'.[37]

The broken mirror

*'I think of life as meaningless; but we give
it meaning during our own existence.'*[38]

Despite complaining that 'people have been dying around me like flies and I've had nobody else left to paint but myself', Bacon continued to make portraits of friends and lovers during the 1980s.[39] These included images of the French philosopher Michel Leiris, the American

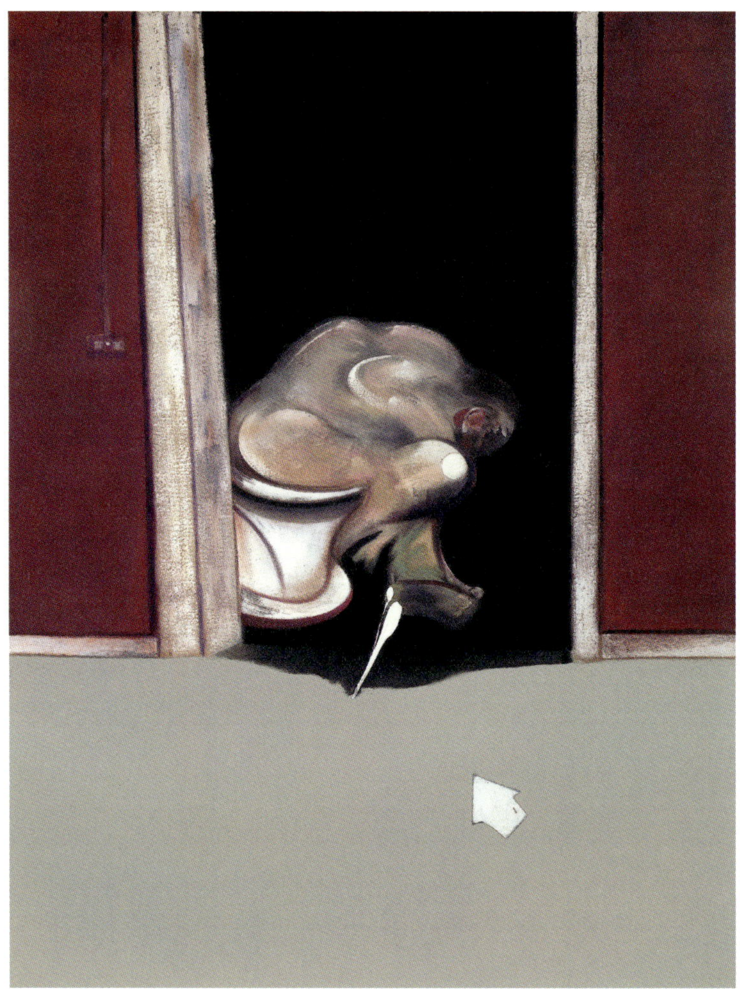

Fig.9 Francis Bacon *Triptych May–June 1973* 1973 Oil on canvas 1980 × 1475mm (each panel)

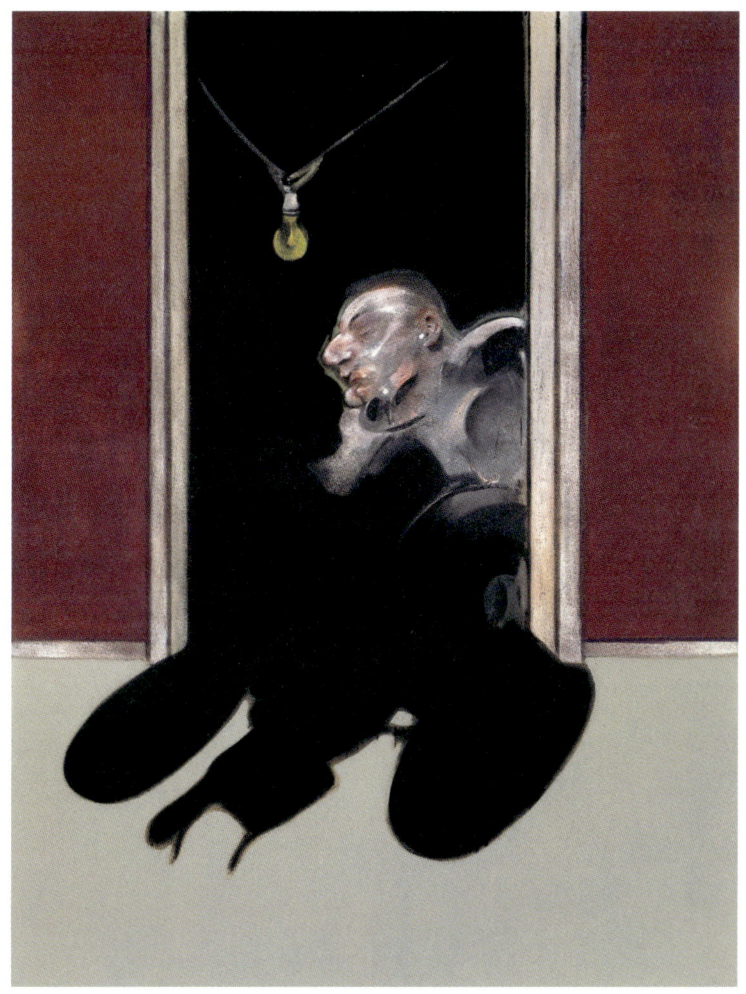 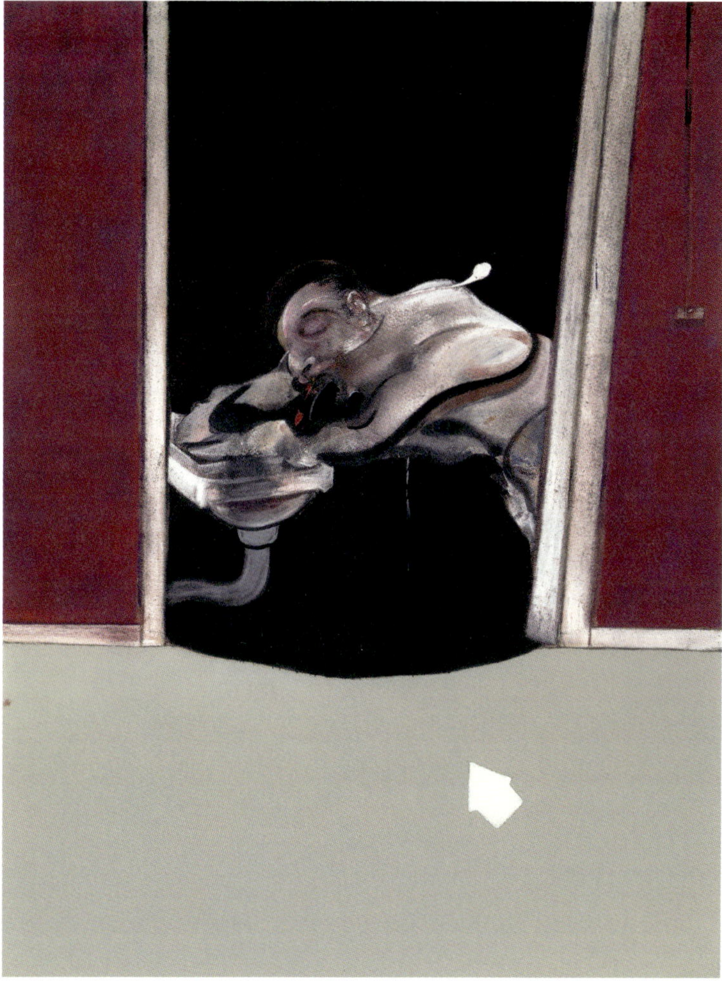

photographer Peter Beard and the Spanish banker José Capelo, representatives of the sophisticated international milieu of the artist's later years. Bacon made over 20 portraits of his companion John Edwards, a bartender whom he had met in 1974 (p.165). Edwards, known as 'Eggs', became Bacon's executor and arranged for Bacon's studio at Reece Mews in South Kensington to be dismantled and recreated at the Hugh Lane Art Gallery in Dublin.

Reece Mews was a wholly idiosyncratic working environment that has come to define both the artist and his practice, as James Hall describes in his essay (p.68). It was also the place where Bacon made his greatest portraits. Over time, this studio became a living self-portrait, freighted with memory and experience:

'... the places I live in, or like living in, are like an autobiography; I like the marks that have been made by myself, or other people, to be left. They're like memory tracks for me ... For instance, that door, somebody broke it in a rage over something; well I've left it because I like it like that, also the broken mirror and the papers on the floor'.[40]

To his last, Bacon challenged the conventions surrounding portraiture, dispensing with identifiable settings and attributes, and appealing instead directly 'to the nervous system'. This publication not only demonstrates Bacon's expansive and innovative approach to portraiture, but also the importance of the subjects he chose to paint – individuals whose vivid presence on the canvas enabled him to reimagine the genre.

The Portrait Emerges

'You could say that a scream is a horrific image; in fact, I wanted to paint the scream more than the horror.'

In 1949 Francis Bacon presented a group of six paintings in an exhibition at the Hanover Gallery in London. Each entitled *Head*, they shocked and impressed visitors in equal measure. This series of paintings employed and subverted centuries-old conventions of formal portraiture, in which individuals would sit composedly against darkened backgrounds. The subjects here are not dignified or flattered: two works in the series represent barely human creatures who blindly thrash and flail, teeth gnashing within their gilded frames. The last of the series, *Head VI* (1949; cat.1), was the first painting in which Bacon directly referenced the great seventeenth-century portrait *Pope Innocent X* (1649–50) by Diego Velázquez (p.14), which was to become a touchstone for his work for another two decades. Velázquez's grand and perceptive portrait includes all the trappings of wealth and status expected in a representation of one of the most powerful men of his time. Bacon's painting is an homage to Velázquez's masterpiece, but also a complete reimagining in which the Pope is distressed, in pain or furious. A small tassel dangling from the top of the canvas that tickles the subject's nose seems to mock him further. Crucially, Bacon renders him impotent: trapped within a transparent cage that muffles his cries.

The representation of a scream in this painting is carried through to other works made in the late 1940s and early 1950s. The smartly dressed man in *Study for a Portrait* (1949; cat.2) cries out from within a transparent box, his wrists shackled as they would be in an electric chair. Bacon deployed a number of sources in making these extraordinary images: in addition to Velázquez's Pope, he looked to illustrated books and photographic reproductions from magazines, as well as a still from the 1925 Russian film *Battleship Potemkin* depicting a screaming woman with crushed and shattered metal-framed glasses, her face covered in blood (p.31). These glasses reappear in other small 'screaming heads', including *Study for a Portrait* (1952; cat.3). Despite the papal robes and smart suits, Bacon's sitters appear framed within a nightmarish parallel universe where traditional signifiers of status count for nothing. Together, these works serve to destabilise our traditional understanding of portraits of powerful and successful men.

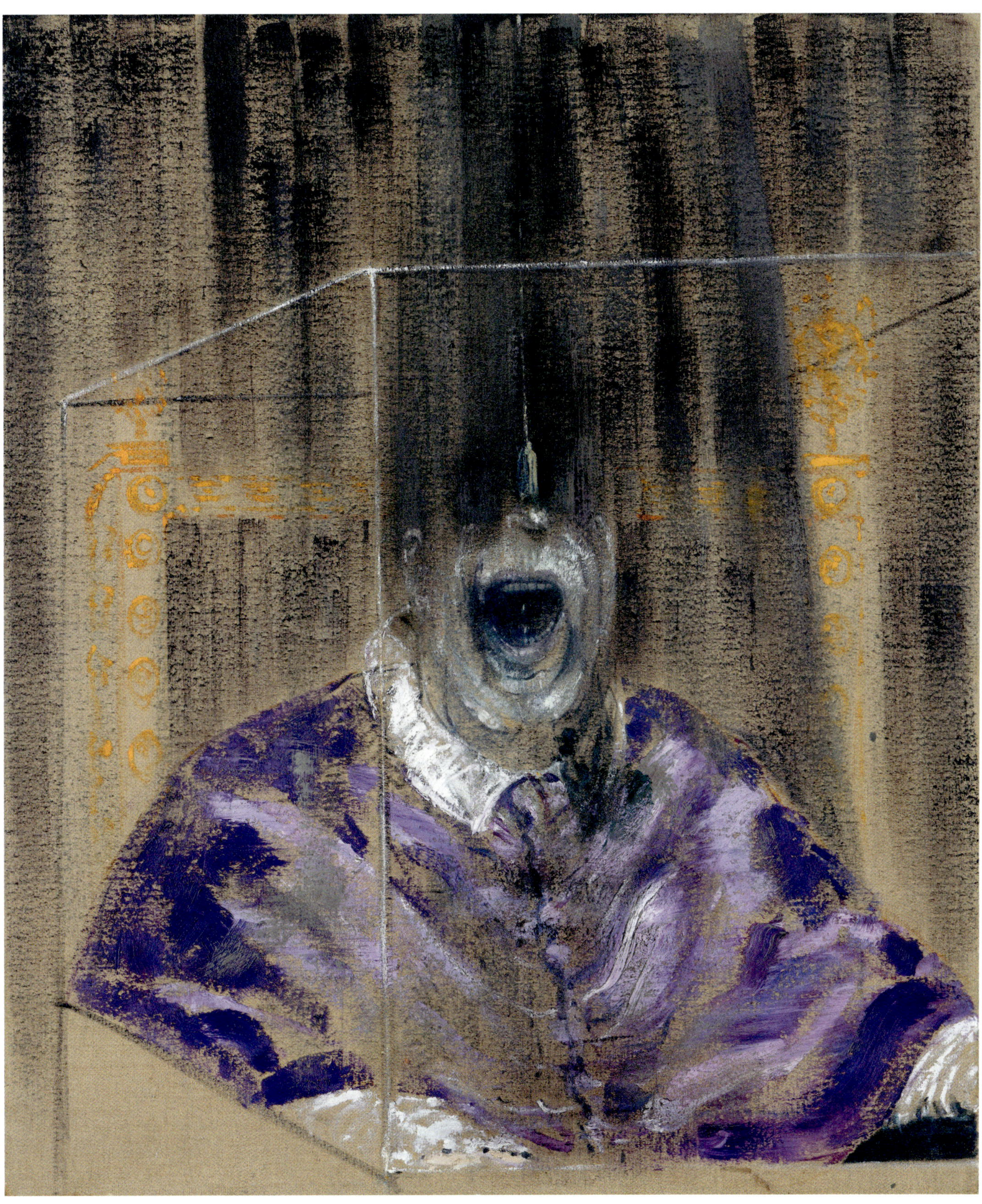

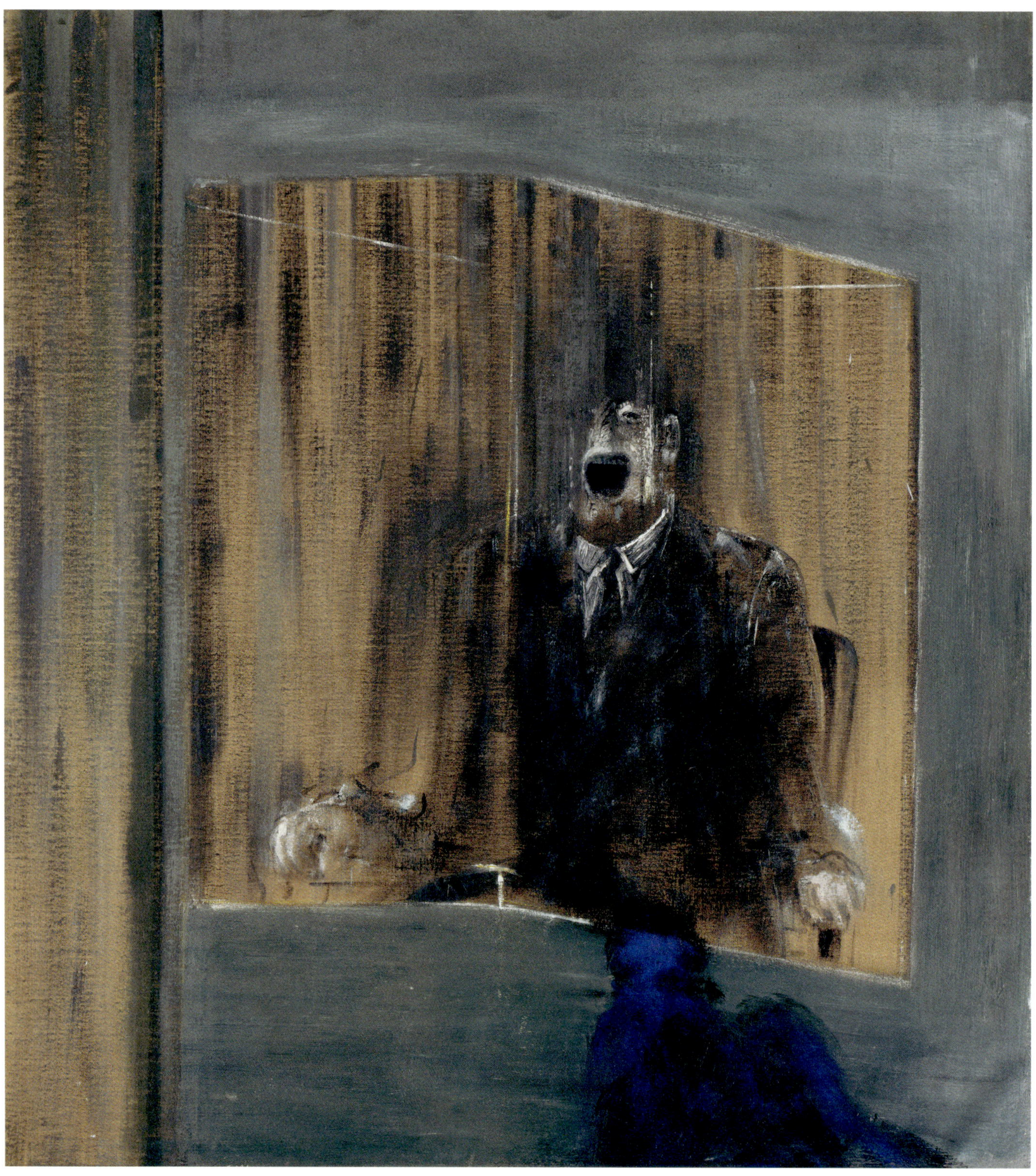

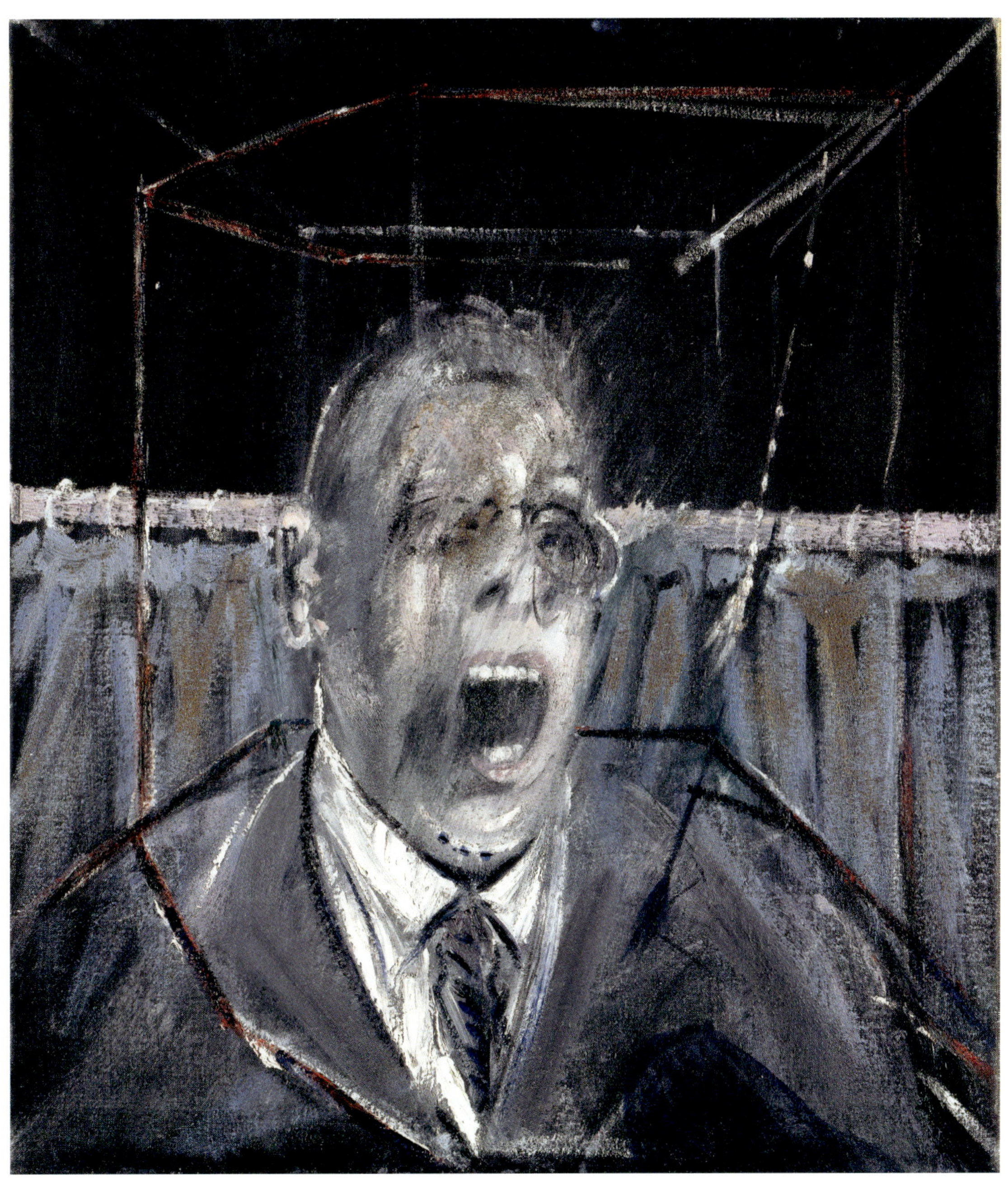

Francis Bacon: Painting in the Era of the Photograph

Martin Harrison

While Bacon was alive, he shielded the photographs and magazines that littered his studio floor from public scrutiny, and he had periodic culls of them. The transfer of the studio's contents from London to the Hugh Lane Gallery, Dublin, in 1998 sparked a considerable interest in this material, most of which was previously unknown, even to his friends. What was revealed generated the presumption of a causal relationship between photograph and painting, but this is over-simplistic and misleading. Bacon sometimes made rough, quick, compositional sketches, but he did not make preliminary drawings. Photographs, or images that he encountered in printed media, were, therefore, an effective alternative in formulating paintings. Yet the paintings themselves always renounce their photographic source(s); they are not dictated by them and are patently not photorealist facsimiles.

This raises the question of what 'the photograph' meant to Bacon. Photography has been with us for nearly 200 years, altering our perceptions of space, time and memory, and changing the course of art and representation. Bacon was not alone in his alertness to photographs, or as a consumer of magazine imagery, for artists since Degas had maintained a creative dialogue with these new media. Yet while acutely conscious of the cultural significance of photography, Bacon was nonetheless ambivalent about the value of 'great' photographic images: certainly, he was unmoved by what has become known as 'art photography'. Photographs functioned mainly as a means to an end, and he was indifferent to the distinction between original photographs and mechanical reproductions of them. On the other hand, for Bacon photographs were poignant witnesses of the passage of time, tracing the inevitability of mortality.

Few of Bacon's earliest paintings escaped his tendency to destroy work that dissatisfied him, but among the handful of survivors there is no evidence they were inspired by photographs. Until 1945 he was, in any case, revisiting Picasso's 'forms', as he called them, painted between 1927 and 1933, which had no direct basis in reality. The first of Bacon's paintings that depended on photographs date from 1945; four of them (all later abandoned) were variations of images he found in books on Nazi Germany. *Figure in a Landscape* (1945; fig.1) was, he told art historian John Rothenstein, painted from a snapshot of his friend Eric Hall dozing in a chair in Hyde Park. Although he turned his lack of formal art training conspicuously to his advantage, it is evident that initially he lacked confidence in his ability to render a satisfactory likeness

Fig.1   **Francis Bacon**   *Figure in a Landscape*   1945   Oil on canvas   1448 × 1283mm

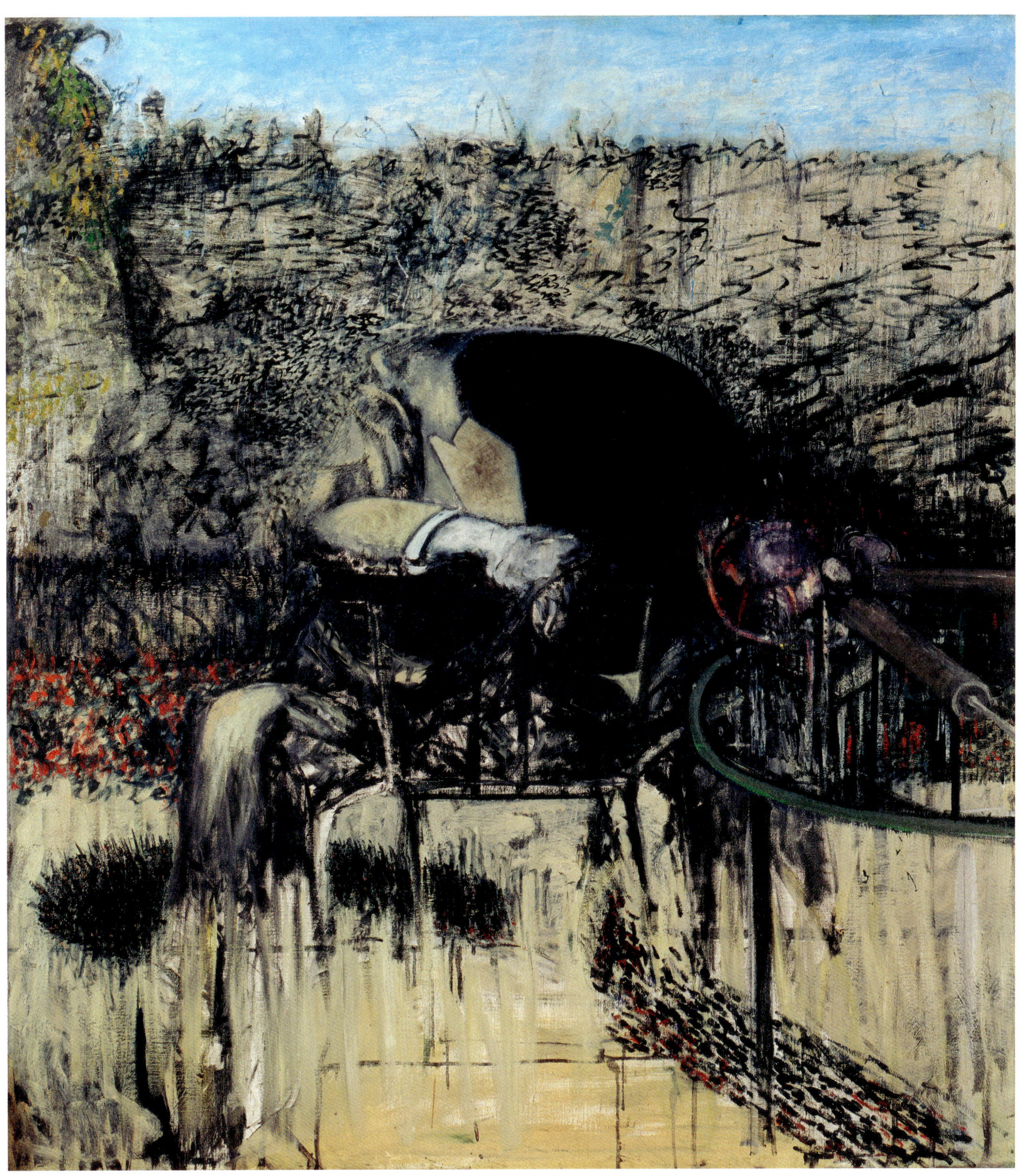

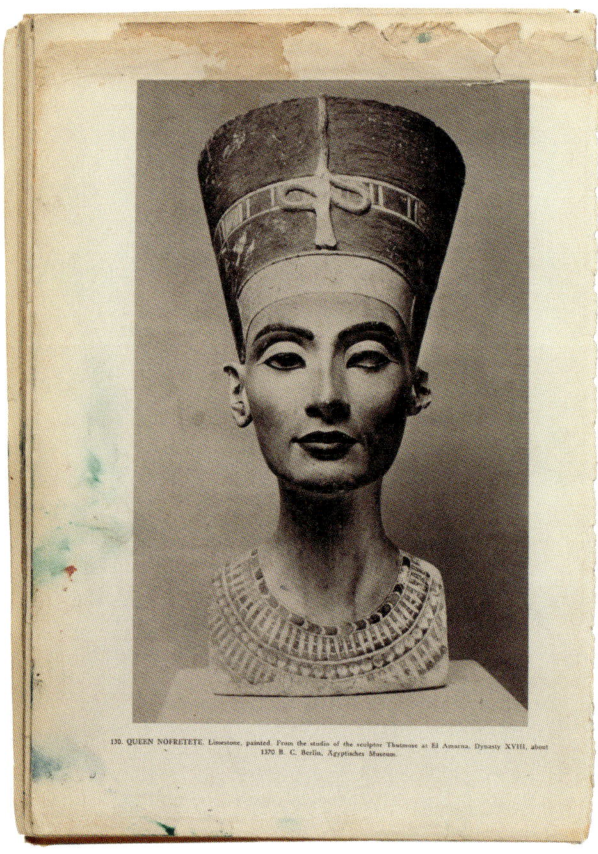

Bacon based Freud's pose on a photograph of Franz Kafka, and although Freud sat for the painting, it was already almost complete when he first arrived. Freud considered it a good likeness, but in a literal sense the physiognomy is unconvincing. Bacon felt inhibited by having a sitter in front of him, and seldom subjected himself to the embarrassment after 1960. Consequently, photographs would play a decisive role in his portrait paintings. It seems improbable that Bacon considered his portrait of Freud a success, and in 1952 he addressed the problem of painting heads: this he rapidly solved, as *Study for a Portrait* (1952; cat.3), attests. The need for reference photographs of specific individuals became more urgent when he was commissioned by Robert Sainsbury to paint his portrait in 1955 (cat.32); the Sainsburys were already becoming major collectors of Bacon's paintings, and this was the first portrait commission Bacon undertook. Lisa Sainsbury sat for several of the eight paintings Bacon made of her between 1955 and 1957 (four of which he destroyed), but he would not let her see them while they were in progress; her immediate presence was less important to him than his visual stimuli, which were photographs of ancient Egyptian sculpture (fig.2).

in a portrait. Thus, it is unlikely to be an accident that Eric Hall's head is obliterated in *Figure in a Landscape*. As the range of photographs that Bacon assimilated expanded, by 1949 he was appropriating gestures and body positions from Eadweard Muybridge's photo-sequences in *The Human Figure in Motion*; they were his substitute for life drawing, fulfilling Muybridge's intention that they would form a resource for artists.

Bacon's portraits followed a different trajectory. During the six years after *Figure in a Landscape*, the heads in his paintings were mostly obscured or turned away from the viewer; then, in 1951, he painted the large, ambitious *Portrait of Lucian Freud* (cat.4) – the first of his paintings to formally announce it was a portrait in the title.

The Grand Manner paintings that Bacon paraphrased were accessed mainly through photographs in books. *Head VI* (1949; cat.1) his renovation of Velázquez's *Portrait of Pope Innocent X*, was perforce based on reproductions. The screaming mouth that Bacon fused onto the Pope was famously inspired by the Odessa Steps sequence in Eisenstein's film, *Battleship Potemkin* (1925; fig.3): the pulse and flicker of early movies powerfully resonated with Bacon, but he adapted the woman's anguished howl from a still in a cinema magazine. Few art books in the 1940s had plentiful colour plates; a young audience today may be unfamiliar with publishers who used to boast, '130 photographs, four in full colour'. Thus, Innocent's cape in *Head VI*, painted from a monochrome reproduction, is purple and lavender, rather than the red Velázquez had painted. When colour reproductions started to predominate in magazines during the 1950s, Bacon's palette, as Lawrence Alloway first suggested, switched from virtually monochrome Prussian Blue to the intensity and explosive abandon exemplified in the Van Gogh series of 1957 (cats 13–4).

From 1958 Bacon commissioned John Deakin to take photographs of Peter Lacy when he visited London. Lacy had moved to Tangier in 1955, but Bacon, who was still attached to his former lover, continued to paint him until 1962. In *Study for Three Heads* (1962; cat.38), painted immediately after Lacy's death, two heads of Lacy based on Deakin's photographs

Fig.3 Film still from *Battleship Potemkin* 1925

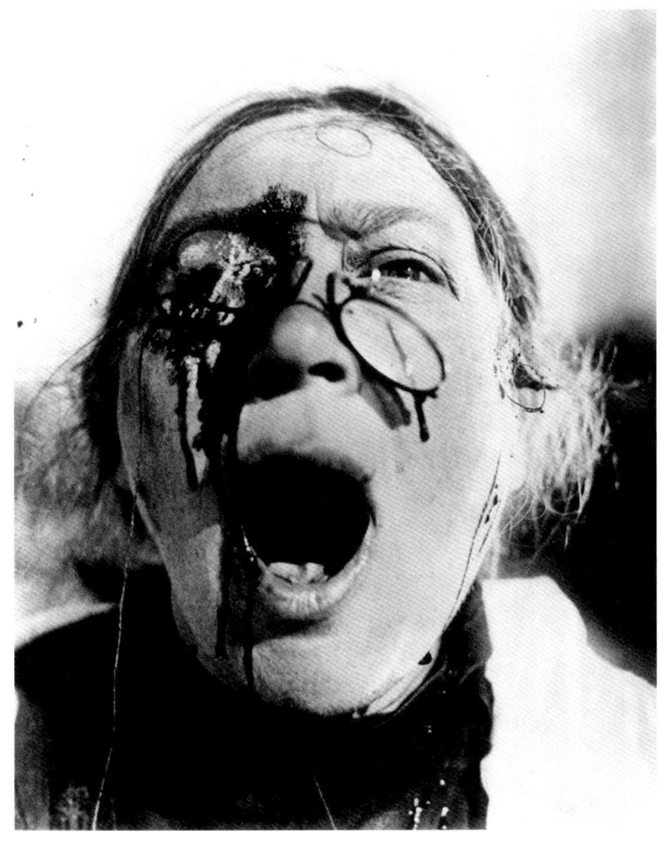

flank a disconsolate Bacon in the centre panel. Bacon was refining his modus operandi, and from 1963, in addition to his large 'subject' paintings, he painted portrait heads, on one, two or three canvases, each 355 × 305mm. This would remain a significant category in his *oeuvre* until 1990.

At the same time, he also started to commission John Deakin to photograph the close friends who were the subjects of a majority of his portraits, both small and large, well into the 1970s – Henrietta Moraes, Lucian Freud, Isabel Rawsthorne and George Dyer. Deakin's photographs were artless, relatively neutral records, not the incisively graphic portraits that had made his reputation; Bacon preferred to characterise them as aides-memoires, despite the paintings themselves being conspicuously non-mimetic. His careless treatment of them – or modifications, sometimes accidental – was adroitly translated in his paintings. He performed a balancing act in 'twisting the image', as he put it, away from the 'mere illustration' he abhorred. After the damage he inflicted, both to the photograph and to the image he painted, we are left to gaze at the irreducible essence of the person. He painted alone, and one can imagine him contemplating Deakin's photographs of George Dyer before carrying out the manipulations that anticipated the spectral paint attack in, for example, *Three Studies for Portrait of George Dyer (on light ground)* (1964; cat.52).

All Bacon's paintings are, in a sense, portraits. Irrespective of the distortions, or the expressive vigour of the brushstrokes, the identity of the person being represented is never in doubt. He captures their life force, their individual aura, simultaneously with their mortality, while invariably bringing the image back to appearance.

Francis Bacon's Close-up Heads: An Overlooked Source

Richard Calvocoressi

Much has been written about Francis Bacon's prodigious use of film stills and photographic imagery in his work – from press cuttings and reproductions torn from books to commissioned portraits. To list just two, indispensable texts: Martin Harrison's monograph *In Camera. Francis Bacon: Photography, Film and the Practice of Painting* and David Alan Mellor's essay 'Film, Fantasy, History in Francis Bacon'.[1] Both authors mention the photographer Helmar Lerski, whom Bacon claimed to have met by chance in Berlin in 1927. Lerski photographed Bacon's effeminate, 18-year-old face in profile, close-up and dramatically lit (fig.1). Bacon must have kept a print of the portrait since it was later published in the first *Catalogue Raisonné* of his work by John Rothenstein and Ronald Alley (1964). But little has been written about the consequences for Bacon's art of this chance encounter (if chance it really was) with Lerski in Berlin.

Helmar Lerski is little known in Britain today outside specialist photography circles, yet his work was hailed as revolutionary during the 1920s and 1930s, attracting the attention, after the Second World War, of Edward Steichen, who was interested in acquiring some of his photographs for the Museum of Modern Art in New York.[2] Lerski spent the years from 1893 to 1914 in the USA, initially in the theatre, but in 1910 he opened his own photographic studio. He specialised in portraits of actors in character roles, using 10 × 12-inch (254 × 305mm) plates at a distance of less than half a metre from his models. Following the outbreak of the First World War, he returned to Europe, settling in Berlin in 1915. He came to the notice of the silent film industry and, from 1916 to 1928, pursued a full-time career as cameraman on a number of films. He was director of cinematography for Robert Reinert's *Ahasver* (1917), Paul Leni's *Waxworks* (1924) and Berthold Viertel's *The Wig* (1925), and was a cameraman and special effects expert on Fritz Lang's *Metropolis* (1927). It was his manipulation of light and shadow in close-ups of the human face that earned him his reputation: his use of 'black velvet [backdrops] and wide-angle lenses to eliminate all superfluous information' was particularly noted.[3]

If the teenage Bacon was interested in avant-garde cinema in 1927, he could have met Lerski in Berlin through some mutual film connection. However, as Harrison points out, beyond his professed admiration for early Eisenstein, especially *Battleship Potemkin*, and early Buñuel, there is scant documentation on what films Bacon actually

Fig. 1   Helmar Lerski   *Francis Bacon*   1927   Gelatin silver print   290 x 230mm

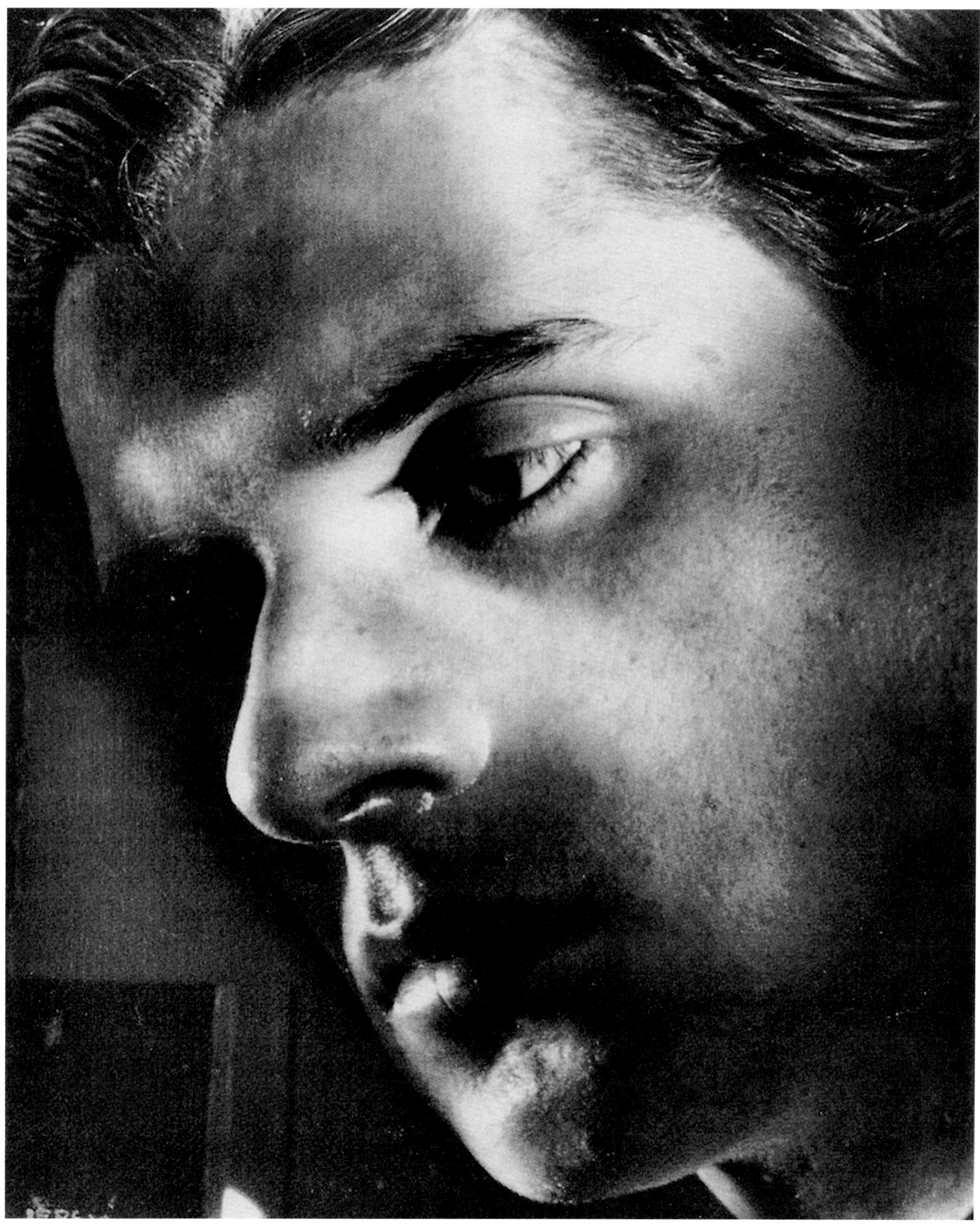

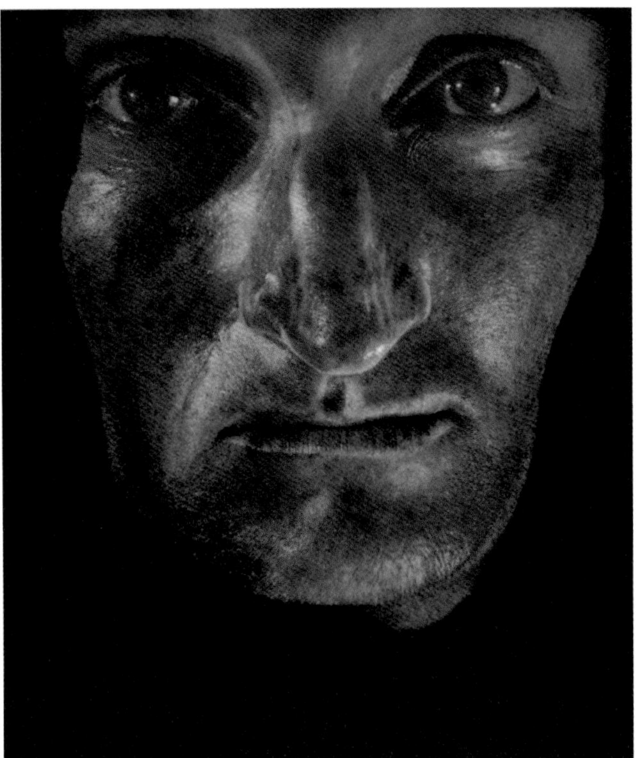

Fig.2   Helmar Lerski
Photograph from *Verwandlungen durch Licht*
(Metamorphosis through Light)   1936

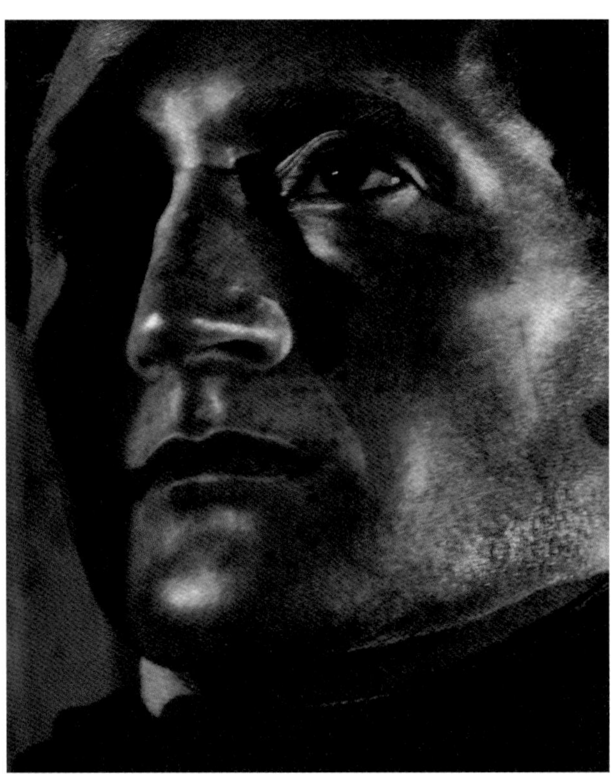

Fig.3   Helmar Lerski
Photograph from *Verwandlungen durch Licht*
(Metamorphosis through Light)   1936

saw and when he saw them.[4] Mellor claims that Bacon was 'astonished' by *Metropolis* but does not say when or where he watched it.[5] Intriguingly, in early 1930 Bacon sent a card from London announcing his new interior design showroom to Tilla Durieux, the Austrian film and stage actress who was a prominent figure in Weimar Berlin.[6] She was a friend of the Berlin photographer Frieda Riess, who specialised in taking portraits of actors and artists, and who in 1930 exhibited her work alongside Lerski's.

Lerski also photographed celebrities from the arts, including some of the same subjects. Durieux acted in Fritz Lang's 1929 science fiction film *Woman in the Moon.* All this would seem to suggest that, during his stay in Berlin, Bacon was moving in, or at least had been introduced to, advanced film circles.

By 1925 or 1926 Lerski was combining his work for the film industry with portrait photography. In the late 1920s, in addition to his portraits of well-known figures from Berlin cultural life, he began his series of photographs of anonymous Berlin workers. These were collected and published as a book, *Köpfe des Alltags* (*Heads from Everyday Life*), in 1931. The following year, Lerski and his second wife moved to Palestine. In 1936 he created what he later regarded as his masterpiece, the 'Metamorphosis through Light'.[7] Over a three-month period, on the roof terrace of their flat in Tel Aviv, he took 175 black and white photographs of the head of the same unnamed young Jewish labourer – again, no more than 20cm from his subject (figs 2 and 3). By means of numerous mirrors, he was able to reflect harsh, probing sunlight onto the man's face. The intention with *Heads from Everyday Life* had been to reveal abstract or archetypal 'truths' rather than individual physiognomies. This time Lerski created multiple images of a single face as opposed to multiple images of 30 faces. The astonishing thing about the 'Metamorphosis', 80 of which Lerski felt were of great significance, is how different each photograph looks – how Lerski has employed light to disclose structure and transform facial expression.

Bacon would have had an opportunity to become reacquainted with the English-speaking Lerski between 1937 and 1939, when the latter spent extended periods in London. On his first visit, Lerski brought with him the 'Metamorphosis'. Through one or other of his friends in the German-Jewish émigré community, he made contact with Elsie Cohen, who in 1931 had founded the art house Academy Cinema in Oxford Street. And so, every day for five weeks from late June to early August 1938, 12 images from the 'Metamorphosis' were projected onto the Academy's screen as a short before the main feature. The public reaction was by all accounts ecstatic. 'Enthusiastic audiences have been holding up the show at Oxford Street's Academy with thunderous applause for a series of pictures, twelve studies of a man's face, projected on the screen by slides', wrote the reviewer for *Cavalcade*, under the heading 'Camera Genius: Photographer who paints with Light'.[8]

Since Bacon frequented the Academy and knew Elsie Cohen, it is reasonable to assume that he may have been one of those who saw the shortened version of 'Metamorphosis' in London in the summer of 1938.[9] If so, it is equally feasible that its serial, cinematic format appealed to him as much as Lerski's extreme close-ups of the human face. Bacon later said that he visualised paintings in sequence like a slideshow and occasionally thought of making a film.[10] The nearest he came to this was the triptych format, which he first used in *Three Studies for Figures at the Base of a Crucifixion* (*c*.1944), but which he did not adopt more generally until the 1960s for his portrait heads. Each of these

Fig.4   Dyk Rudenski
Page from *Gestologie und Filmspielerei*
(Gestology and Movie Tricks)   1927

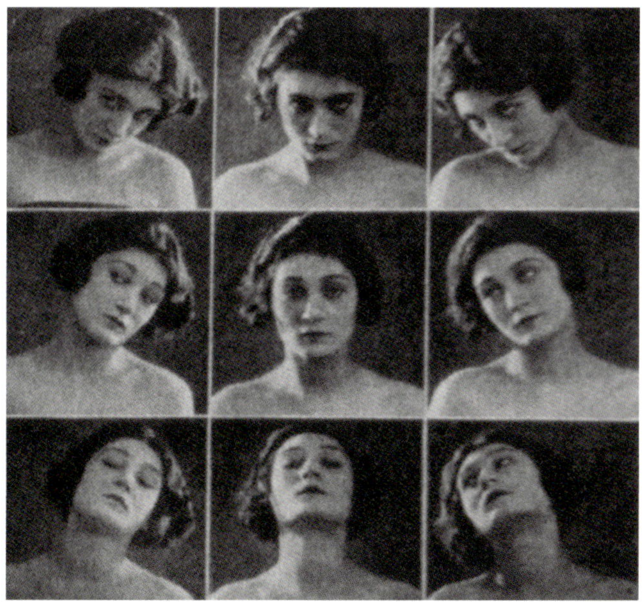

Fig.5   Helmar Lerski
Publicity stills of Carl de Vogt
for the film *Ahasver*   1917

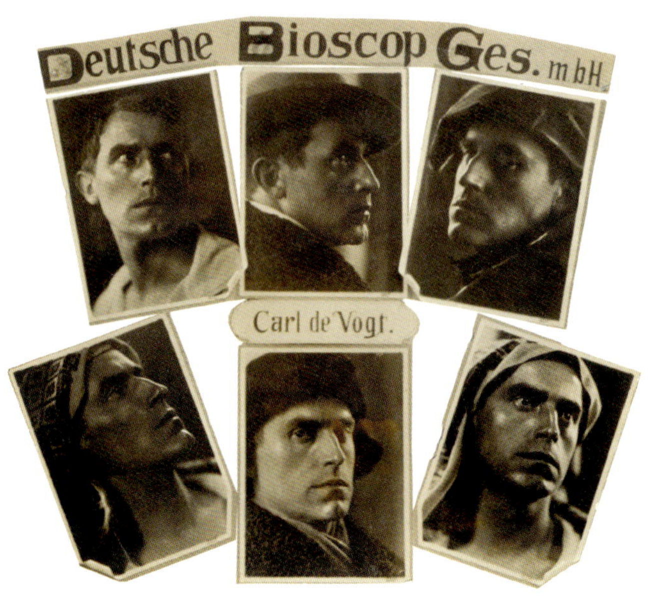

small heads, whether singly or grouped in threes, is painted on a 14 × 12-inch (356 × 305mm) canvas, allowing the head to be depicted at roughly life size. Bacon painted some 40 small triptychs of heads. The format enabled him to explore different aspects of the same face – profile, full-face and three-quarter view – or contrast images of three different people, usually close friends or lovers. In the very first triptych, *Study for Three Heads* (1962; cat.38), the artist's face is flanked by two views of his lover's, Peter Lacy, who had recently died. In this instance the triptych has an explicitly commemorative, almost devotional function, underlined by its background of mourning black.

European books on portrait photography and physiognomic expression in the 1920s and 1930s – for example, Dyk Rudenski's *Gestologie und Filmspielerei* (1927) – often illustrated three different views of the same head in triptych format (fig.4). Lerski himself used this technique in his publicity still for Carl de Vogt (fig.5), who acted the leading role of the Wandering Jew in *Ahasver*. If there is a connection between the exaggerated facial language of silent cinema and the development of avant-garde black and white portrait photography, it is epitomised in the career of Lerski himself. Lerski's background as an actor, and his early studio work photographing actors, influenced his highly subjective approach to both cinematography and portraiture. His faces are contrived, each one a pose or mask performing a different role. Instead of make-up or disguise, Lerski uses light to sculpt and transform appearance.

Bacon also had a theatrical side. He wore make-up, dyed his hair and posed in photo booths, using the resulting strips as the basis for self-portraits.[11] In his small triptychs, Bacon seems to have absorbed, consciously or not, the more dramatic aspects of Lerski's work: multiple views of the same face evoking

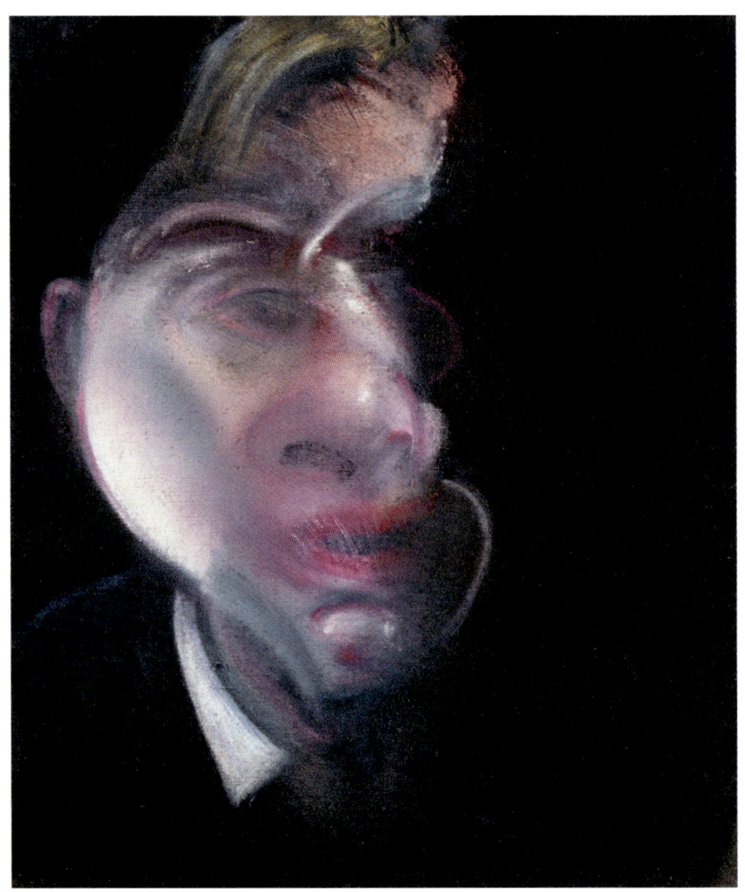

Fig. 6 *Three Studies for Self-Portrait* 1979 Oil on canvas 375 × 318mm (each panel)

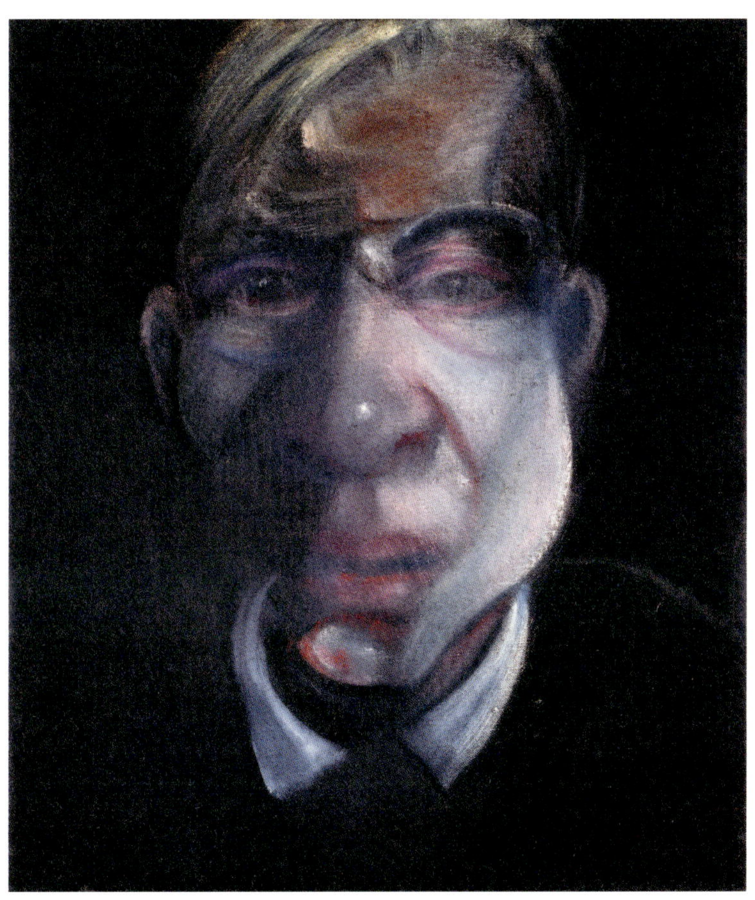 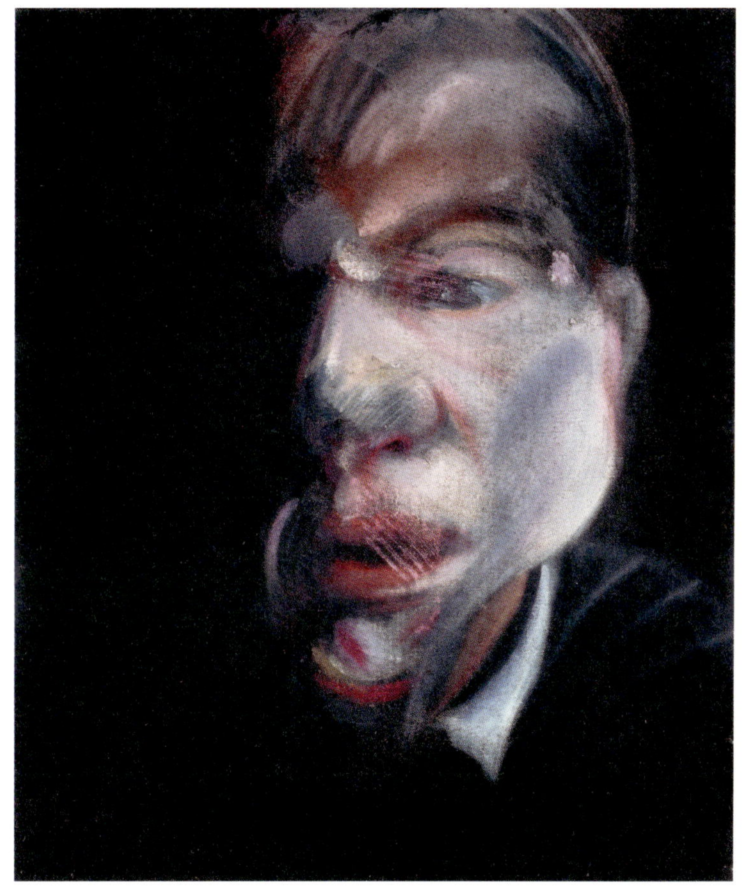

an existential idea of human identity as fluctuating and contingent; close-up heads, tightly framed and occasionally cropped, their contours often sharply outlined; and blank, sometimes black, backgrounds that isolate the subject and throw it into even sharper relief.

What might have stimulated Bacon's interest in Lerski again was the exhibition *Neue Sachlichkeit and German Realism of the Twenties*, shown at the Hayward Gallery from November 1978 to January 1979. Given his fascination with the Weimar period, not to mention the Third Reich that supplanted it, it is hard to imagine Bacon missing this large and important show, which brought masterpieces by Beckmann, Dix, Grosz, Schad and others to London, many for the first time. As revelatory as the paintings, drawings and prints were the photographs and photobooks – 138 items in all, including five photographs by Lerski from *Köpfe des Alltags* and a copy of the book itself.[12]

Shortly after the Hayward exhibition closed, Bacon, then in his seventieth year, painted *Three Studies for Self-Portrait* (1979; fig.6). It is one of the starkest and most frontal of his late triptychs of heads, its poignant sense of mortality recalling the first, 1962 triptych, commemorating Peter Lacy.[13] Except for subtle passages of colour in the skin and hair, Bacon's palette is restricted to black and white, with black predominating. In the left and right panels, one side of the artist's ageing face is in complete darkness; in the centre, it seems to loom towards the spectator. It would be nice to think that, half a century after their first meeting in Berlin, Lerski's close-up heads, black velvet backgrounds and contrasts of light and dark still resonated with Bacon and played a part in his own extraordinary metamorphosis through paint.

Beyond Appearance

'I hate a homely atmosphere ... I would like the intimacy of the image against a very stark background.'

While Bacon was working on screaming heads, he was also beginning to engage with portraiture more directly by working from live sitters in his studio. His first painting of a named individual represented his friend and fellow painter Lucian Freud, *Portrait of Lucian Freud* (1951; cat.4). Bacon preferred to paint his sitters alone and untethered by the familiar surroundings of a home or the studio: 'I hate a homely atmosphere' he stated, 'I want to isolate the image and take it away from the interior and the home'.[1] He placed his subject against a dark background articulated by a white frame, and ghostly double shadows infiltrate the canvas at the base. Freud's own recollection was that by the time he arrived for his sittings the portrait was almost complete and that Bacon had used a reproduction of an old photograph of the writer Franz Kafka when young as a reference.[2] Consequently, the painting is not quite a portrait of either Freud or Kafka, but a conflation of sitters that would become a characteristic of Bacon's *oeuvre*.

It is possible that Lisa Sainsbury had Bacon's portrait of Freud in mind when she commissioned a portrait of her husband Robert, *Portrait of R.J. Sainsbury* (1955; cat.32), who, like Freud, sat for Bacon in his studio.[3] Robert's appearance no doubt appealed to Bacon:

he wore glasses reminiscent of those Bacon had incorporated in his series of screaming figures. Furthermore, in his dark suit he could be mistaken for any of the anonymous men populating the *Man in Blue I–VII* series begun the previous year (see cat.6).

Lisa herself became Bacon's first female sitter. While Bacon later claimed to finding the presence of a sitter in the studio too inhibiting, Lisa proved to be a conducive companion sitting for eight canvases, of which four survive.[4] In *Sketch for a Portrait of Lisa* (1955; cat.33), Bacon employs vertical white painted stripes, a device he described as 'shuttering', which sometimes served to trap or conceal a figure but which here seems more like a veil. It is possible that this usage is in keeping with Bacon's wish that 'the sensation doesn't come straight out at you but slides slowly and gently through the gaps'.[5] Lisa's presence in the studio may account for a more sympathetic treatment in her portrait. Other likely points of reference for this painting have been identified, including black and white photographic images of ancient Egyptian art, specifically sculpted portraits of the Pharoah Akhenaten and Queen Nefertiti (p.30) – further evidence of Bacon's magpie-like appropriation of sources when making portraits.[6]

4   *Portrait of Lucian Freud*   1951   Oil on canvas   1983 × 1371mm

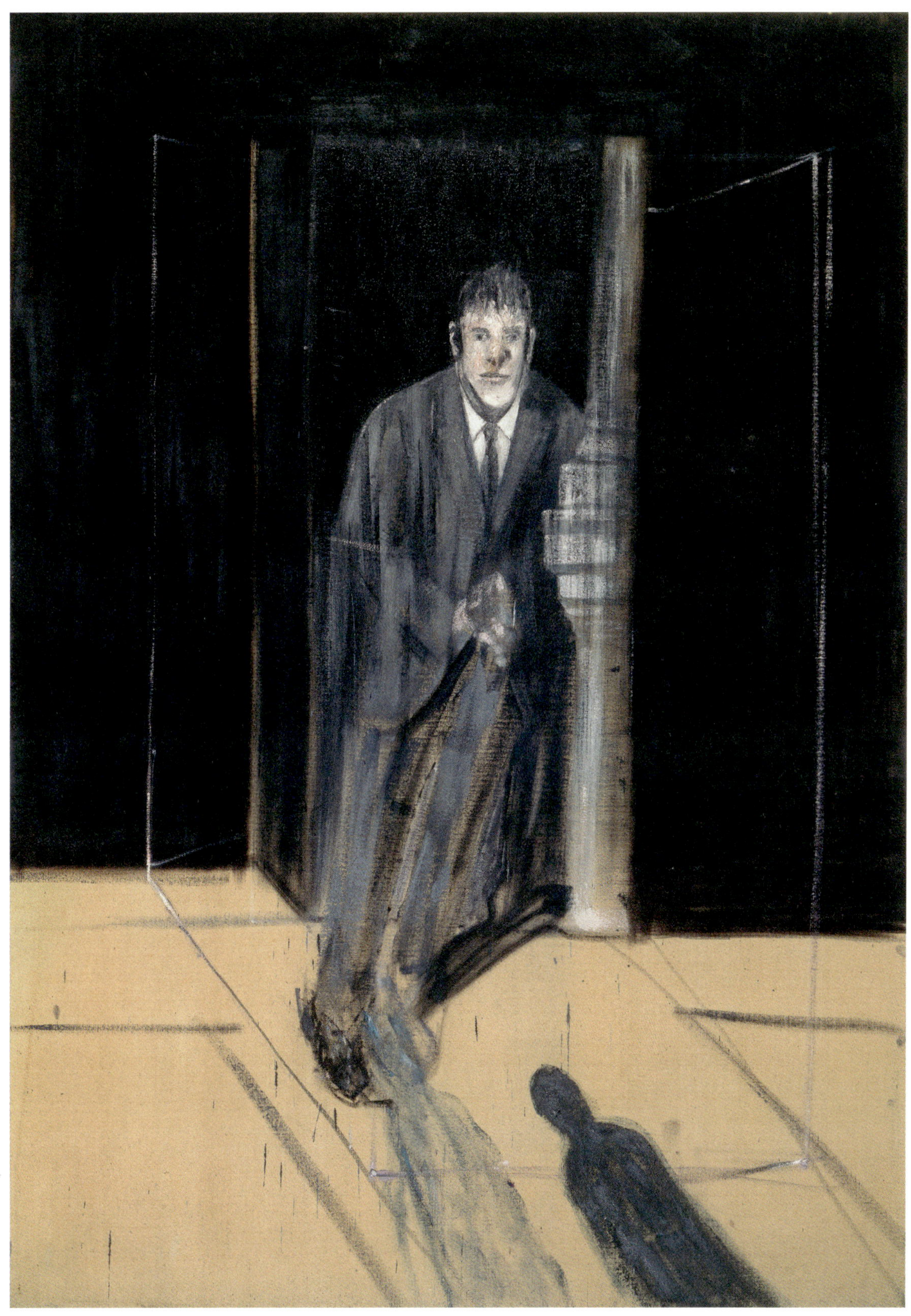

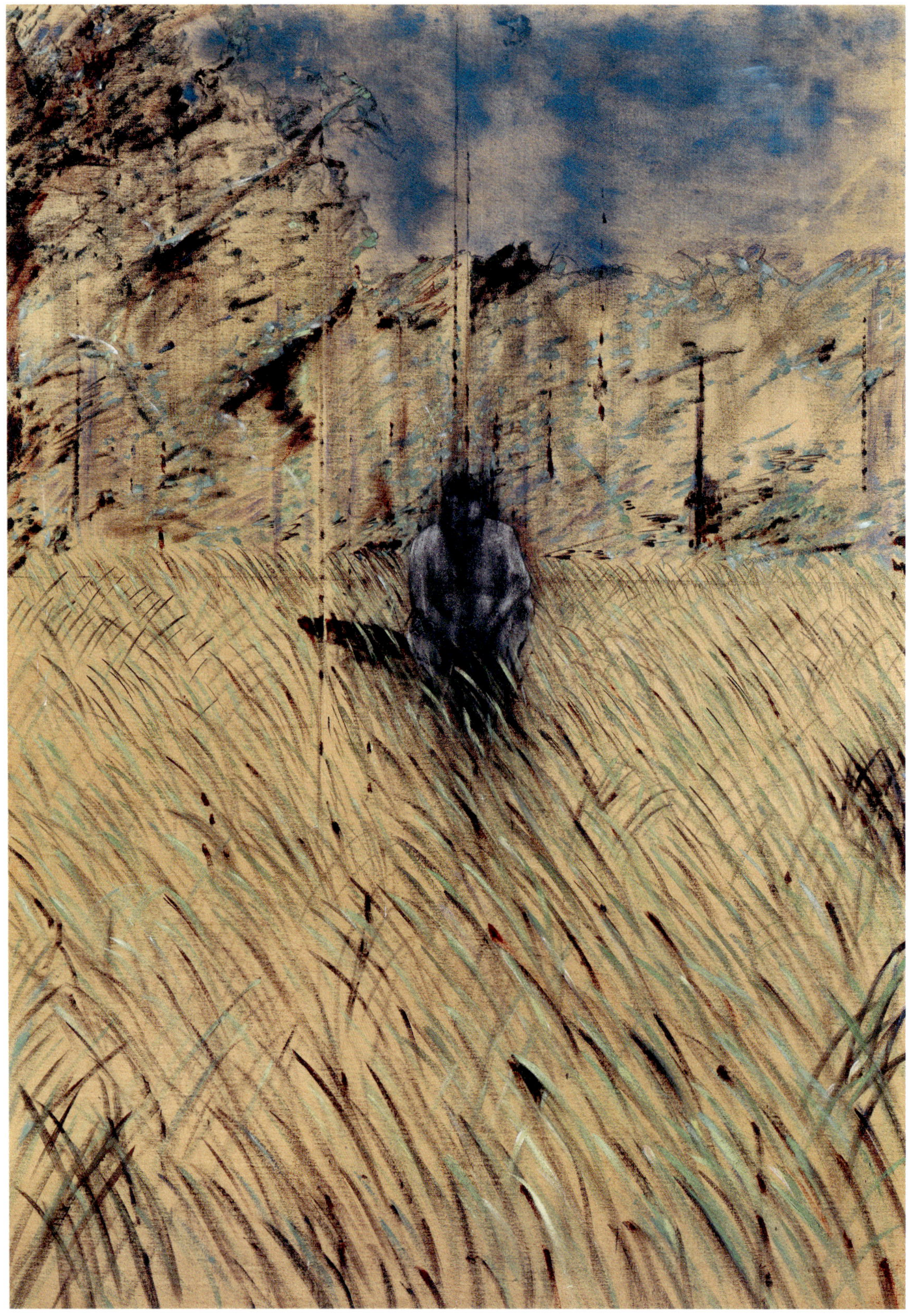

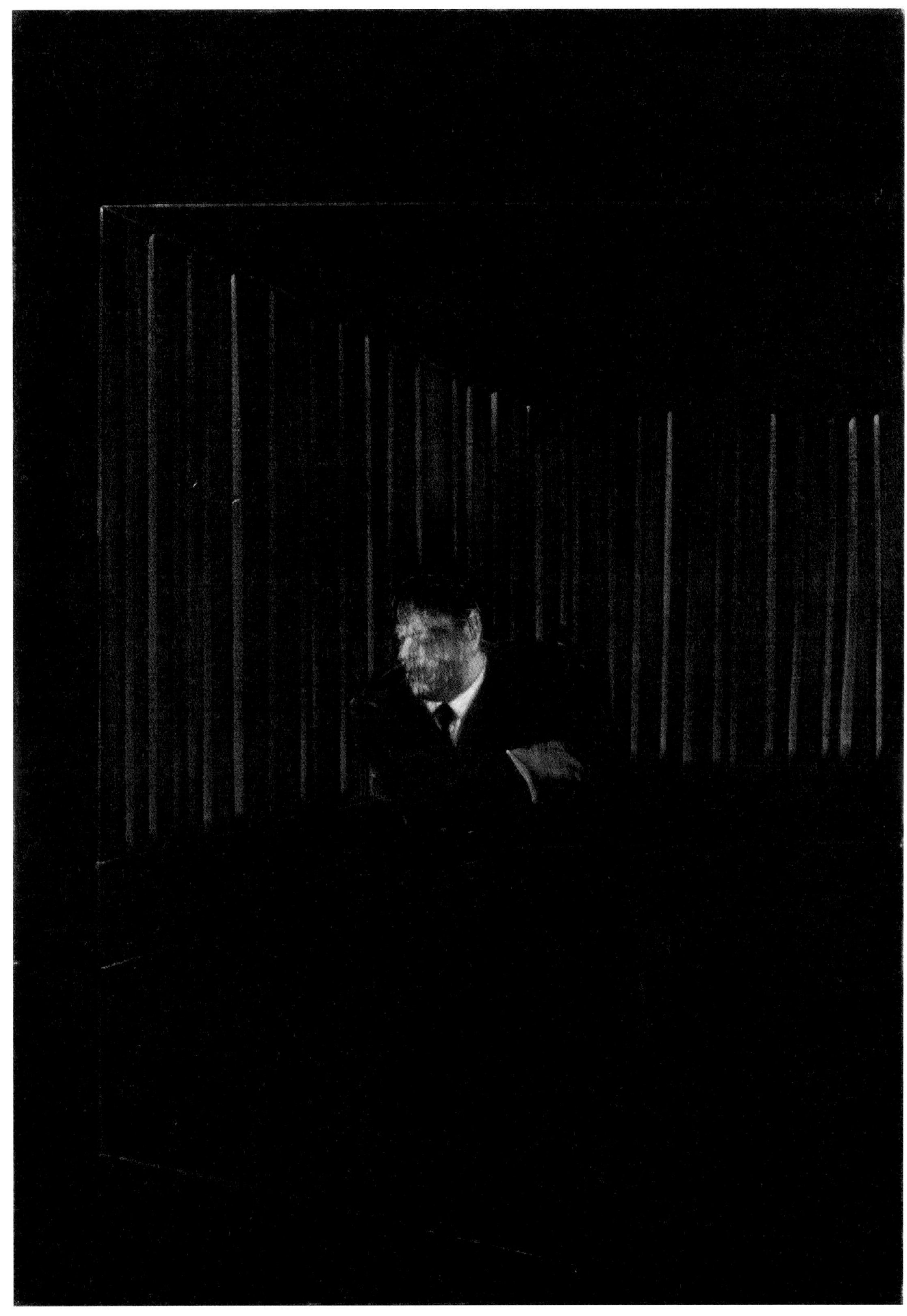

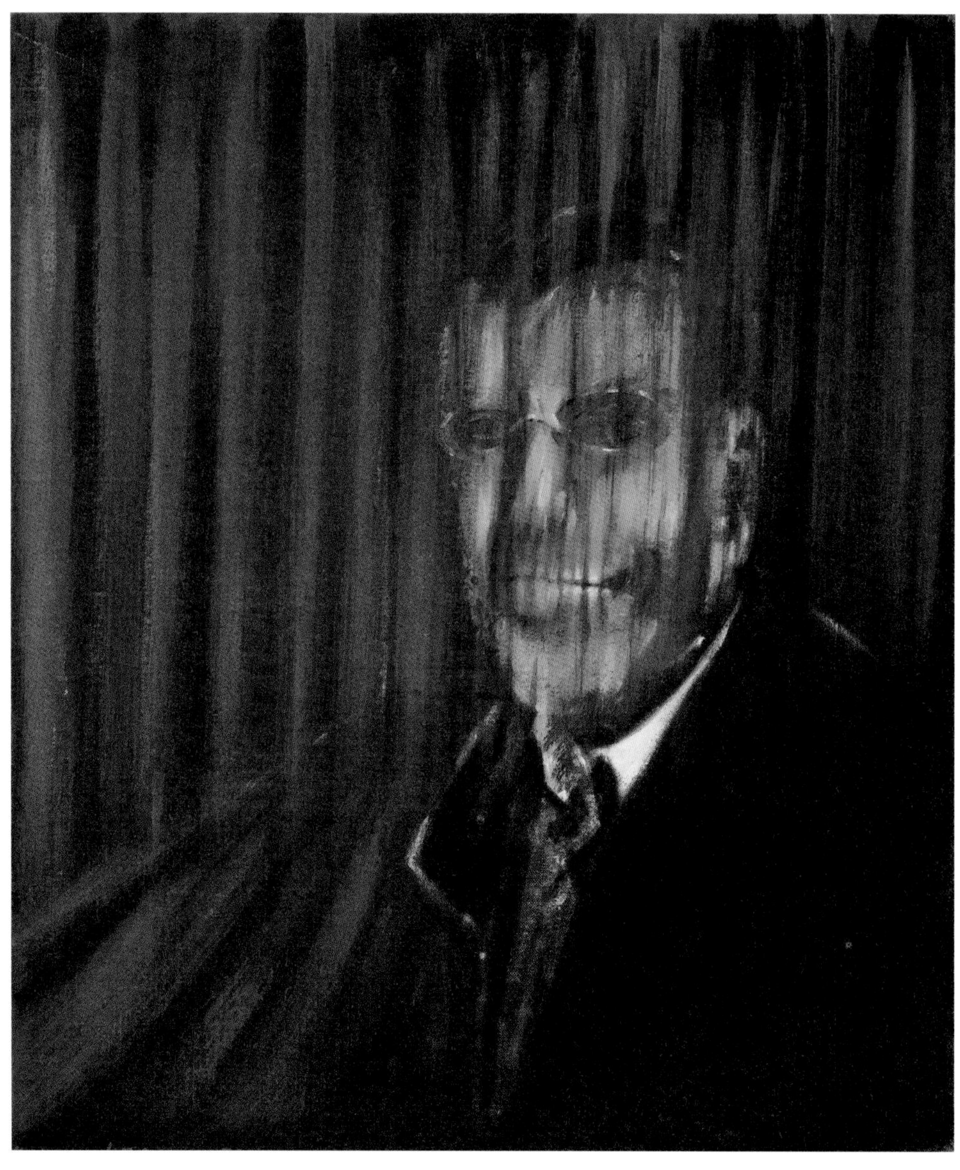

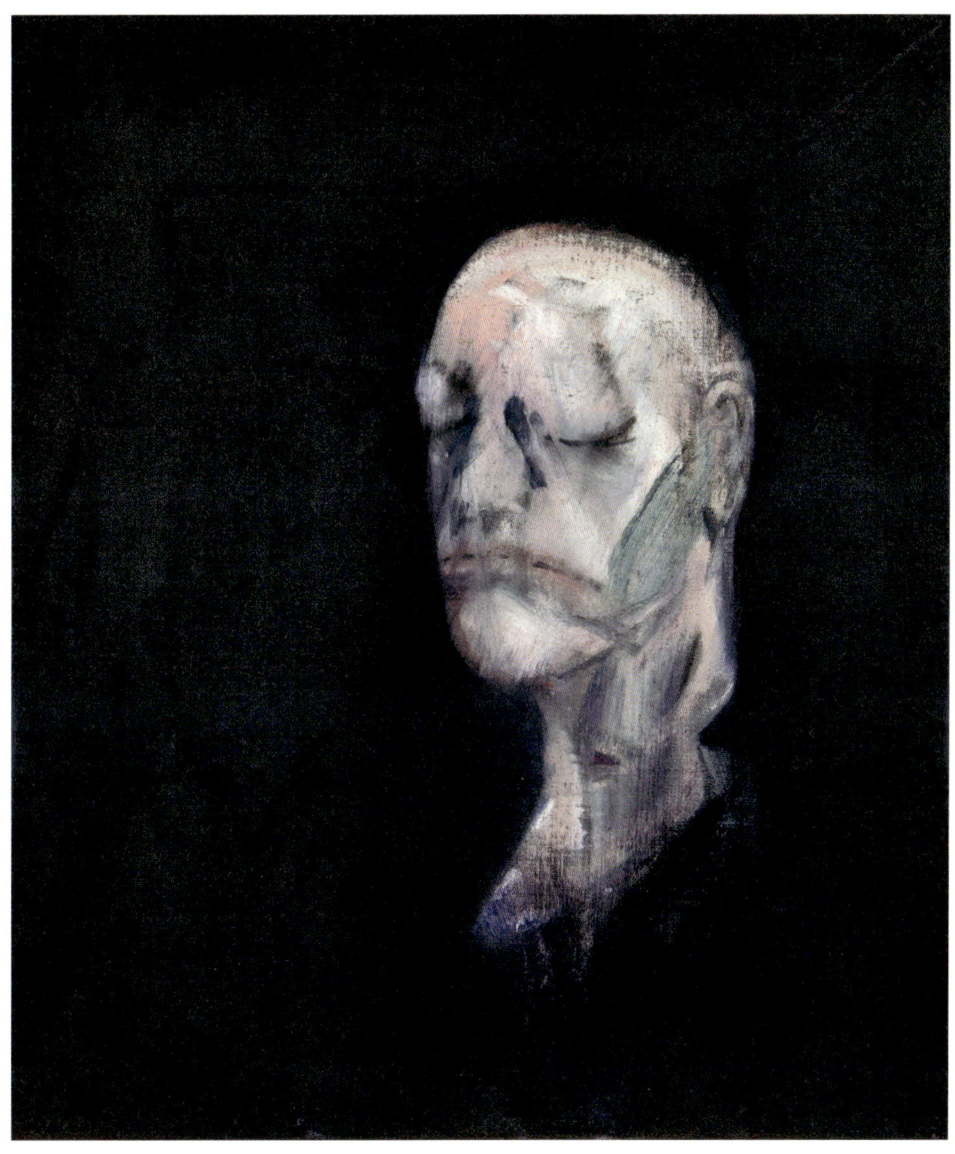

9   *Portrait of Man with Glasses I*   1963   Oil on canvas   343 × 292mm

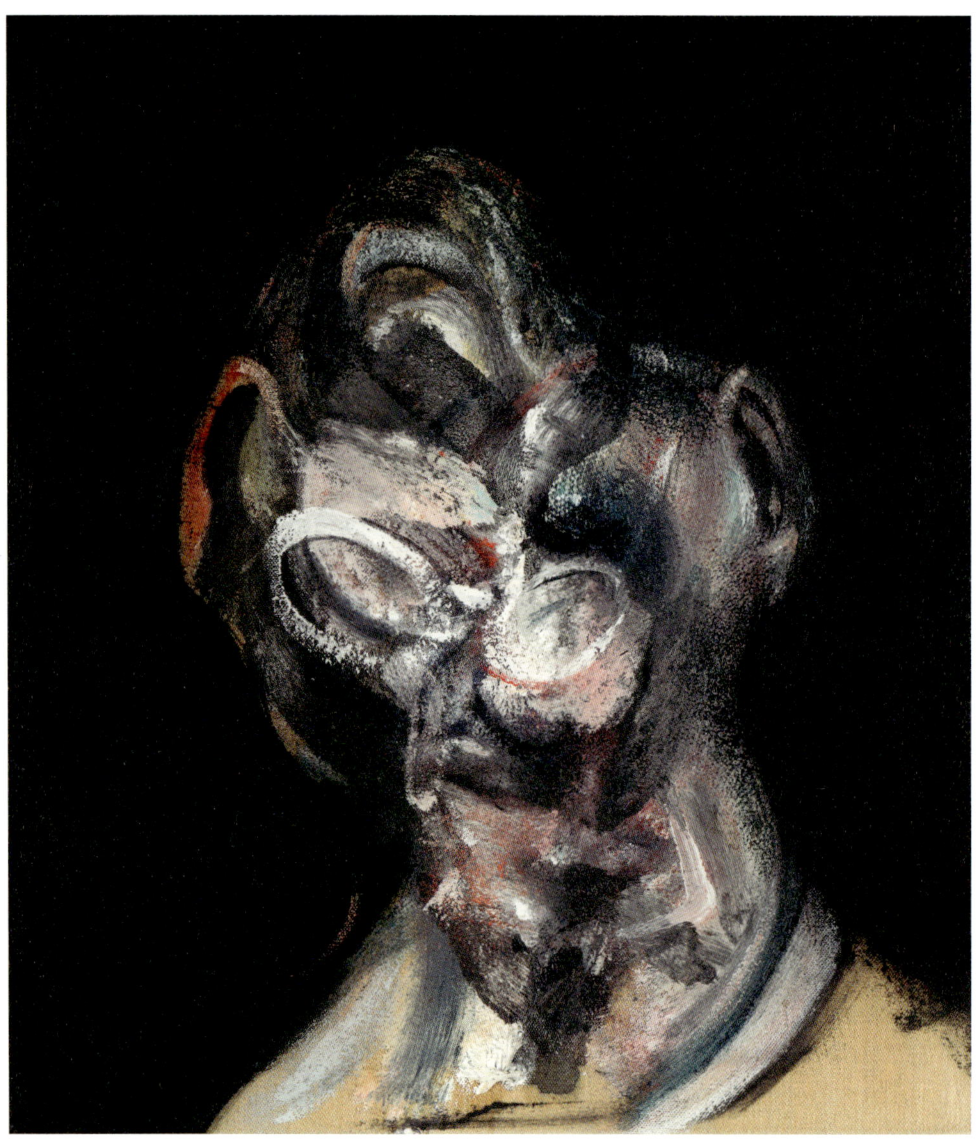

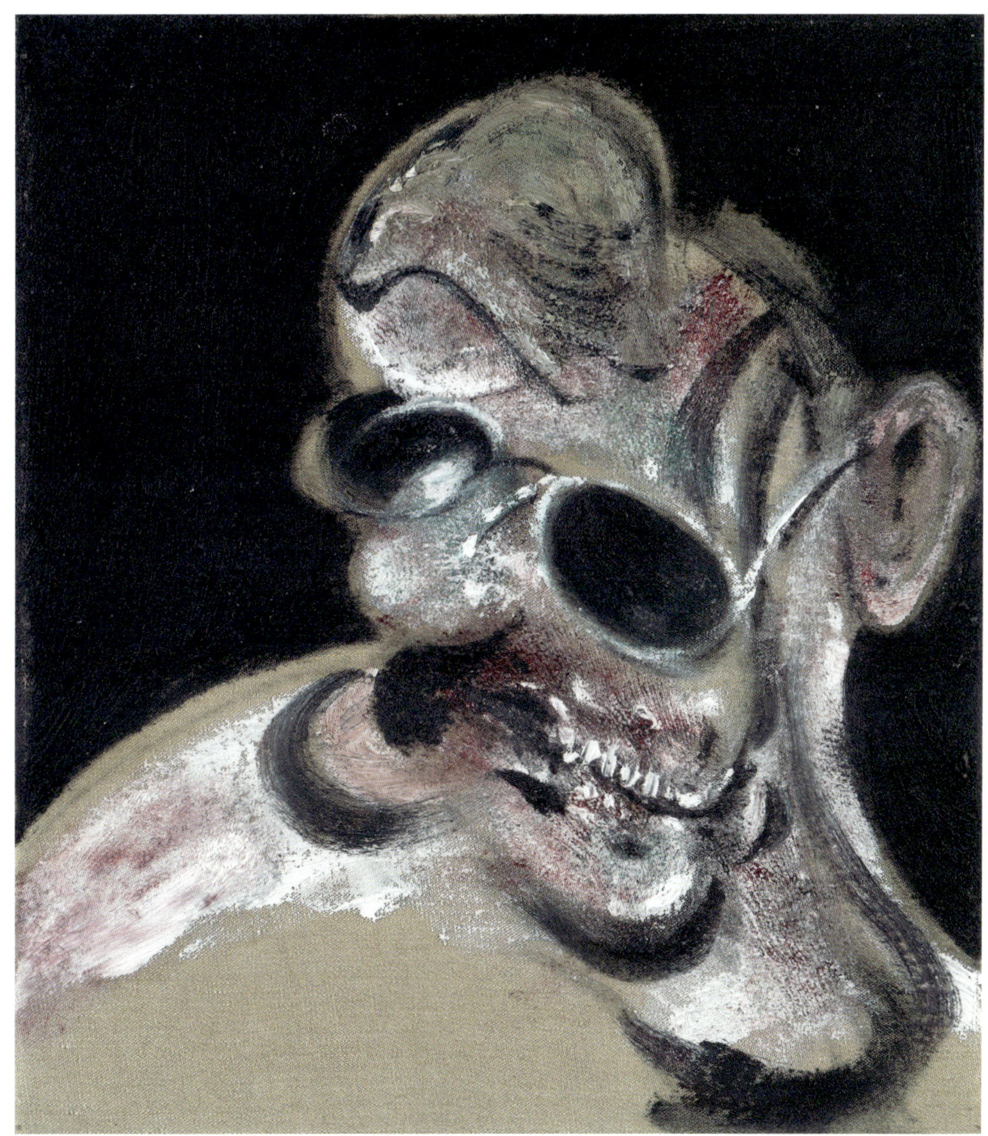

Queer Attachments to Francis Bacon

Gregory Salter

In the November 1993 issue of the gay and lesbian publication the *Pink Paper*, alongside previews for the first full UK production of Tony Kushner's play *Angels in America* at the National Theatre and a Wolfgang Tillmans photography show in Hackney, the writer James Cary Parkes drew readers' attention to an exhibition of Francis Bacon's portraits staged at the Marlborough Gallery. Bacon's portraits, he explained, 'involve a very peculiar and difficult negotiation as to what an aesthetic expression of insights into people can conjure up'.[1] In one glance, you might encounter 'a very cruel surface of profound distortions and inner neurosis', while in another there resides a certain intimacy and empathy.[2] This turmoil results in the paintings 'begging constantly alternating interpretations that eventually return to their primary source', Bacon himself.[3] This description reflected the unsteady, dynamic relationship that audiences had with Bacon's portraits, and indeed with Bacon as an artist. Yet the prominent placement of Cary Parkes's review underlines that by 1993 Bacon had become a touchstone in the gay and lesbian press, a recognisably queer figure of interest to a mass audience. How, then, did Bacon's paintings come to mean something to queer audiences, and how have these meanings shifted over time?

In recent years, more general gay and lesbian attachments to Bacon have been joined by an increase in scholarship on 'queer' Bacon.

This work has read Bacon's painting as engaging with imagery and practices recognisable to men beginning to think of themselves as homosexual in Britain in the years after the Second World War.[4] We might, for instance, interpret Bacon's frequent depictions of spaces where forms of public intimacy between men could take place, such as the bar-like settings of the series *Man in Blue I–VII* (1954; see cat.6) as being connected to increasing police crackdowns on such practices in the post-war years. Or we might think of his engagement with interior spaces, such as in his *Study for a Portrait* (1953; fig.1), as gesturing to the emergence of domesticity as, potentially, the acceptable realm for homosexuality, particularly following the publication of the Wolfenden Report in 1957, which recommended that sex between men in private could be decriminalised. In these ways, the 1950s paintings appear to embody a certain ambivalence relating to navigating public and private spaces, particularly as they became fraught with expectations about and limitations on sexual intimacy and sociality.[5] They become resonant with a certain atmosphere prior to the partial decriminalisation of homosexuality in England and Wales in 1967, touched by tones of discretion and quiet anxiety, though never reducible solely to them. There is intimacy too, quiet, gut-churning moments of contact between men, which are made visible and appear to implicate us in their dynamics.

Fig.1 Francis Bacon *Study for a Portrait* 1953 Oil on canvas 1525 × 1180mm

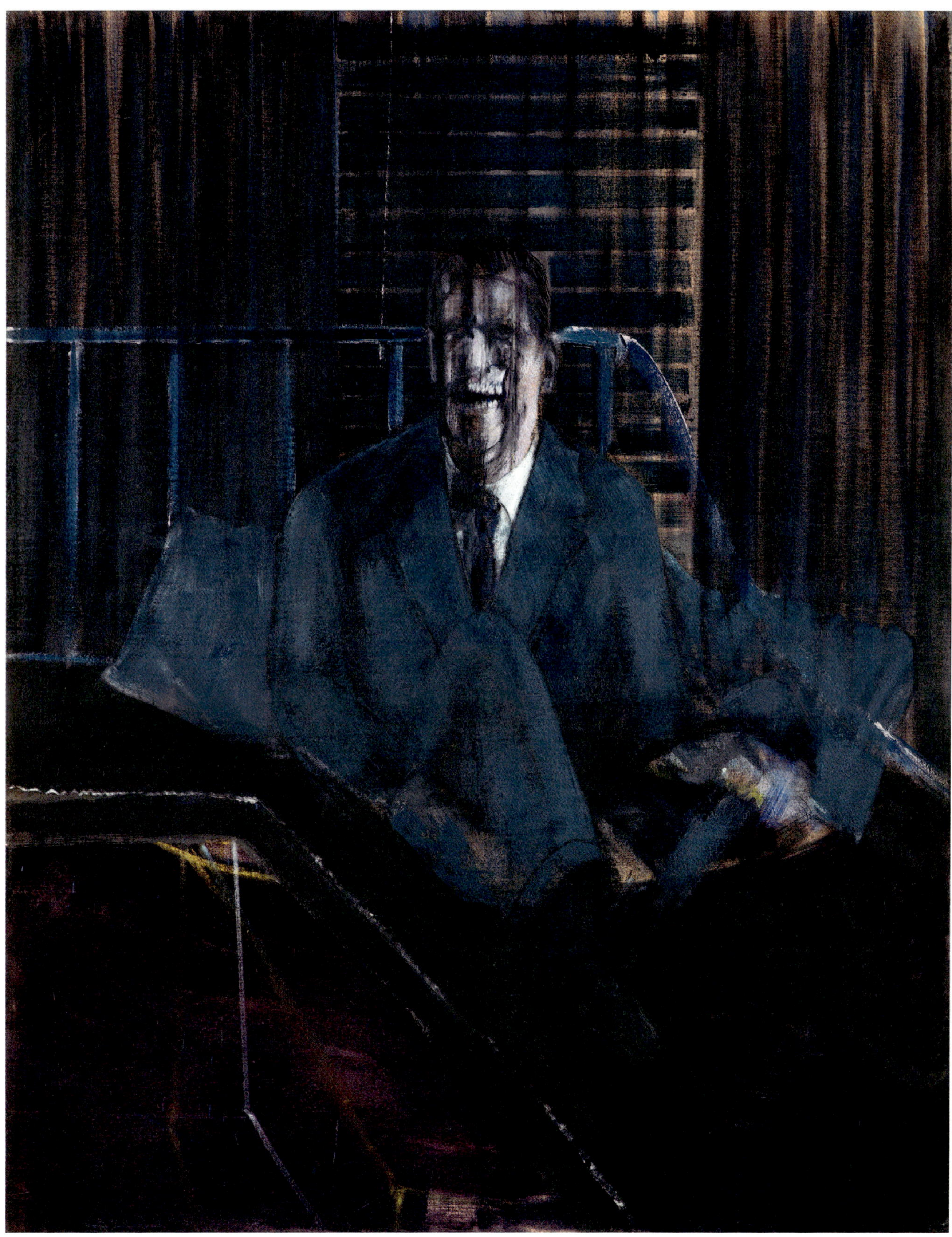

In the wake of partial decriminalisation and
Gay Liberation, Bacon's art could be included
as one aspect of the emergent idea of a 'gay
culture'.[6] By 1978, Emmanuel Cooper, the art
critic for *Gay News*, made Bacon's practice a
focus in an article that explored whether such
a thing as 'gay art' existed, illustrating and
discussing *Two Figures* (1953; fig.2) as 'an
important step in the recognition of the male
homosexual subject'.[7] In this period, *Two
Figures* was a frequent touchstone for writers
seeking to think about Bacon's work as 'gay
art', a perhaps unsurprising development
given that it is one of his more explicit images
of apparent sexual intimacy between men.
Another repeatedly referenced painting
following this reading of Bacon's work is
Triptych May–June 1973 (1973; pp.20–1),
a piece that explicitly memorialises the suicide
of Bacon's partner George Dyer. The US-
based gay and lesbian magazine the *Advocate*
mentioned the 'searing autobiographical'
painting in its overview of 'gay art' in 1980,
and the Dyer works become frequent reference
points alongside *Two Figures* in further
coverage later in the decade.[8] It is instructive
that particular paintings in Bacon's *oeuvre*
– those depicting homosexual intimacy most
explicitly and those that can be related to
a particularly tragic relationship – became
a focus in the 1970s and 1980s, as a gay
identity formed and solidified in a particular
way in the West. They speak to questions
of the increasing yet fraught visibility of
homosexuality and its liminal position in
public life. Yet as gay audiences sought
to secure a particular image of Bacon, his
interviews with art critic David Sylvester,
published for the first time in 1975, avoided
any explicit discussion of the relationship
between his sexuality and his art.

In the late 1980s Bacon's paintings took
on further resonances with gay and lesbian
viewers. Just over a month before the passing
of Section 28 of the Local Government Act

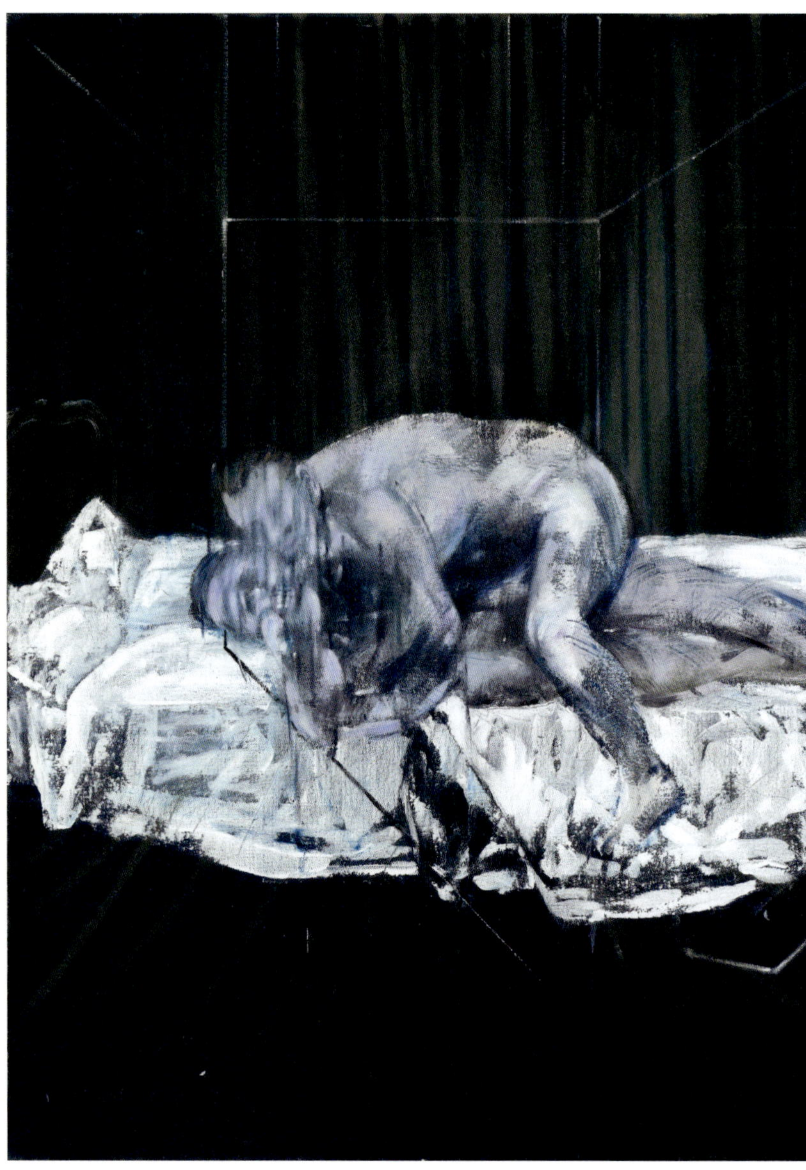

Fig.2 **Francis Bacon** *Two Figures* 1953
Oil on canvas   1525 × 1165mm

in May 1988 – a piece of legislation that
outlawed the 'promotion' of homosexuality
by local authorities and denigrated gay men
and lesbians as operating in '"pretended"
family relationships' – an article in *Gay Times*
noted that Bacon was one of several artists,
alongside Derek Jarman, Maggi Hambling
and Howard Hodgkin, who signed an open
letter published in the *Sunday Times* warning
that the legislation would lead to 'self-
censorship by libraries, museums, galleries
[and] theatres' and amounted to an 'erosion

of civil liberties'.[9] This is not to say that Bacon explicitly connected his art to the contemporary struggle over gay and lesbian rights, but he may well have recognised that his artwork could fall foul of the new legislation. A few months later, in September 1988, the *Pink Paper* recorded that an episode of ITV's *The South Bank Show* was going to focus on 'Homosexual Art'. The programme's producer, Tony Knox, explained that the idea had come from an article by the writer Edmund White that commented that 'some of the best post-war British art had been produced by gay men', naming Bacon as one such example.[10] Knox continued:

> It seemed to us on the programme that this association between art and homosexuality had long been made in peoples' minds but that the time had come to address that connection directly and ask if there was, in fact, a direct link. The discussion seemed particularly appropriate as at that time Clause 28 was going through parliament and there was a pressure on gay artists to leave that area.

While Section 28 had not been the catalyst for the programme's focus, it was shaping a renewed and more mainstream engagement with 'gay art' and Bacon's relationship to it. In this light, it is reasonable to assume that works like *Two Figures* and *Triptych May–June 1973* took on new resonances as works that might, respectively, trouble the culture of censorship and attest to the complexity of gay relationships at a moment of their denigration.

Over the decades since Bacon emerged onto the London art scene at the close of the Second World War, his art has been understandable as having particular meanings for queer subjects and their histories, whether that be pre-decriminalisation cultures and networks that flourished prior to 1967, the solidifying of a gay identity and the search for something like a 'gay art' after the early 1970s, or debates about censorship and family life in the late 1980s. Bacon's paintings, which so frequently concern themselves with portraiture, have become ways for individuals and audiences to orientate themselves in particular moments, despite the paintings' ambivalences and contradictory brutalities and intimacies. All this is, in one sense, to make a rather simple point – that the meanings of artworks change over time, that the encounters viewers have with Bacon's portraits in 1953, or 1975, or 1988, or indeed 2024 will be different. But it is also to draw out the position of Bacon's paintings in the continuous structuring and restructuring of sexual cultures and their histories, to note that encounters with Bacon's portraits have been, and will continue to be, sites where queer audiences have remade themselves.

Lucian Freud & Francis Bacon: A Friendship of Two Halves

Tanya Bentley

In June 2001, shortly before his Tate retrospective, Lucian Freud organised what can perhaps be described as his only ever performance art piece. In a carefully staged stunt, 2,500 posters designed by Freud were plastered around Berlin. Each featured an image of a stolen painting under the words 'WANTED' in red, and offered a reward of up to 300,000 Deutschmarks (almost £100,000) for information on its whereabouts (fig.1).[1]

The painting in question was Freud's exquisite 1952 portrait of Francis Bacon. The painting was bought by Tate but was then stolen while on loan to the Neue Nationalgalerie in Berlin in May 1988. Freud allowed the painting to be reproduced on the poster only in black and white, explaining that this was 'partly because there was no decent colour reproduction, partly as a kind of mourning'. He joked that it was 'equivalent to a black arm band. You know – there it isn't!'[2] Freud released a tongue -in-cheek statement pleading for the thief to consider at least lending the picture to his upcoming Tate exhibition.[3] The appeal and poster campaign, although unsuccessful, made the front pages of several major German and UK newspapers. Freud carefully preserved all the clippings.[4]

The friendship, and presumed rivalry, between Bacon and Freud has become enshrined in the mythology of twentieth-century British art. The artist Graham Sutherland introduced

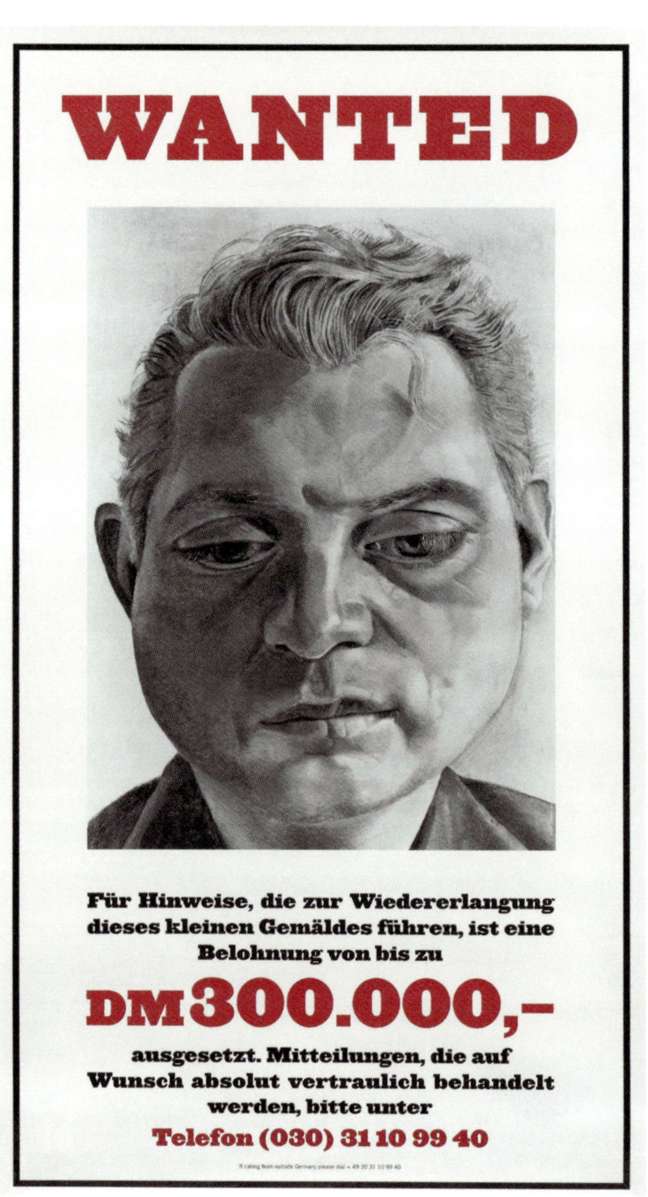

Fig.1 Lucian Freud Finished 'Wanted' poster 2001 Colour lithograph 1533 × 840mm

Fig.2 **Harry Diamond** *Francis Bacon and Lucian Freud in Soho* 1974
Gelatin silver print 172 × 264mm

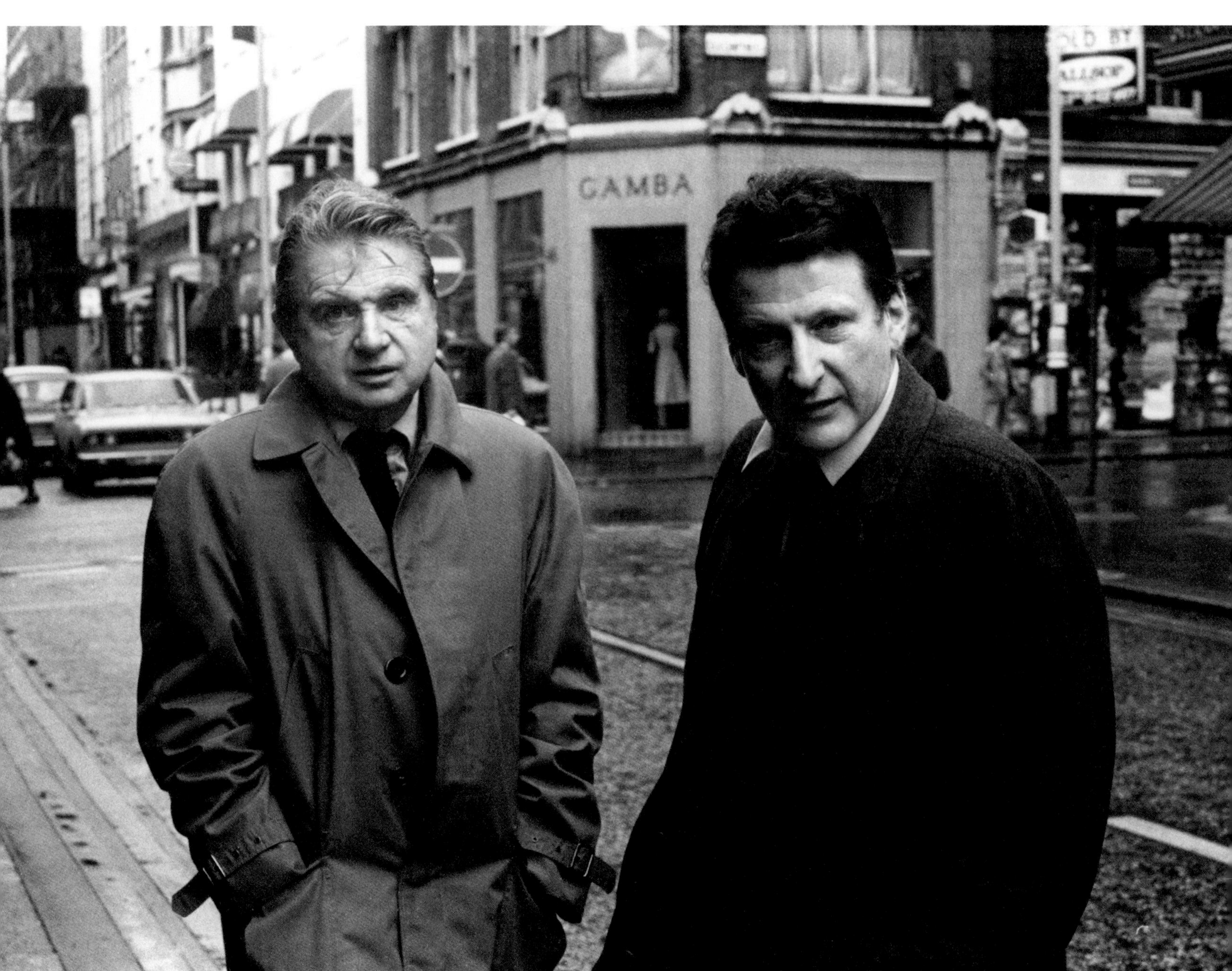

them in late 1944 or early 1945. During the 1950s, they were known to have been almost inseparable. In their art they shared a commitment to the human figure. They also shared a passion for gambling, and spent many afternoons and evenings together in Soho restaurants and bars, such as Wheeler's, the Gargoyle and the Colony Room (fig.2). At these gatherings, Freud's eldest daughter, the writer Annie Freud, later recalled how their intense connection was 'a kind of public verbal love-making – telling stories … being absolutely scandalous and looking fantastic'.[5]

Freud looked up to Bacon, who was 13 years his senior, and later reflected: 'Francis opened my eyes in some ways. His work impressed me, but his personality affected me.'[6] Some have attributed Freud's shift in painting style in the late 1950s from linear to broader brush strokes to his relationship with Bacon. The artist Sophie de Stempel, who was a model and close friend of Freud, noted how Bacon gave Freud a 'freedom and a possibility', which was reflected in his more expressive mark making.[7]

The exchange of ideas that naturally came about from their almost daily meetings led to them making portraits of one another. However, their methods were extremely different. Freud worked only from life, and his subjects, including Bacon, had to endure arduous sittings lasting several months. By contrast, Bacon worked quickly and preferred to base his portraits on photographs. Between 1951 and 1973 he completed 17 paintings of Freud, often using John Deakin's photographs as a starting point (p.128). Bacon's portraits of Freud varied from intimate portrait heads, and an uneasy diptych of Freud with fellow artist Frank Auerbach, to sprawling triptychs, both small-format and monumental (cats 41–3). In a rare surviving letter dated 15 April 1964, Bacon wrote to Freud whilst on holiday

in Malta with George Dyer explaining his new idea for a portrait: 'I have written to John Deakin, would you mind having some more photographs taken … I would like to do a very large serial portrait of you if you don't mind, it suddenly came to me here how I could do it.'[8] The 'serial portrait' probably referred to the three striking works produced the same year of an angst-ridden Freud on a pale green bench (cat.41).

If Freud was enamoured of Bacon, the quantity and quality of the Freud portraits bear witness to the way Bacon took inspiration from the passion, intelligence and magnetism of the younger artist. Bacon would often incorporate elements of himself into his portraits of his sitters, and this was especially the case with his portraits of Freud. Freud noticed that Bacon 'always gave me his legs when he painted me'.[9] There were also self-portraits by Bacon, such as *Study for Self-Portrait* (1964; cat.18), which borrowed the pose and clothing almost entirely from Deakin's photographs of Freud. The ease with which Bacon interchanged and conflated their body parts in the portraits alludes to the intertwined nature of their relationship at this point in their friendship.

In 1951, the same year that Bacon painted his first portrait of Freud, Freud made three elegant line drawings of Bacon in his sketchbook at his home in Clifton Hill, Maida Vale, London. Bacon posed with his shirt unbuttoned, his sleeves rolled up and trousers unzipped to expose his hips. When Freud was later asked about the sitting, he said that Bacon was directing the scene as much as his own hand, instructing him 'to do this because I think that's rather important'.[10] This insight highlights the flow of inspiration between the two artists and gives the sense of Bacon as collaborator. Then, in the following year, came the miniature-like head and shoulders portrait of Bacon on copper painted in the linear and

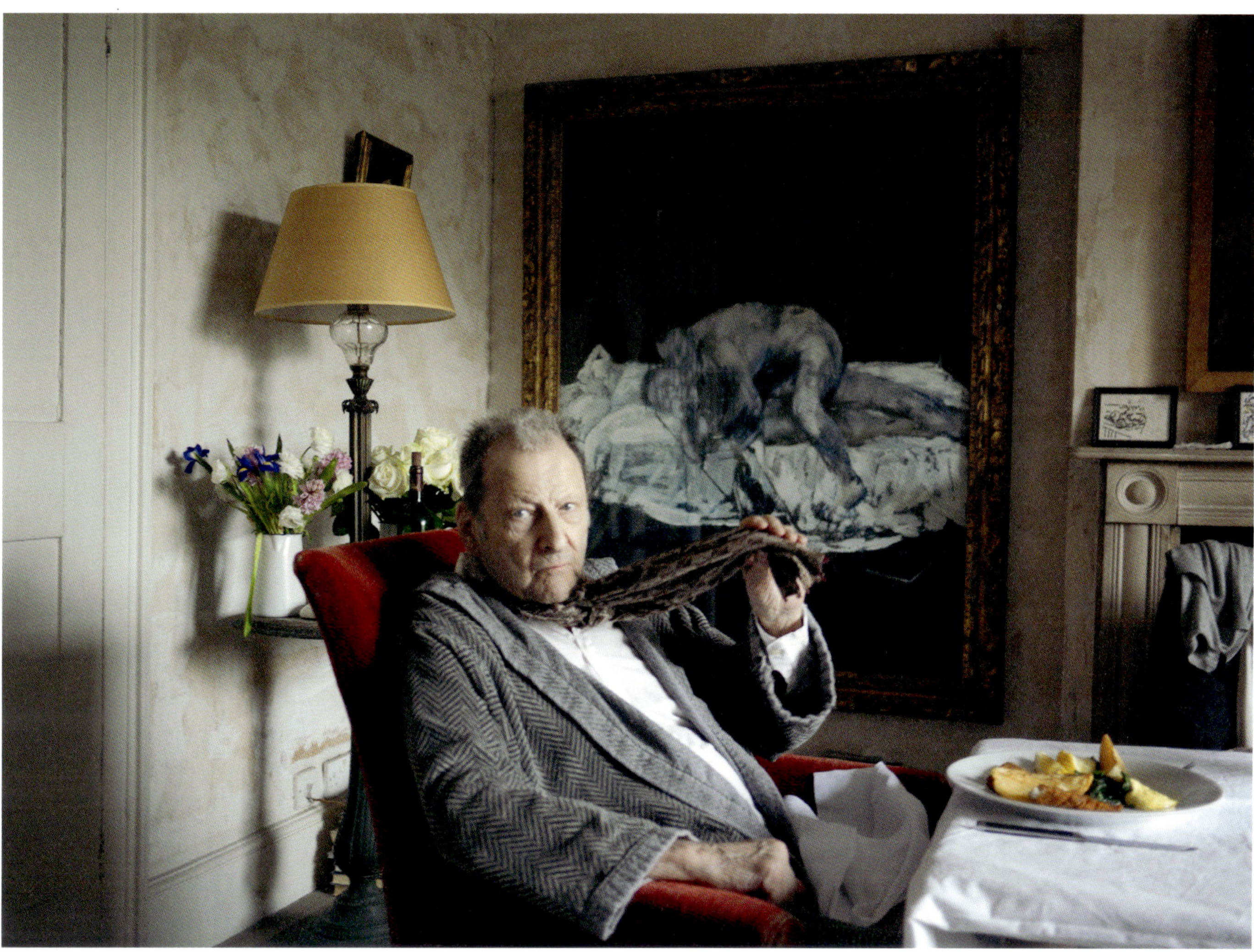

hyperrealist style Freud had perfected at the start of his career.[11] It was now Freud who seemed to be commanding the sitting. He recalled how he 'sat very close to him, face-to-face', with the copper plate on his knees. He remembered 'wanting to bring Bacon out from behind the blur. I wanted to know him not just as an art world person, but as … a friend I suppose'.[12] This time, Bacon was not posing. In contrast to the earlier drawings, Freud caught him unawares, with his eyes downcast, capturing a rare moment when Bacon was not performing, as was often the case when entertaining his friends at a Soho gathering. Freud was relieved to find out that Bacon approved.[13]

Freud appeared to be particularly affected by the loss of the painting in his birth town in 1988. As the 2001 poster campaign demonstrated, he was still trying to recover it years later. By this point, Freud and Bacon's friendship had come to an end for reasons that have never been, at least publicly, fully understood. According to De Stempel it had turned into something 'very painful for both of them … like any intensely strong relationship that [had] failed.'[14] This may have been in part due to an unhealthy competitiveness as Freud's reputation grew, particularly after his acclaimed exhibition at the Hayward Gallery in 1974, as well as increasing disparagement of each other's later works. Although Freud

Fig.4   Lucian Freud   Design before 'Wanted' poster in *John Berryman's Sonnets* (1967)   *c.*2001
Charcoal on paper   222 × 290mm

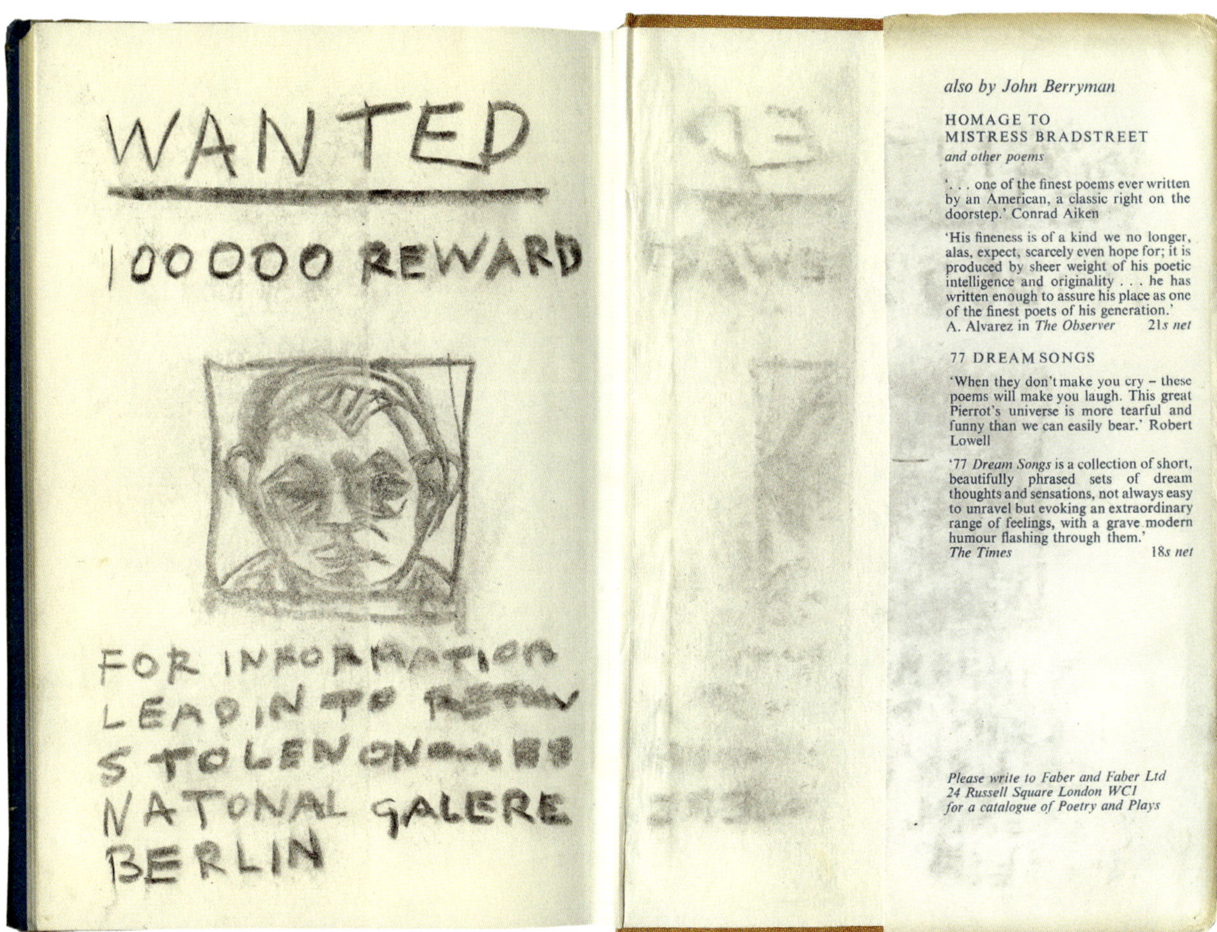

clearly still admired much of Bacon's earlier work and, over the years, owned nine of his paintings, including *Two Figures* (1953; p.50), a ground-breaking depiction of homosexual intimacy. It hung in his home for most of his life and became another point of contention as Freud in later years refused to lend it, claiming that 'it wouldn't be the same when it came back' (fig.3).[15]

Freud's unrelenting attempts to find the 1952 painting reflects his remorse not only for the lost work, considered one of his early master-pieces, but also for a souring friendship, remnants of which were immortalised in his tender portrait of Bacon. Freud drew a design for the poster on the back page of a copy of the American poet John Berryman's sonnets, now kept in the National Portrait Gallery's archive (fig.4).[16] In the quick sketch, completed almost 50 years after the original painting, he draws his former friend once again; not simply as a perfunctory task to complete his design, but to revisit the memories of their intimate and exhilarating friendship. A crumpled and paint-splattered reproduction of the painting was also kept by Bacon in his studio.

Painting from
the Masters

‘It is thrilling to paint
from a picture which
really excites you.’

For Bacon there were a small number of artists from the past whom he held in high regard. He was discriminating, sometimes singling out for admiration just a few works by one artist. The way in which he drew from this small and specific canon was not a straightforward matter of emulation. Artists such as Diego Velázquez, Rembrandt van Rijn, Vincent van Gogh and Pablo Picasso provided a lexicon of imagery to use and reuse, as well as solutions to technical problems that arose when painting figurative works. Two portraits in particular provided Bacon with a rich resource of imagery and possibility: Velázquez's portrait of *Pope Innocent X* (1649–50; p.14) and Van Gogh's self-portrait, *The Painter on the Road to Tarascon* (1888; p.17). The Pope went through various transformations in Bacon's hands during the 1950s and 1960s, including the powerful series represented here with *Study for a Pope I* (1961; cat.11). He returned to the theme with dramatic aplomb with *Study for Portrait (With Two Owls)* (1963; cat.12).

Given Bacon's obsession with both of these remarkable paintings it seems extraordinary that he knew them only through reproductions. He chose not to see the Velázquez's masterpiece when visiting Rome,[1] and Van Gogh's painting had been destroyed by Allied bombing on Dresden during the Second World War. However, this degree of separation gave Bacon a certain licence and freedom to reimagine them – much as he felt more able to paint portraits in the absence of his subjects. Furthermore, Bacon valued the insights that these artists brought to their human subjects. For Bacon, Velázquez's greatness was 'his interest in people ... Velázquez came to the human situation and made it grand and heroic and wasn't bombastic'.[2]

Van Gogh's *The Painter on the Road to Tarascon* did not represent to Bacon what appears at first glance to be a tenacious *plein-air* painter, loaded down with painting equipment and in search of a motif. Rather he saw it as a more intangible presence, 'a phantom of the road'.[3] It fascinated him to the extent that he was inspired to paint a series of eight paintings. The central figure in Bacon's series is distinctly and increasingly abject: this phantom figure is part man, part shadow, apparently bound to the lava-red road (cats 13–4). For these works Bacon employed vigorous, lively brushwork in a way that was wholly new in his *oeuvre*, coupled with vibrant colour, triggered by Van Gogh's own sun-drenched palette, which was evident in modern colour reproductions. Bacon identified a kindred spirit in Van Gogh, whose desire to 'change and remake reality'[4] through his work resonated with Bacon's own ambition to 'unlock the areas of feeling, which lead to a deeper sense of the reality of the image'.[5] Each time Bacon reimagined Van Gogh's painting, he offered a fresh and personal perspective on the artist's predicament.

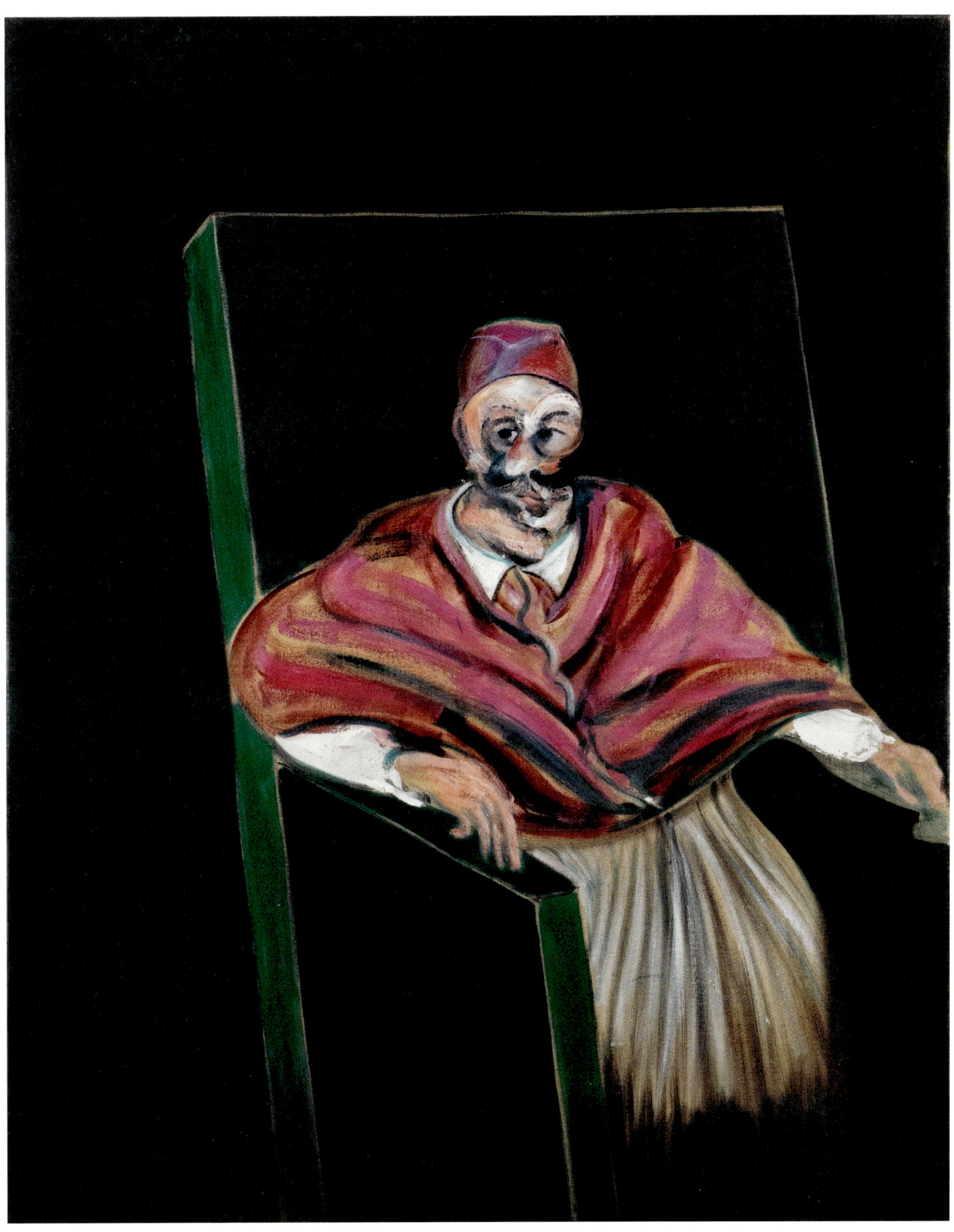

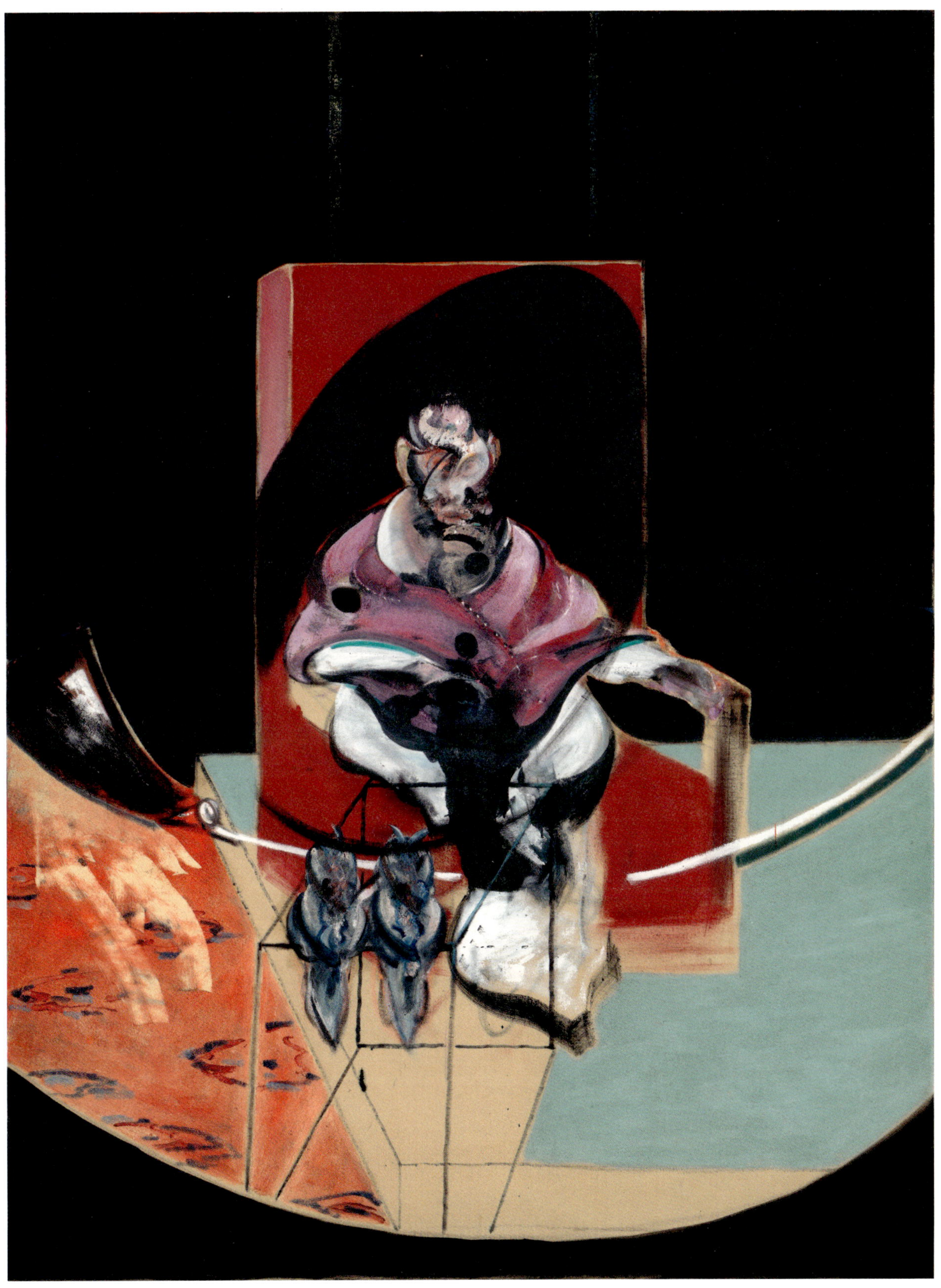

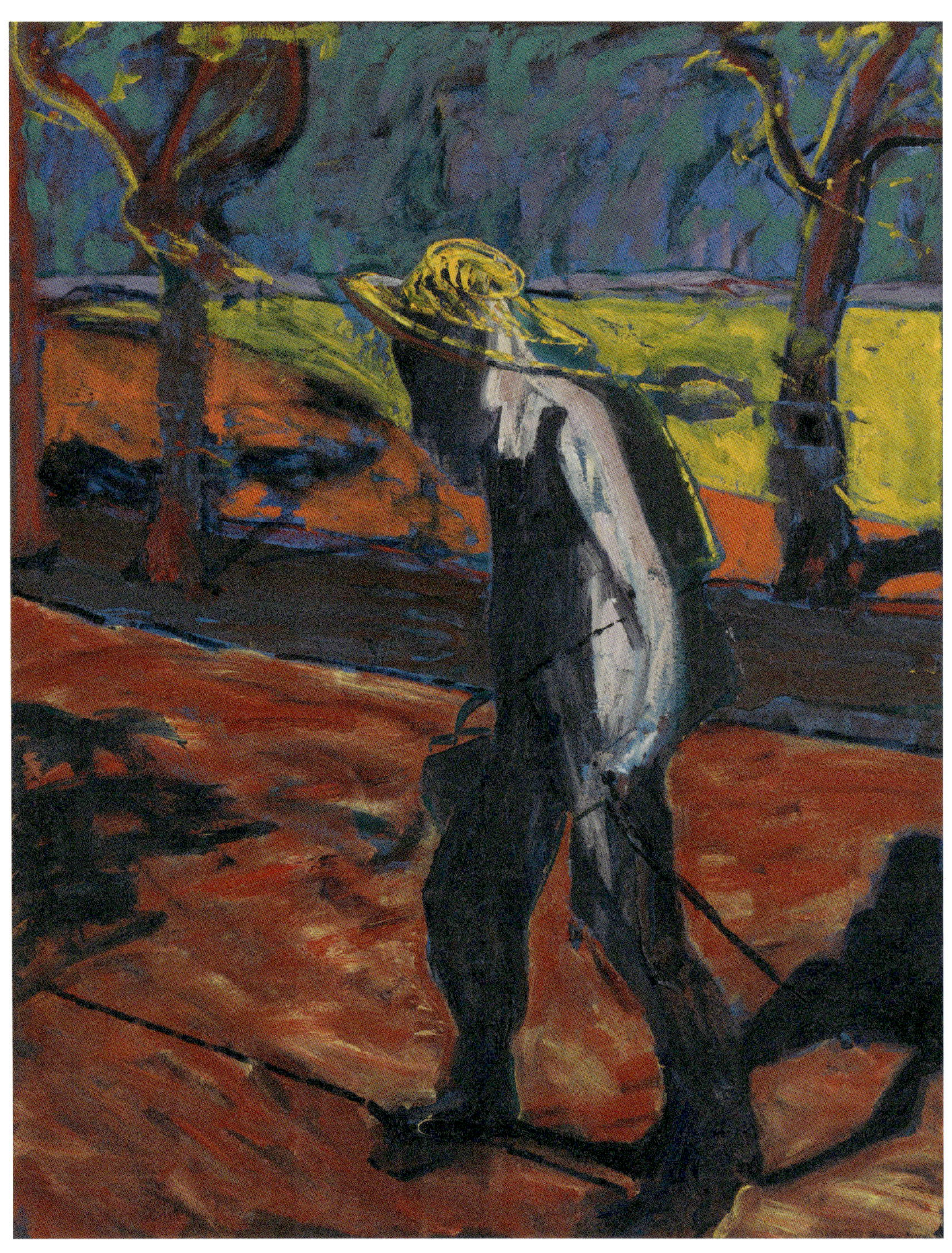

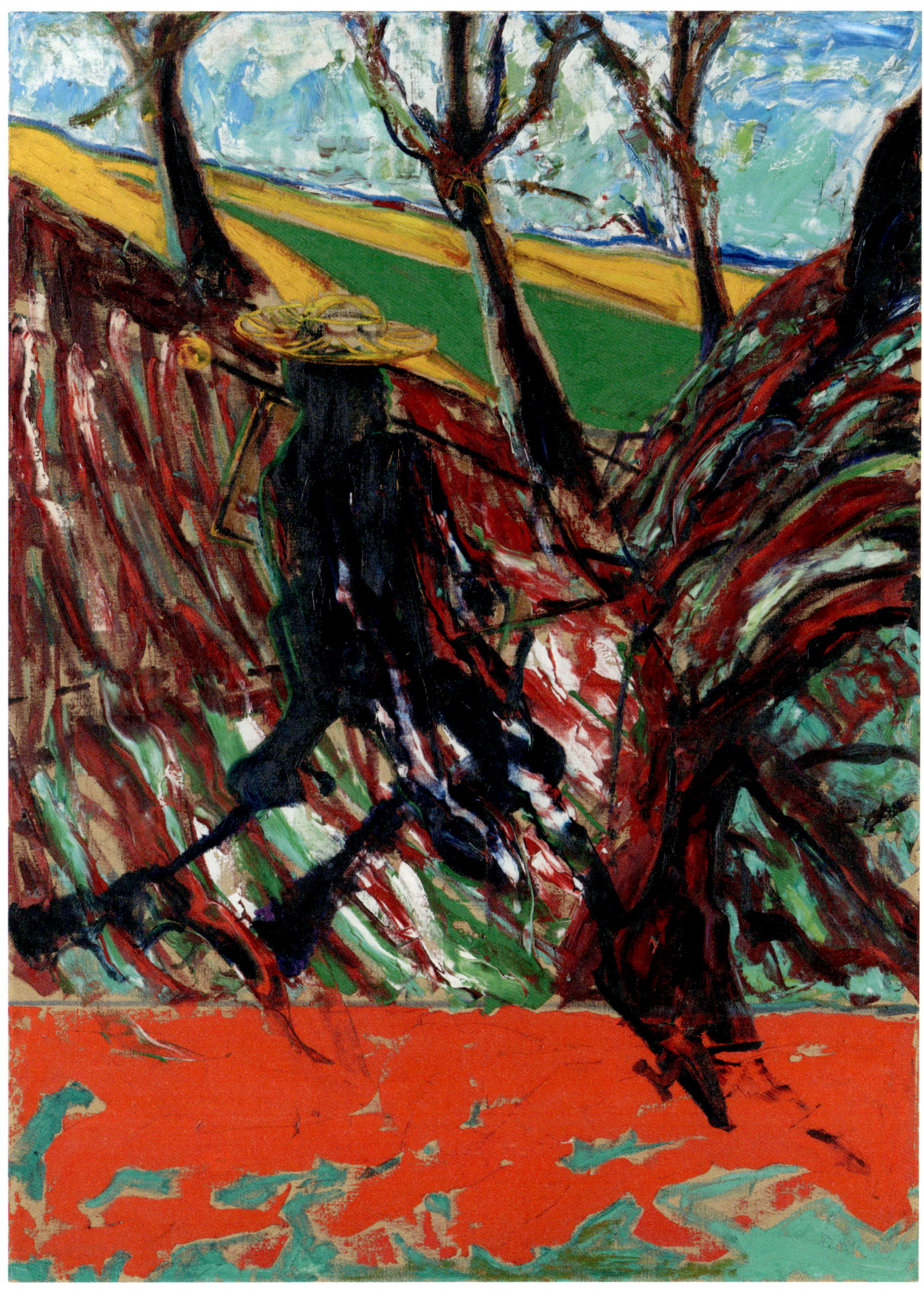

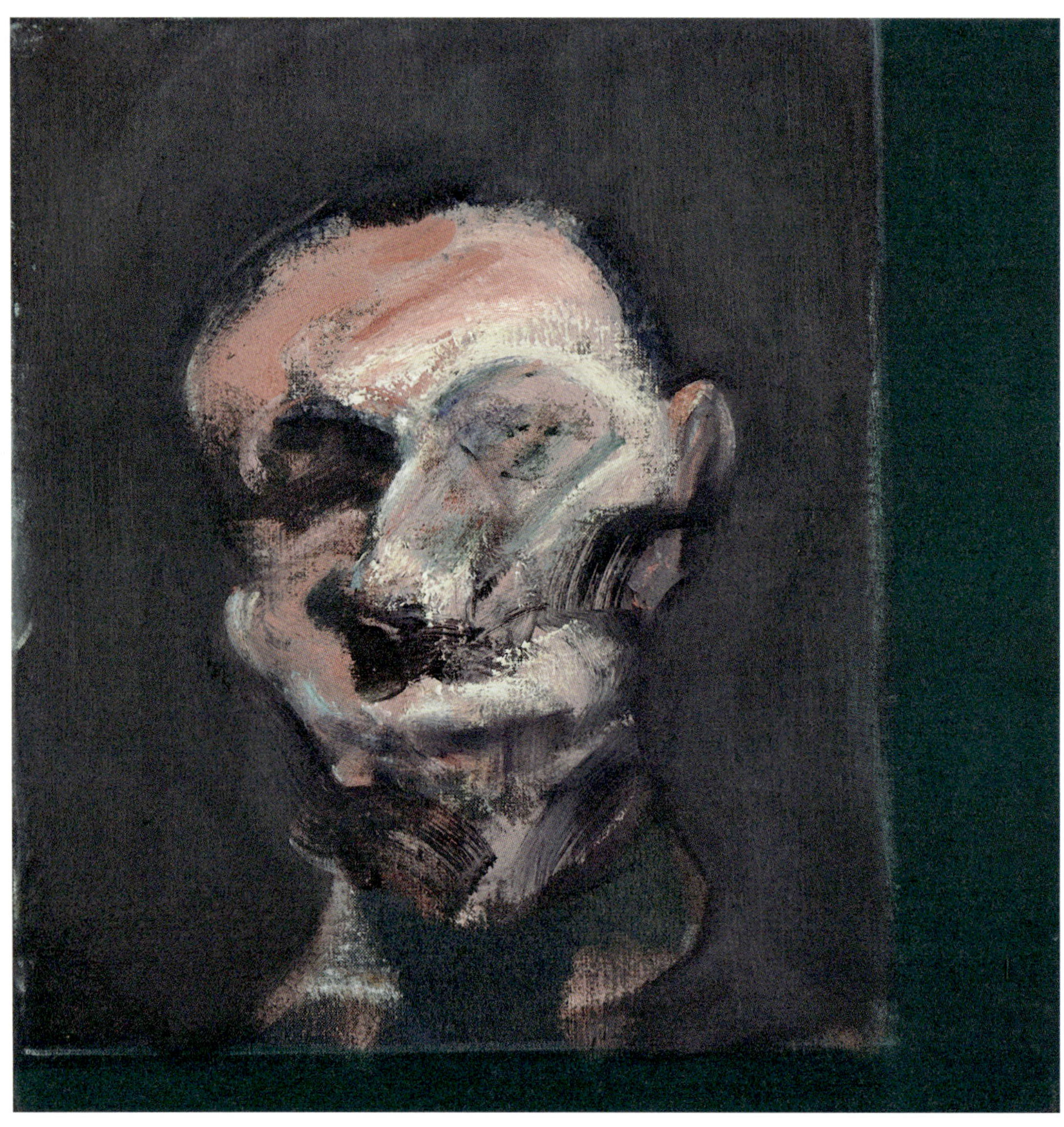

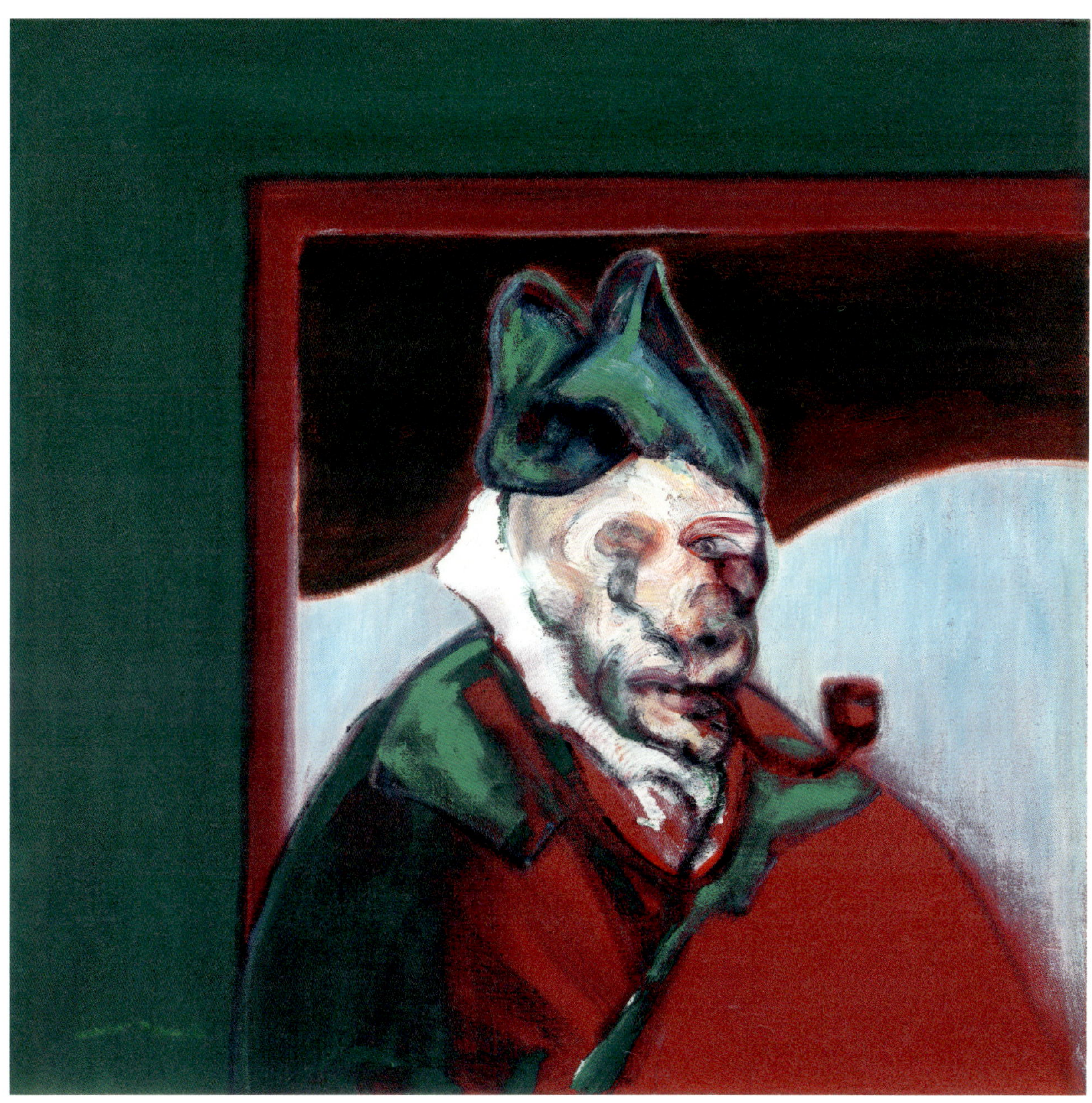

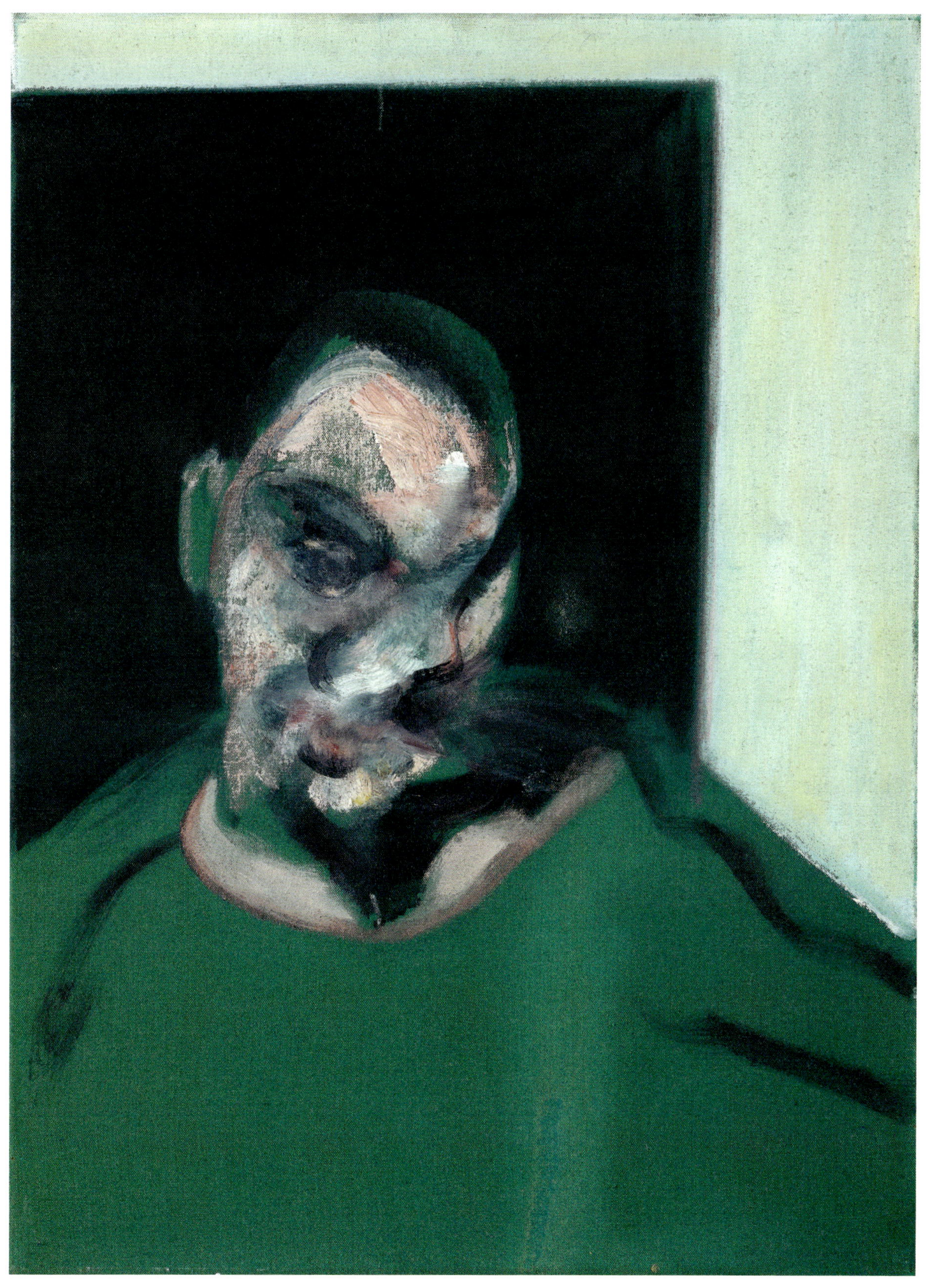

Corners of Filth & Fantasy: Francis Bacon's Studios as Self-Expression

James Hall

Francis Bacon's Reece Mews studio, which he occupied from 1961 until his death in 1992, shaped perceptions of his art and persona long before its triumphal translation to Dublin. Bacon was always adept at using studios as photogenic stage sets that screamed 'edgy', 'outcast', 'reckless' and 'bohemian'. During his early years, he cultivated a post-cubist angularity using furniture, canvases and easels, before swamping Reece Mews with shabbily apocalyptic, image-rich landfill. In this section, his studios will be put in historical context, while demonstrating how they reinforced Bacon's self-image and provided inspiration.

The Australian painter Roy de Maistre undoubtedly alerted Bacon to the potential of the studio as a catalyst for, and subject of, art. In 1930, when they met in London, Bacon was forging a career as a modernist designer and decorative painter. De Maistre painted two images of Bacon's large, modernist showroom-cum-studio in Queensberry Mews, where he sleekly displayed his furniture and rugs. In 1932 and between 1933 and 1934, de Maistre painted at least six more pictures of Bacon's studios in Fulham Road and/or Royal Hospital Road.[1] Unpopulated by human forms, they focus unerringly on a corner of the studio filled with Bacon's stored artefacts. The most surrealist (evoking Giorgio de Chirico's

Metaphysical Interiors) include a corner entrance or exit point – a barely visible enclosed staircase in Queensberry Mews, and a pitch-black open attic doorway in another studio, itself rendered inaccessible by canvases partially blocking it (fig.2).

The 'corner of the studio' had become an avant-garde ideal in the second half of the nineteenth century. Emile Zola, pioneer of the naturalist novel, claimed the work of art was 'a corner of creation seen through a temperament'.[2] The 'corner' meant a marginal area where unvarnished and subversive truths could be found. In contrast to history painters composing vast staged tableaux in cavernous studios, Zola praised the artist Édouard Manet for being 'happy to place a few objects and people in a corner of his studio and paint them with care'.[3] Such works might equally be regarded as a 'corner of fantasy', disrupting the status quo. Indeed *coin*, the French for 'corner', also means 'wedge'. (Bacon was fluent in French.)

Corners were often dark and dirty. Vincent van Gogh, whose letters Bacon devoured, idealised such places: 'In the poorest little house, in the filthiest corner, I see paintings or drawings. And my mind turns in that direction as if with an irresistible urge.'[4] Artists such as Paul Cézanne, Edgar Degas, Henri Matisse

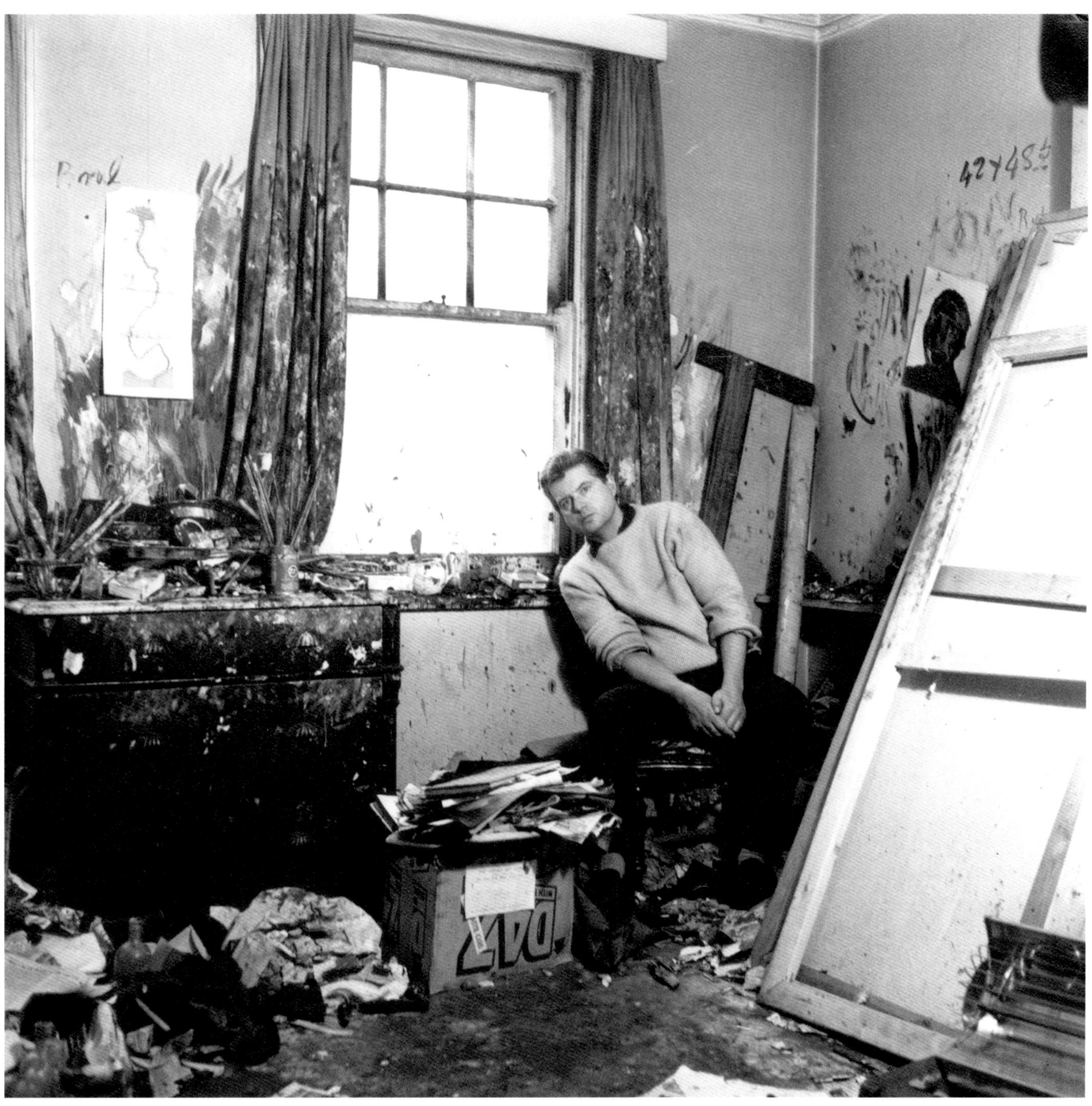

Fig.2   Roy de Maistre   *A Corner of Francis Bacon's Studio*   1932
Oil on canvas   910 × 760mm

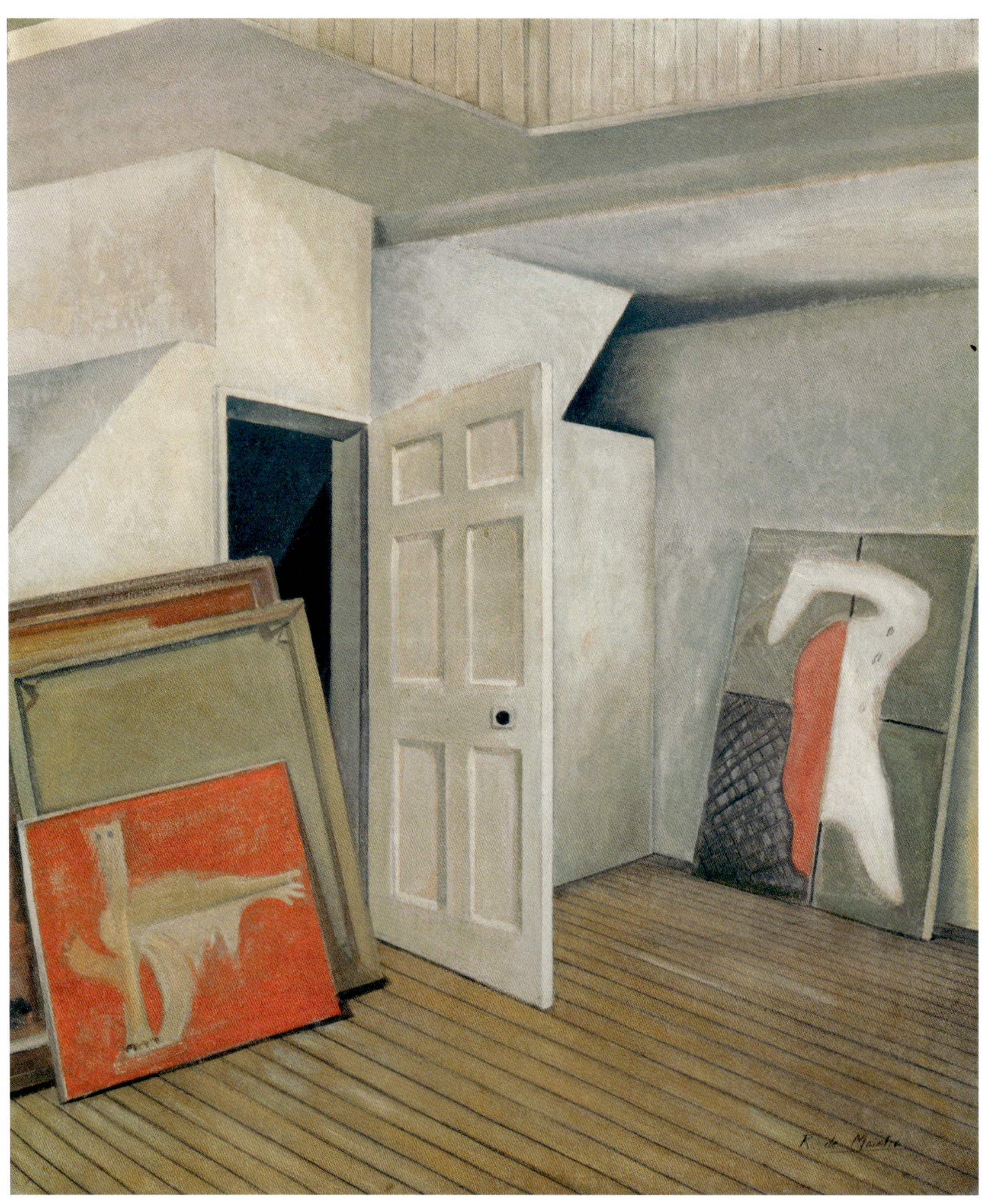

70

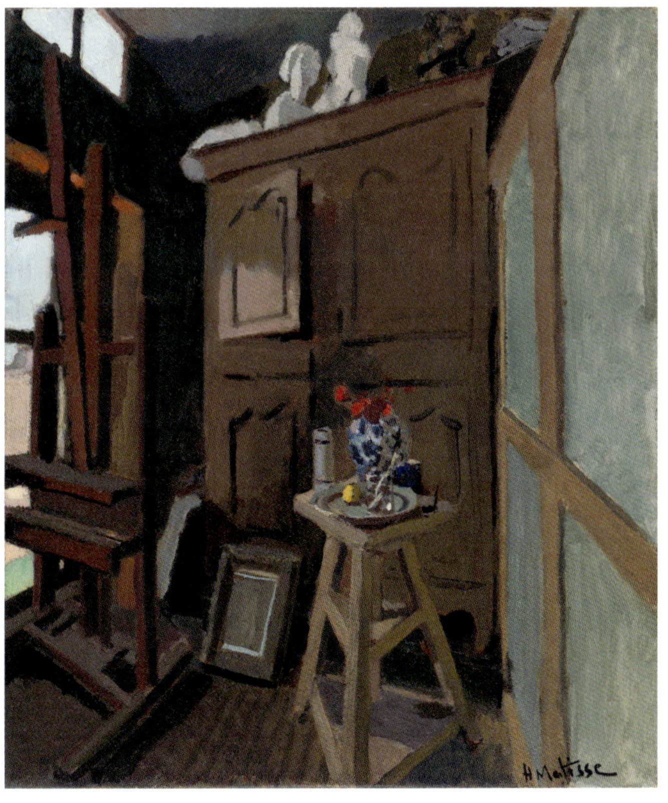

Fig.3   Henri Matisse
Studio Interior / Studio Corner   c.1903–4
Oil on canvas   550 × 460mm

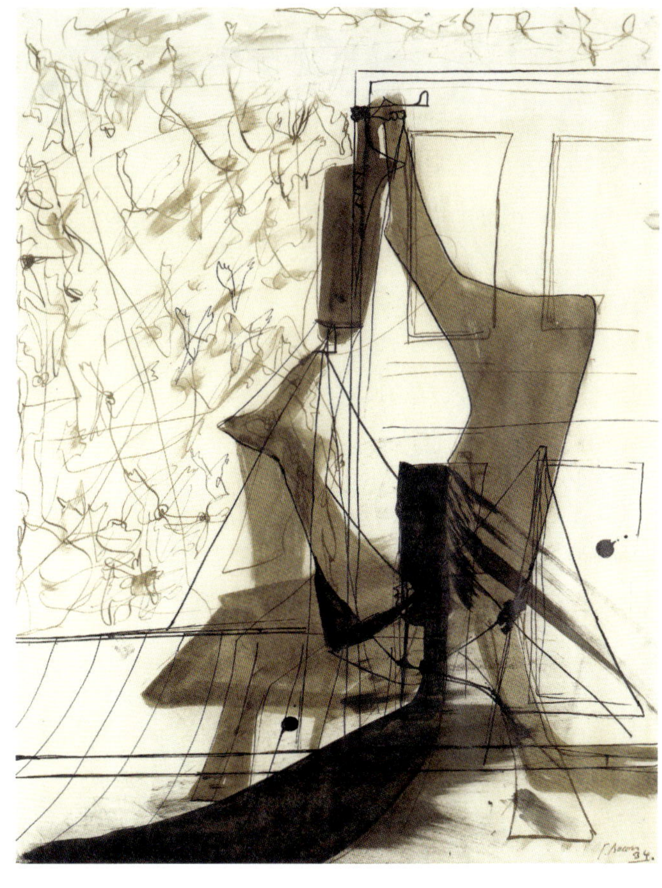

Fig.4   Francis Bacon
Corner of the Studio   1934
Pen and ink and wash on paper   527 × 398mm

and Walter Sickert had painted their own 'studio corners', treating them as inhospitable backstage areas, disorientating fragments of missing wholes (fig.3). In de Maistre's paintings, it is the enigmatic staircase and doorway, as well as Bacon's artworks, that make it a corner – and wedge – of fantasy. John Edwards, perhaps following Bacon's lead, would later call Reece Mews 'a little corner of South Kensington'.[5]

Bacon's large drawing in ink and wash, *Corner of the Studio* (1934; fig.4), shows a Picasso-style figure mixed with geometric lines evoking the form of an easel. Placed before a closed door, the figure occupies the right half of the page. In 1934 Bacon was renting a dingy basement in Sunderland House, Curzon Street, built by William K. Vanderbilt in 1905. The basic *mise en scène* was inspired by Picasso's *The Studio* (1927–8), where a painter stands before a closed door, blocking it. But Bacon has sullied that bright, clean-contoured picture, creating a seedy surreal underworld. He covered the wall in tendril-like automatic writing that evokes birds, genitalia and damp stains. These pre-empt the paint-wiped curtains

of post-war studios, and the smeared colour tests daubed on the walls of Reece Mews. An edgy corner ideal would pervade Bacon's mature paintings via space frames and perspective lines, apparently as portable and free-standing as the folding screens he made in his designer days. These create dislocating force fields of multiple internal corners and wedges, while making the portrayed figures seem 'cornered'.

A second depiction of a studio, *Studio Interior* (mid-1930s), shows a white canvas on an easel in the studio corner with a pink figure hurtling towards and into it – doubtless a sardonic self-portrait. In around 1960 Cecil Beaton sat for Bacon in the latter's Battersea studio. Beaton went on to describe the experience in his diaries: 'Francis started work with great zest, excitedly running backwards and forwards to the canvas with gazelle-springing leaps – much toe bouncing.'[6] Beaton photographed the studio with Bacon the classic 'cornered-artist-in-his-studio-corner', surrounded by what Beaton called an 'incredible mess' (fig.1).[7] He leans sideways out of his lair, peering at the alien world from an odd angle, wedged into the corner.

Henri Cartier-Bresson photographed Bacon in 1952 in a large studio at Cromwell Place. The studio was, however, made small and inhospitable by recently inherited antique furniture and painter's equipment packed higgledy-piggledy into the corner, rendering it unusable. The barricaded space was presided over by a gilded mirror casting enigmatic reflections. Miraculously, Bacon always presents himself in pristine clothes, with clean hands and fingernails. The diabolical dandy rises up from his fallen studio world like one of the blessed on Judgement Day.

The filthy, chaotic studio has a long history, mostly as a symptom of social and artistic failure rather than of principled asceticism.

Fig.5   Aert van Waes
Painter Disgusted at his Art   1645
Etching   163 × 215mm

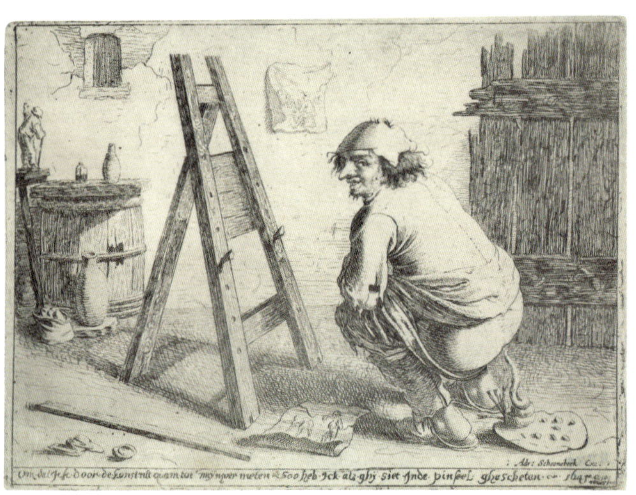

Leonardo da Vinci, in his *Notebooks*, contrasted the working conditions of the painter with those of the sculptor: 'The painter sits before his work at the greatest of ease, well dressed and applying delicate colours with his light brush. His residence is clean and adorned with delightful pictures.'[8] Conversely, the sculptor in his noisy workshop is dirty and his house 'is in a mess and covered in dust and chips from the stone'.[9] Michelangelo, Bacon's favourite artist, countered by giving a heroic spin to the back-breaking privations he experienced while sculpting *David* and frescoing the ceiling of the Sistine Chapel. He was said to live in squalor, and to sleep in his work clothes, like a hermit. But Leonardo's luxurious vision of the painter's home studio was to remain the ideal for four centuries.[10] The association of failure with squalor is brutally encapsulated by Adriaan Schoonebeek's *The Painter Disgusted at his Art* (1645), where an artist in a crumbling hovel defecates on his brushes and palette (fig.5).

Squalor became fashionable among artists during the nineteenth century as part of a romantic cult of high-minded suffering rather than selling out, and of art as a new religion. Henry Murger's *Scenes of Bohemian Life* (1851) charted the precarious lives of young artists renting unfurnished garrets in Paris's Latin Quarter: 'They are the race of obstinate dreamers for whom art has remained a faith and not a profession … They live, so to say, on the outskirts of life, in isolation and inertia …'[11] A key attribute was a lack of furniture, with one artist telling his prospective landlord that he sleeps not on a bed but 'on a good conscience'.[12] He will use his boot as a chamber pot (in Cartier-Breton's photograph, Bacon *disables* the fine furniture, which he soon sold). When Van Gogh rented a bare room in The Hague in the winter of 1881, he was determined to sleep on the floor under a woollen blanket. The young James McNeil

Whistler and his English artist friends aspired to live in Paris as simply as possible. Whistler made do with a camp bed, chair, basin and jug. One of them drew fine furniture onto the walls of an otherwise empty garret. Making unsellable art on bare walls was another marker of bohemianism.

These, though, were artists at the start of their careers. In the first half of the twentieth century, it became more fashionable for successful artists to cultivate saintly squalor. Bacon admired the great mess-makers Sickert, Picasso and Giacometti. Giacometti's tiny Paris studio-home was grey with dust, often compared to a monk's cell, and contained only a few rudimentary pieces of furniture. Every wall was covered in drawings (which have been preserved). Rebecca Daniels has strikingly compared Bacon's Reece Mews studio with a 1938 photograph of Sickert in his Broadstairs studio, every surface covered in piles of newspapers and assorted detritus, a gilded Victorian mirror propped behind the seated artist partially blocking the doorway.[13] The magpie Picasso always lived in unbelievable chaos and clutter, never allowing anything to be thrown away or moved. He would buy another house when he ran out of space.[14] For both Sickert and Picasso, the accumulated 'detritus' was source material.

Alexander Liberman, in *The Artist in His Studio* (1960), said that Picasso 'needs all the memorabilia, all the art and sculpture of the world to inspire him, but to produce he needs little. All has to be reduced to essentials as uncluttered as the inspirational sources were cluttered'.[15] He compared Picasso to a gambler, embracing chance and accident, with the chaotic studio as emblem. The same might be said of the gambler Bacon's winnowing processes as he sifted through his image bank like a rag-picker, embracing chance discoveries – the more torn, creased and besmirched the better. 'I feel at home here in this chaos because the chaos suggests images to me', he claimed of what he called his 'dump'.[16] 'Other implications' were added by the source material being walked over and crumpled.[17] The Reece Mews studio measured a meagre eight by four metres. The furniture in his small bedroom-cum-sitting room was plain, apart from a fine inlaid chest of drawers on the landing.

Prior to Reece Mews's removal to Dublin, archaeologist Edmond O'Donovan made a plan of the contents of the studio floor in three layers, with elevations of walls and shelves. He found around 7,500 items, all of which were catalogued. They included 129 photos commissioned from John Deakin of Bacon's lover George Dyer, and hundreds of pages torn from illustrated books, magazines and newspapers. Archaeological metaphors were central to Sigmund Freud's conception of psychoanalysis, and it has been prevalent in all branches of subsequent psychoanalytic work. Freud told a patient that 'the psychoanalyst, must uncover layer after layer of the patient's psyche, before coming to the deepest, most valuable treasures'.[18] There is little discernible hierarchy to Bacon's 'dump', but its damaged treasures were a living record of his life and mind. Great paintings emerged like exotic plants from a dung heap.

Self-Portraits

'I've done a lot of self-portraits, really because people have been dying around me like flies and I've had nobody else left to paint but myself.'

Francis Bacon painted over 50 self-portraits throughout his career, from small single heads to full-lengths and large triptychs. Despite saying that he 'loathed' his own face and that self-portraits were something of a last resort, they remained a presiding theme in his work and one that enabled him to articulate an artistic vision that became increasingly personal.[1] These images offer an extraordinary range of responses to the artist's own body, psyche and ego across three decades. They each correspond to a different phase in Bacon's artistic development, his artistic pre-occupations, professional success and personal relationships. Almost always intended for public exhibition and sale, they are also bound up in the mythology of his life and the artistic persona that Bacon perpetuated.

Bacon's reworking of Van Gogh's self-portrait *The Painter on the Road to Tarascon* (1888; p.17) marked not only a turning point in his approach to paint and colour, but also of the idea of the self-portrait in his work.[2] He identified with Van Gogh in such a way that his variations on Van Gogh's painting can be read as a portrait of Bacon himself. This conflation of the artist with his subject, often a close friend or lover, became an important aspect of Bacon's self-portraits, which often seem to represent two individuals simultaneously. An example of this can be seen in Bacon's *Study for Self-Portrait* (1964; cat.18), which derives as much from Bacon as it does from photographs of the artist Lucian Freud,

with whom he had a close friendship during this period.

Bacon's extraordinary decade-spanning body of self-portraits is rivalled only by that of Rembrandt, who intensively documented his appearance through the highs and lows of his life. Bacon was intimately familiar with Rembrandt's *Self-Portrait with Beret* (1659; p.18), having studied it during his time in Aix-en-Provence in France.[3] He also kept several reproductions in his studio and particularly admired the way in which the paint and the subject completely coalesced. This remarkable quality distinguishes the self-portraits Bacon made towards the end of his life, in which his painted visage seems to float from the canvas.

Some of Bacon's most poignant and introspective self-portraits were undertaken shortly after the deaths of the people closest to him. When his long-term partner Peter Lacy died in 1962, Bacon responded with a small triptych of portraits that memorialised their relationship: the two outer panels represent Peter, his features obscure, while the central panel is a moving self-portrait (*Study for Three Heads*, 1962; cat.38). A decade later, Bacon lost his lover George Dyer, another potent presence in so many of his paintings. Dyer's death seems to have compelled Bacon to make a remarkable group of self-portraits (see *Self-Portrait*, 1973; cat.24) that capture his grief and isolation and become a way to reckon with his own mortality.

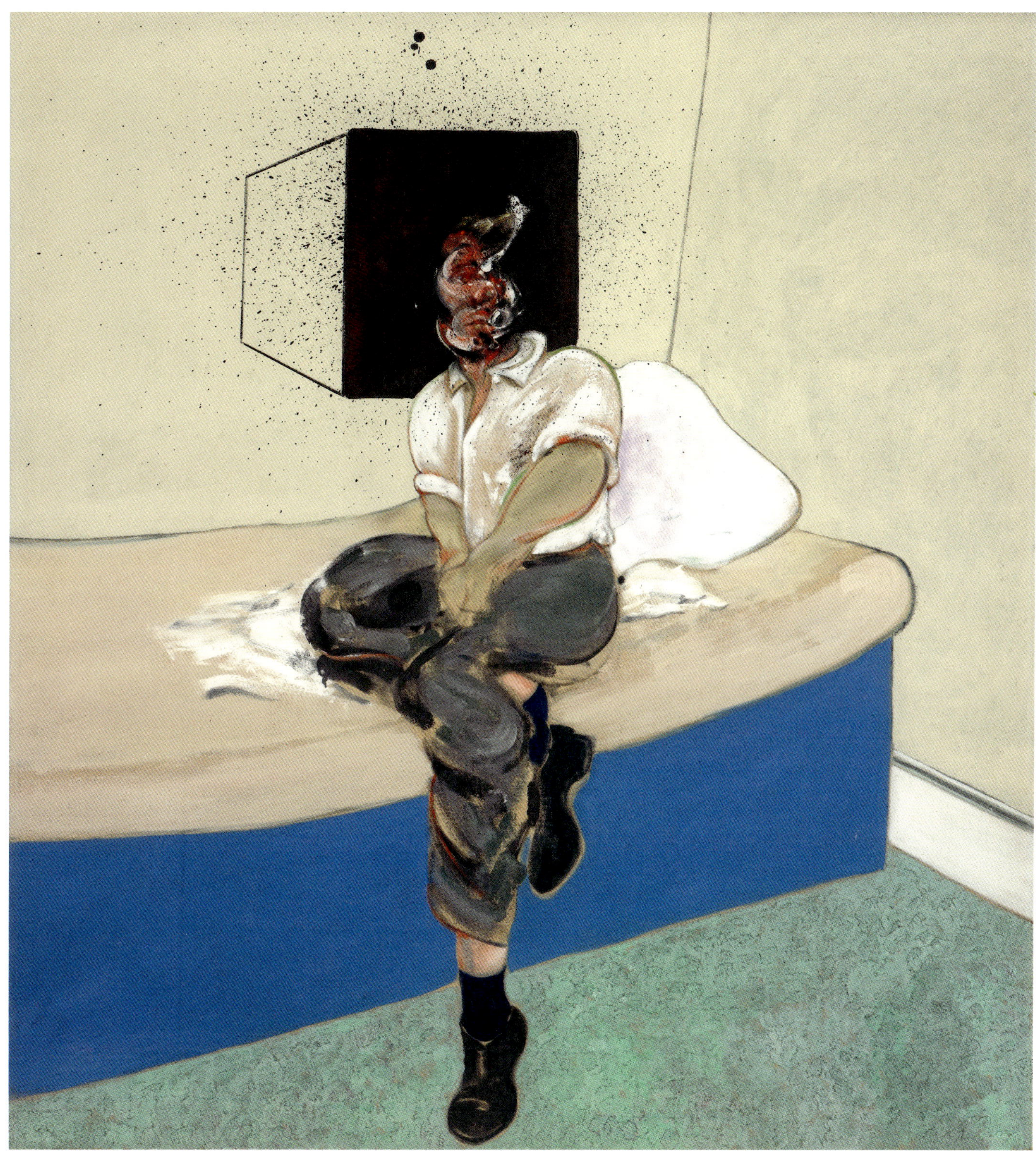

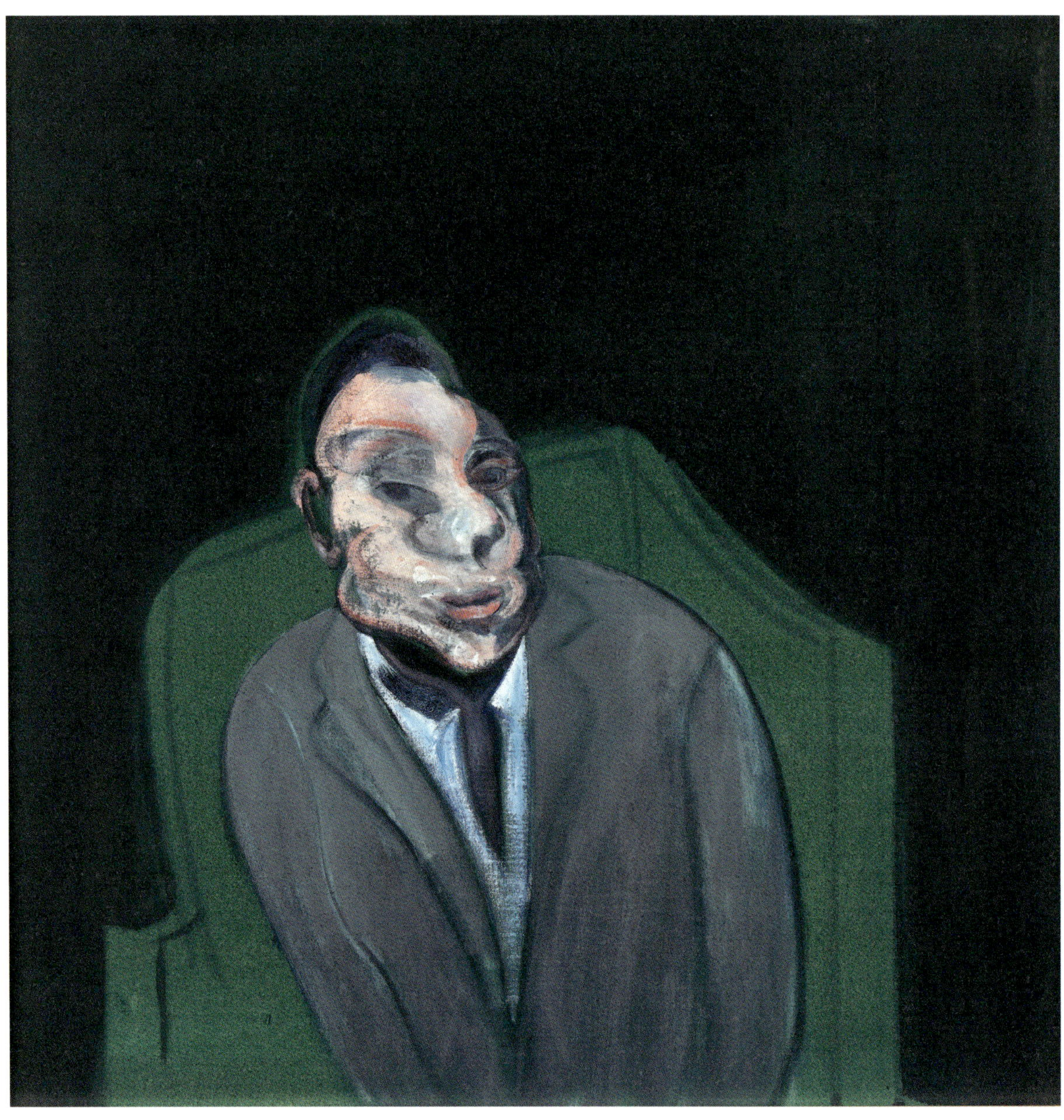

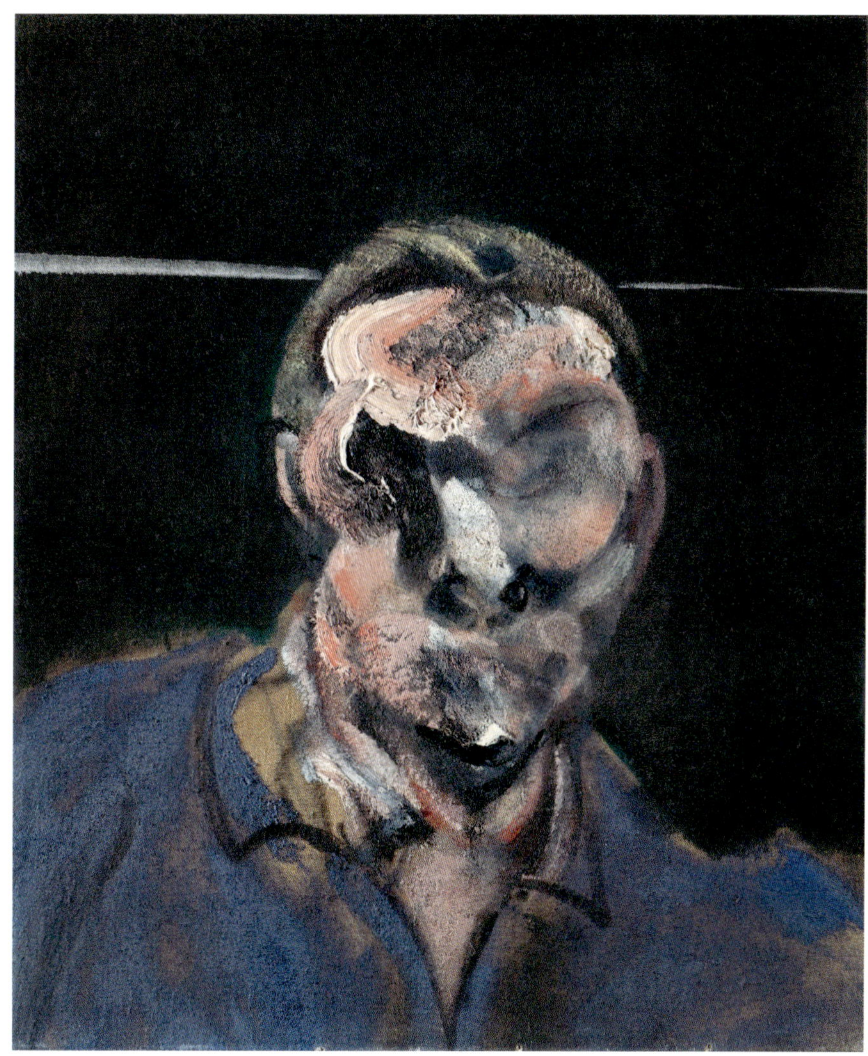

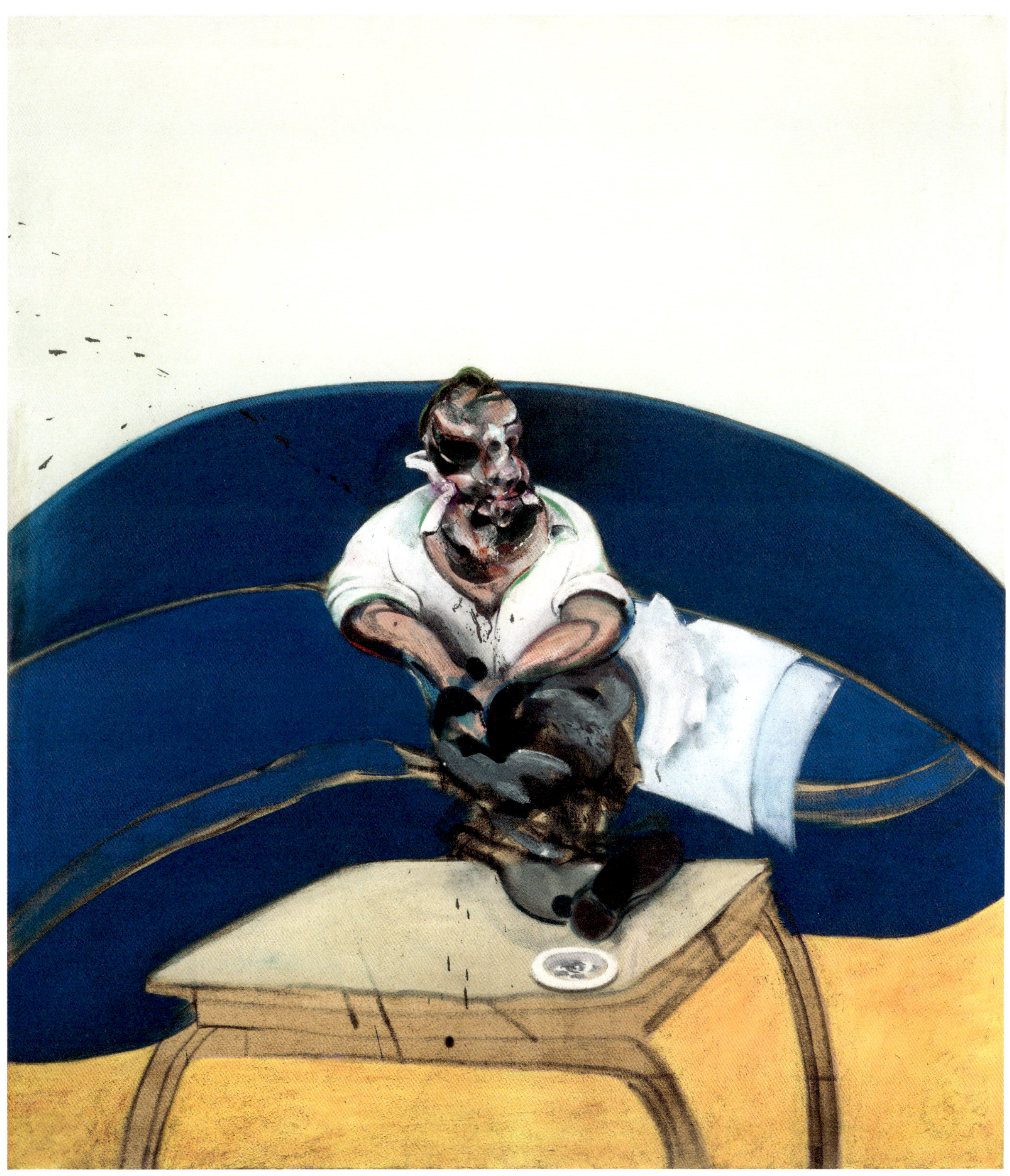

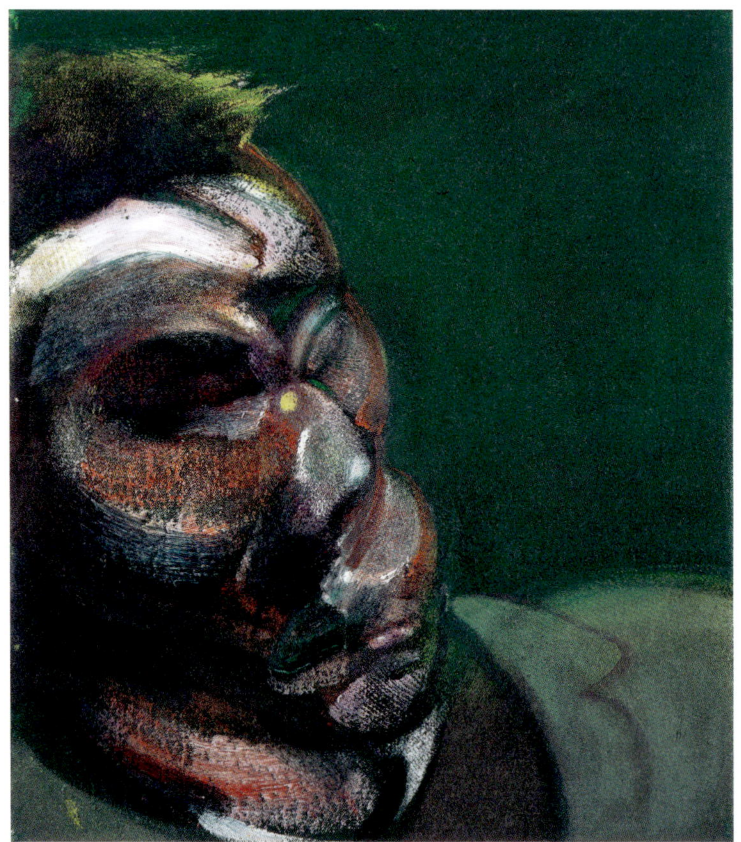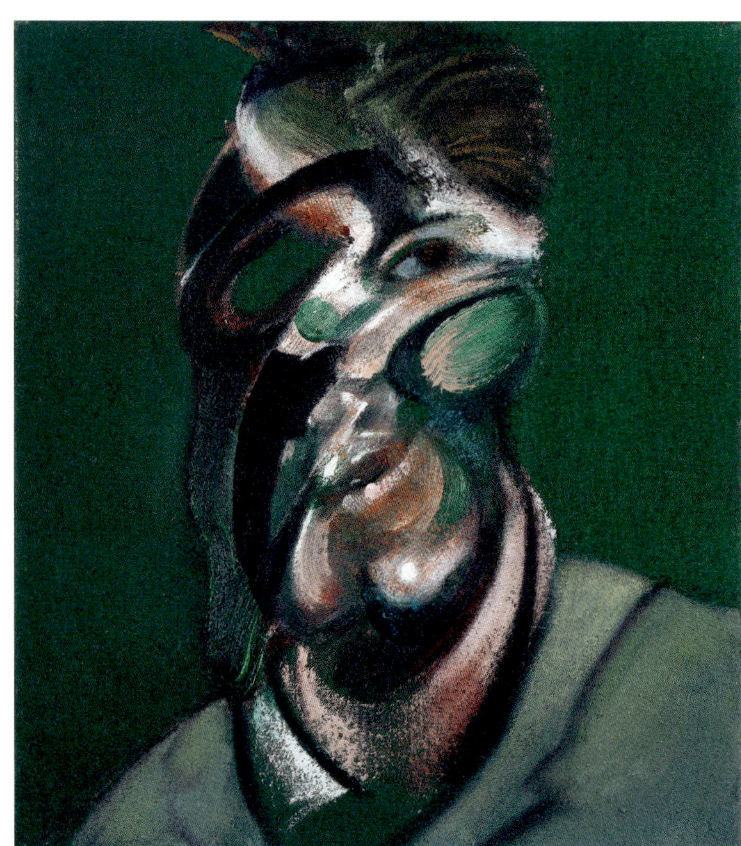

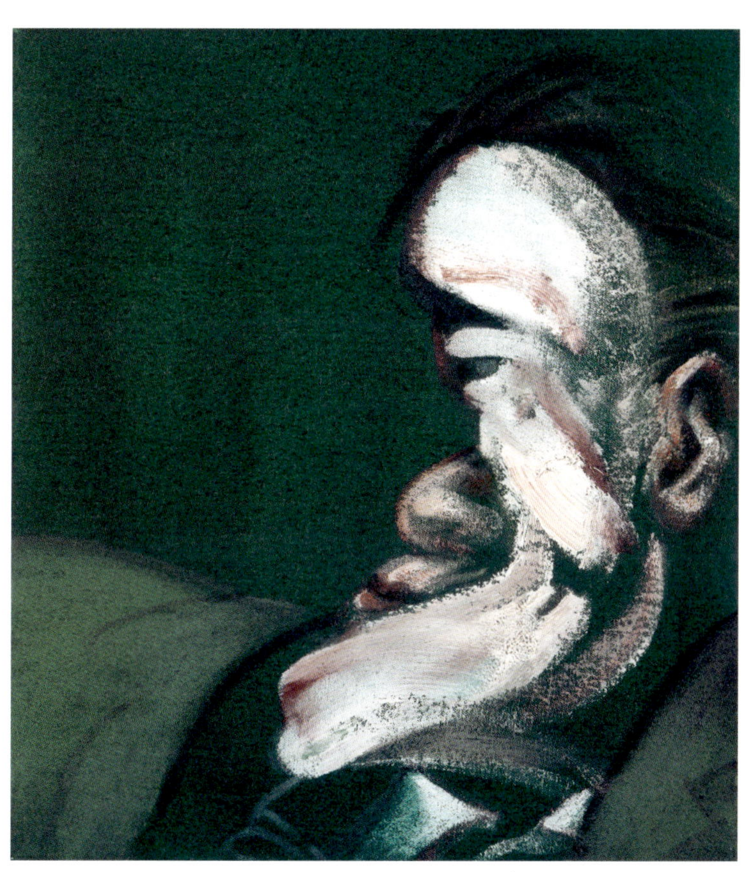

23   *Self-Portrait*   1972   Oil on canvas   355 × 305mm

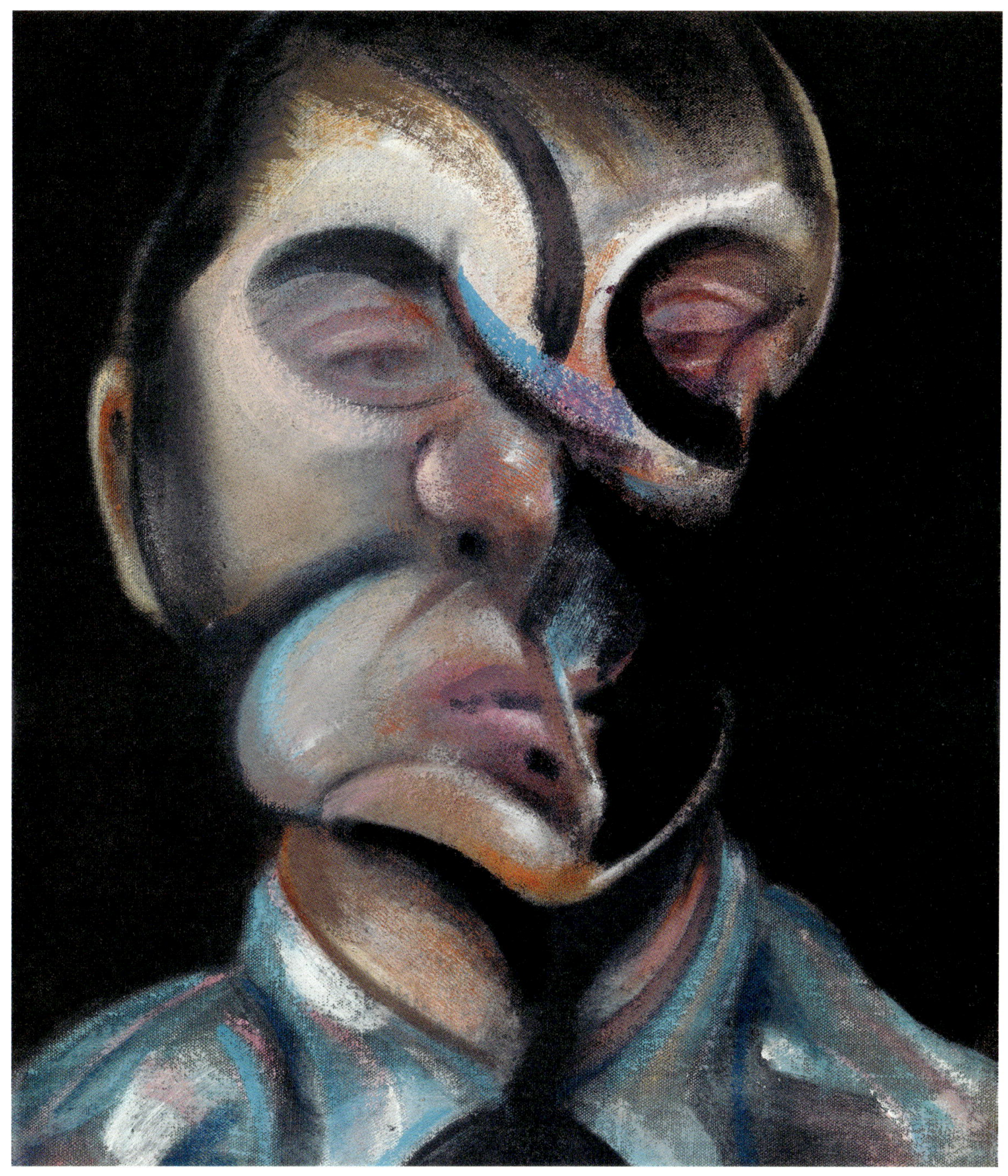

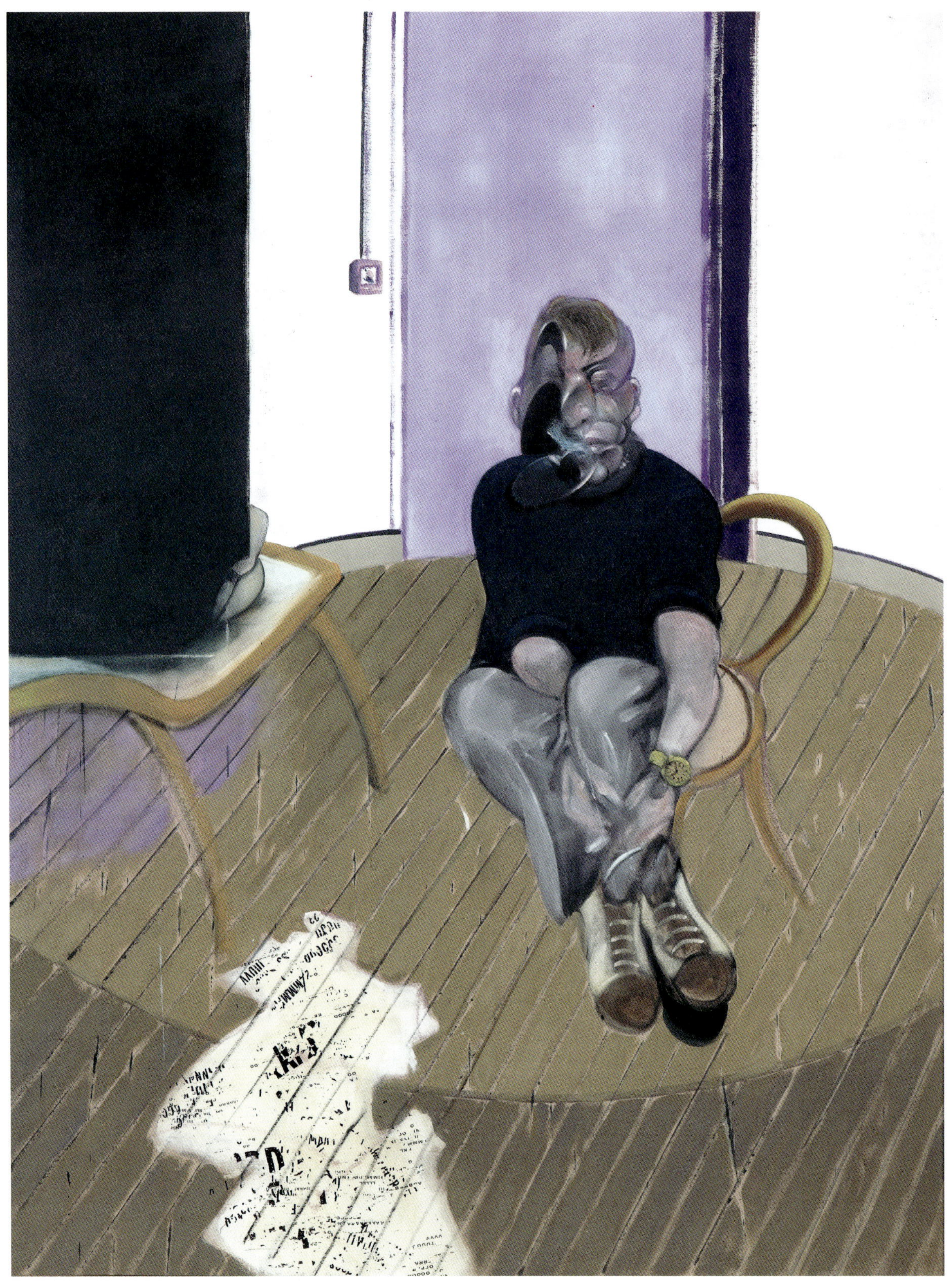

25 *Self-Portrait, 1973*   1973   Oil on canvas   355 × 305mm

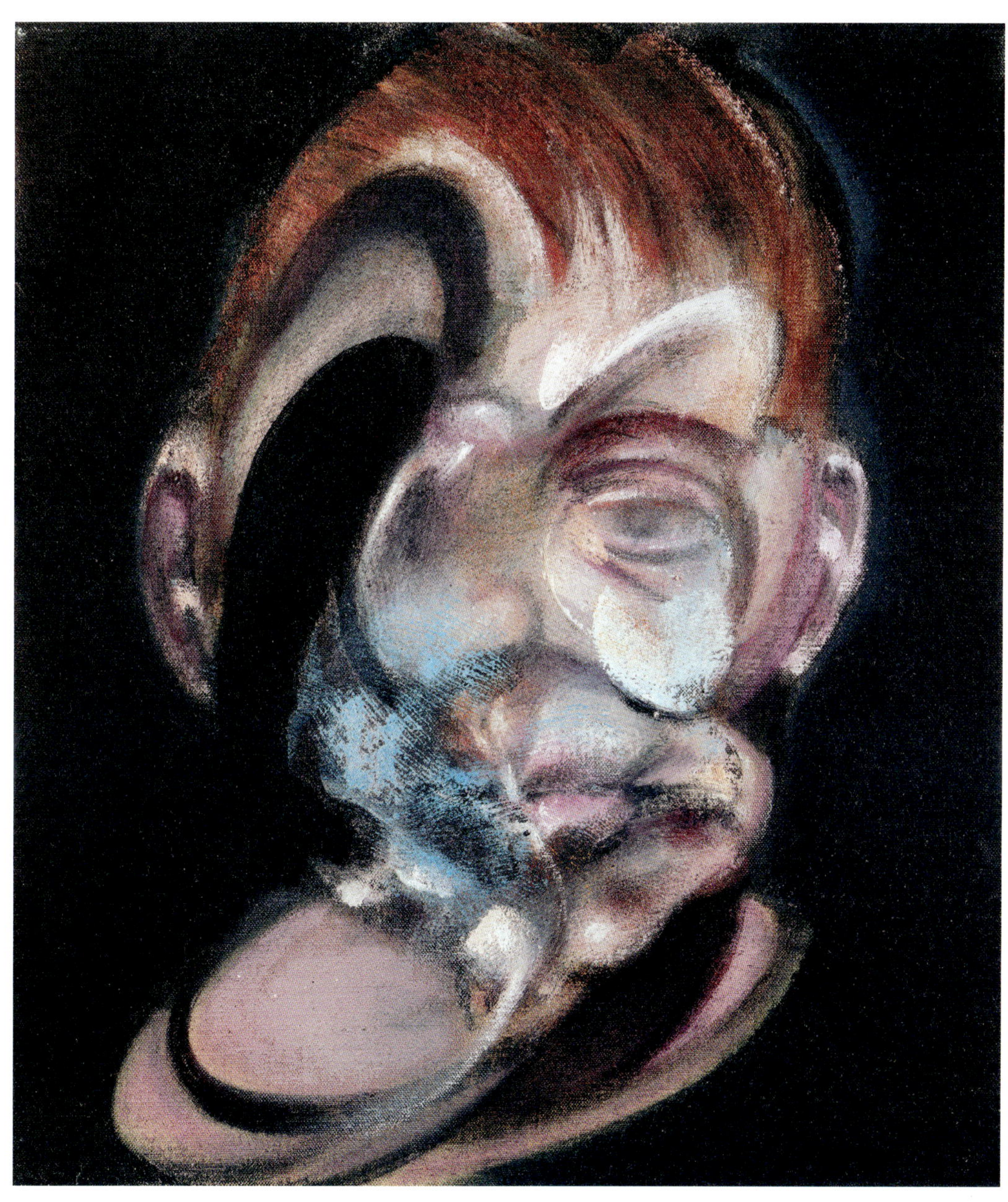

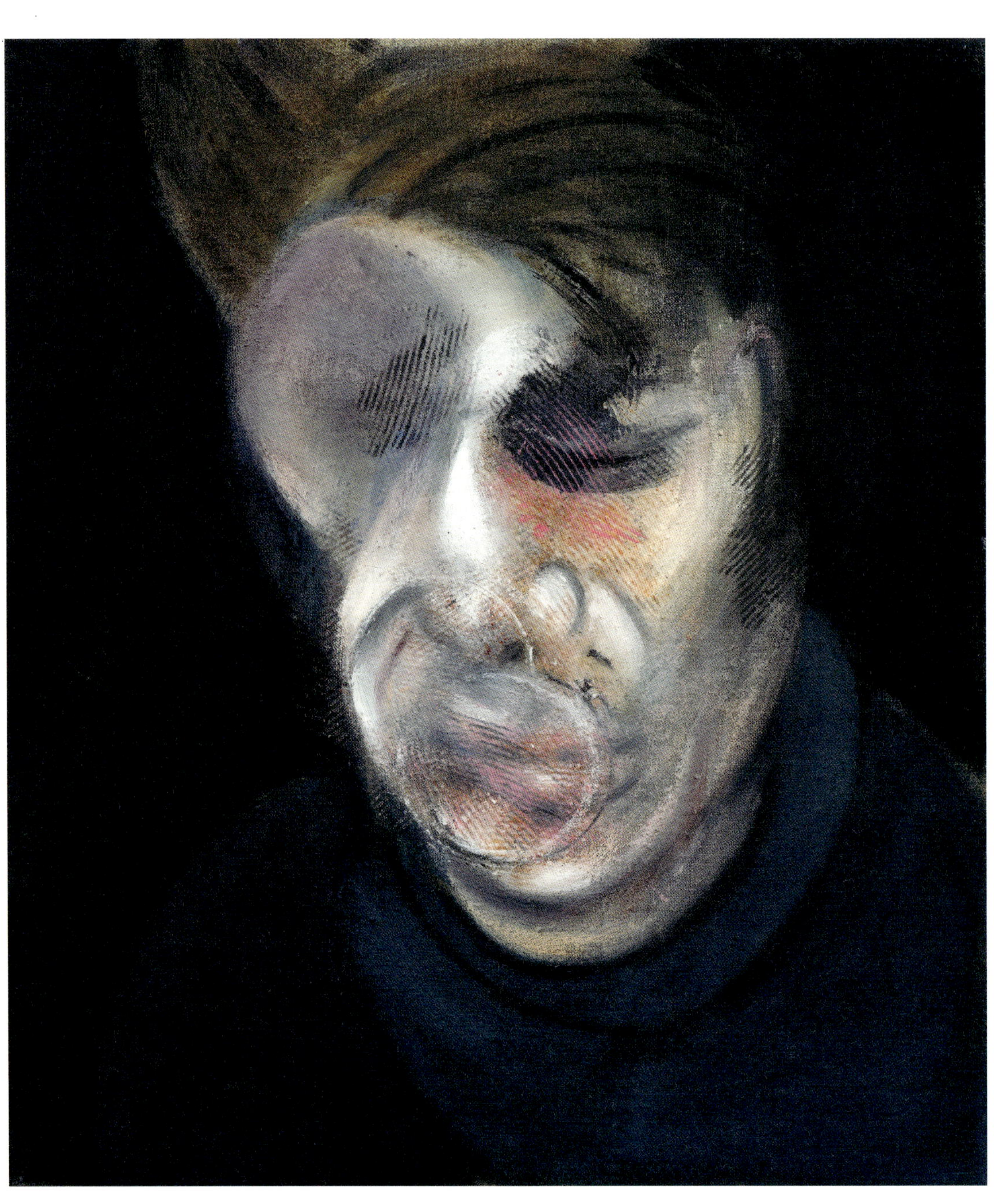

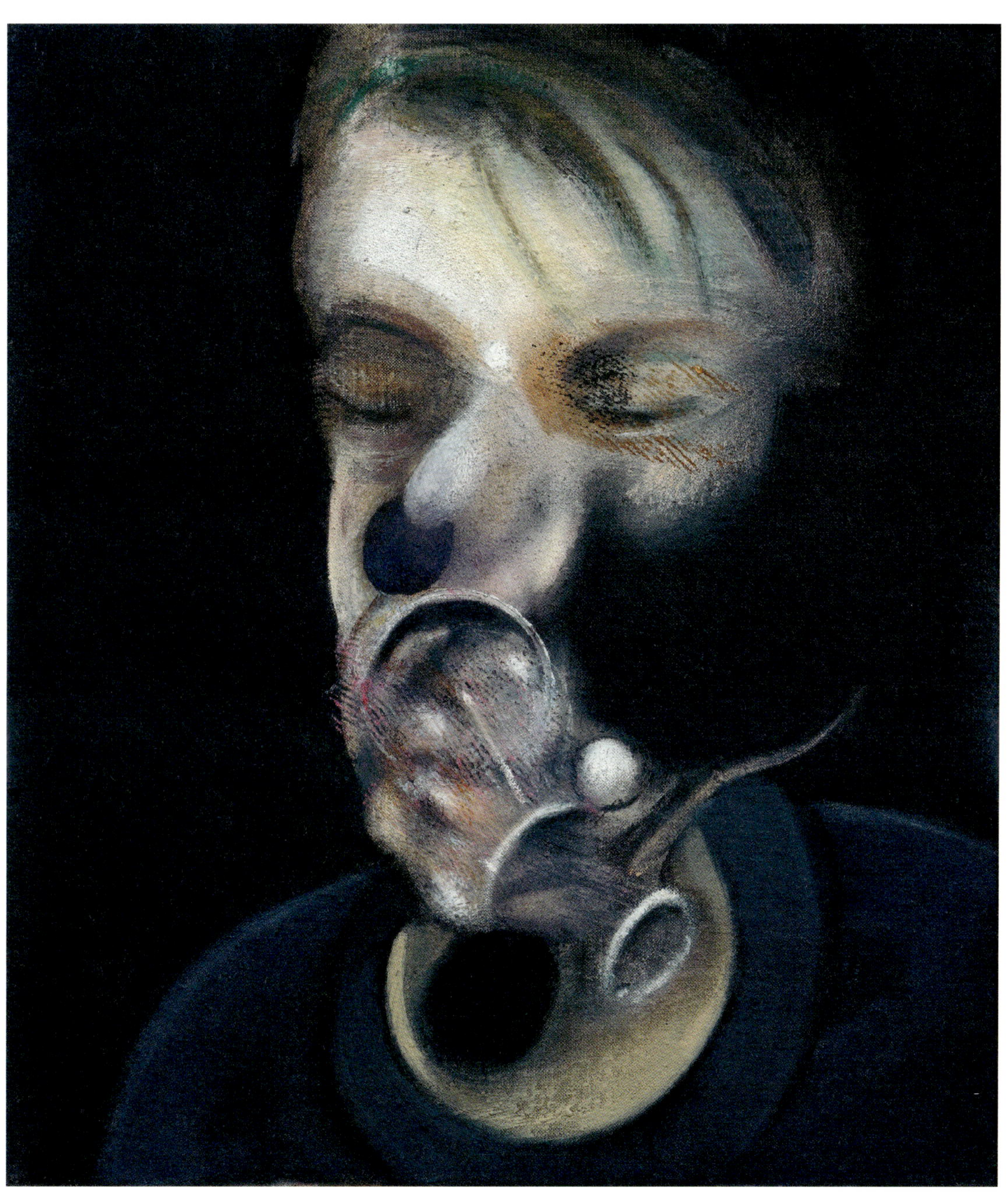

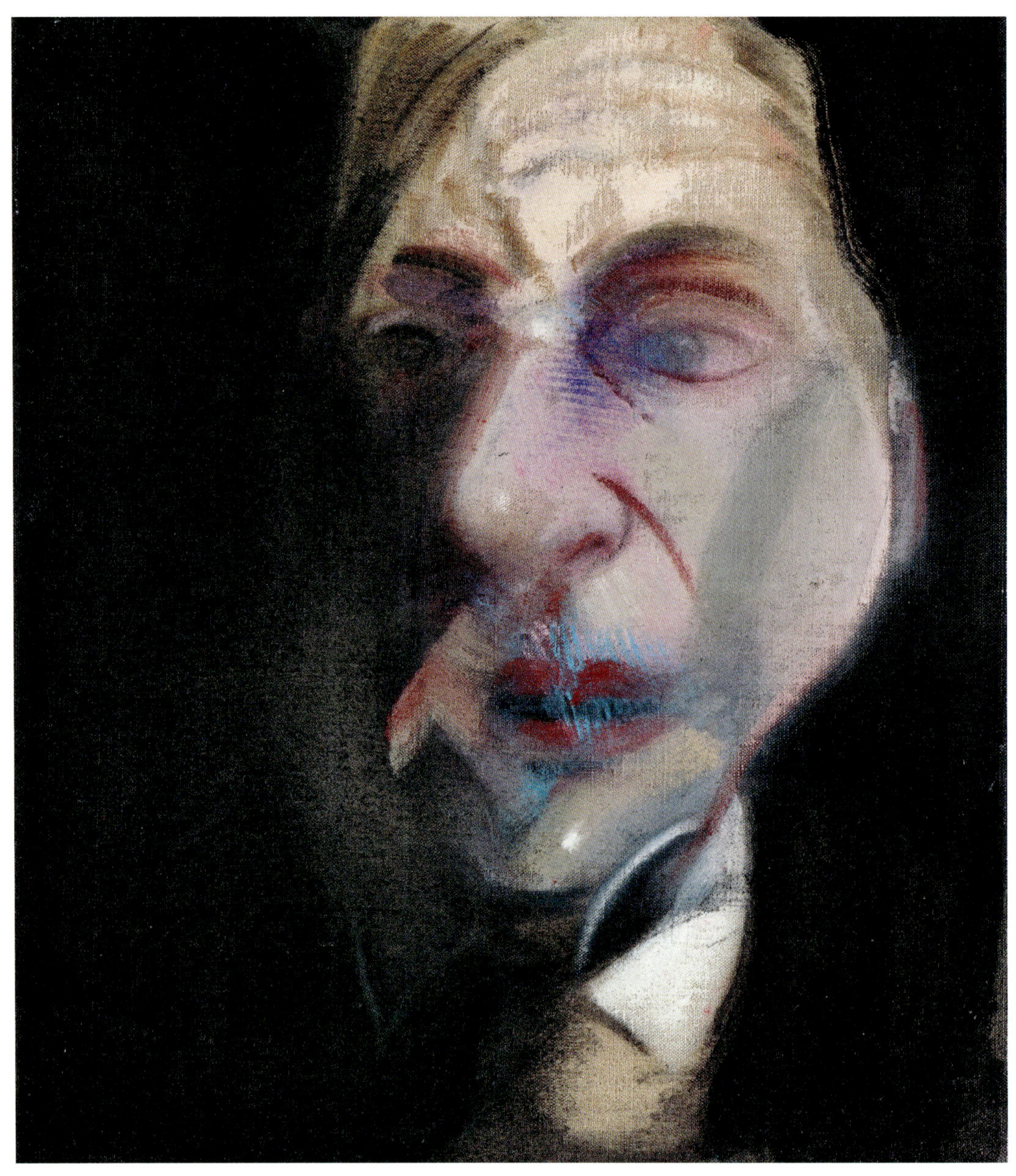

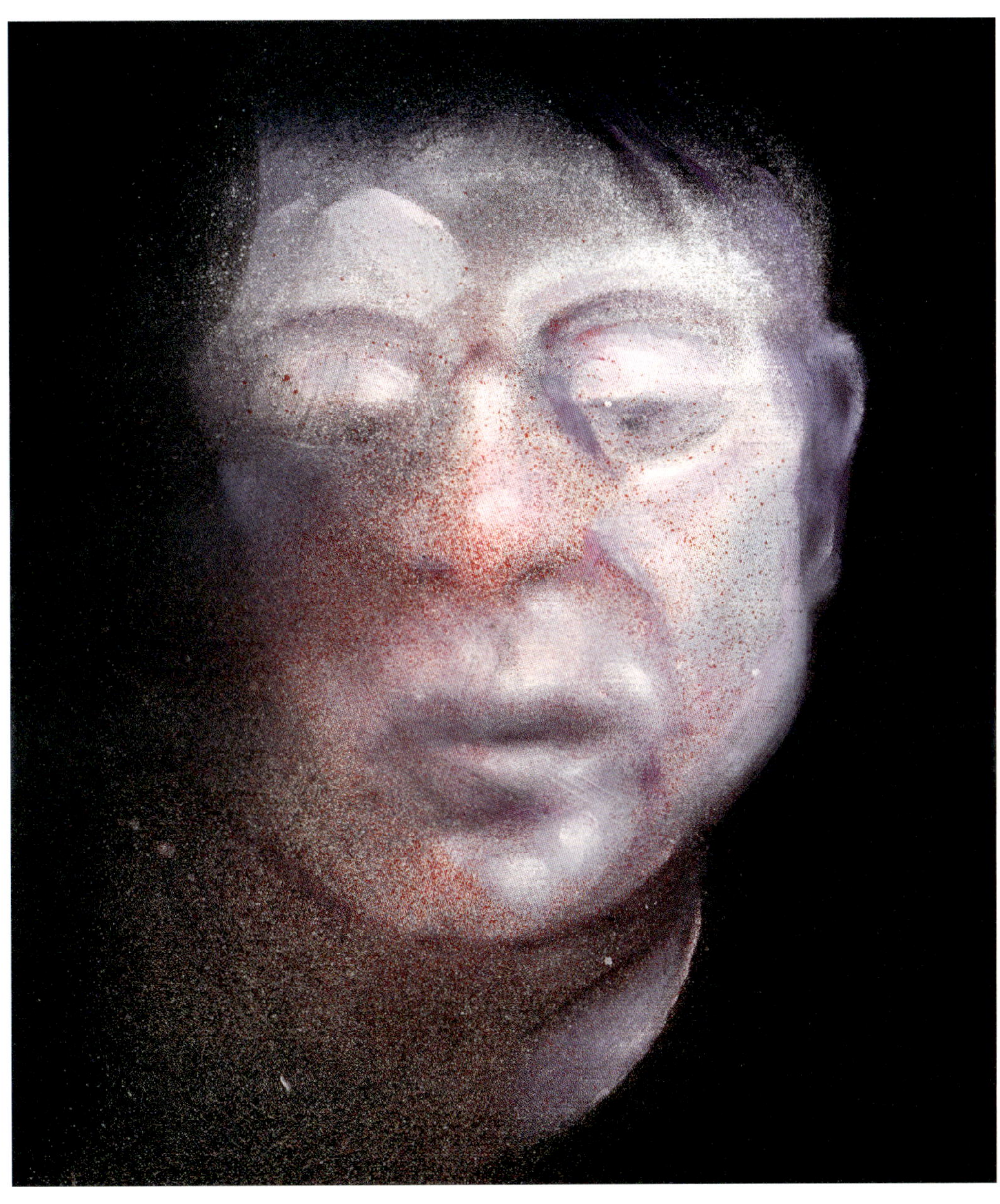

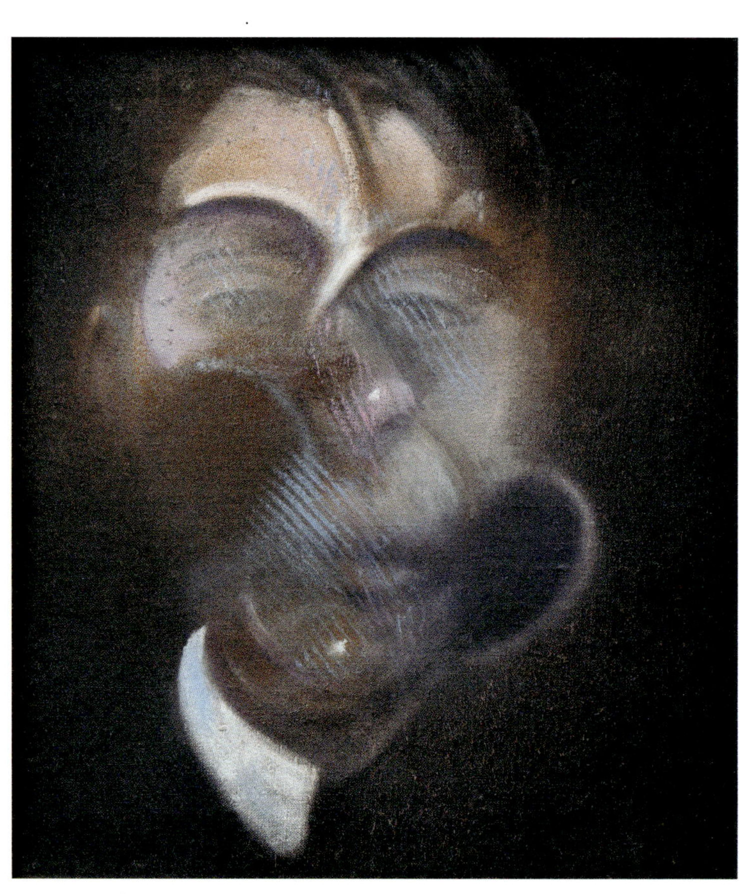

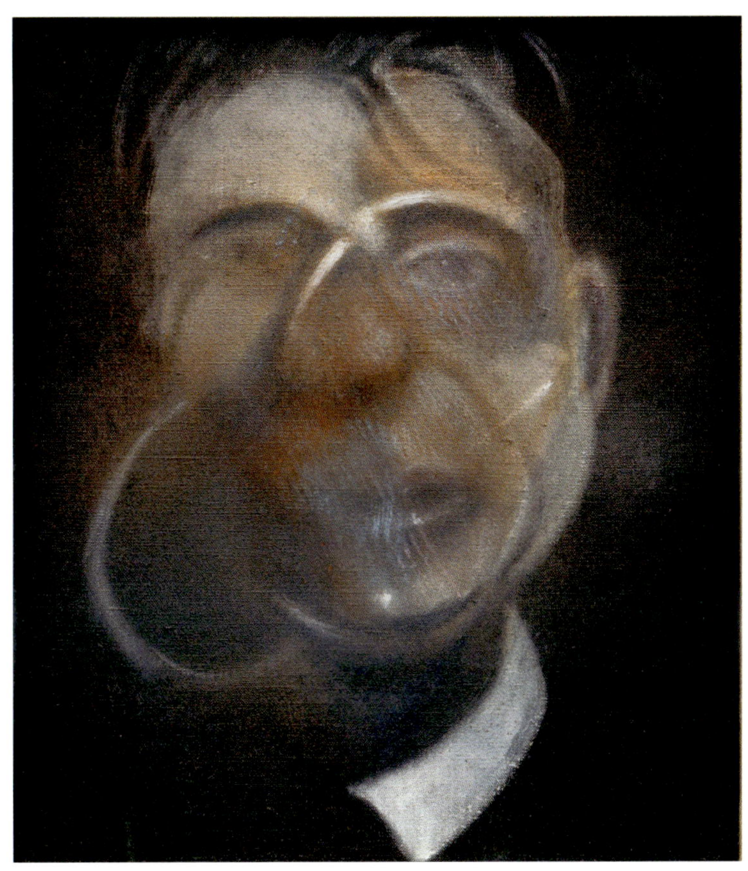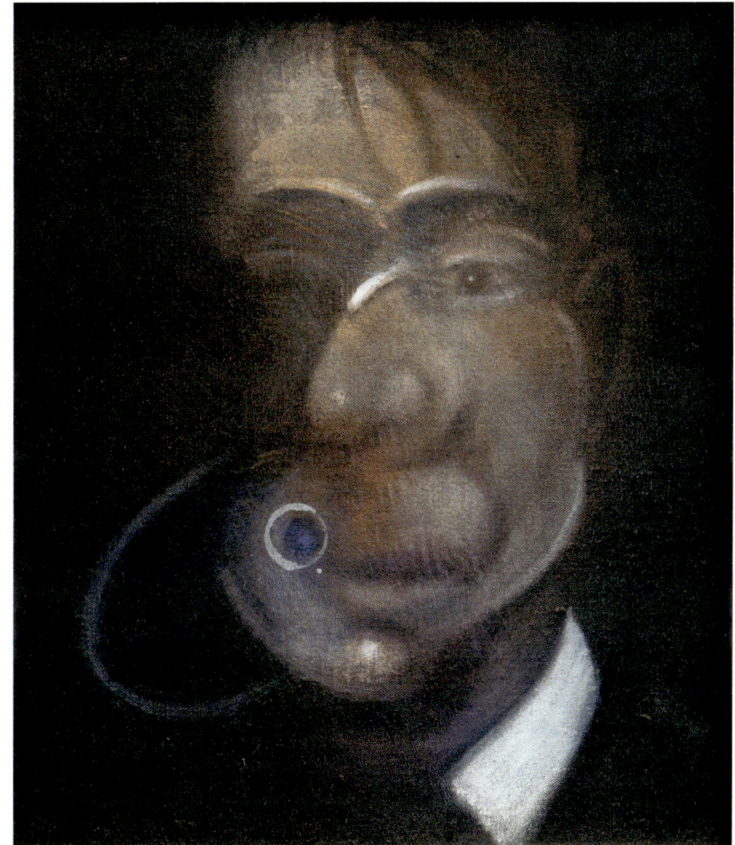

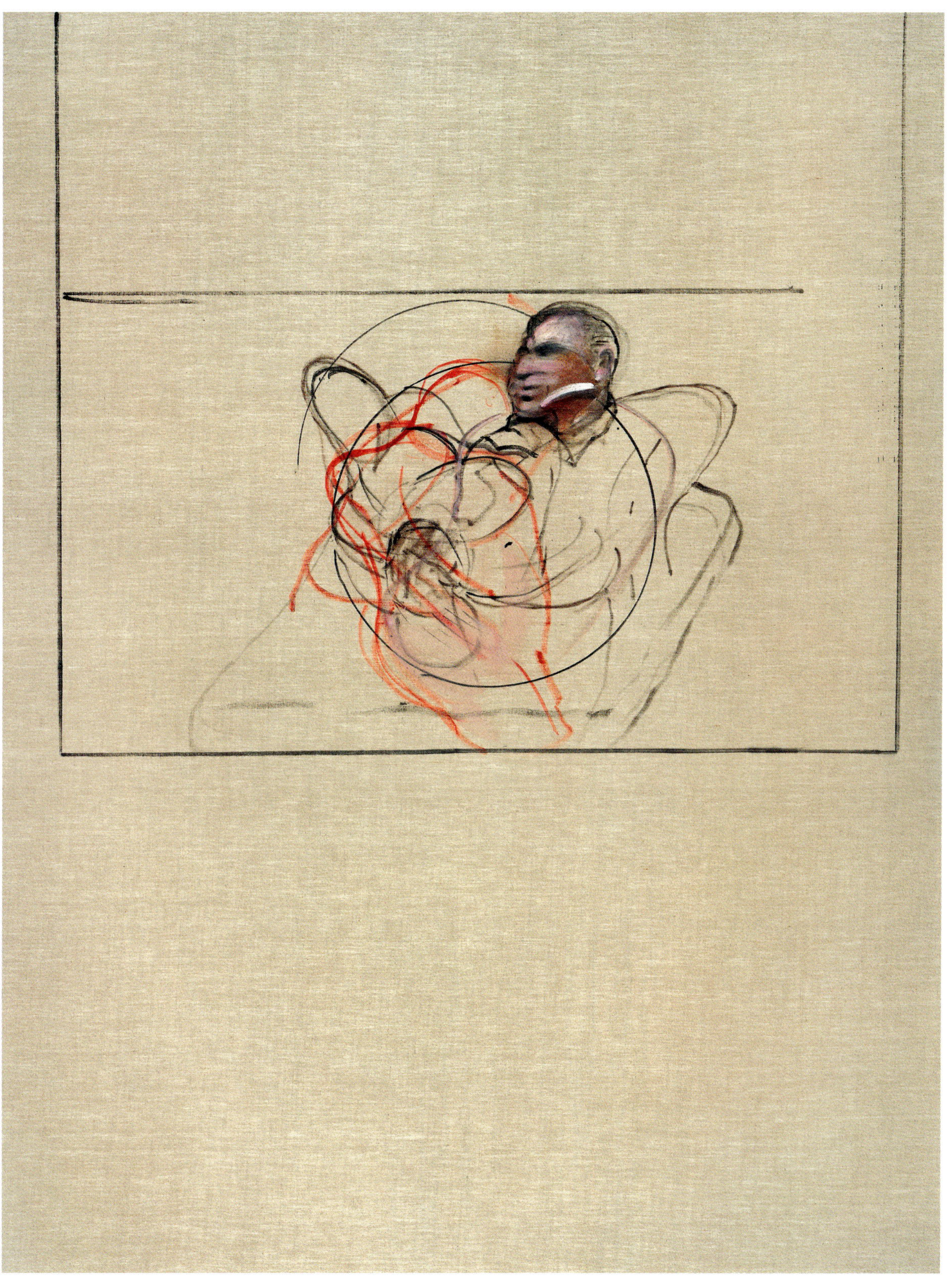

30 *Self-Portrait* 1991–2 Oil on canvas 1980 × 1475mm

Study from a Human Body: Francis Bacon & Medical Self-Portraiture

Sophie Pretorius

*'Listen, we live, how are we going to make our body,
our experience between birth and death, into an image?'*[1]

It is most unusual for the body of a painter of bodies to become available and known to an interested audience, particularly to the degree that Francis Bacon's body has become. In 2018 his medical records were kindly donated to the Estate of Francis Bacon in the name of Dr Paul Brass. They document, in minute detail, Bacon's extraordinary ill health and his attitude towards it.[2]

Dr Paul Brass was Bacon's private physician, a role he inherited from his father, Dr Stanley Brass. Brass senior had begun his care of the artist in 1935, shortly after Bacon moved to the Kensington and Chelsea area. Thus, the doctors Brass cared for Bacon from his twenty-sixth until his eighty-second year. For more than half a century they acted as the most consistent male presence in his life. Through their notes a portrait of Bacon emerges, one whose similarities to and differences from the portraits that Bacon himself painted are instructive. Perhaps more than that of most artists, Bacon's *oeuvre* has about it the air of a self-portrait. In his paintings boundaries are porous: bodies morph into shadows, shadows into animals, animals into women, women into men, men

into landscapes, and all his sitters' faces blend into each other and into his own likeness. At their most successful, Bacon's canvases, no matter their subject, capture a charitably honest glimpse into the truth, amplified through distortion, of a singular human condition. As the quote above illustrates, Bacon's goal was to make his body, or what he would sometimes call his 'nervous system', into an image, 'abbreviate[d] into intensity' (fig.1).[3] What the medical records provide us with, alongside useful anecdotal information, is an image of the body and mind of the painter, proto abbreviation.

The extent to which Bacon used his illnesses and injuries as models for his notoriously disquieting and medically graphic paintings has often been speculated. He frequently spoke of working from images in books about medical diseases, such as George Hector Percival's *Atlas of Regional Dermatology* (fig.2), and in interviews he occasionally alluded to utilising his ailments as inspiration. For instance, in 1977 he stated to the journalist Edward Behr, 'I'm allergic to turpentine and wear gloves when I'm painting. But nevertheless, I occasionally get rashes on

Fig.1   Francis Bacon   *Study from the Human Body*   1949
Oil and cotton wool on canvas   1475 × 1310mm

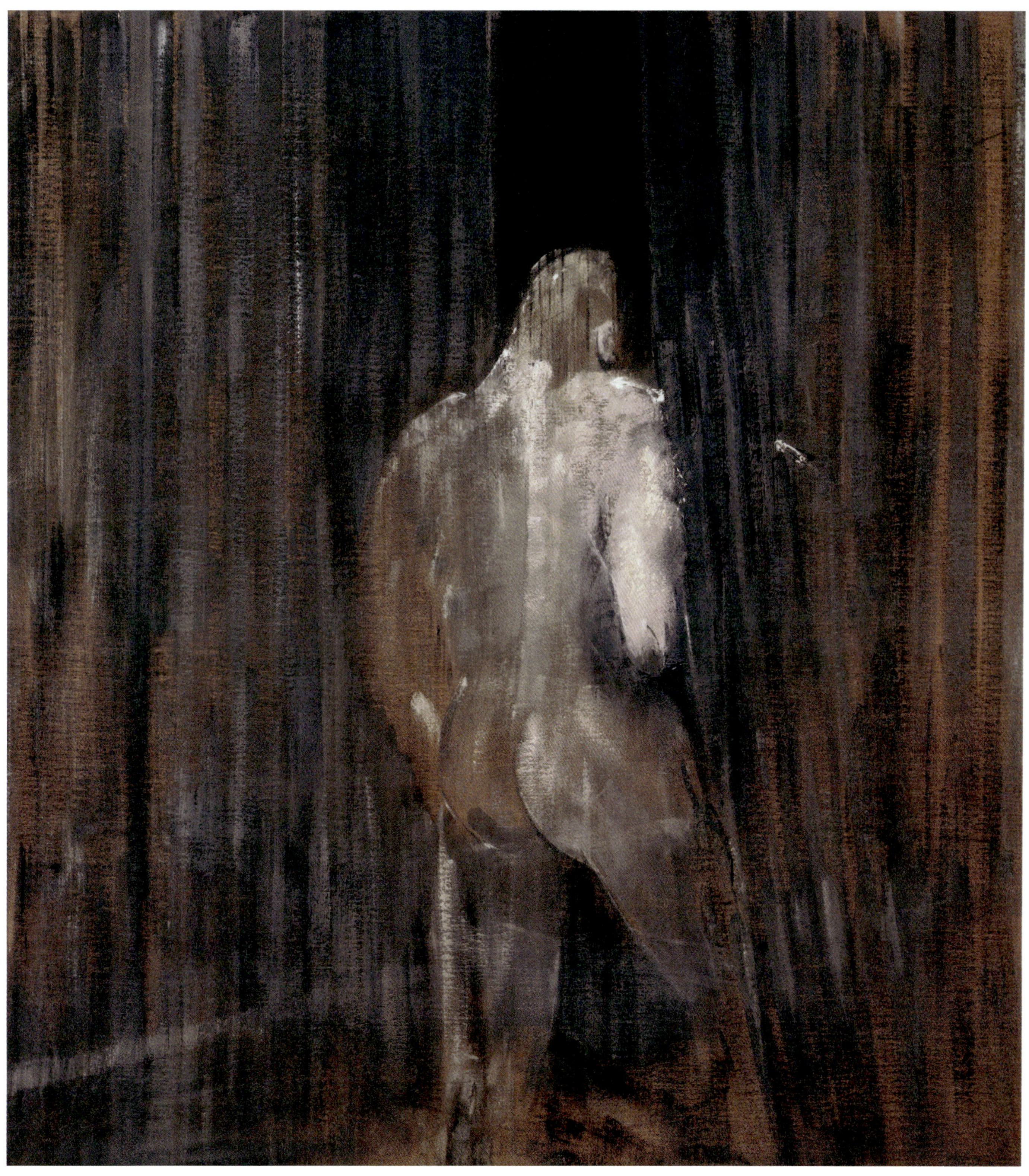

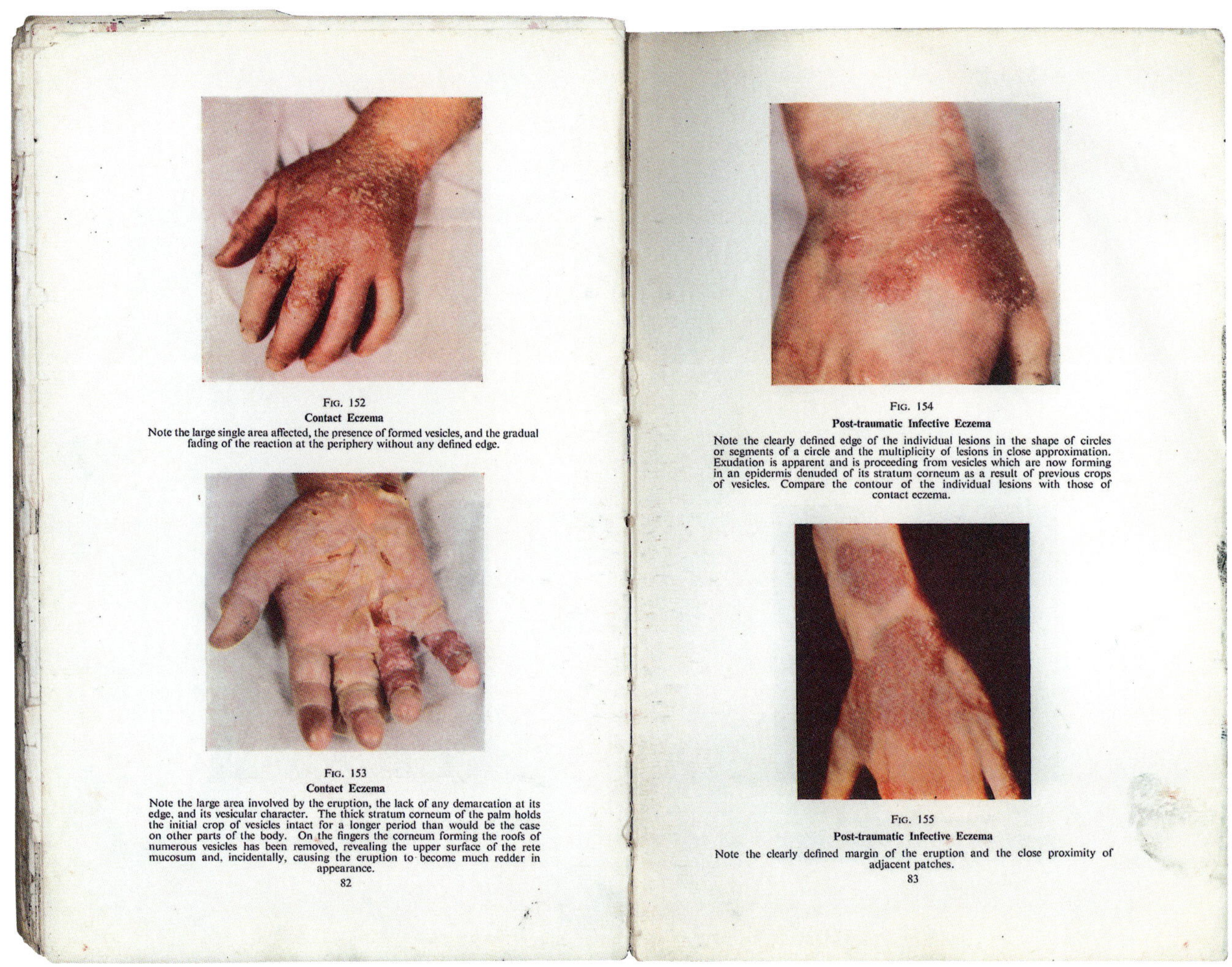

my hands and their color [*sic*] is tremendously suggestive to me, not necessarily horrific.'[4] Comments such as this turn even Bacon's few landscapes, such as *Sand Dune* (1983; fig.3), into potential self-portraits.[5] So too with Bacon's less fleshy ailments. One need only look at the 'Screaming Heads' on show in this exhibition to understand how the large and terrifying prospect of asphyxiation for the asthmatic might have come to influence his portraits of himself and others.

While a consideration of Bacon's chronic health conditions is useful to bear in mind in a general, thematic sense when considering his paintings, what the medical records provide is specificity. In these records we find direct evidence of Bacon's literal transposition of his injuries from his physical body onto his painted one, and onto those of his subjects. A strong example of this may be seen in the work Bacon completed in 1972. Early that year, just over three months after his lover, George Dyer, in a state of distress at least partially brought on by Bacon, died of a barbiturate and alcohol overdose, and two months after Dr Paul Brass described Bacon as being 'depressed about George's death', Bacon visited his doctor again. What follows is the resulting record of that visit (explanatory text mine).

Fig.3   Francis Bacon   *Sand Dune*   1983
Oil, pastel and dust on canvas   1980 × 1475mm

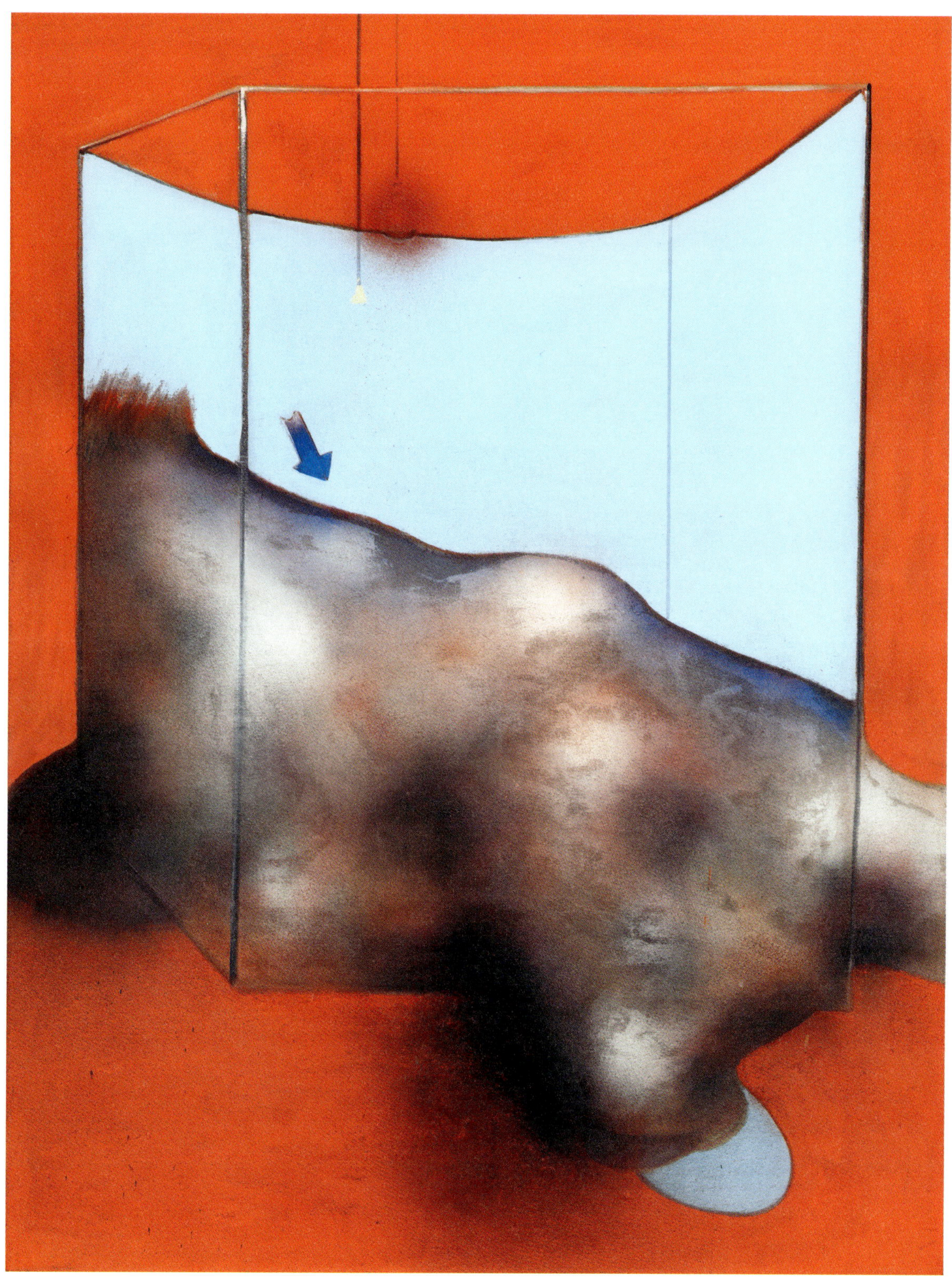

7/2/72.

Fell 10 days ago – knocked out for
20 minutes.
Injured **L** [left] side of face – laceration
of **L** cheek. and outer end of eyebrow.
Followed by **L** facial & frontal headaches.
Now M.I. [much improved] but still ou.
[*oculus uterque* (both eyes)] on waking.
In middle of work, doesn't want to be
disturbed.
Sub conjunctival hematoma **L** eye
and skin oedema of **L** cheek
1. # [fracture] maxilla bone.

also – sickness has returned.

O.E. [on examination]
abdo [abdomen] – N.A.D. [nothing
abnormal discovered] lungs HT ✓. 160/100
ʀ [prescribed] Maxolon [Metoclopramide
– for the treatment of nausea] 1/1 t.d.s.
[three times daily]

Bacon's doctors made it clear in their writings elsewhere that they knew what Bacon might have meant by his having 'fallen', and that it had something to do with his being a sexual masochist. After this 'fall' in 1972, ten of the 15 paintings Bacon completed were self-portraits and all of them show a somewhat exaggerated interest in the human eyelid and swelling, and with gouged-out segments of the face. Significantly, he gifted one of these self-portraits to Dr Paul Brass. The above medical record proves that the most literal of these paintings, *Self-Portrait with Injured Eye* (1972; fig.4), as well as those that followed, were autobiographical.

In this painting, Bacon presents the left side of his face coquettishly and accusingly to the viewer. The skin on his cheek is taut and shiny, lending a certain sensuousness to the swollen injury. Bacon made minor changes to the work between February, when it was first photographed, and April 1972 (fig.5).[6]

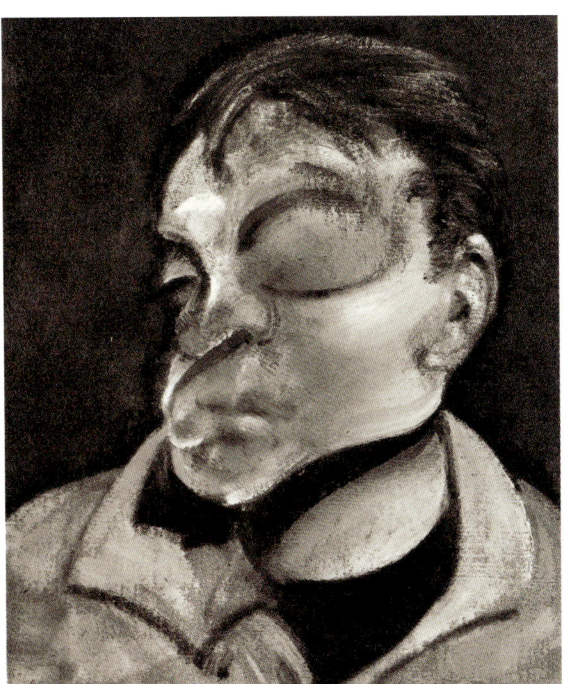

Fig.4　Francis Bacon
First version of *Self-Portrait with Injured Eye*　1972
Oil on canvas　355 × 305mm

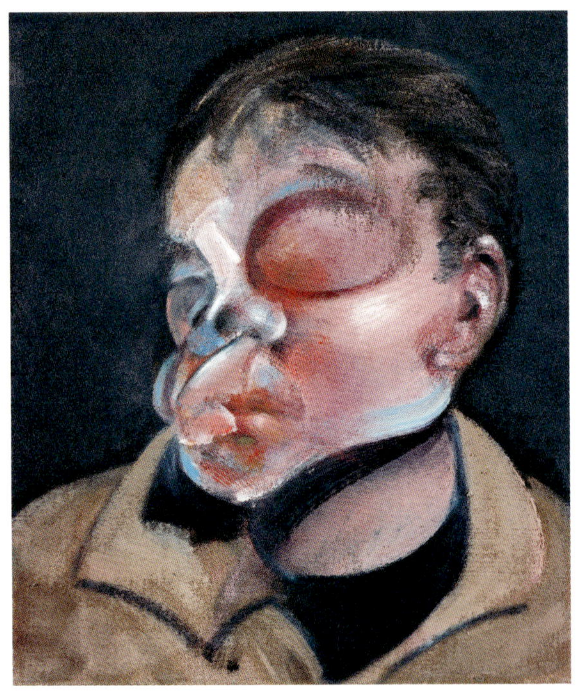

Fig.5　Francis Bacon
Self-Portrait with Injured Eye　1972
Oil on canvas　355 × 305mm

While the painting was back in his studio, and probably while he was working through still-swollen eyelids, Bacon emphasised the bones within his nasal aperture, making it more skull-like, and deepened the indentation surrounding his eye, accentuating the suggestion of facial oedema. In April 1972, Bacon made changes to another work in this series, *Self-Portrait* (1972; figs 6 and 7). In his revisions to this painting, Bacon was more drastic. He stressed the seductive parting of his lips in the work and darkened the already almost non-existent background into nothingness, extending it into the right side of his face, making an island of his right eye. The shadow cuts through his maxilla bone, significantly the bone that Dr Paul Brass notes as having been fractured by his 'fall' earlier in the year.

Martin Harrison records in his 2016 *Catalogue Raisonné* that Lucian Freud (who was then friends with Bacon) told a former owner of this painting that he believed it to be a portrait of himself, and not of Bacon.[7] Although it seems improbable in this instance that Bacon intended a likeness of Freud, it appears that even when Bacon was at his most autobiographical, his and his subjects' bodies seemed equally close to the tip of his brush. Note, too, the shocking redness of the eyes in this portrait, which evokes the sub-conjunctival hematoma that Dr Paul Brass recorded Bacon having sustained earlier in the year, as well as the eye redness associated with over-consumption of alcohol.

Painting the sclera of the eyes red was a device Bacon used repeatedly throughout 1972, both in self-portraits and in portraits of others.[8] *Portrait of a Man Walking Down Steps* (1972; cat.55) is an example of this. Although Dyer is not named in the title, on 15 May 1972 Bacon recorded starting this painting and referred to it as 'Portrait of George walking down steps'. These slippages, of Freud and

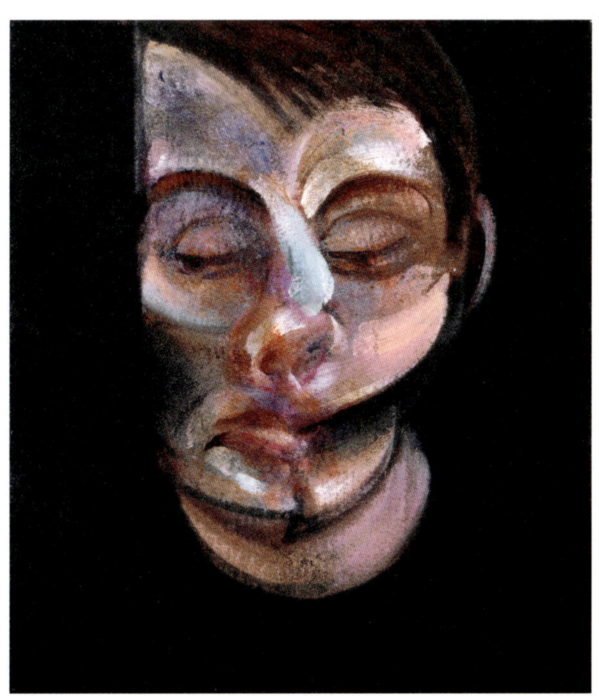

Fig.6   Francis Bacon
First version of *Self-Portrait*   1972
Oil on canvas   355 × 305mm

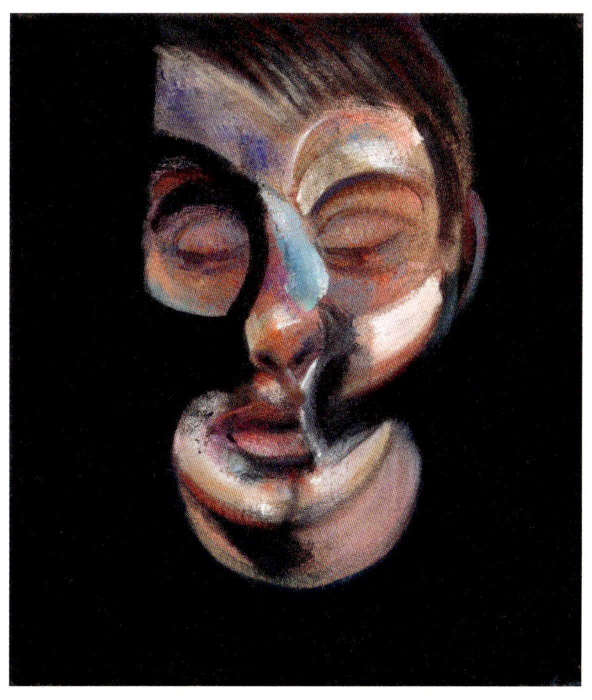

Fig.7   Francis Bacon
Self-Portrait   1972
Oil on canvas   355 × 305mm

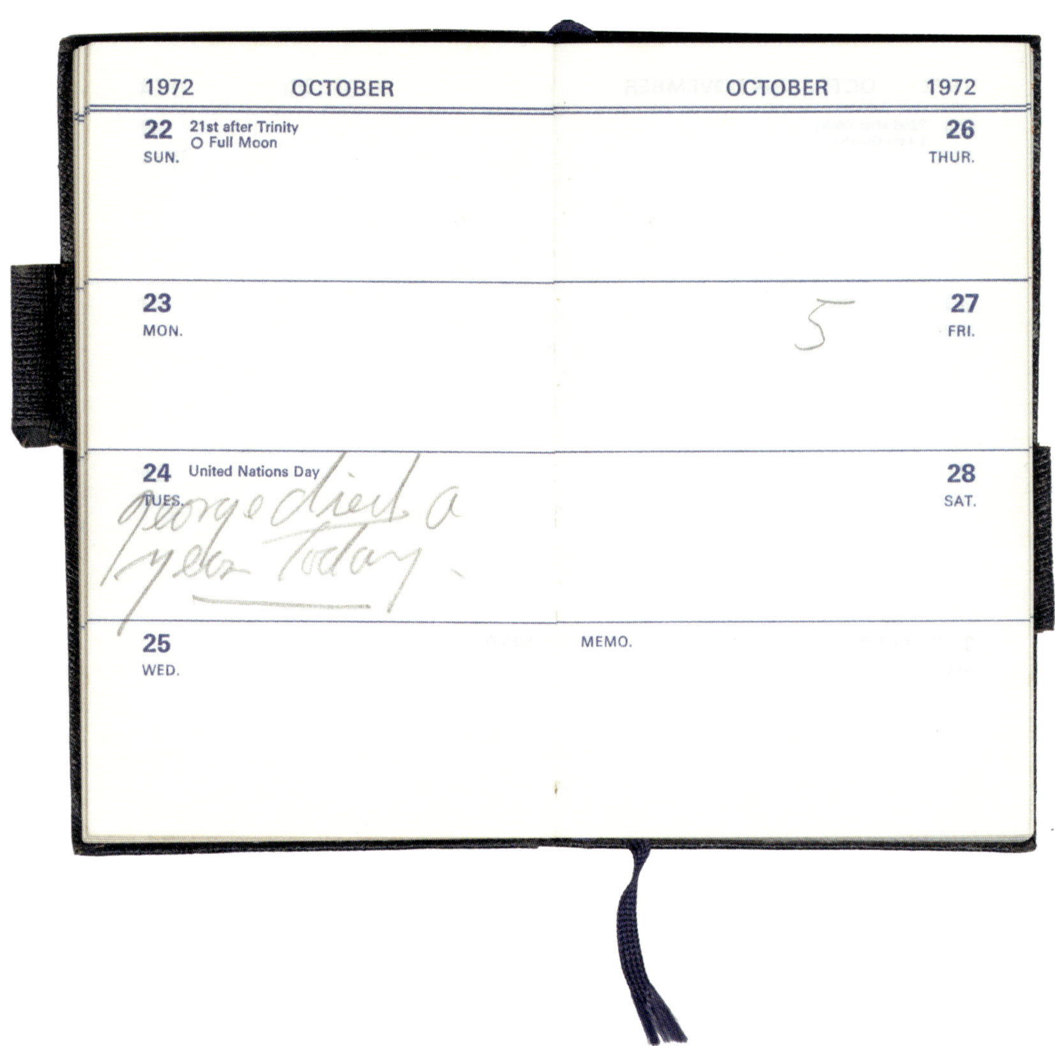

Bacon's faces, of Bacon's injuries onto the bodies of others, of Dyer's identity away from him, were all enacted within what must have been a difficult year for Bacon, one filled with guilt, mourning and perhaps masochistic coping strategies; they bring to mind the brutal maxim 'an eye for an eye'. Later in the year, on 24 October 1972, in the same diary, Bacon poignantly notes 'George died a year today' (fig.8).

Bacon's health, or lack thereof, not to mention the medication of it and the side effects of this medication, affected every aspect of his creative practice. Although the medical records by no means explain Bacon's pictures, they paint an unprecedentedly detailed portrait of the body that served as medium to Bacon's genius, and come as close as I believe we ever shall to an objective perspective on the work. My preceding exploration of the implications of half of a single card from Dr Paul Brass's records illustrates the potential of this archive to deepen our understanding of the motives behind some of Bacon's creations.

Friends & Lovers

'I couldn't [paint] people
I didn't know very well ...
It wouldn't interest me to
try to ... unless I had seen
a lot of them, watched
their contours, watched
the way they behaved.'

An important shift in Bacon's approach to portrait painting can be traced through representations of his charismatic and troubled lover Peter Lacy, whom he met in 1952. Lacy's presence is implicit in the numerous anonymous businessmen painted during the early years of their relationship, when Lacy was working as a stockbroker in his family firm. By the end of the decade, and as Bacon adopted a more expressive style of brushwork and colour palette, portraits of Lacy had become more emotionally charged, such as *Sleeping Figure* (1959; cat.35), in which his subject is depicted tenderly. These more personal paintings signal the emergence of the artist's desire to capture the 'emanation' of a particular sitter.

This new phase of Bacon's portraiture centred on representations of lovers and friends, many of whom had entered Bacon's orbit via the drinking establishments of Soho. While most of these friendships began in the post-war period, sitters such as his great friend the artist Isabel Rawsthorne appeared and reappeared in portraits across the subsequent three decades. When it came to sitters, Bacon was selective, preferring attractive people who, like him, dwelt on the fringes of conventional society and traversed boundaries of social class. In the early 1960s Bacon commissioned the photographer and fellow Soho stalwart John Deakin to take pictures of potential sitters, including Rawsthorne, Lucian Freud and Henrietta Moraes. Deakin's images became integral to Bacon's practice to secure a likeness and, when torn and crumpled on the studio floor, the photographs suggested new and startling images. In depicting his sitters, Bacon used memory, sensation and chance to convey a sense of presence that transcended illustration.

Some of Bacon's greatest portraits represent his lover George Dyer, whom he met in 1963. In *Portrait of George Dyer in a Mirror* (1968; cat.53) Dyer's reflected visage, based on a Deakin photograph, is brutally sliced. This portrait is part of a series of large canvases featuring Dyer made at the end of the 1960s. While the two men's relationship had always been fraught, Dyer's death prompted Bacon to produce the so-called black triptychs, extraordinarily moving portraits that commemorate Dyer's tragic last moments, whilst conveying the full force of Bacon's grief at his loss. Dyer continued to be a potent and poignant presence in Bacon's work, even in the decades after his death.

31 John Deakin George Dyer and Francis Bacon on the *Orient Express* 1965
Gelatin silver print 203 × 202mm

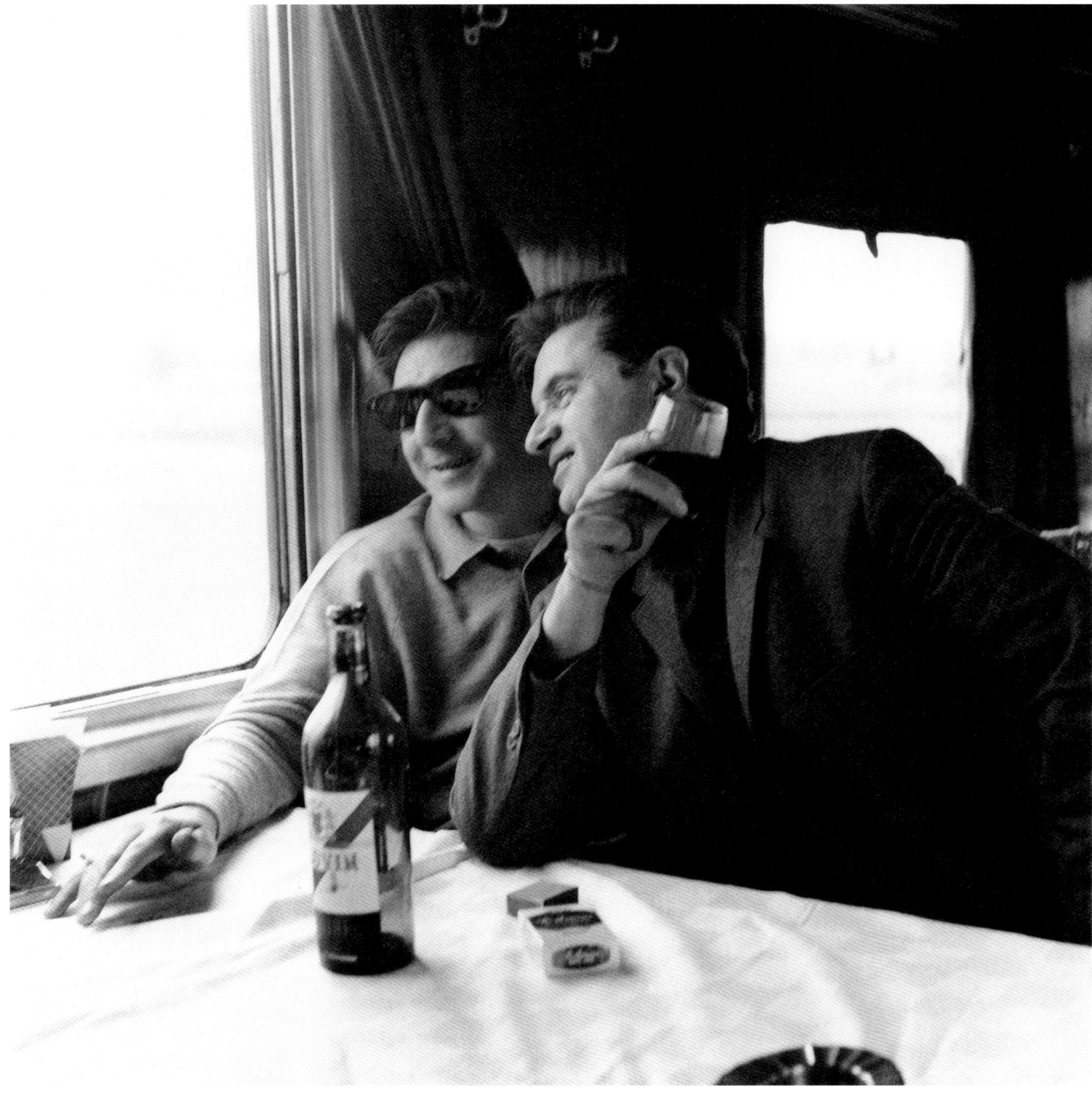

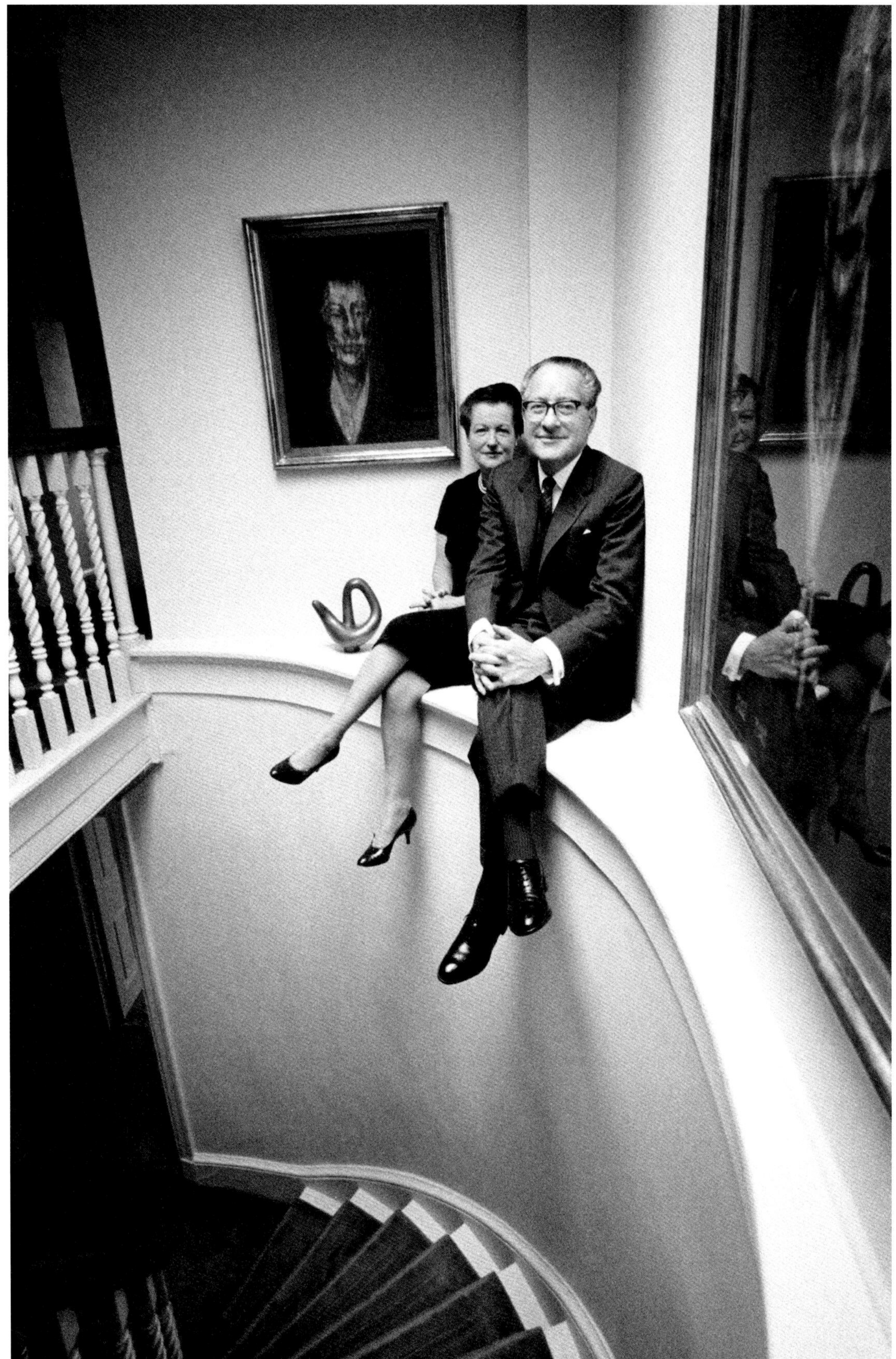

Lord Snowdon   *Robert and Lisa Sainsbury*   1965   Gelatin silver print   382 × 258mm

Robert & Lisa Sainsbury

Sir Robert Sainsbury (1906–2000) and Lady Sainsbury (1912–2014) were influential British art patrons and collectors. In 1930 Robert joined the eponymous family business, a grocery-store chain then known as J. Sainsbury. In 1937 he and Lisa married, a relationship that in 1989 was compared to 'a well-balanced classical sonata where the pianist does not overshadow the string-player but where she is consistently much more than an accompanist'.[1] The art dealer Erica Brausen brought Francis Bacon to the Sainsburys' attention, and from the mid-1950s, they became instrumental in supporting the artist. They bought their first work, *Study of a Nude* (1952–3) in 1953, and eventually owned 13 paintings by Bacon.[2] The artist was known to have petitioned the philanthropic couple in times of financial insecurity, and at one point asked them to guarantee overdrafts at the bank.[3] When Bacon's major Tate retrospective of 1962 was thrown into doubt, the Sainsburys agreed to support the show, such was their faith in his work.[4]

In the 1950s Lisa commissioned Bacon to create a portrait of her husband (*Portrait of R.J. Sainsbury*, 1955; cat.32). Robert sat during his lunch-breaks in Bacon's studio in Mallord Street, London, over a series of nine sessions.[5] It was Bacon's first commissioned portrait. Lisa herself sat for Bacon between September 1955 and 1957; one resulting portrait, *Sketch for a Portrait of Lisa* (cat.33), is visible in the photograph shown opposite. They would have lively discussions, gossiping about life and art. Lisa told the art critic and curator David Sylvester in an interview in 1996 that 'they were all done not as a commission but as an act of friendship'.[6] Describing the studio in Battersea where she sat, she said, 'It was rather difficult to sit in that room ... there was so much on the

floor and it was jolly difficult to get to the
chair without being covered in paint.'[7]

The Sainsburys remained lifelong friends
and supporters of Bacon, as they had been to
other artists, such as the sculptor Henry Moore.
In 1973 they gifted the majority of their rich
art collection, including works by Bacon,
Alberto Giacometti, ceramist Lucie Rie
and a vast collection of art from Africa, the
Pacific and Asia, to the University of East
Anglia in Norwich, now housed, since 1978,
in the Sainsbury Centre for the Visual Arts.

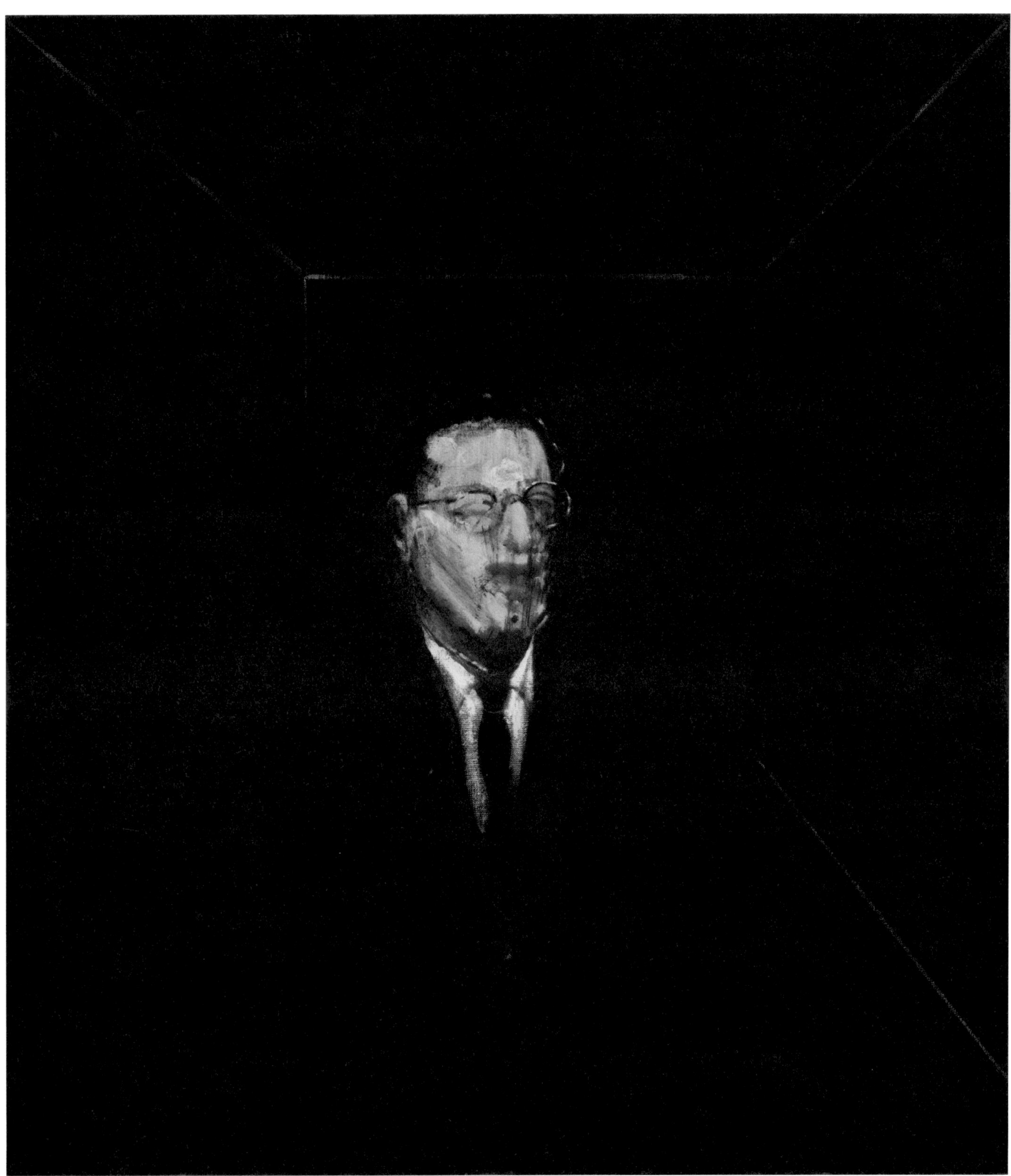

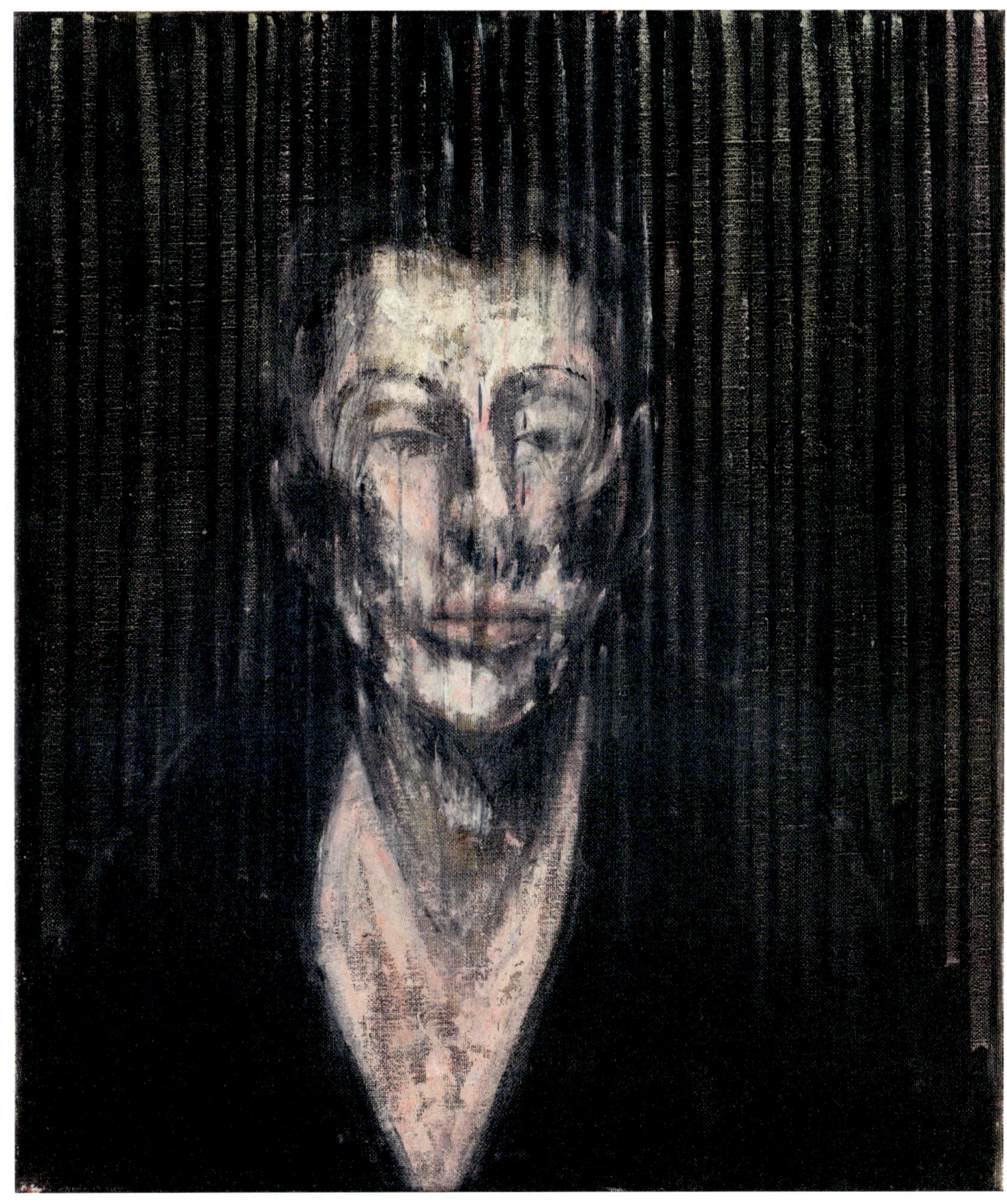

John Deakin *Peter Lacy* 1959 Gelatin silver print 248 × 185mm

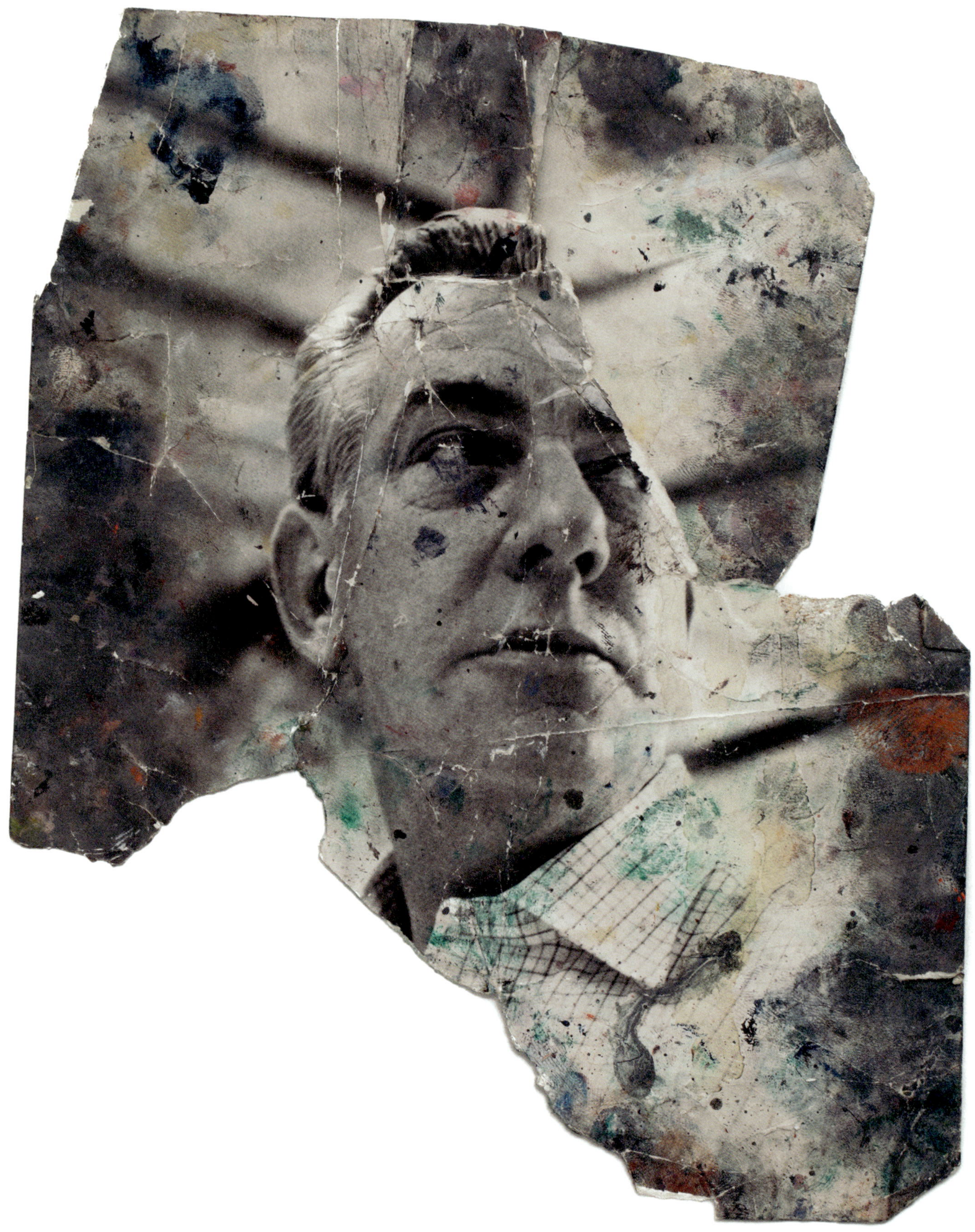

Peter Lacy

Peter Lacy (1916–1962) has been described as the love of Bacon's life.[1] This is despite the complications, suffering and episodic violence that characterised their relationship. Lacy was tall, fine-boned and elegantly dressed, with swept-back hair. Bacon met Lacy in Soho in 1952 and their relationship stretched over most of the 1950s. Reflecting on the relationship years later, Bacon said, 'Being in love in that way, being absolutely physically obsessed with someone, is like an illness.'[2]

Both men came from wealthy Midlands families with Irish heritage. Like Bacon, Lacy was raised in a strict and repressive religious household in which his homosexuality would have been condemned. His experience in the aircraft industry led him to join the RAF in June 1941, working as a mechanic and test pilot.[3] He was not, as is often stated, a fighter pilot during the Battle of Britain.[4]

Lacy squandered his considerable inheritance from his father on a bad investment. Some of the fortune enabled him to live, for a time, in a Moorish house in Barbados. Following a request from Lacy, Bacon painted the house with uncharacteristic realism from a black and white photograph as a love token (*House in Barbados*, 1952).

After living for some time in London, Lacy relocated to the small town of Henley-on-Thames, and then in 1955 to the expatriate community in Tangier, where drugs and homosexuality were briefly tolerated. Bacon would visit regularly for long stretches but, despite numerous attempts, they were unable to live successfully with one another. During these visits, Lacy's uncontrollable rage coupled with Bacon's masochistic desires, often led to violent encounters. Bacon was beaten and assaulted by Lacy, and his canvases slashed.[5]

Lacy had a passion for jazz music, admiring, in particular, the American jazz pianist Fats Waller.[6] Lacy himself was a talented pianist, playing in the Music Box club in Soho during wartime, and then at Joseph Dean's notorious bar in Tangier during the late 1950s. The novelist Robin Cook, a visitor to Dean's in July 1956, evoked the bitter-sweet scene of Lacy at the piano: 'This cigarette-scarred instrument produced an inspired stream of music which I had never known to end before seven in the morning, at which hour the performer would sway and his face collapse gravely into the keys with a faint but haunting discord.'[7]

Bacon painted Lacy continuously throughout the 1950s. In *Study of Figure in a Landscape* (1952, cat.5), Bacon depicts Lacy in South Africa, where he had visited family in 1951. Lacy had not been with Bacon in South Africa, so his source was a black and white holiday snap taken in the Mediterranean. The artist replicated the tonal qualities of the photograph in

this painting, as though to emphasise the incongruity of Lacy in that location. The monochrome figure appears spectral amongst the strokes of green and the earthy brown of the unpainted canvas, as wild and vulnerable as the 'big game' Bacon had observed in South Africa. Other portraits range from the psychologically interrogating *Seated Figure* (1961; cat.34), depicting Lacy twisted on a couch, to more intimate and tender depictions of Lacy in repose such as *Sleeping Figure* (1959; cat.35), or the more sexually explicit and menacing *Portrait* (1962; cat.37).

Lacy died from alcoholism in May 1962, the evening of the private view of Bacon's career-defining Tate retrospective. After Lacy's death, Bacon painted his first small-format triptych, *Study for Three Heads* (1962; cat.38) bringing together two portraits of Lacy with a central grief-stricken self-portrait. *Landscape near Malabata, Tangier* (1963) represents another memorial to his lover, who was buried in Tangier, and whose spirit is alluded to through the restless black forms in the painting.

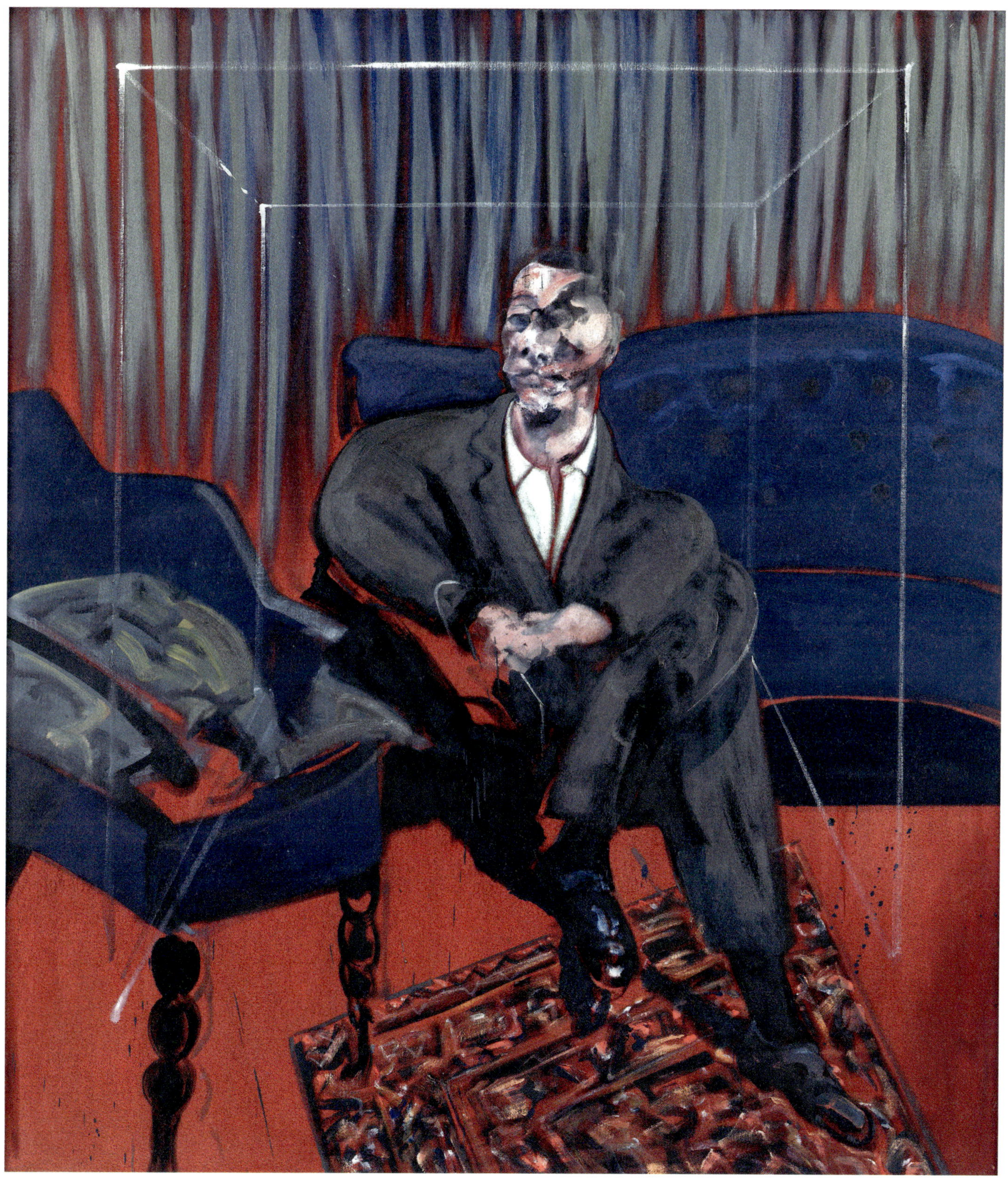

34 *Seated Figure* 1961 Oil on canvas 1651 × 1422mm

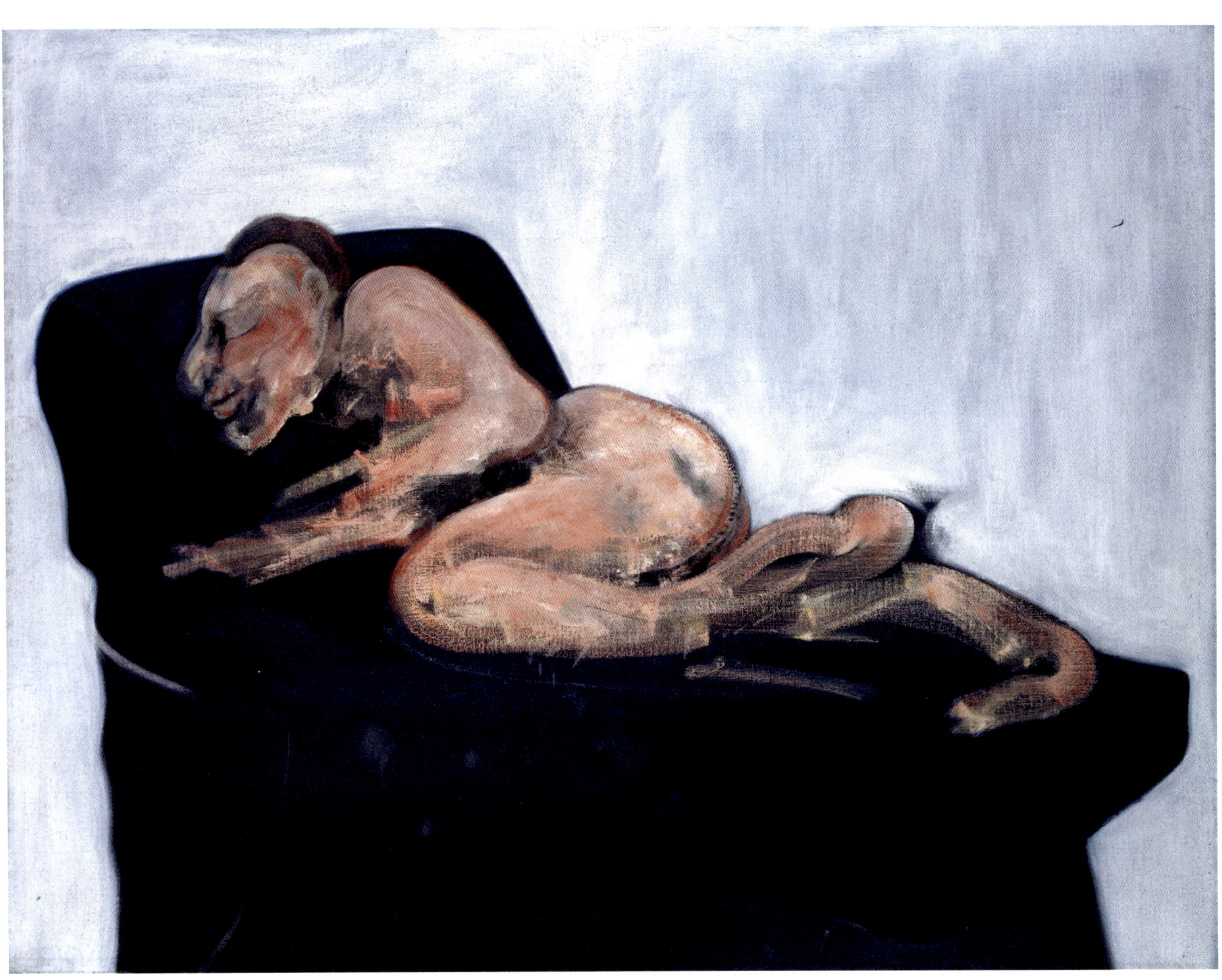

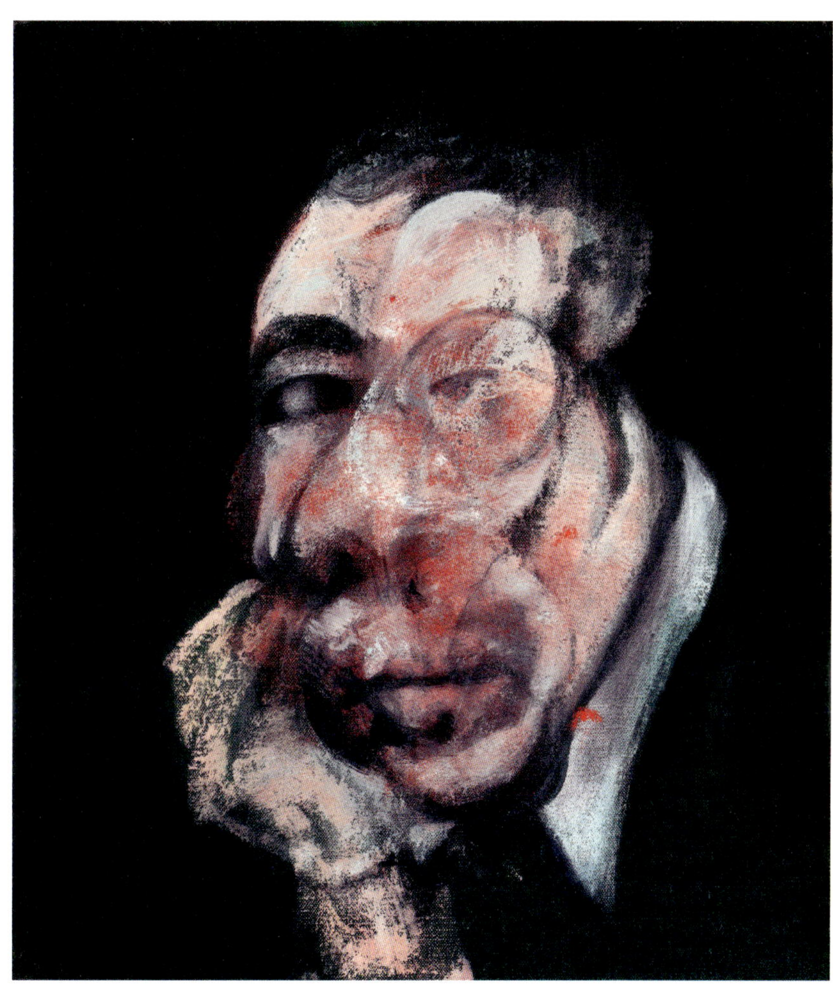

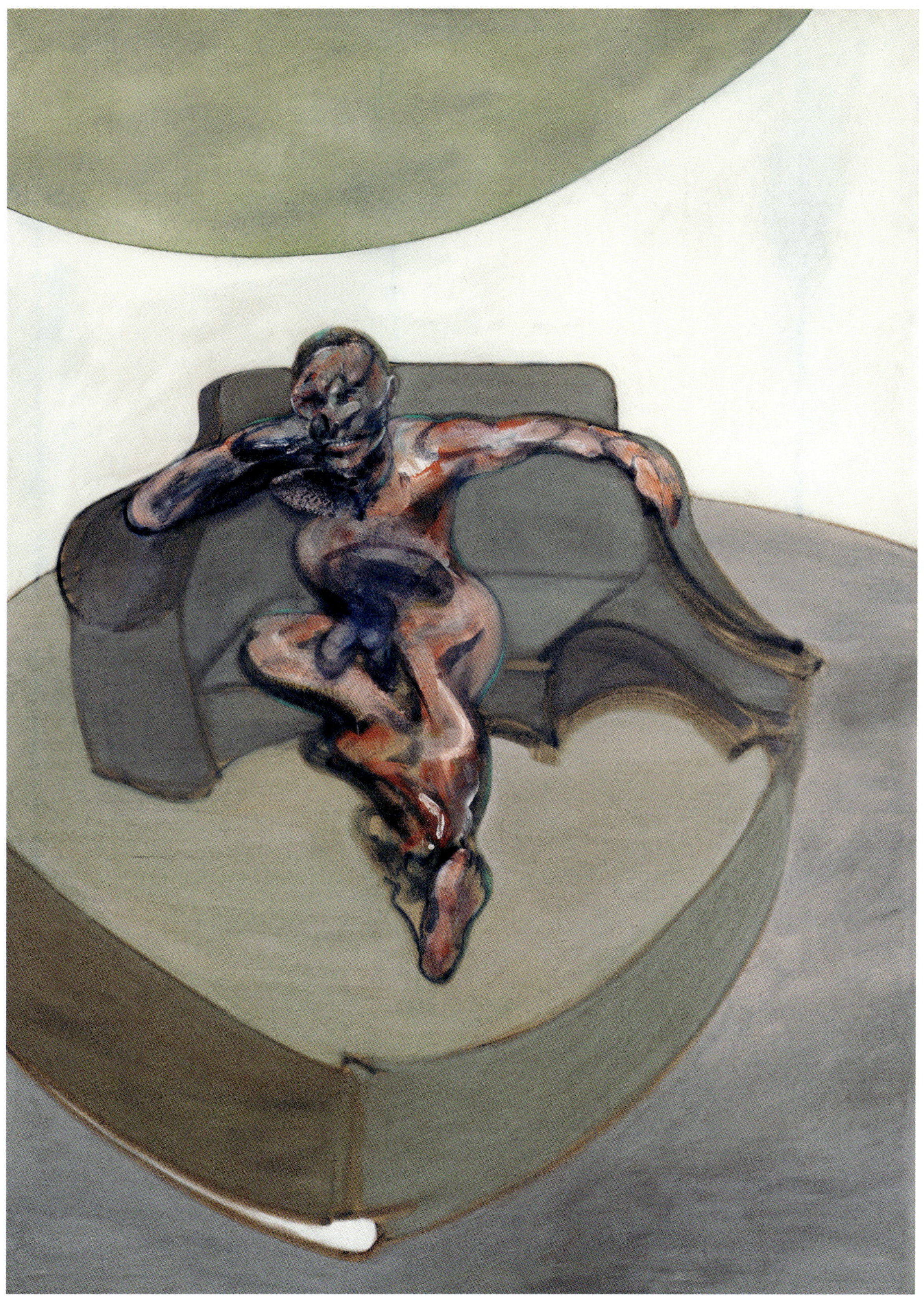

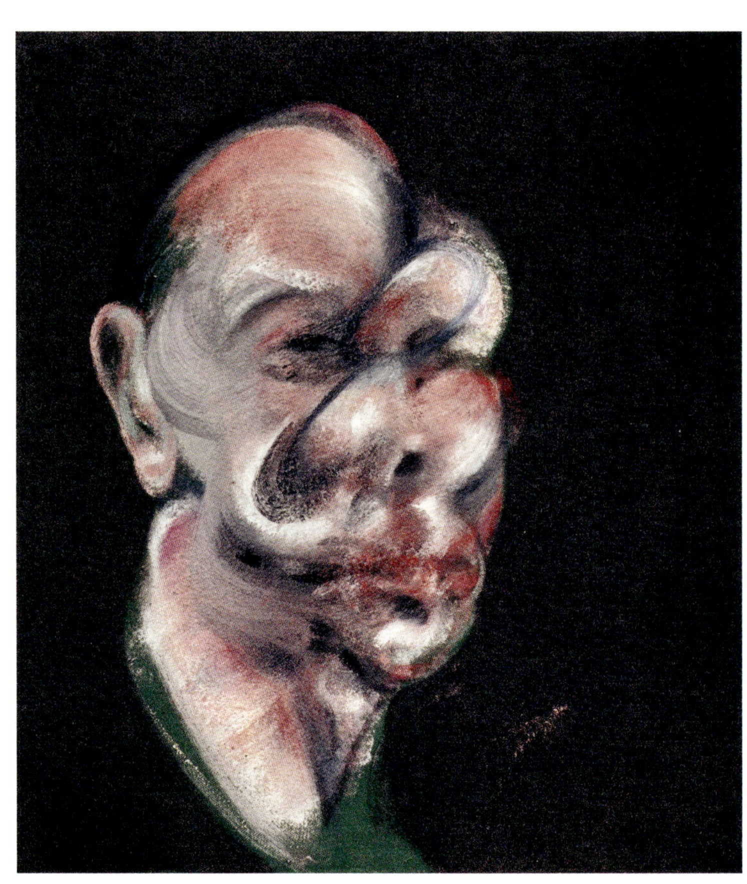

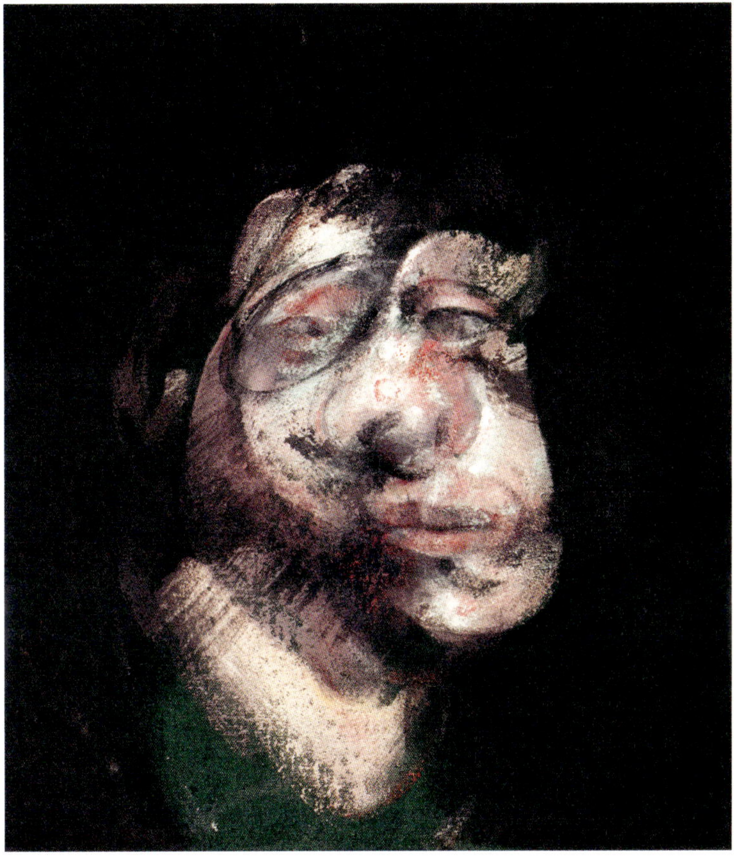 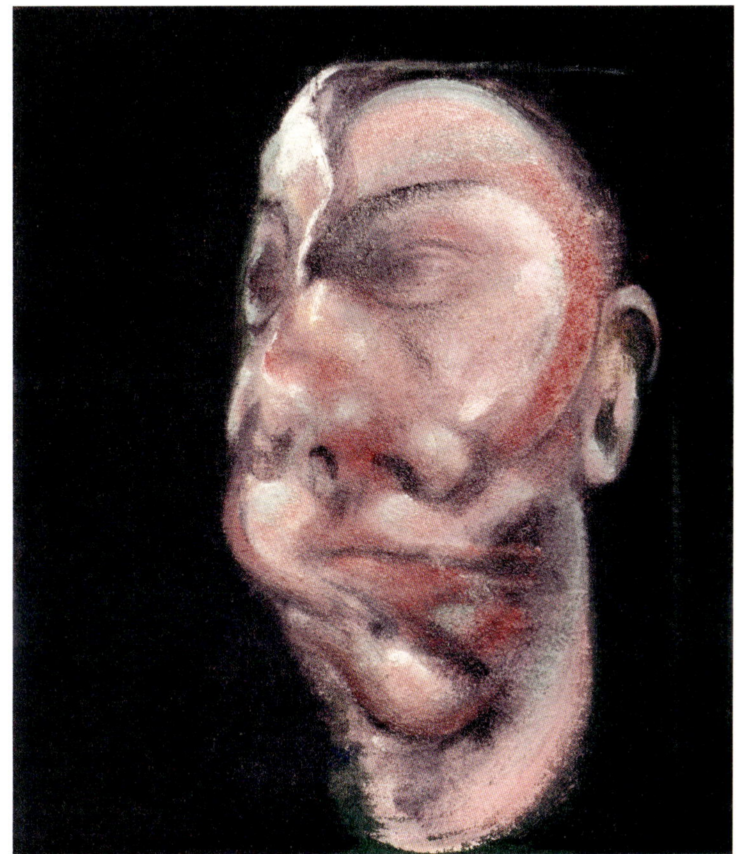

John Deakin   *Muriel Belcher*   c.1965   Gelatin silver print   295 × 254mm

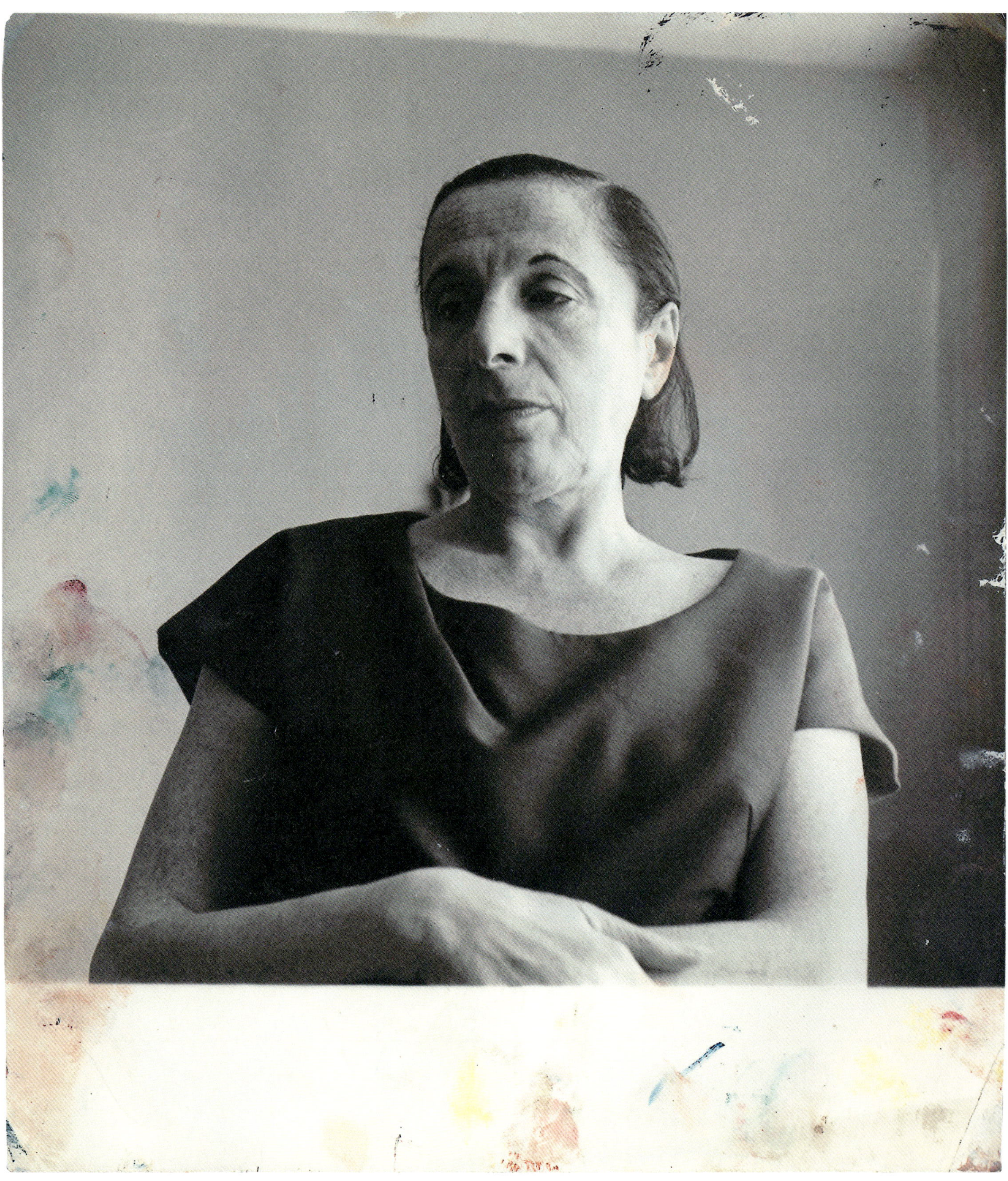

Muriel Belcher

Muriel Belcher (1908–1979) was the founder
of the Colony Room, a private members' club
in Soho frequented by artists, writers, radicals
and free thinkers, many of whom would become
synonymous with the post-war British art scene.
Belcher first came to London from Birmingham
in about 1937 to run The Sphinx, a gay club
on Gerrard Street, with her business partner
Dolly Mayers. They then went on to run the
Music Box off Leicester Square.

Described as a 'delinquent saint', Belcher
was known to have been dedicated to her
patrons, yet ruthless to those she disliked.[1]
The Colony Room was a safe haven for sexual
non-conformers, a place, as Francis Bacon
described, 'to lose your inhibitions … to go
where one feels free and easy'.[2] It brought
together people from different ranks, races
and sexualities, helping to break down social
barriers entrenched in post-war London.

Bacon came across the Colony Room shortly
after it opened in 1948, and it remained one
of his favourite drinking spots. Belcher offered
the charismatic and gregarious artist £10 a week
and free drinks in return for attracting clientele
into the club. Belcher's habit of transposing
the genders of her patrons, including Bacon,
who she called 'Daughter', was seen to be a sign
of affection, as was her vulgar greetings to her
members upon arrival ('Hello cunty!').

Michael Andrews's painting *The Colony Room I*
(1962) provides a snapshot of the community
that would gather alongside Bacon and Belcher,
who are depicted perched on stools at the
bar. These included the writer Jeffrey Bernard,
the photographer John Deakin, shown in
heated conversation with Henrietta Moraes,
the photographer Bruce Bernard in profile,

Lucian Freud, glass in hand, staring back knowingly at the artist, Ian Board the barman, and Belcher's girlfriend, Carmel Stuart.

Belcher was the subject of four portraits by Bacon, including *Miss Muriel Belcher* (1959), painted from memory while Bacon was spending time in St Ives, Cornwall, a full-length nude *Seated Woman* (1961; cat.39) and the triptych *Three Studies of Muriel Belcher* (1966; cat.40), for which Bacon used Deakin's photographs of her as the starting point. Bacon's final painting of her, *Sphinx – Portrait of Muriel Belcher* (1979), was in progress when Belcher fell ill and died. It acted as his parting memorial to her. When asked why he painted her, Bacon answered: 'She's a very beautiful woman. It's as simple as that.'[3]

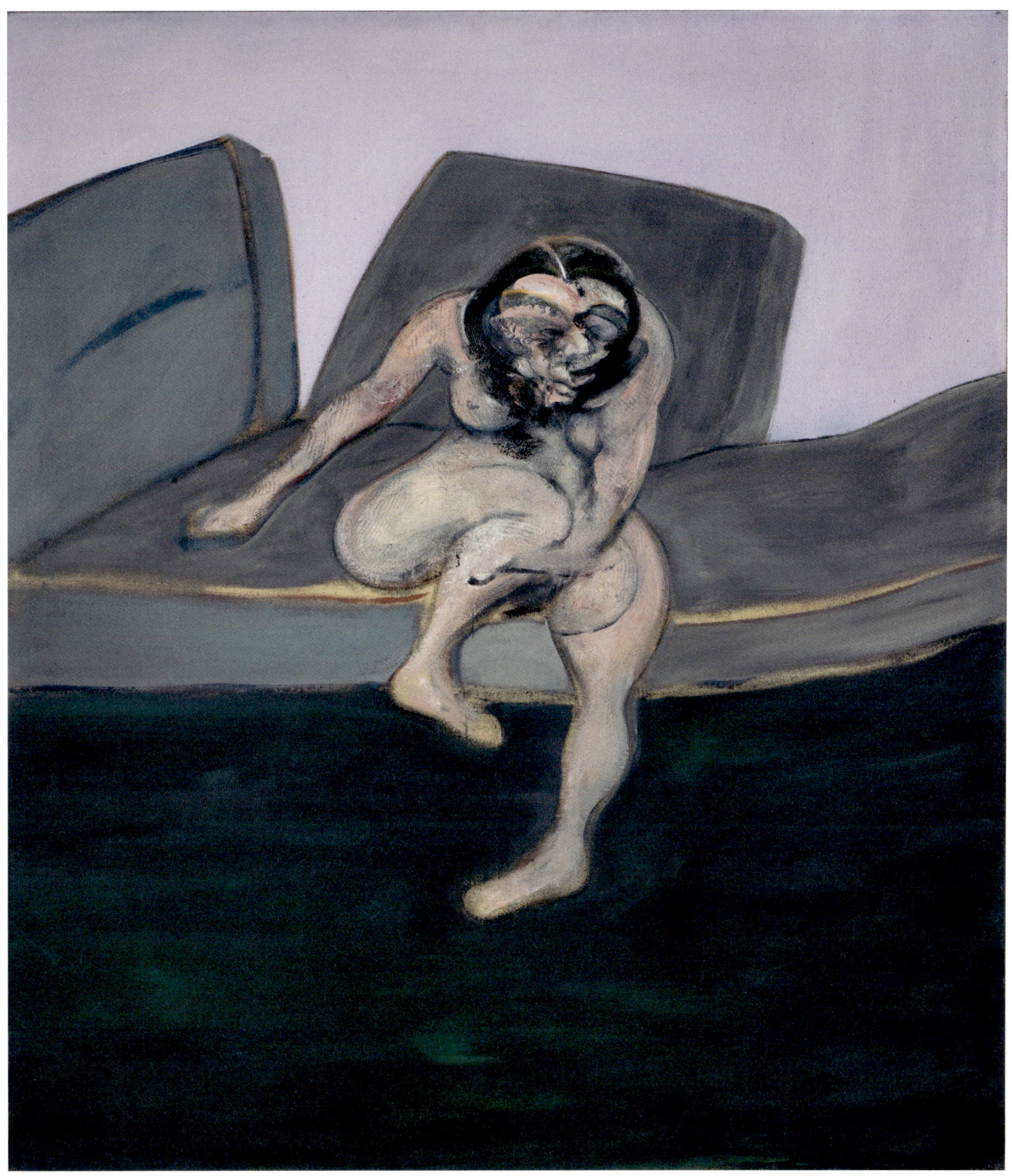

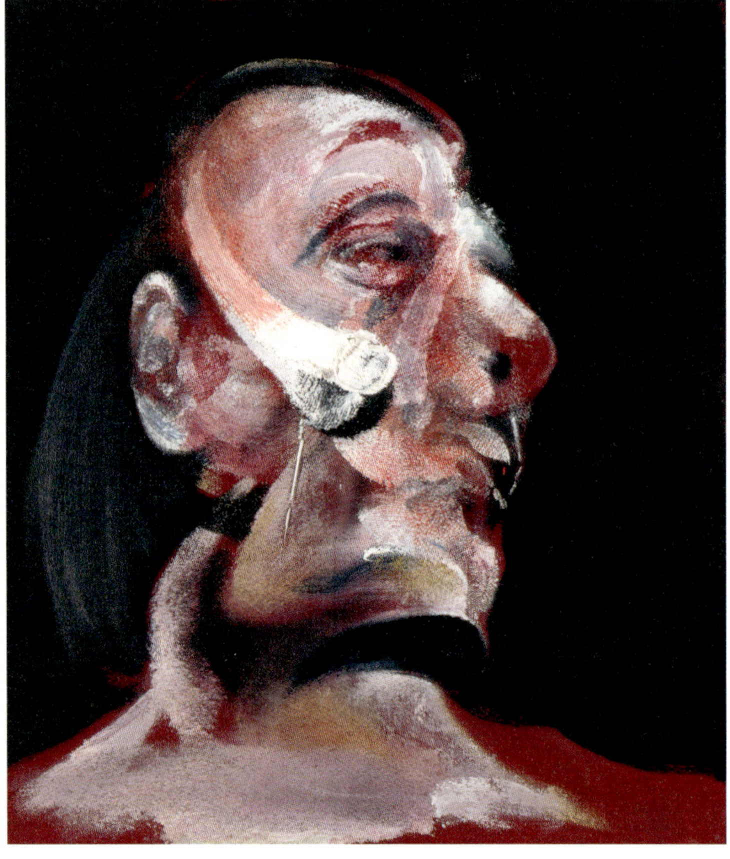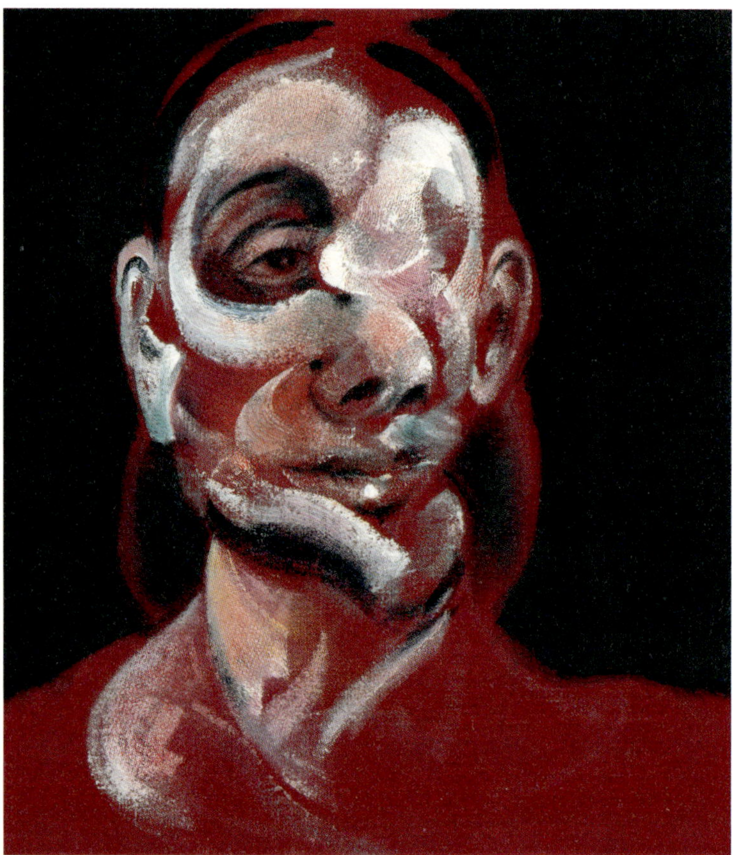

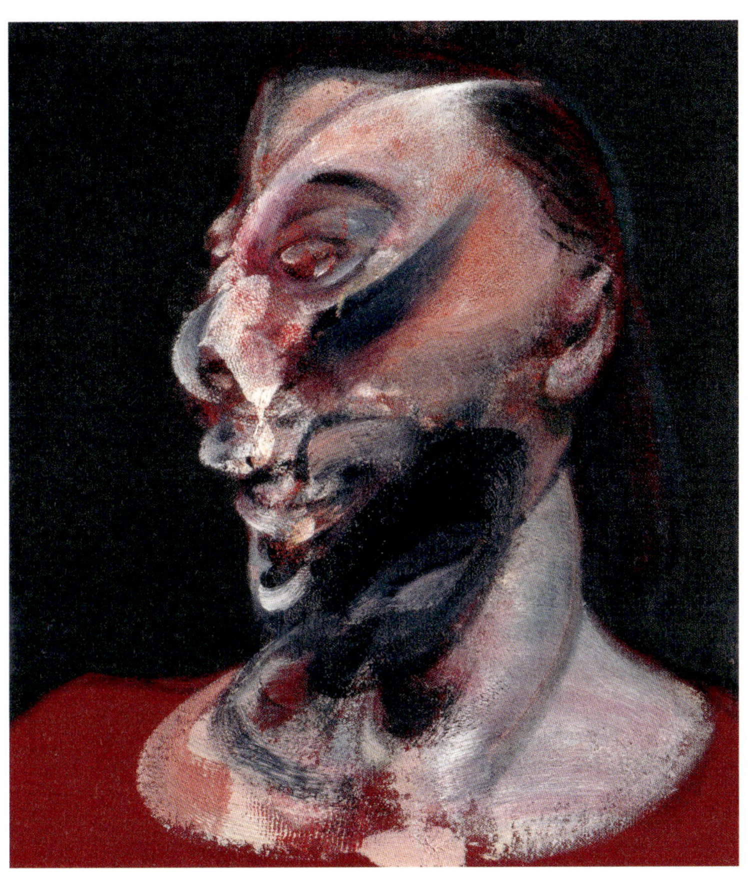

John Deakin   *Lucian Freud*   *c*.1964   Gelatin silver print   302 × 305mm

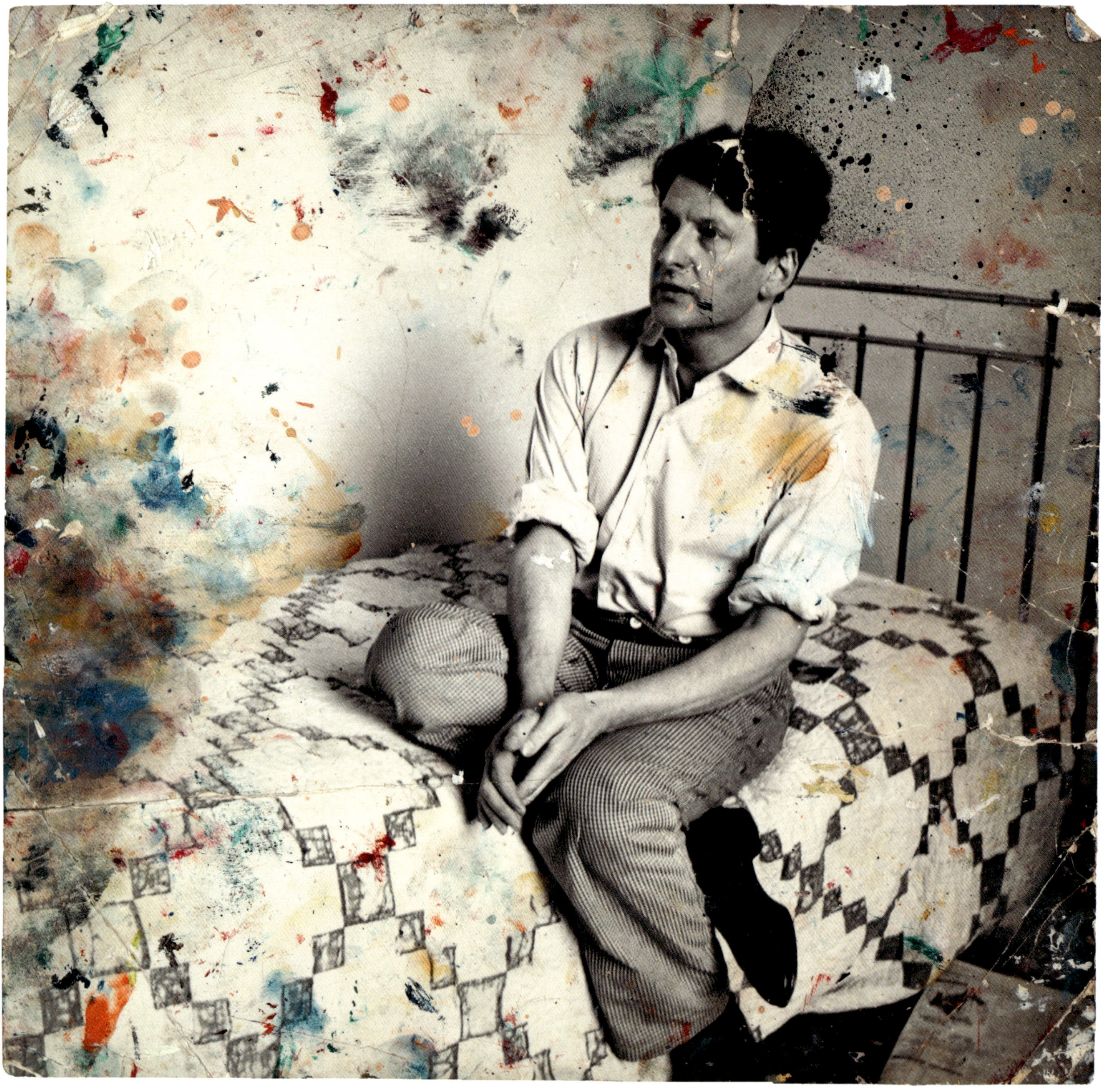

Lucian Freud

Lucian Freud (1922–2011) was one of Britain's foremost figurative artists, known for his closely observed and psychological portraits of his lovers, patrons, friends and children. He was born in Berlin on 8 December 1922 to a wealthy, liberal, non-observant Jewish family. His parents, Ernst and Lucie, decided to move their family to the UK in 1933, following Hitler's rise to power in Germany. Freud was passionate about drawing from a young age and his mother always nurtured his creative talents.

Along with his two brothers, Freud went to the progressive boarding school Dartington Hall in Devon, where he spent much of his time looking after the animals on the school farm. He later attended Bryanston School in Dorset. It was here that he carved the three-legged horse that gained him entry to the Central School of Arts and Crafts in London, where he studied briefly. In spring 1939, aged 16, he joined the East Anglian School of Painting and Drawing, run by artists Cedric Morris and Arthur Lett-Haines. In March 1941, during the Second World War, Freud enrolled in the Merchant Navy. Taking his inks and paints with him, he drew the crew on the SS *Baltrover*, heading for Nova Scotia. However, he was soon invalided home due to ill health.

Freud's work gained recognition as early as 1940 when the newly established literary and arts journal *Horizon*, run by the art editor Cyril Connolly and art patron Peter Watson, published one of his self-portrait drawings. Following the war, Freud established himself in the London art scene, gaining renown in part due to the fame and reputation of his grandfather, Sigmund Freud. Beyond his family name, there were many who were drawn to his intelligence and beguiling personality. The art critic John Russell described him as a 'magnetic adolescent'.[1] Freud felt at ease both in the working-class district of his Paddington studio and with the dons of the British art world, such as Sir Kenneth Clark, who, while he was Director of the National Gallery, had paid the 20-year-old Freud a visit.

Principally a draughtsman in the early stages of his career, Freud made controlled and highly finished drawings, and was commissioned to make book illustrations. In 1944 he had his first solo exhibition at the Lefevre Gallery in London. In 1948 he married Kitty Garman, daughter of the sculptor Jacob Epstein. His earlier paintings, including a number of Garman, were often fraught with tension. They were made while sitting very close to his subject 'using absolute maximum observation and maximum concentration', as he described it.[2]

Freud met Francis Bacon in the mid-1940s through a mutual friend, the artist Graham Sutherland. They remained extremely close for several decades and would meet regularly in their studios, or favourite Soho restaurants and bars. Bacon was present at Freud's second marriage to the Irish writer Lady Caroline Blackwood in December 1953. Blackwood recalled having 'dinner with Bacon nearly every night for more or less the whole of my marriage to Lucian [1953–7]. We also had lunch.'[3]

From the late 1950s Freud's painting technique gradually shifted from being linear and detailed to a looser, more textured style, using broad painted strokes. This change was in part achieved by abandoning his soft sable brushes in favour of larger brushes made from coarse hog's hair. His first major institutional exhibition took place in 1974 at the Hayward Gallery, London, when Freud was 51 years old. His fame and recognition continued to grow thereafter, as did the ambition and scale of his paintings, many of them naked portraits. His recurring sitters included himself, his mother, his many children and his pet whippet, as well as close friends and models, such as artist Sophie de Stempel, Susanna Chancellor, the performance artist Leigh Bowery, job centre manager Sue Tilley and his studio assistant David Dawson.

By the end of his life, Freud had become a celebrity figure. In 2001 he painted Queen Elizabeth II and had major exhibitions at Tate Britain in London (2002) and the Centre Pompidou in Paris (2010), the latter the last exhibition in his lifetime. After his death in July 2011, the majority of his sketchbooks, letters and material relating to his childhood was allocated to the archives of the National Portrait Gallery in London.

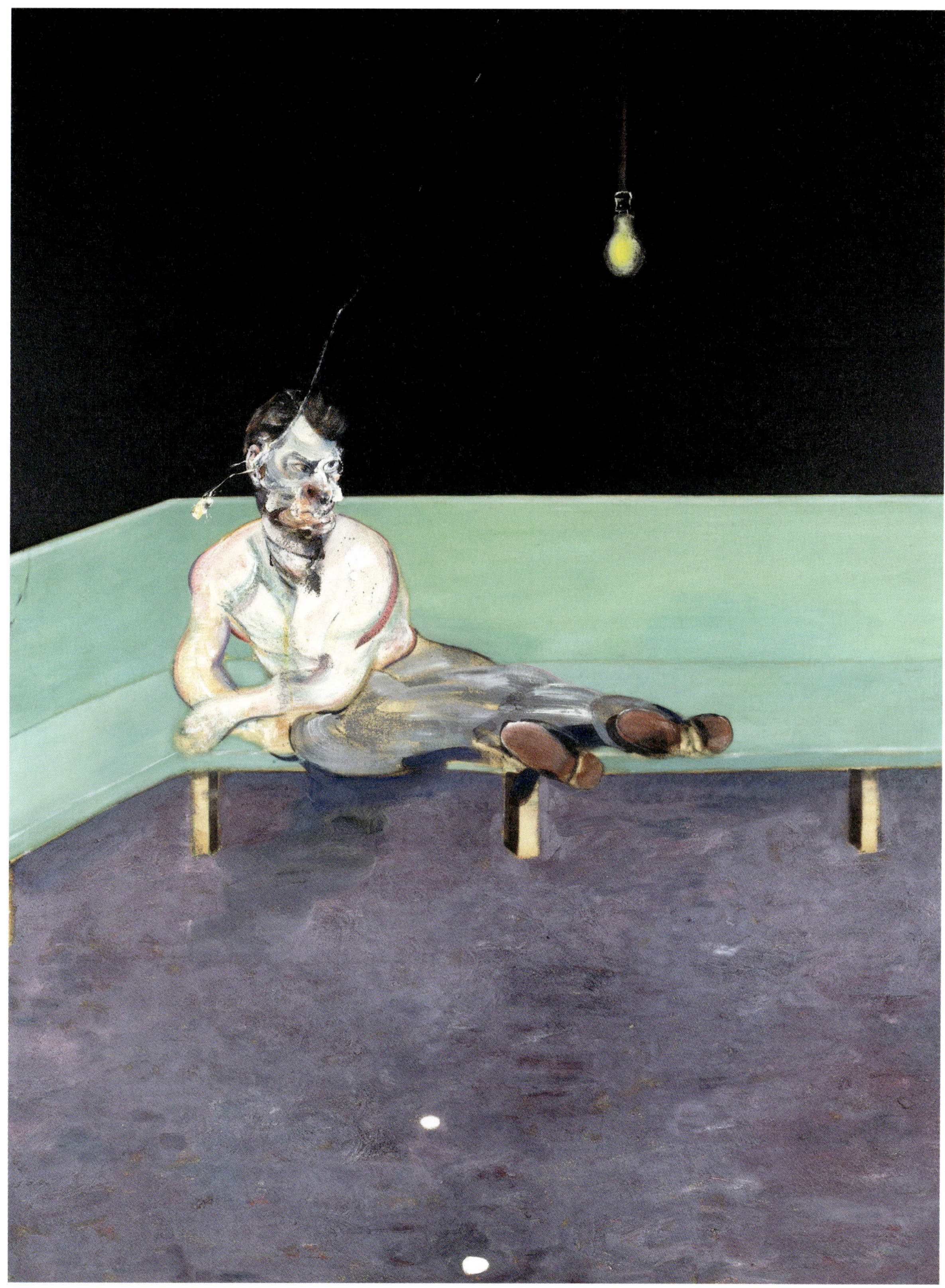

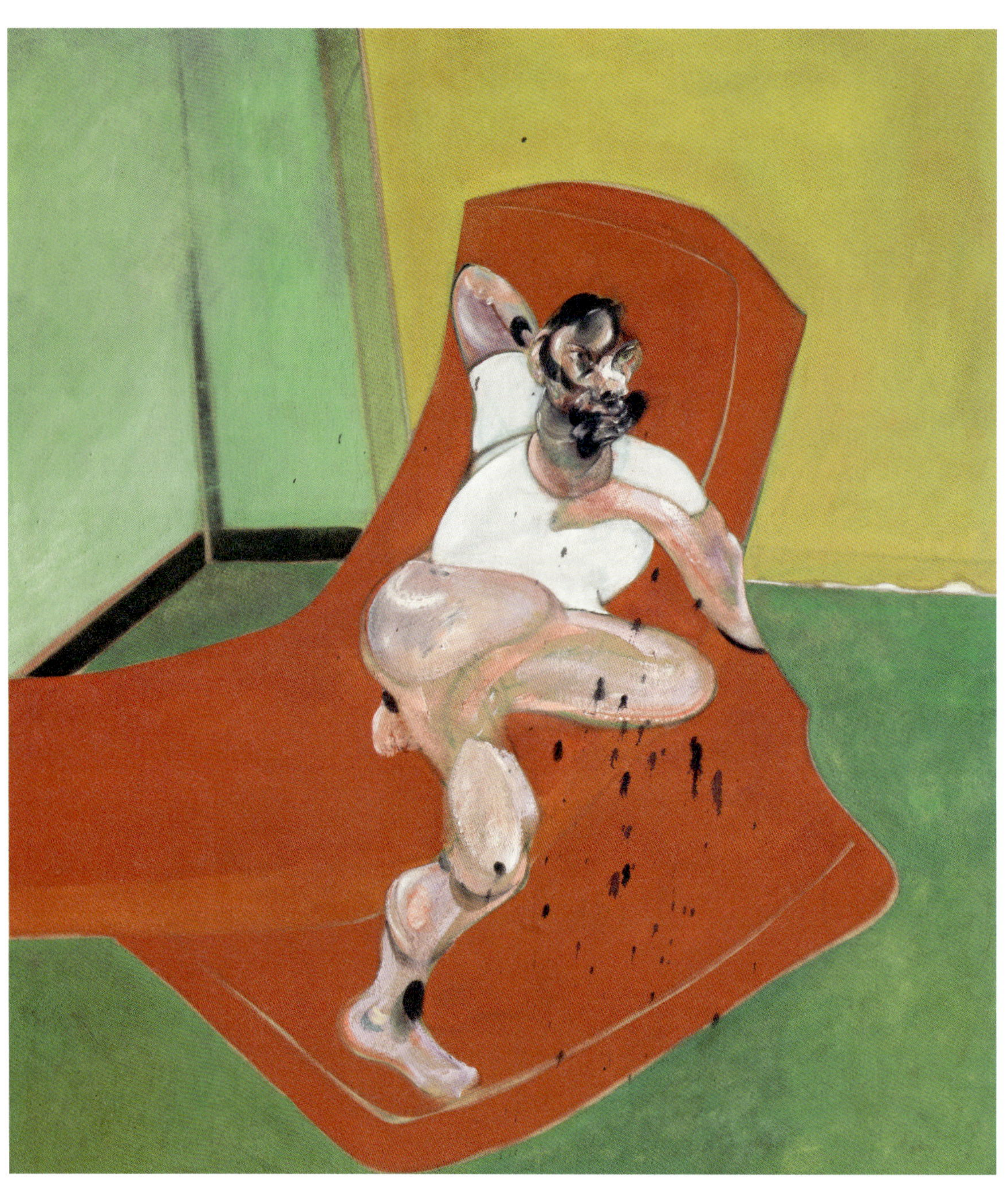

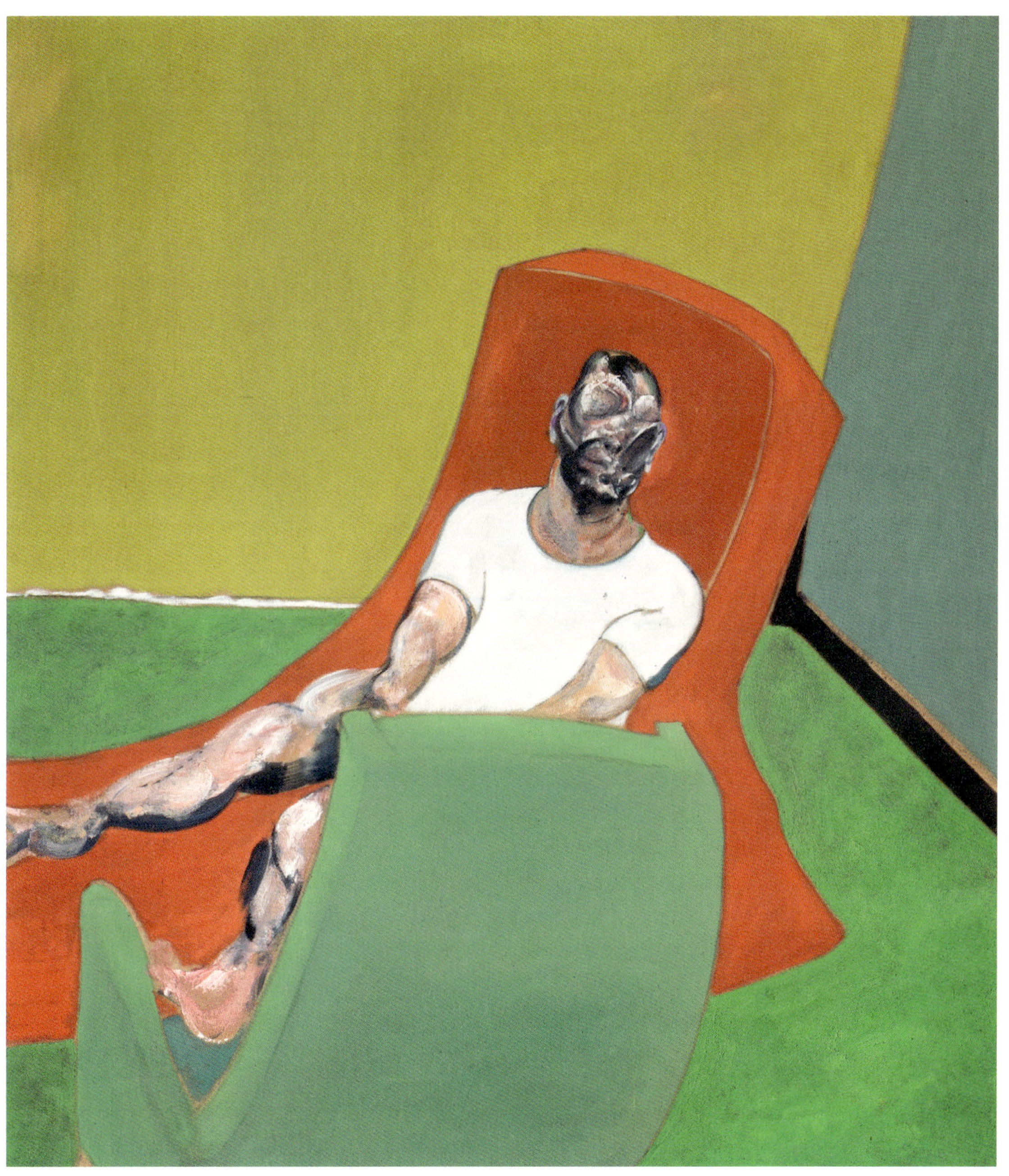

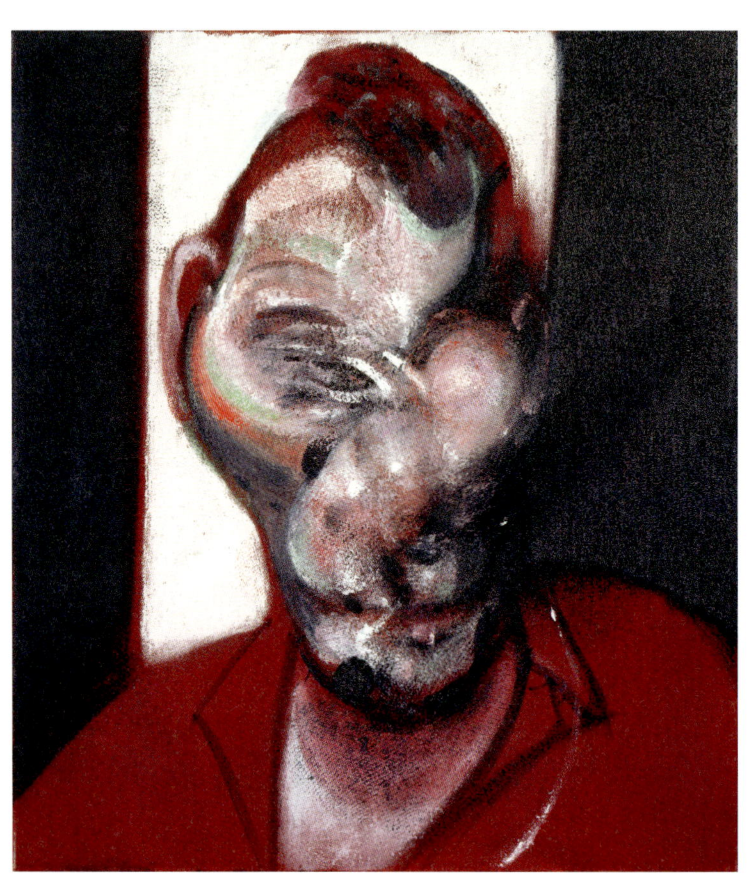

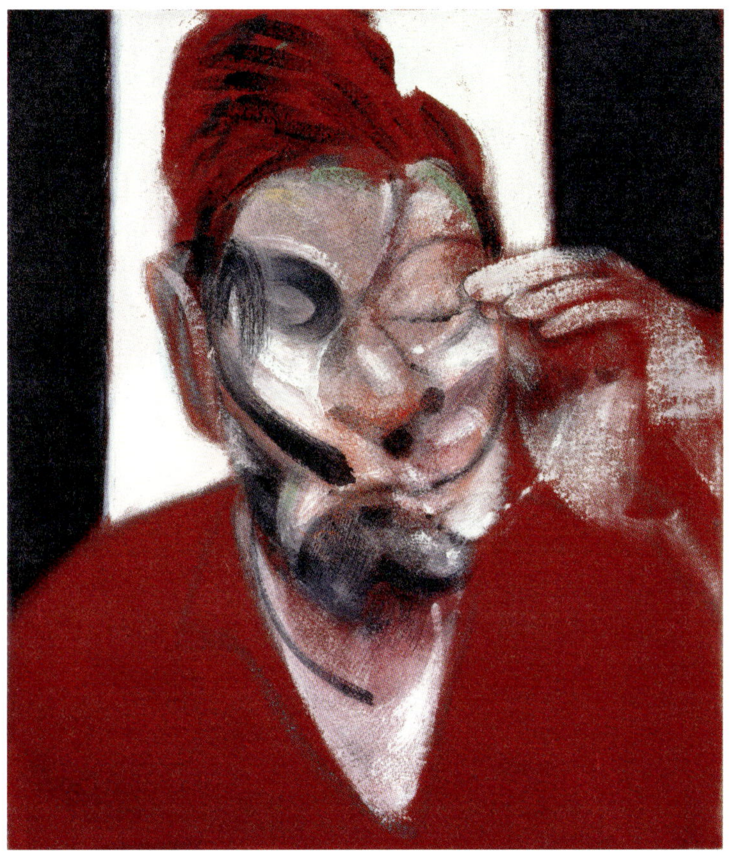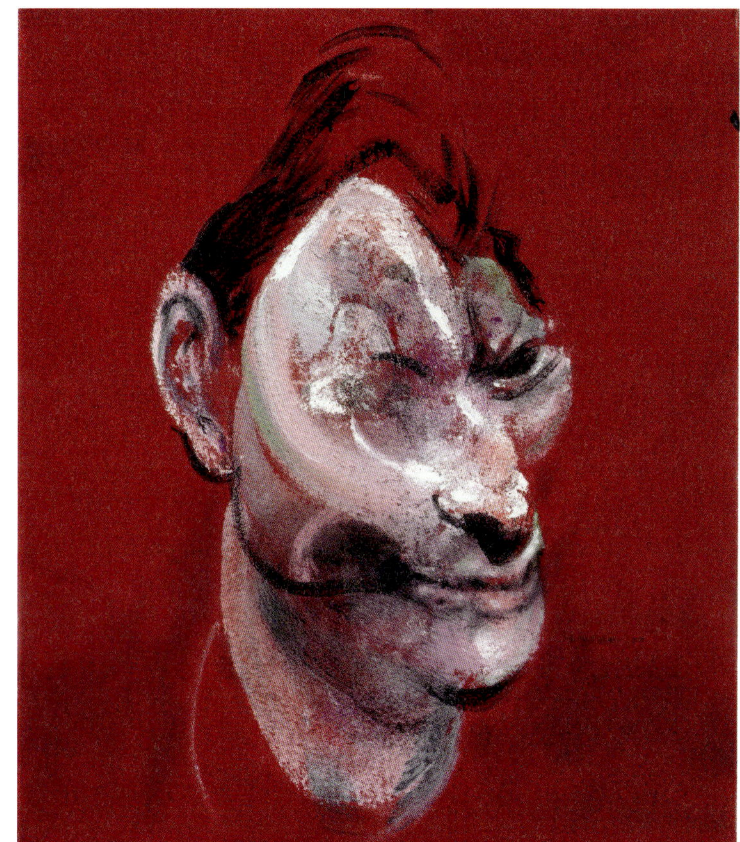

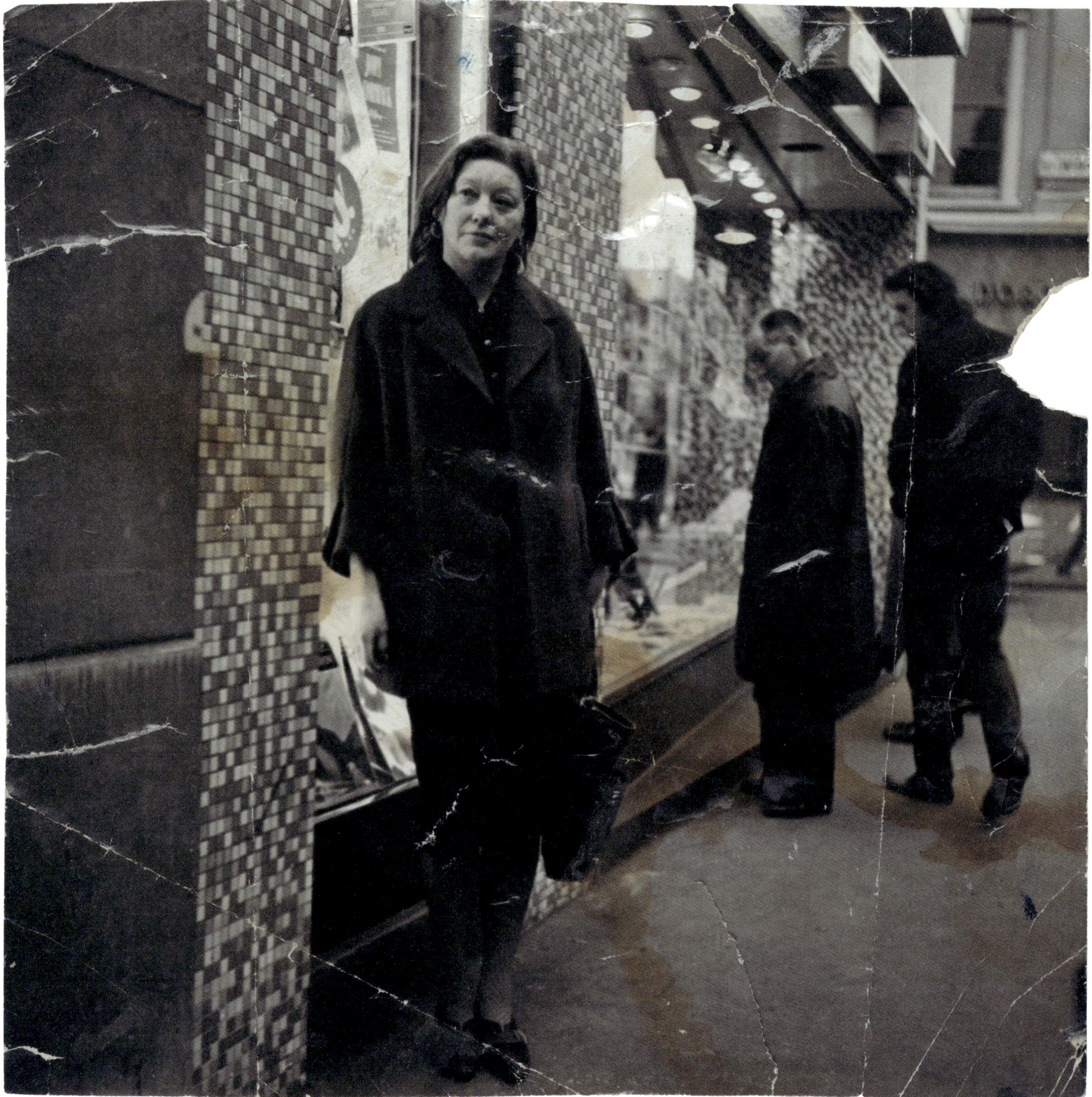

Isabel Rawsthorne

The painter Isabel Rawsthorne (1912–1992) (born Isabel Nicholas) worked for over 60 years, creating art about the body, human and animal, that pushed figuration in new directions such as phenomenology and ethnography. From a modest background, she entered the Liverpool College of Art aged just 16 to study fine art. While there, she and a small group of male and female students defied the gendered segregation of life classes by posing for each other nude.[1] In 1931, she won a life drawing scholarship to the Royal Academy in London. However, poverty led her to leave after a year to work as a studio assistant to the sculptor Jacob Epstein. By the time she was twenty-one she had held two successful exhibitions. She gave birth to a son, who was claimed and brought up by Epstein and his wife, Margaret.

A Francophile, she moved to Paris in 1934, studying at the life room of the Académie de la Grande Chaumière in Montparnasse. She was painted by André Derain and Pablo Picasso and joined an alternative Parisian artistic avant-garde who were rejecting abstraction and surrealism to explore the figure. This included a long artistic and romantic relationship with Alberto Giacometti. Her presence preoccupied him through and beyond the Second World War, inspiring the etiolated figures for which he became famous.

Rawsthorne met Francis Bacon in Paris, soon after the War.[2] They became close friends from the late 1940s when they both returned to London, socialising in Soho, exchanging ideas about art and visiting each other's studios. In February 1949 Rawsthorne was one of the first artists to have an exhibition at the newly established Hanover Gallery, run by the visionary émigré art dealer Erica Brausen.

Bacon also had a show there later that same year. In 1950 Rawsthorne was selected as one of five London painters 'of outstanding talent', alongside Bacon, Lucian Freud, John Craxton and Peter Lanyon, in an exhibition curated by David Sylvester for the Institute of Contemporary Arts.[3] During the 1950s she created set and costume designs for the Royal Ballet and the Royal Opera House.

Rawsthorne and Bacon inhabited an overlapping social network of writers, intellectuals and artists, including Giacometti, Michel Leiris, and Diane and Georges Bataille. Their art took inspiration from similar sources, such as films by Sergei Eisenstein and degraded reproductions and photographs. They could both also be extremely self-critical, frequently destroying their paintings if they did not consider them good enough.

Bacon first painted Rawsthorne in 1964, decades after they met. Like Picasso's portraits of Rawsthorne, such as *Le Chapeau à Fleurs* (*Buste de Femme*) (1940), Bacon's depictions were not painted from life.[4] He made use of John Deakin's photographs of Rawsthorne, taken in Soho around 1965, opposite their regular meeting spot, The French House, as well as existing portraits of Rawsthorne by Derain and Giacometti, which she had in her home.[5] In total, Bacon made 19 paintings of her between 1964 and 1983 (cats 44–7).

Beginning in the 1950s, Rawsthorne embarked on a 20-year study of dancers in motion and series of portraits in parallel with Bacon, exhibited at solo shows at the Hanover Gallery and at the Marlborough Gallery in 1968. A snapshot records Bacon and his lover George Dyer at the private view. Bacon is clutching an exhibition catalogue, and would purchase a large oil by Rawsthorne called *La Bayadère II* (1967).[6] In later life, struggling with alcoholism and glaucoma, Rawsthorne became an environmentalist and returned to painting animals and birds. Her final series, *Migrations*, explored themes of mortality through the wildlife in the surroundings of her cottage in Little Sampford, Essex.

Despite having been an essential contributor to twentieth-century Parisian and London artistic culture, Rawsthorne's life and art, for decades, was eclipsed by the male artists with whom she was associated. She died in January 1992, just weeks before Bacon. Her work is now in the Tate, the Centre Pompidou in Paris and other galleries, including 200 drawings and paintings donated to The New Art Gallery Walsall and her life work has begun to regain recognition.

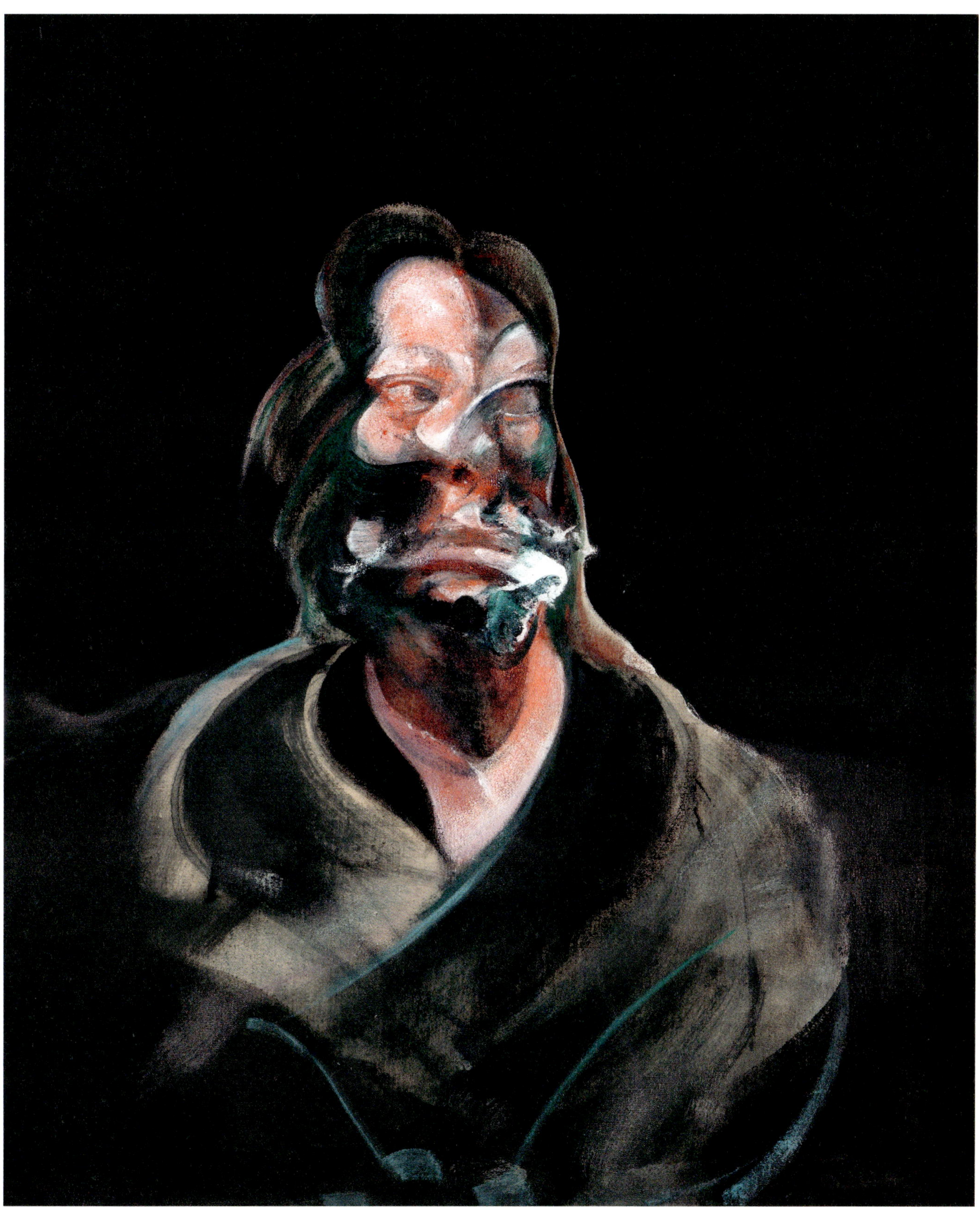

45 *Three Studies for a Portrait of Isabel Rawsthorne*   1965
Oil on canvas   356 × 305mm (each panel)

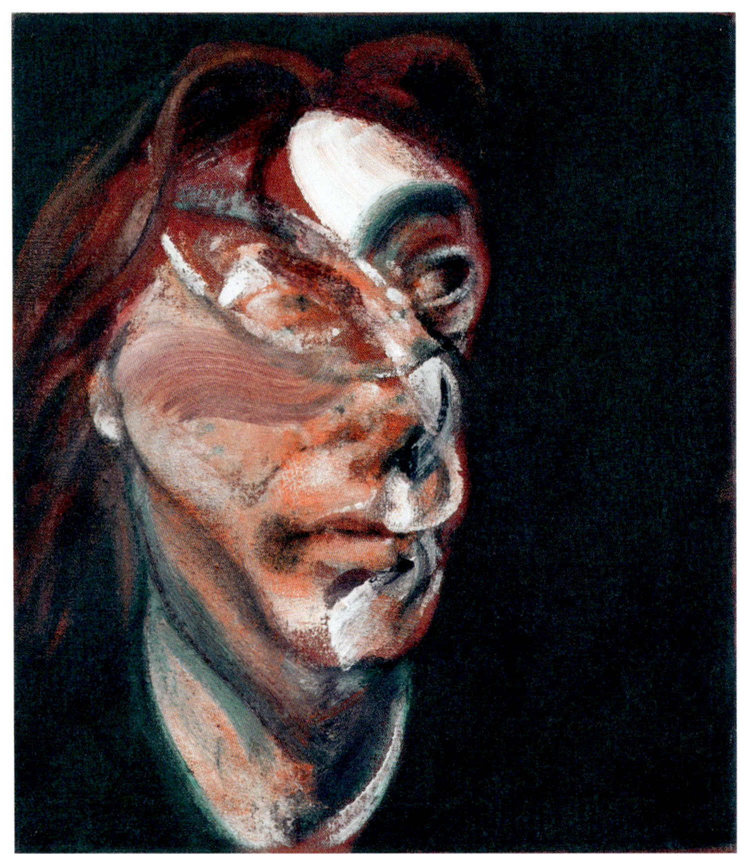 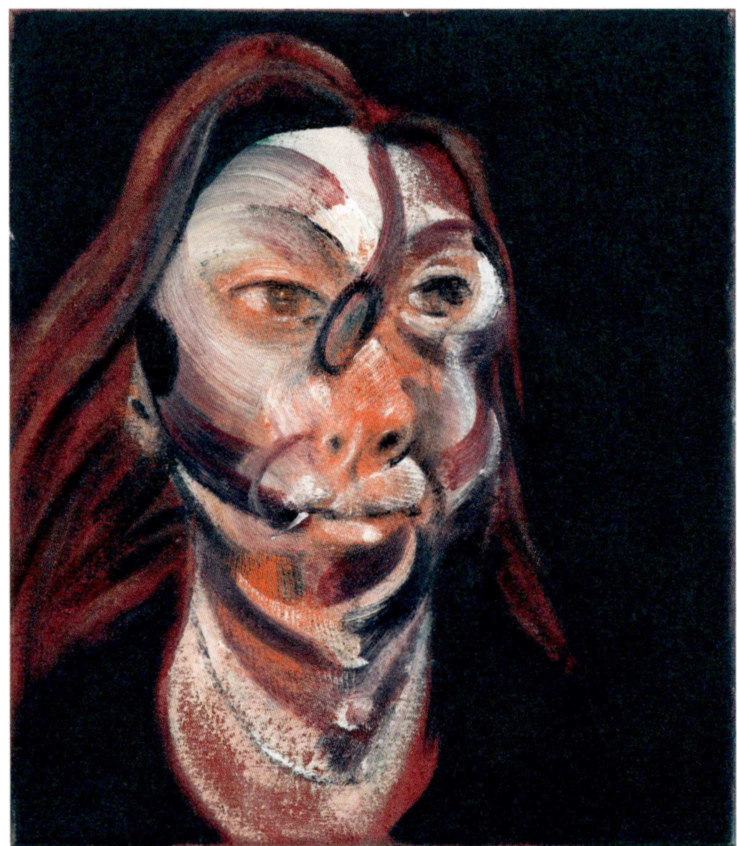

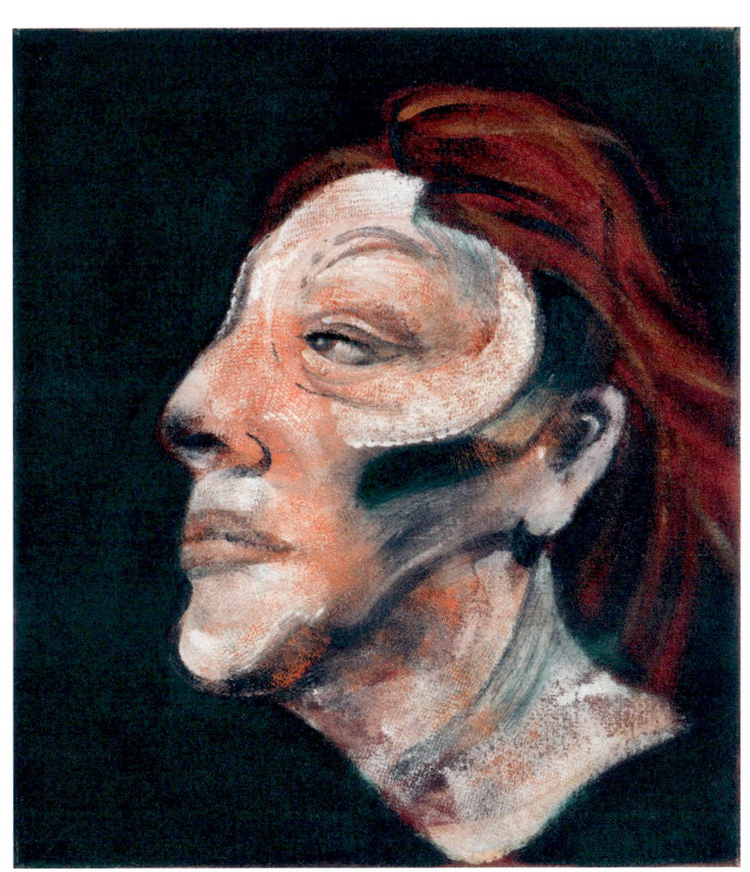

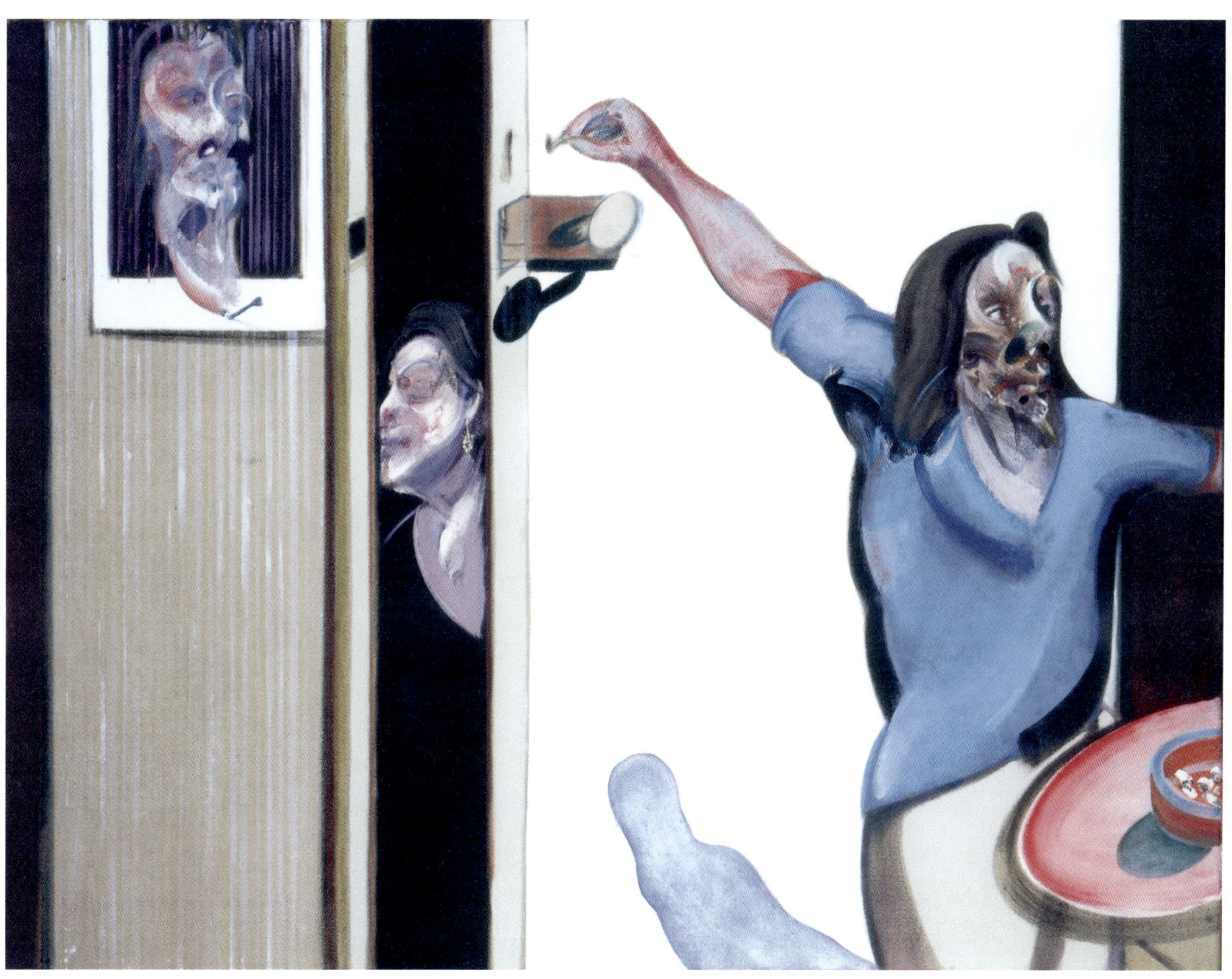

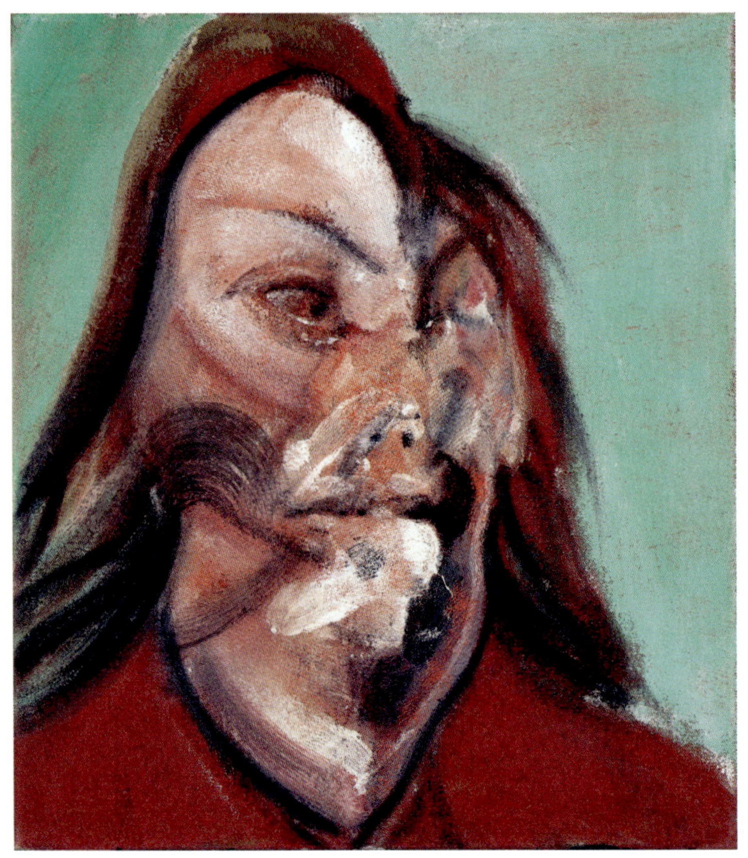 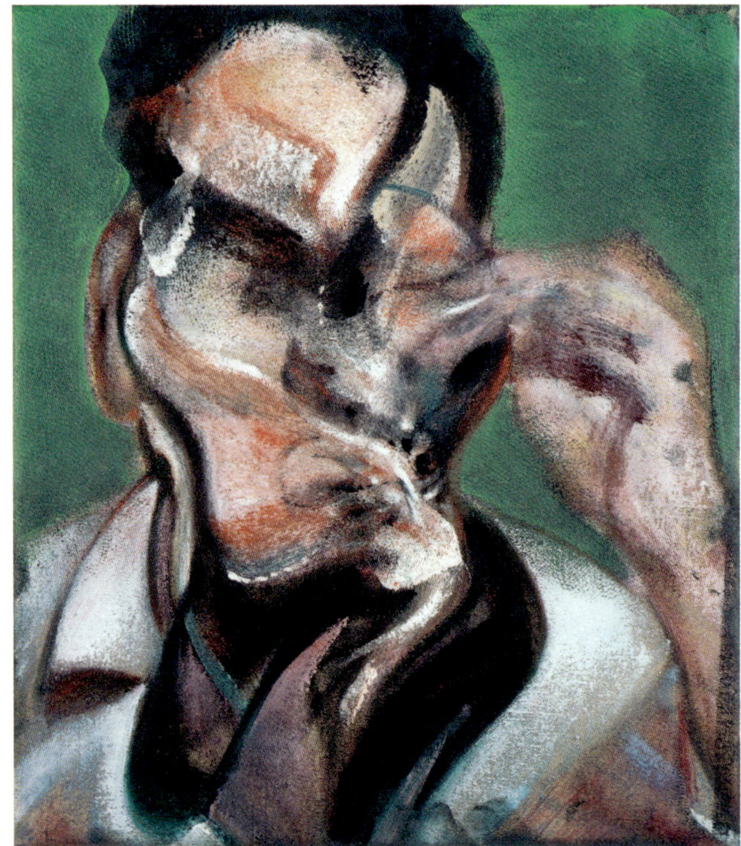

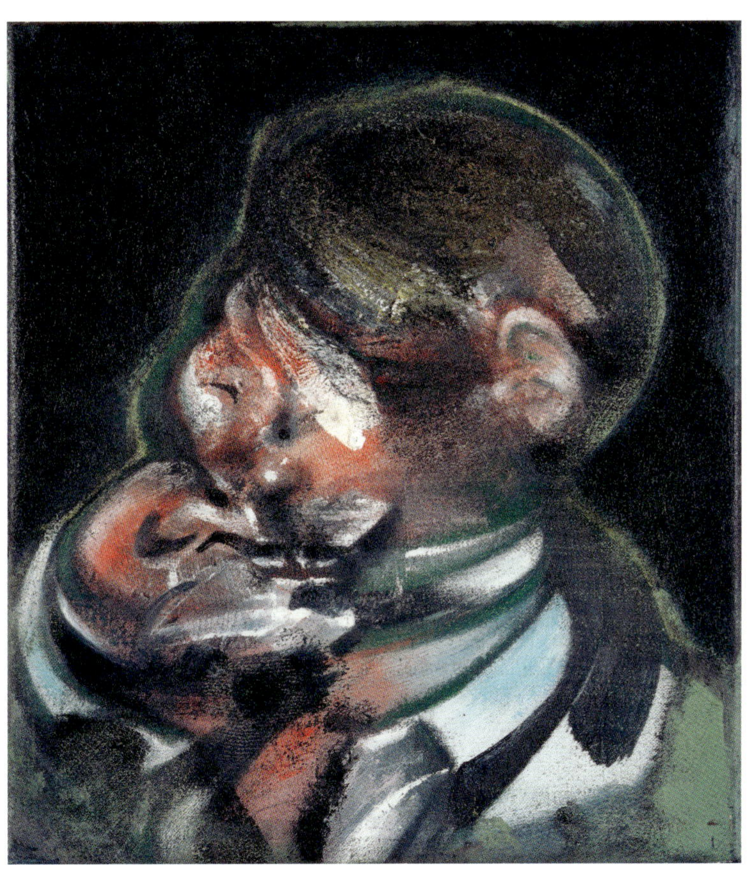

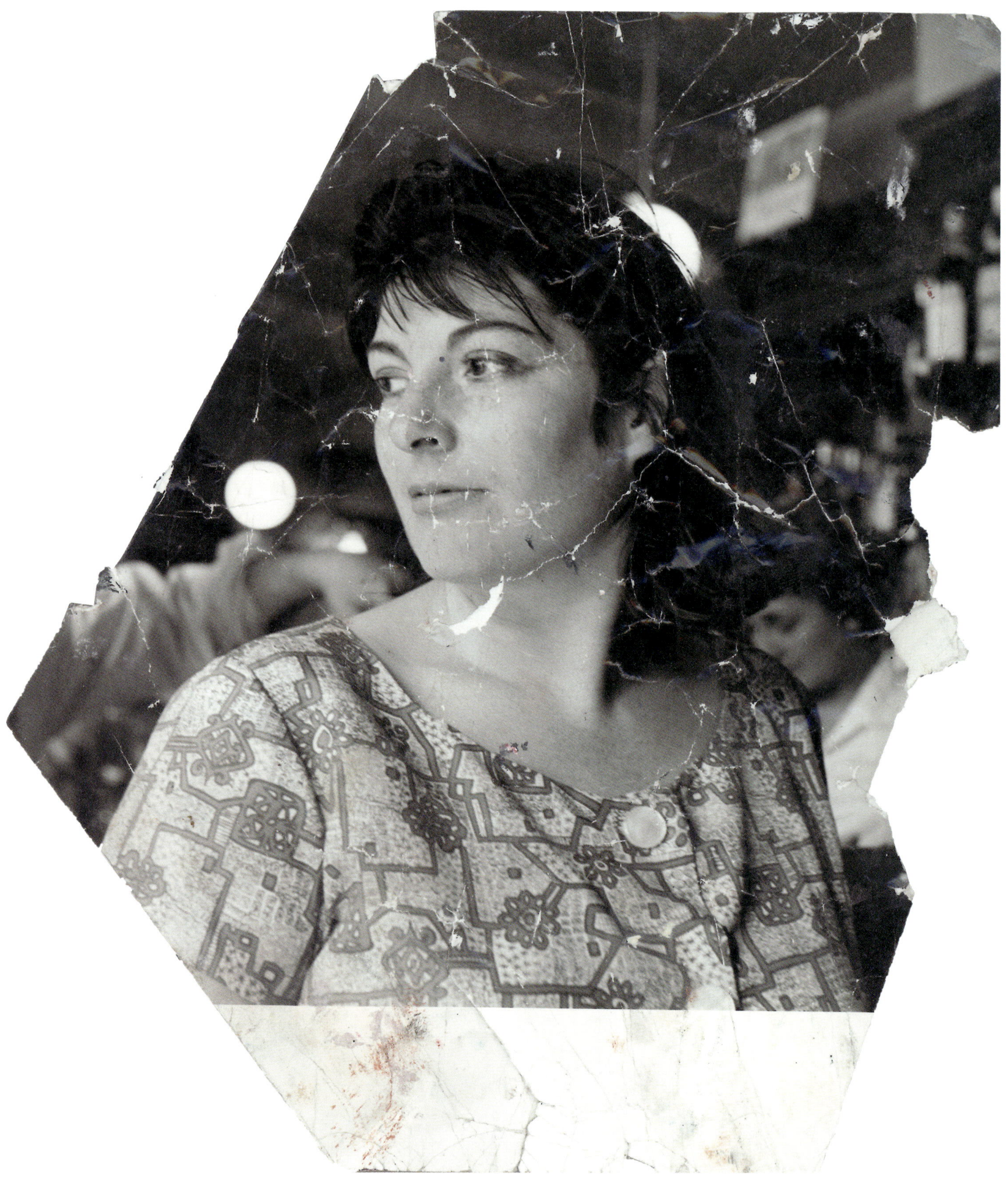

John Deakin   *Henrietta Moraes*   late 1950s   Gelatin silver print   294 × 253mm

Henrietta Moraes

Henrietta Moraes (1931–1999) met Francis Bacon in the late 1940s when she was 18 years old. For a time, they would spend all day together in Soho at Wheeler's oyster bar or drinking champagne at the Gargoyle Club. In her memoirs she recalled: 'At every meeting I had learned something new from him, been captivated, spellbound. Wherever he appeared, the air brightened.'[1]

Moraes was born Audrey Wendy Abbott in Simla, India. She never knew her father and her mother, a nurse, was largely absent from her early childhood. Brought to England as a baby, she was left in the care of her violent grandmother and was sent intermittently to strict convent schools. She moved to London to go to a secretarial college in South Kensington. It was then she discovered London's carousing bohemian scene in Soho, where she would become a regular fixture throughout the 1950s and 1960s. It was her first husband, the filmmaker Michael Law, who suggested she adopt the name 'Henrietta', and 'Moraes' was the surname of her third husband, the Bombay-born poet Dom Moraes.

Both chaotic and charming, she surrounded herself with artists and fell in love with Lucian Freud, who painted her in his Paddington studio. She was also close with the artist John Minton, who, following his suicide, left her his Chelsea house, where she later lived with her two children.

Throughout her life, she was variously a figure model in London's art schools, a coffee bar manager in David Archer's bookshop on Greek Street, Soho, and an assistant at a TV advertising agency. In the 1960s she began to take drugs, and an episode as an unsuccessful cat burglar and a spell in Holloway Prison followed. In the 1970s she acted as a companion and assistant to the singer Marianne Faithfull.

Bacon only began to paint Moraes several years after they met. One afternoon in The French House, Soho, he said to her, 'I'm thinking of painting some of my friends and I'd like to do you.'[2] Explaining that he could only really work from photographs, he organised for the photographer John Deakin to take a series of close-up photographs of her naked on a bed, which would form the basis of his paintings. At first, she was reluctant to pose in such an exposing position, but wrote in her memoirs that, after a few drinks, she conceded and said, 'Oh, all right, then, go ahead. It's only images, after all.'[3] She later found Deakin selling copies of the erotic photos to a group of sailors for ten shillings a time.[4]

Bacon went on to paint her around 20 times and, as such, she became one of his most frequent female subjects. As well as several triptychs, Bacon created 11 nude paintings from 1963 to 1969 based on Deakin's photographs of Moraes (cat.48). This included *Lying Figure with Hypodermic Syringe* (1963), which, with the insertion of the syringe in her right arm, foreshadowed her troubled and unrestrained descent into drug abuse. She was sober at the end of her life and took on the role of artist's model once again in her last months, and even in death, for a series of charcoal drawings by her friend, the artist Maggi Hambling.

48 *Henrietta Moraes*   1966   Oil on canvas   1520 × 1470mm

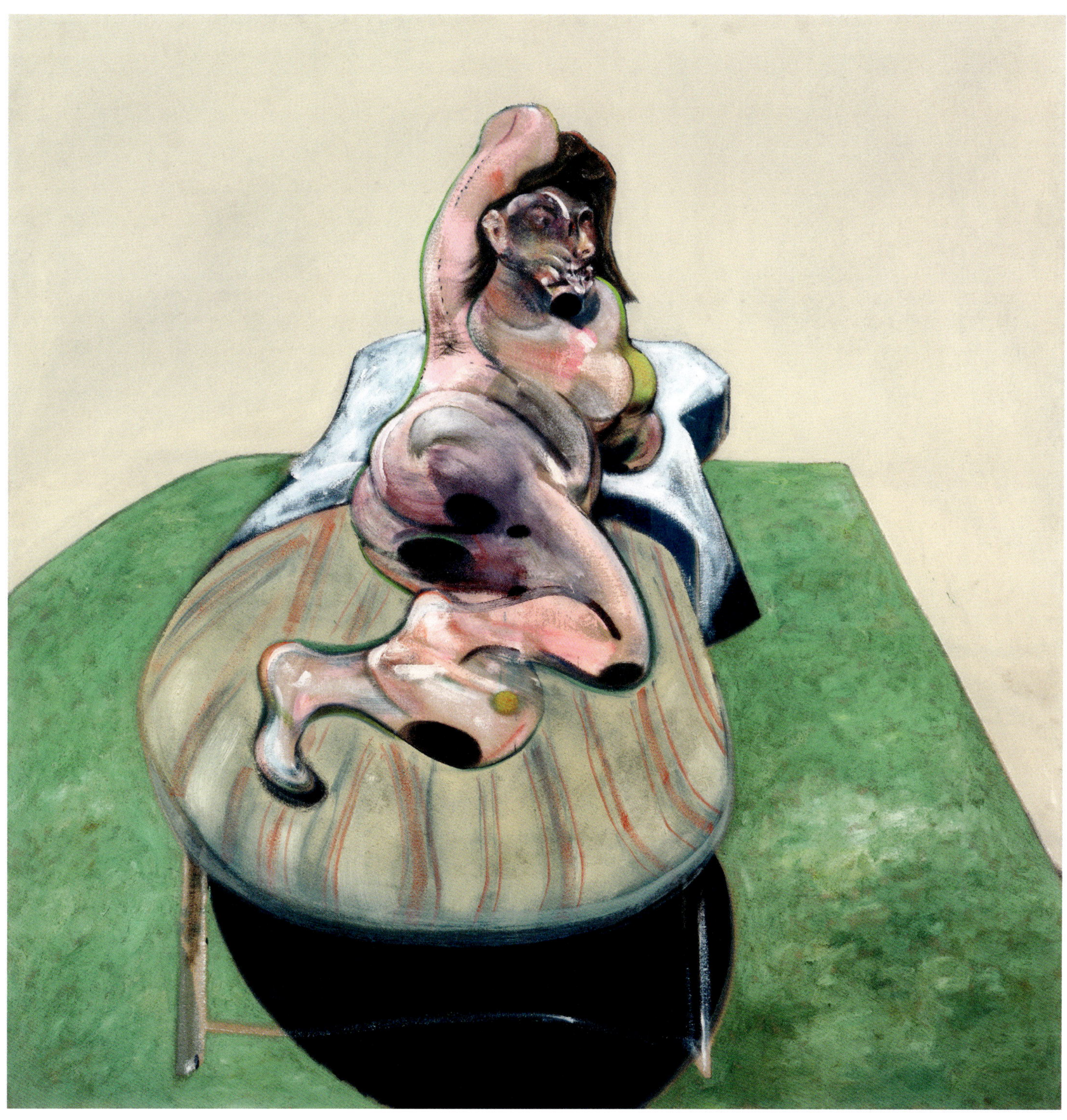

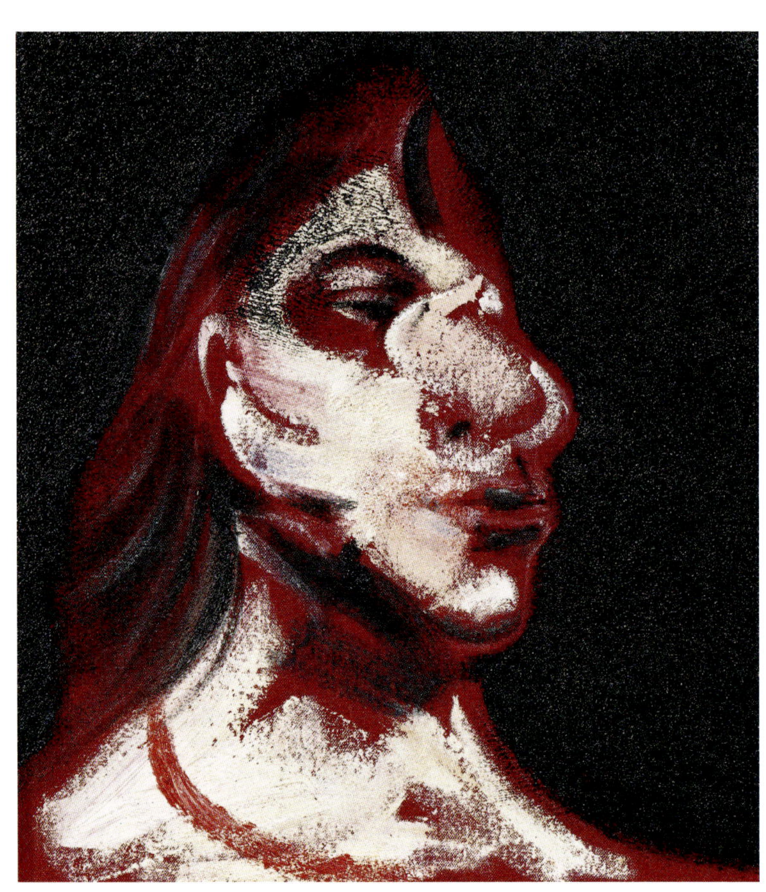

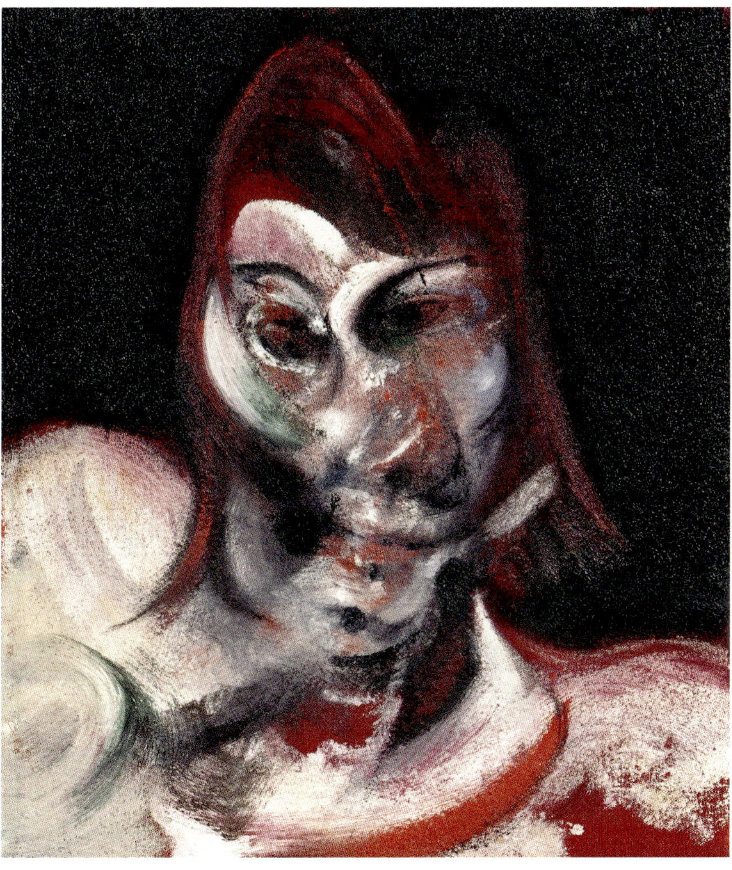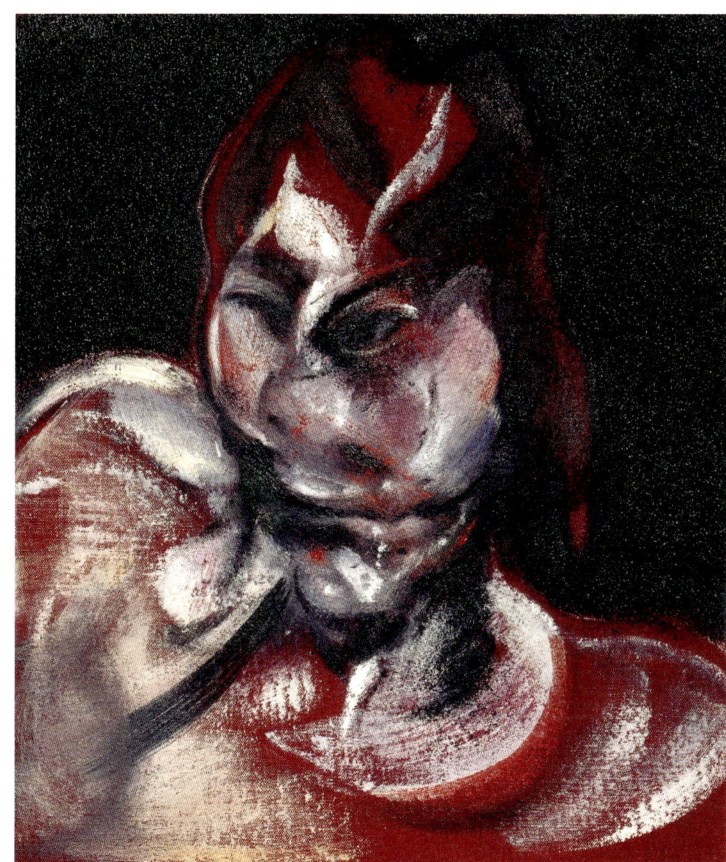

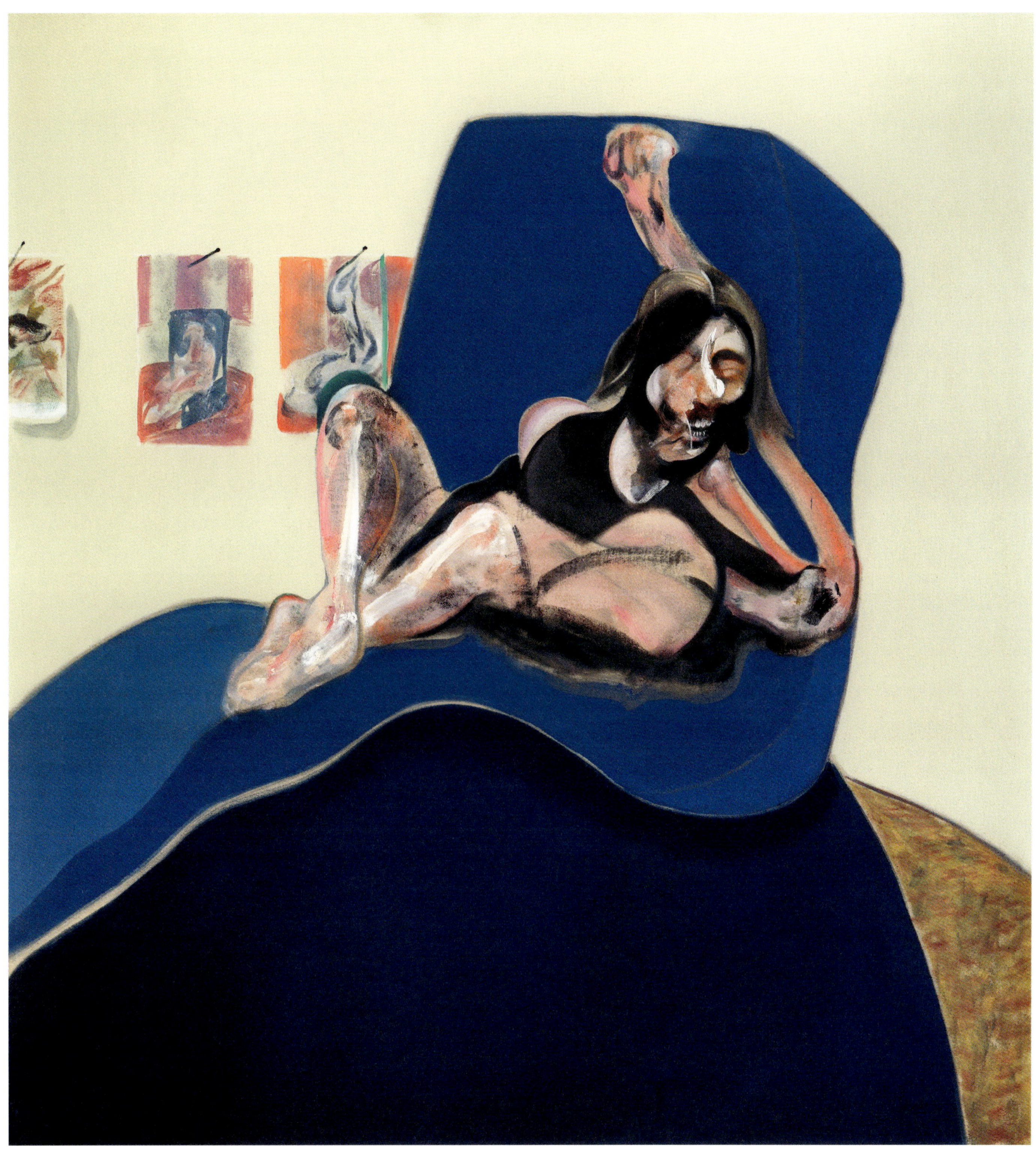

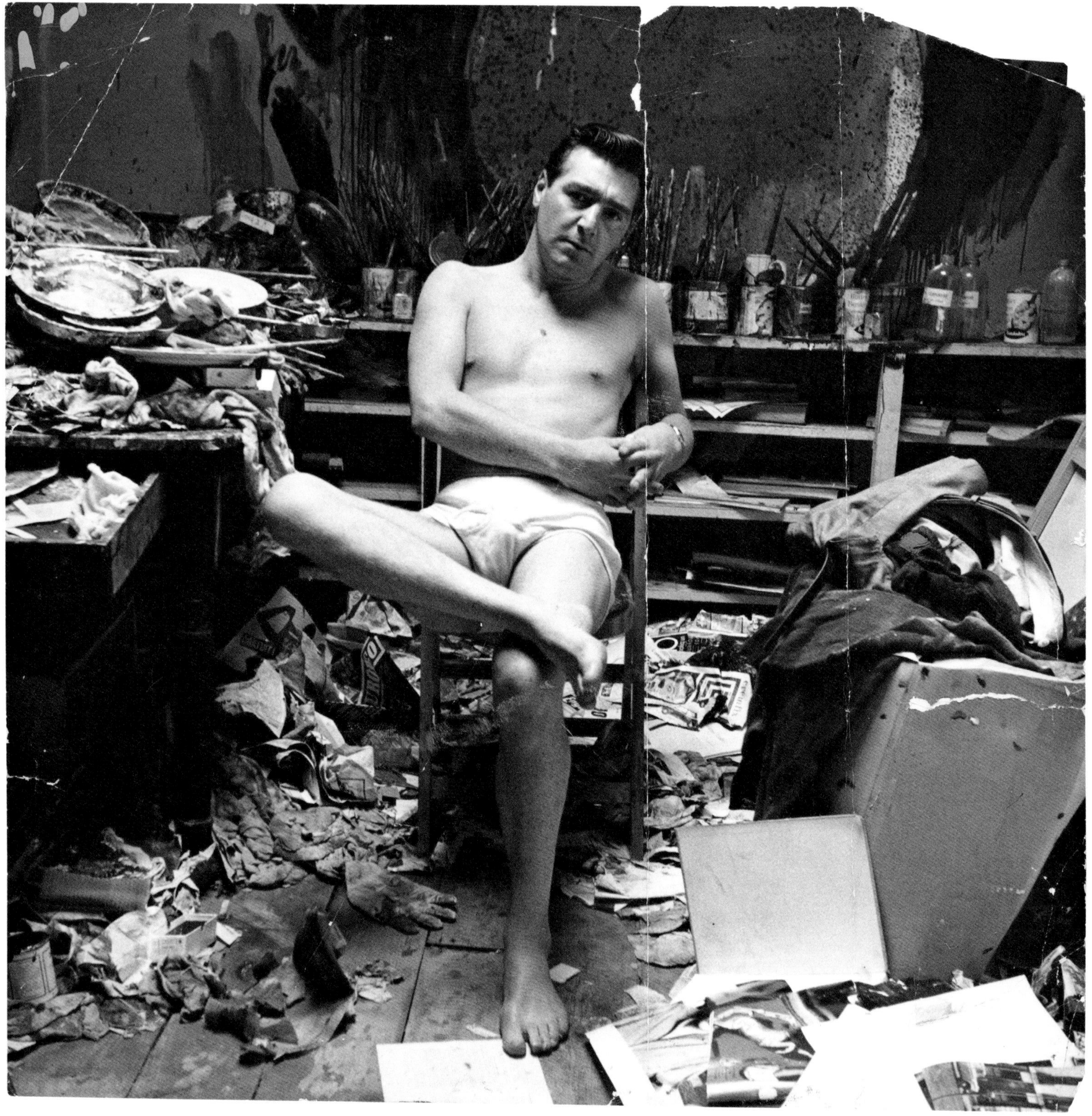

John Deakin *George Dyer* c.1965 Gelatin silver print 300 × 294mm

George Dyer

One of six children, George Dyer (1934–1971) was born in Southwark, south-east London. He was a petty criminal who, with his eldest brother Ronnie, had occasional dealings with the infamous criminal twin brothers, Ronnie and Reggie Kray. His youngest brother, Lee, described him as a 'gentleman', 'quiet … never rude'.[1] Terry Danziger-Miles, who worked for the Marlborough Gallery and knew him well, called him a 'loveable rogue'.[2] His life was uprooted when, in 1963, he met Francis Bacon in a gay bar in Soho with the photographer John Deakin. According to Bacon, Dyer approached them and said, 'You all seem to be having a good time, can I buy you a drink?'[3] Bacon seemed to have been attracted to Dyer's youth and criminal life, as well as his muscular body and distinctive profile. He became the artist's companion and remained devoted to him. Bacon made three small-format triptychs of Dyer within a year of meeting him (*Three Studies for Portrait of George Dyer (on light ground)* (1964; cat.52), and Dyer quickly became Bacon's principal subject.

Although Bacon would not ordinarily paint from life – due in part to the burden of entertaining his sitters – in Dyer he found a patient and unimposing sitter who could sit for hours.[4] Bacon also arranged for Deakin to photograph Dyer so that he had images to refer to when making the portraits. He went on to create around 20 portraits of Dyer in various guises; crouching, talking, riding a bike (*Portrait of George Dyer Riding a Bicycle*, 1966; cat.51) or reflected in a mirror (*Portrait of George Dyer in a Mirror*, 1968; cat.53).

When Dyer accompanied Bacon to parties and private views, he was always impeccably dressed, wearing an Edwardian-style suit and waistcoat, his hair slicked back. In 1964, they travelled together to Malta, Sicily, Naples and Monte Carlo. A series of photographs taken by Deakin in May 1965 recorded their journey to Athens on the elegant *Orient Express* (see cat.31). The happy and romantic shots belie the constant fighting that was to plague the trip.

While Bacon was painting, Dyer had little to occupy his time but drinking in the many Soho clubs. He battled with alcoholism and struggled to stay sober for any length of time. In one attempt to distract him, Bacon asked his friend, the artist Lucian Freud, to take Dyer on as a sitter. The sittings took place in London, as well as at Drummond Castle, Scotland, the estate of Jane Willoughby, where the country air and pleasant lodgings provided a welcome distraction from Soho life.[5] Freud made two paintings of Dyer, including the tender *Man in a Blue Shirt* (1965), which contained none of the violence or theatricality of Bacon's depictions of him.

When Dyer drank, he was prone to violence and would sometimes attack Bacon and his paintings. In one instance, he ripped apart Bacon's canvases and set fire to his Reece Mews studio.[6] In another, he framed Bacon for drug possession, which led to the artist's arrest. Dyer's self-destructive nature culminated in his death on 24 October 1971, aged 37, on the day of the private view of Bacon's retrospective at the Grand Palais in Paris. He was found dead on the hotel toilet after an overdose of alcohol and sleeping pills. His death inspired some of Bacon's most monumental works, including several large triptychs memorialising his lover, (see fig.9, pp.20–1). The first, *In Memory of George Dyer* (1971), was completed soon after a guilt-ridden Bacon returned from Paris.

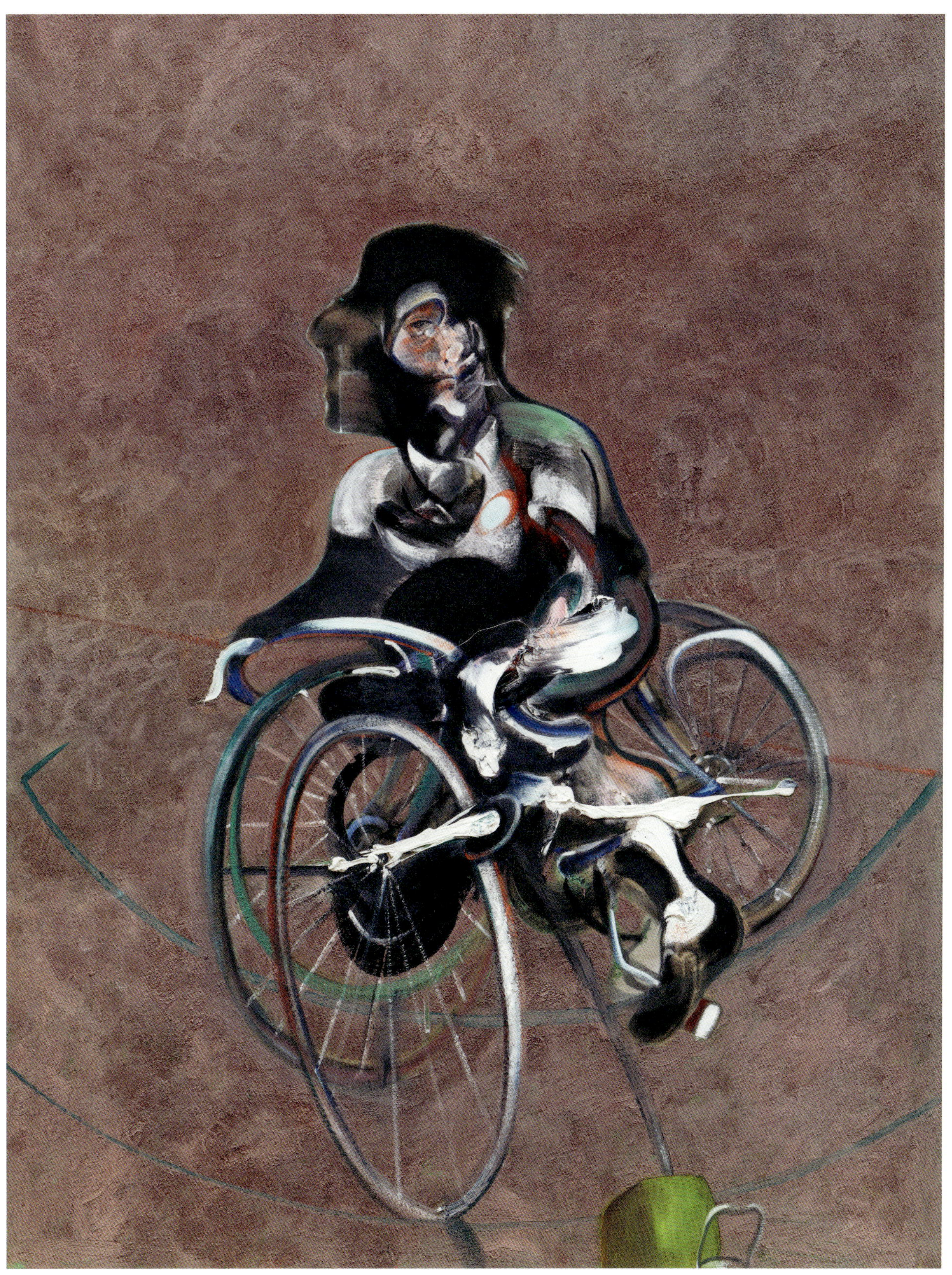

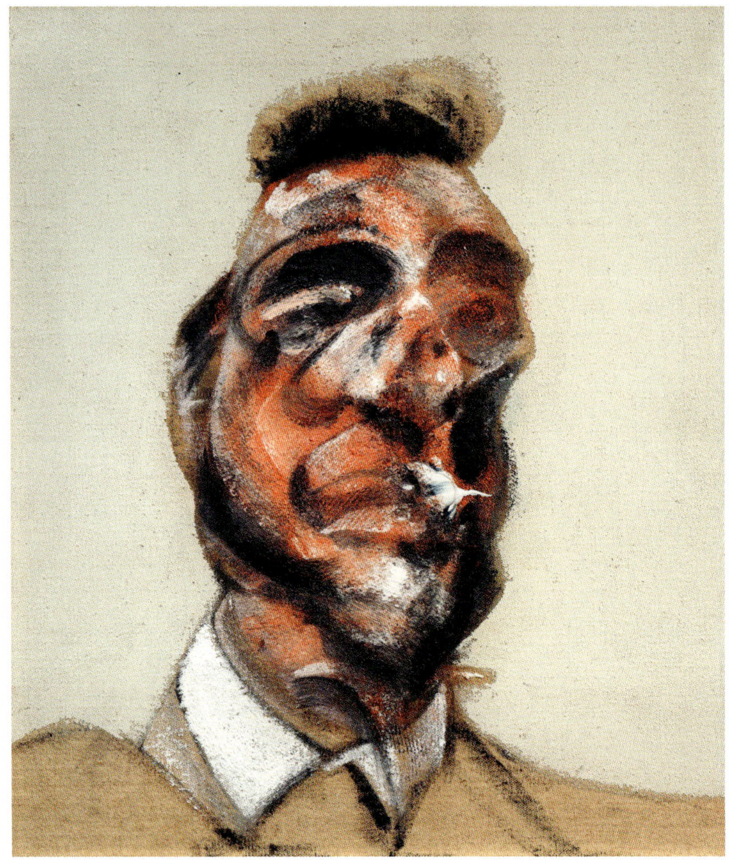 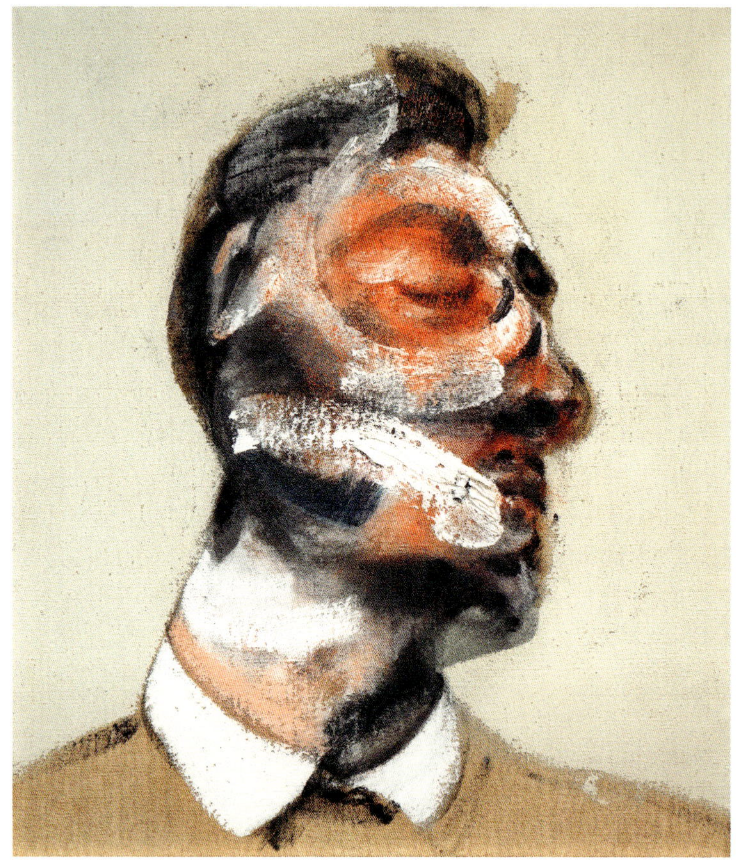

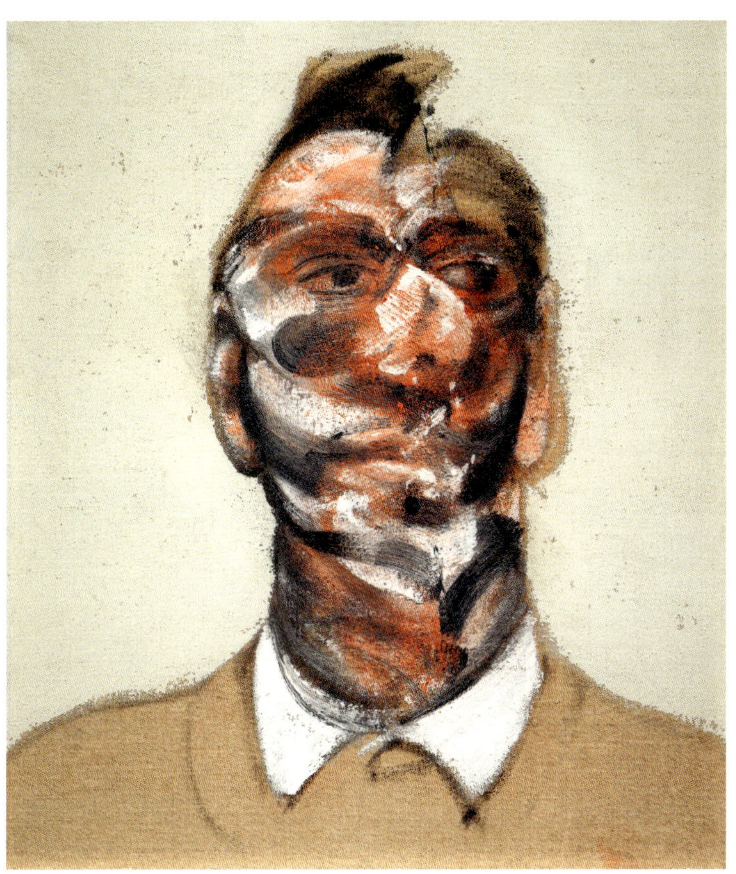

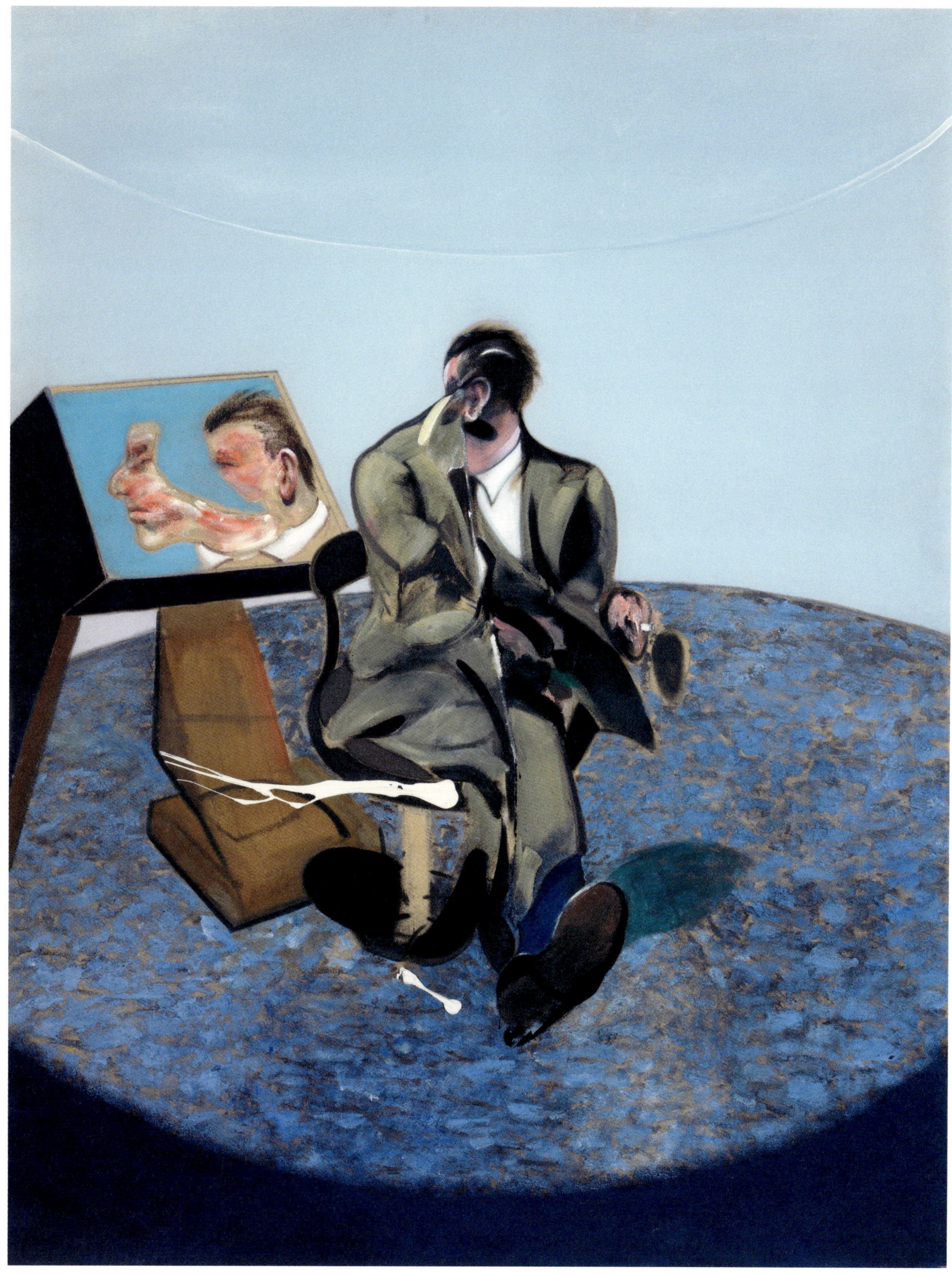

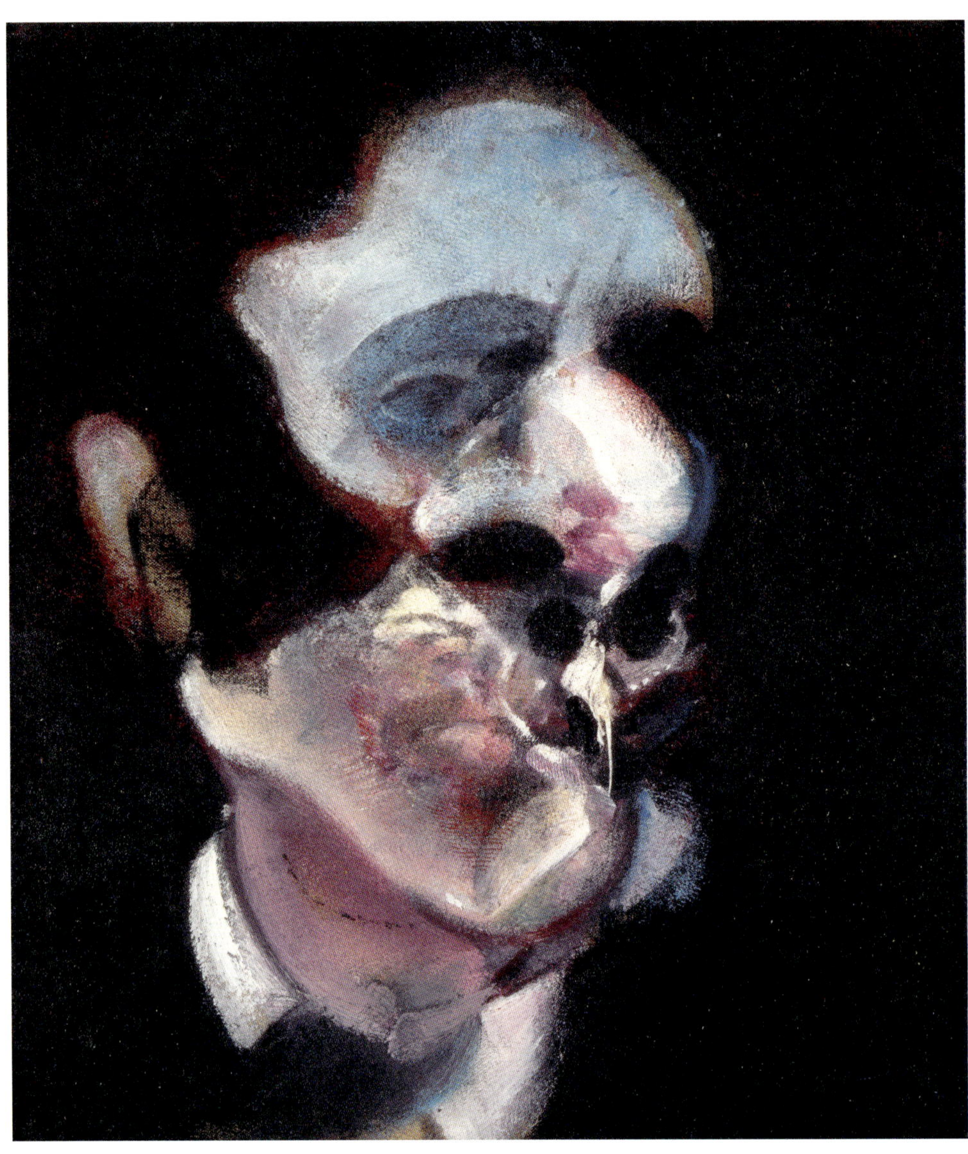

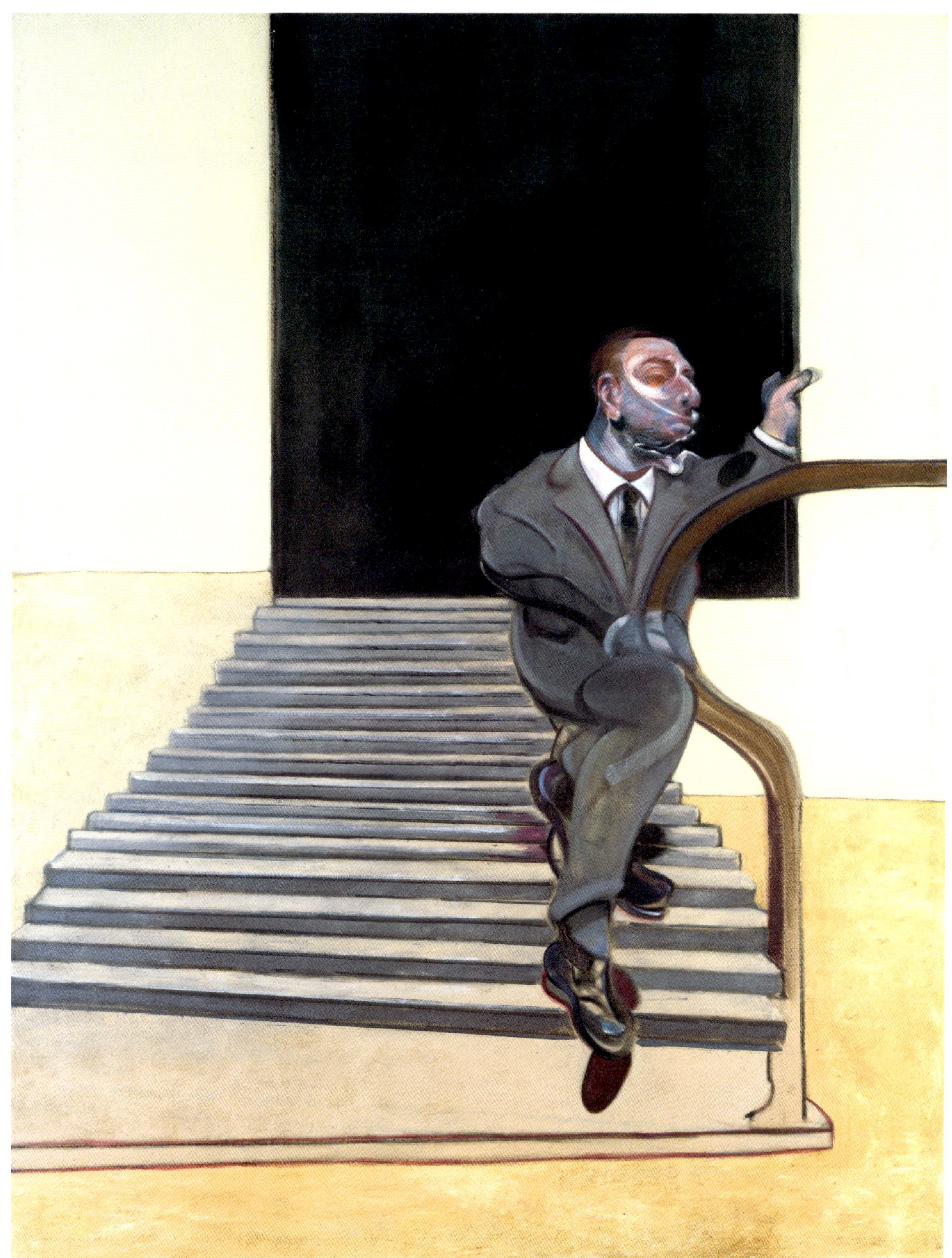

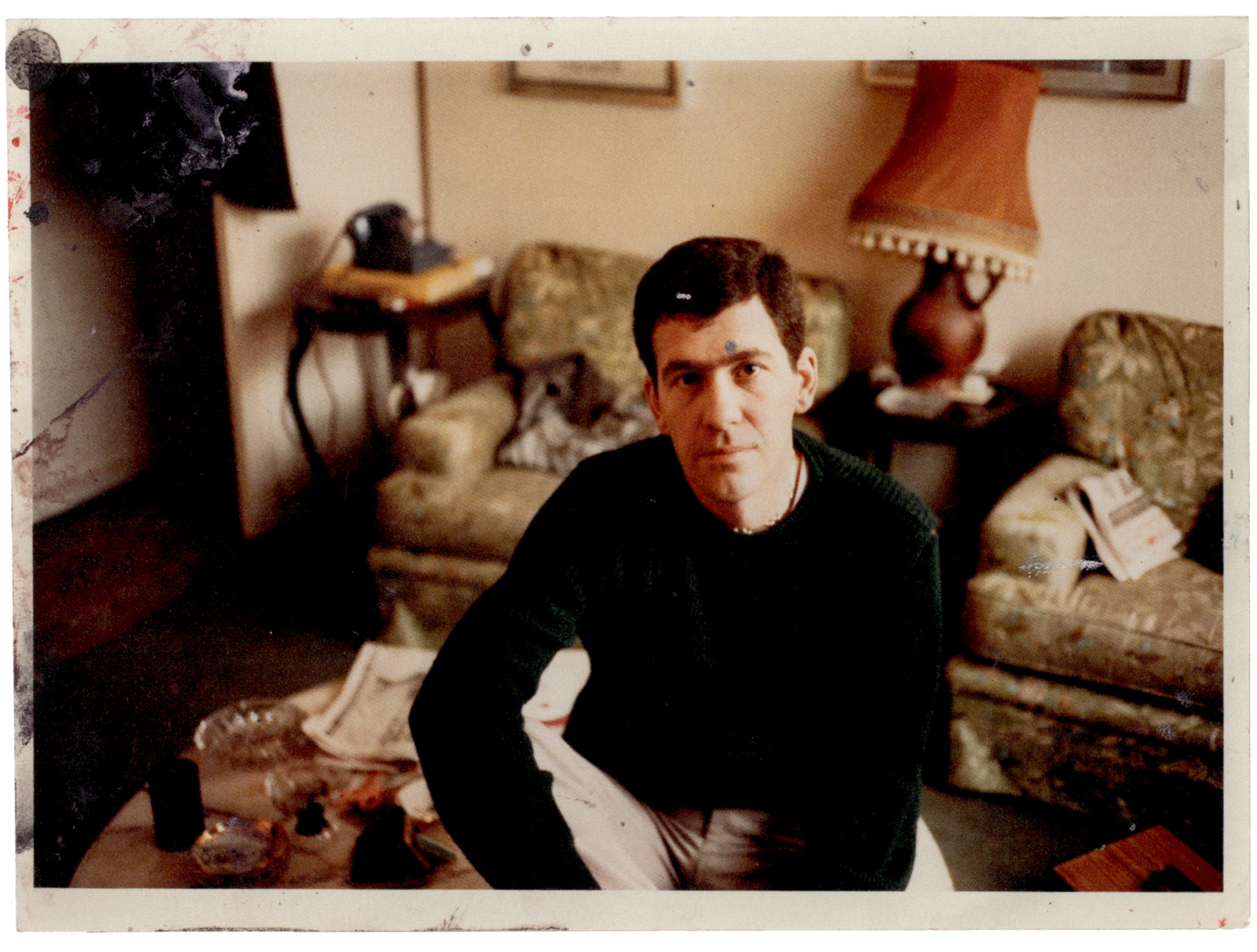

John Edwards

John Edwards (1949–2003) was Francis Bacon's partner in later life. Edwards said that he thought Bacon 'felt very free with me because I was a bit different from most people he knew'.[1] He was a pub manager who had little interest in the art world. One of six children, he was born to a tight-knit family in Stepney in the East End of London. His father, John, was a dockworker and former boxer; his mother, Beatrice, worked in a local shop. He was severely dyslexic and left school aged 14.

He met Francis Bacon in the Colony Room in the mid 1970s; he was in his twenties and Bacon was in his sixties. Edwards apparently confronted Bacon after the latter had failed to turn up to his pub, The Swan in Stratford, after having ordered several crates of champagne in anticipation of his visit. Endeared, Bacon invited him to dinner. Despite Edwards being in a long-term relationship with Philip Mordue, Bacon and Edwards remained companions, travelling widely and frequenting restaurants and bars together. Over the years their relationship became paternal.

Edwards was the subject of many of Bacon's later paintings. *Three Studies for a Portrait of John Edwards* (1980) was the first in which Edwards was named. In 1989, aged 80, Bacon demonstrated his unwavering skill and bravura with one of his last paintings of Edwards, *Study of Portrait of John Edwards* (1989; cat.57).

Bacon left the whole of his estate to Edwards, including the Reece Mews studio, whose entire contents Edwards eventually donated, in 1998, to the Hugh Lane Gallery in Dublin, Bacon's birth town. After Bacon's death, Edwards moved to Thailand, where, in 2003, he died from cancer, aged 53.

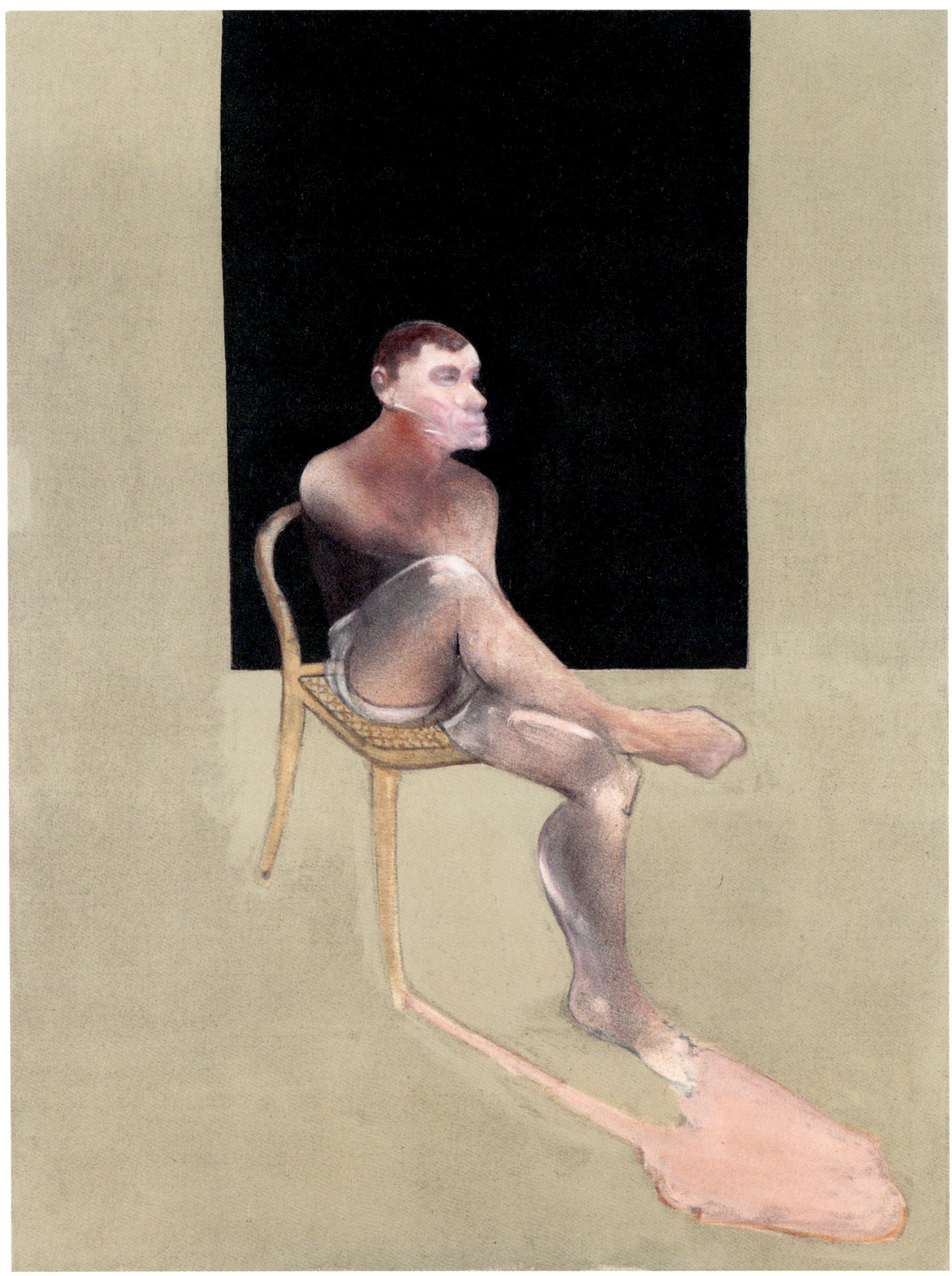

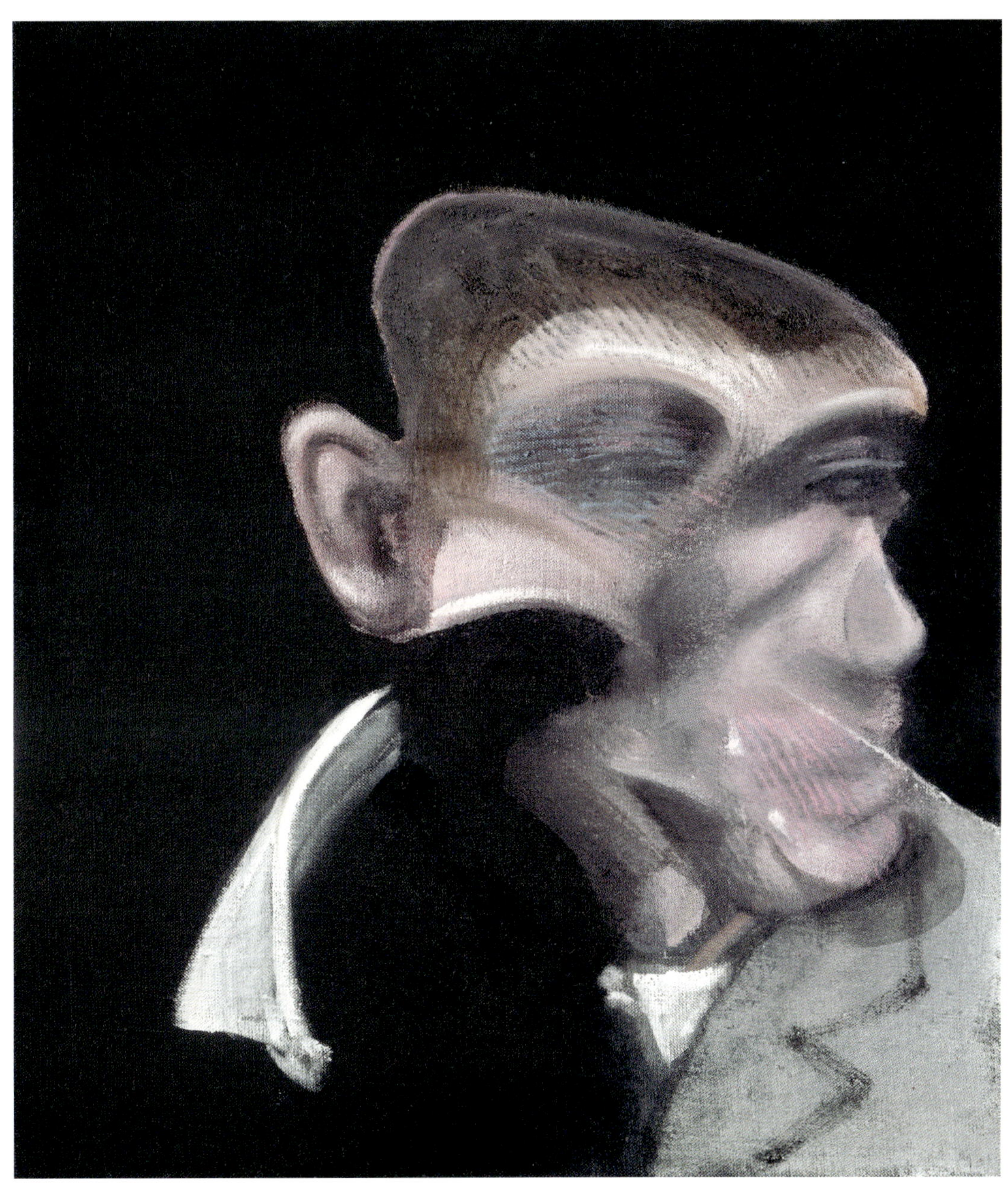

'I've decided to paint a few of my friends': Isabel Rawsthorne & Henrietta Moraes

Carol Jacobi

The term 'Bacon's model' is a misnomer when applied to Isabel Rawsthorne and Henrietta Moraes. Yet, it is a term that has distinguished their portraits from self-portraits and portraits of friends who were men. The difference does not originate from the paintings themselves; rather, it stems from the way in which they have been 'framed' for us to view in the years since their creation. An exception is the 2018 essay, written to accompany the exhibition *Bacon's Women*. Martin Harrison surveyed the artist's relationships with 'strong, independent and intelligent' women from many backgrounds.[1] They included Bacon's grandmother, the wealthy chatelaine Winifred Supple; Jessie Lightfoot, his intermittent carer from childhood to his early forties; his successive gallerists Erica Brausen, Helen Lessore and Valerie Beston; and the editor and archivist Sonia Orwell. Bacon painted seven of his women friends: his cousin, in *Figure in Landscape (Miss Diana Watson)* (1957), four of his patron Lisa Sainsbury (1955–7), four of the club proprietor Muriel Belcher (1959–79), and, perhaps most notably, 19 of his fellow painter, Isabel Rawsthorne (1961–82), and 23 of his close friend and member of the hippie movement Henrietta Moraes (1961–76).

In the twentieth century, Rawsthorne and Moraes were characterised through stereotypes originating in the nineteenth century. Their obituaries, in 1992 and 1999 respectively, cast them according to surprisingly traditional fantasies of the female model, muse and femme fatale. Their lives were celebrated in the context of men's work, not their own: Rawsthorne's for sitting to Jacob Epstein, André Derain, Alberto Giacometti, Pablo Picasso and Bacon (though she never physically sat for Picasso or Bacon); Moraes as a 'timeless incarnation of the bohemian artist's model'.[2] Commentaries, at once prurient and disapproving, foregrounded sexual allure, relationships and the women's oft-mentioned 'three husbands'. Bacon's reclining figures of Moraes (1966; cats 48–9) were infused with her tale of John Deakin tricking her into letting him shoot photographs from a pornographic angle, and his later selling them in the pub. As one obituary of Moraes put it, she 'may have been painted by Bacon and bedded by Lucian Freud, but … could equally well have been a model – and mistress – for Augustus John or Toulouse-Lautrec'.[3] Even Bacon deployed the age-old convention of conflating sex and sitting when he revealed in an interview a few weeks after

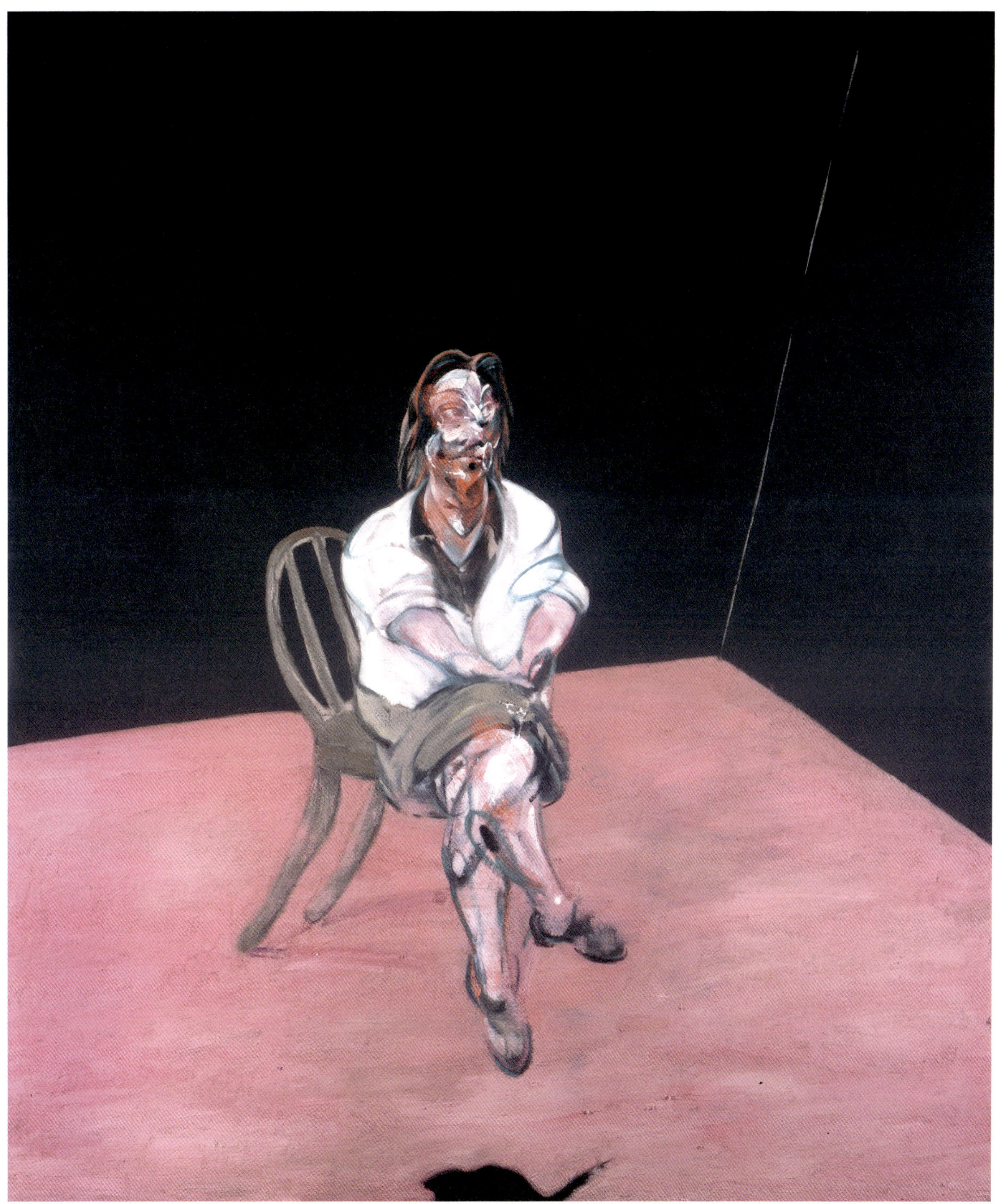

Rawsthorne's death that he had had a brief sexual liaison with her, describing her as, 'a very beautiful woman who was Derain's model and Georges Bataille's girlfriend' (Bataille being known for dark, erotic writing).[4] This traditional typing sits uncomfortably with Bacon, who was challenging traditional definitions of portraiture. By regarding images of Rawsthorne and Moraes as illustrational narrative portraits of 'Bacon's models', we diminish our viewing of his works. This publication is a timely opportunity to become more familiar with them and explore how their familiarity for Bacon informed his artistic process. Rawsthorne's 1985 autobiography, unpublished but informing a substantial monograph in 2021, and Moraes's auto-biography, published in 1994, bring their voices into the picture.[5]

Many accounts give the impression that Moraes and Rawsthorne were without significant professions or passions. In fact, Moraes existed on the margins of the landed upper classes and earned a living variously in bookselling, writing, journalism and adver-tising, with periods as assistant to singer and writer Marianne Faithful, as a gardener, and as custodian of rural Roundwood House in Ireland. Rawsthorne came from an impoverished background and was committed to drawing and painting throughout her life, having her first solo show at the age of 20 and her last at 79. She was also a designer for ballet and opera, and had stints with the Special Operations Executive and in journalism in the 1940s. When Bacon began painting the two women in the early 1960s, Moraes was already a friend of ten years, a single parent in her thirties, working as a TV advertising account manager. Rawsthorne was in her fifties (nearly Bacon's age), friend and ally since they re-launched their careers at the Hanover Gallery after the disruption of the war. The two women are usually described within the frame of Soho, but spent much of

their lives elsewhere in London, the countryside and beyond. Bacon was often a guest at Rawsthorne's Essex cottage, for example.

Bacon and Rawsthorne shared close ties to France. They had met in Paris in 1946, at a time when the French Existentialist circle was lending the portrait new significance as an exploration of the individual human experience. Existentialism's most prominent advocate, Jean Paul Sartre, eulogised the eroded, alienated figures of Alberto Giacometti, an artist with whom Rawsthorne had collaborated and for whom she had sat on many occasions in the late 1930s and 1940s. Rawsthorne introduced Giacometti to Bacon in the early 1960s. Bacon's first named portrait of Rawsthorne, *Study for Portrait (Isabel Rawsthorne)* (1964; fig.1), recalled Giacometti's last portrait of her, *Isabelle in the Studio* (1949; fig.2). In both works

Fig. 2   Alberto Giacometti   *Isabelle in the Studio*
1949   Oil on canvas   1050 × 870mm

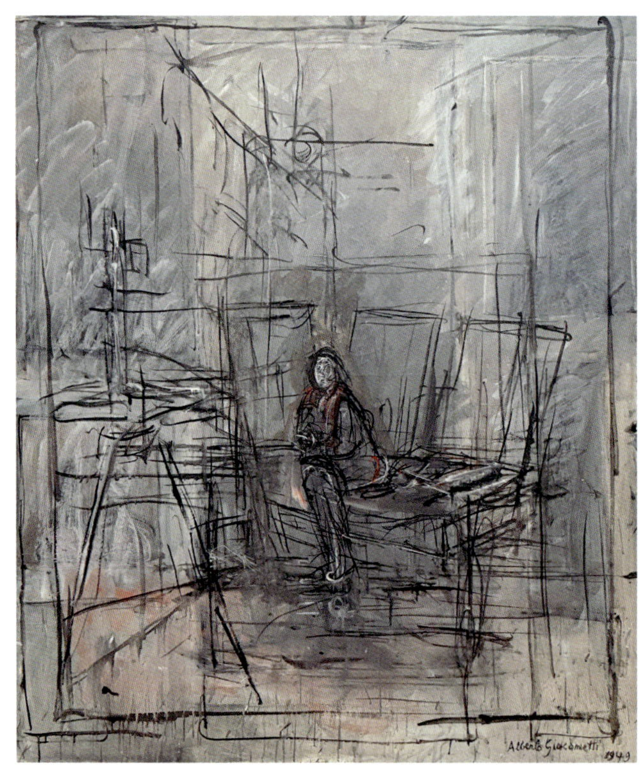

she perches on a chair within a geometric frame, her knees protruding awkwardly from her skirt. For Bacon, portraiture was 'the hardest thing to do in painting', and he and Rawsthorne were both inspired by Giacometti's 30-year search for 'presence'.[6] Giacometti's practice concentrated on a small circle of family and friends. Familiarity with his models helped him to go deeper than their appearance and to synthesise memories, feelings and prior images by himself and others. Bacon and Rawsthorne's repetition of a similarly limited set of portrait subjects was an acceptance of the open-ended imposs- ibility of the project: 'I do absolutely understand what Giacometti meant when he said, "Why ever change the subject?"'[7]

Two years after *Study for a Portrait*, Bacon's 1966 *Portrait of Isabel Rawsthorne* (cat.44) was accepted by the Tate. The notes relating to the acquisition described Rawsthorne as a 'well-known painter and designer'.[8] Yet by the 1980s, which saw a proliferation of interviews with and books about Bacon, Rawsthorne (and Moraes) had been recast as 'muse', her own reputation eclipsed and distorted. Talking about the painting at the Tate retrospective in 1985, Bacon himself chose to introduce Rawsthorne only as a model and token of his connection to other male artists: 'a great friend of Giacometti's. A lot of the very early things Giacometti did are about her.'[9] Although these myths of association contributed to Bacon's fame, they worked against his desire for his work to be read through an anti-illustrational lens, instead returning it to the realms of illustration, something he was keen to avoid. Indeed, when interviewers proposed illustrational interpretations of Bacon's portraits of Rawsthorne and Moraes, he always returned them to purely visual ones, focusing instead on the form, colour and composition of his work. The art historian Hugh Davies recalled asking Bacon whether

the tusk-like forms on the head in a study of Moraes 'might reflect the predatory nature of females', but Bacon 'shook the question off as if I'd missed the point'. Davies later reflected, 'I think my constant leaping to literal interpretations frequently taxes his patience'.[10]

Narrative interpretations of this kind have even been applied retrospectively. Many accounts of Moraes mention heroin, a literal reading of two nude portraits of her entitled *Lying Figure with Hypodermic Syringe I* and *II* (1963; fig.3 and 1969). Yet, as Moraes herself pointed out, the first of these pre-dated her relationship with hard drugs, and there is little evidence that she ever injected heroin. Bacon firmly asserted a formal purpose, emphasising the role of the syringe as a tool within the composition to fix the figure to the bed, rather than as demonstrative of drug-taking: 'I've used the figures lying on beds with a hypodermic syringe as a form of nailing the image more strongly to reality or appearance. I don't put the syringe because of the drug that's being injected.'[11] The motif provides a different kind of insight. It clarifies the role of friendship in Bacon's portrait process, the 'condensation of facts' and their glancing 'implications', sometimes tender, sometimes devastating. Moraes's autobiography is notably frank and thoughtful about addiction and the wider context of drug taking. Bacon's use of the syringe in 1963 is more likely to have been suggested by their talk about heroin users who were then frequenting Moraes's flat, and an article she was writing on the subject for the *Sunday Times*.[12] The Drugs (Prevention of Misuse) Act, passed in 1964, leading to the Misuse of Drugs Act in 1971, was the beginning of the end of the practice of receiving heroin from doctors. Moraes's autobiography traces the shift of the drug to the black market and the rise of the stigma associated with it. While Bacon may have denied the illustrational element of his work in relation to the inclusion of the syringe, he acknowledged that 'everyone reacts to their times'. Moraes's writing and the 1963 painting 'condensed' rather than illustrated their conversation and a moment in London drug culture that year.[13]

When Bacon reprised the composition in 1969 the context had changed, and 'implications' had accumulated. Amphetamines were widely prescribed for everything from weight loss and tiredness to mental illness, contributing to the energy and risk that were part of 1960s culture. Moraes turned to drugs during a period of depression and unemployment that followed the end of her third marriage, the loss of her home and the death of her nanny, who had brought some care and stability to her single-parent household. Initially, she took Dexamyl in tablet form, 'purple hearts', later joining a group who injected methedrine, and her autobiography describes her entering a different social world. Bacon's awareness of this may have added resonance to *Figure with Hypodermic Syringe II*, but, as always, such resonances are glancing. Moraes's rounded contours are accompanied by more apparitional, blacker forms, but there is no literal representation of the extreme emaciation that the drug caused in reality. By 1969 Moraes was no longer ill or dependent; a short imprisonment for breaking and entering brought her to the attention of a social worker, who supported her and her children for many years.

Returning to Rawsthorne, who was a colleague as well as a friend of Bacon, her portraits resonate with conversations about art. *Three Studies of Isabel Rawsthorne* (1967; cat.46) depicts her turning a key in a door. She is accompanied by two head studies, one pinned to the wall and the other outside the room, visible through the door opening. Bacon told Davies that the key had resonances from a favourite poem, T.S. Eliot's

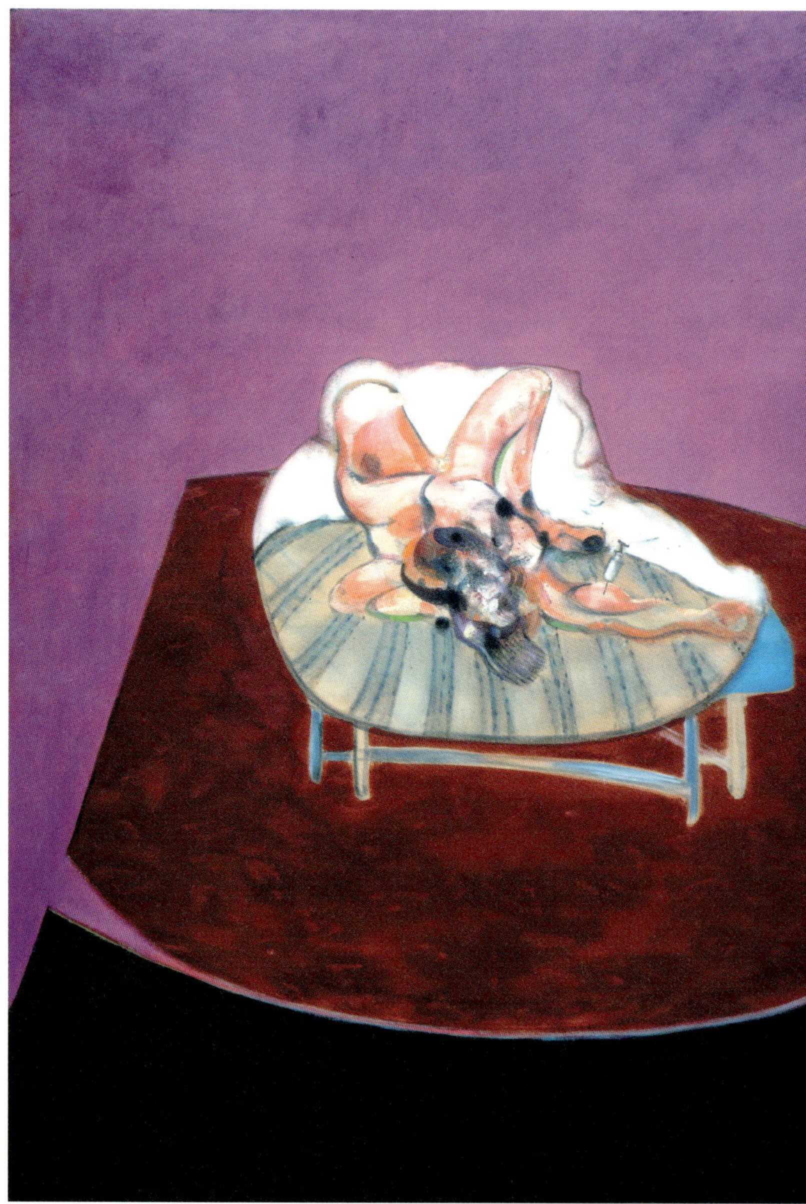

Fig. 3   Francis Bacon
Lying Figure with Hypodermic Syringe   1963
Oil on canvas   1980 × 1450mm

The Waste Land (1922): 'I have heard the key/Turn in the door once and turn once only/We think of the key, each in his prison.'[14] *The Waste Land* was also a key text for Rawsthorne, and it is hard to imagine that the picture does not give a nod to conversations the two artists had about the poem. *Three Studies of Isabel Rawsthorne* can be used to begin to examine how Bacon's and Rawsthorne's practices were intertwined.

Both artists were fascinated by 'life' and 'death' masks. Bacon's 1955 series, including *Study for Portrait II (after the Life Mask of William Blake)* (cat.8), inspired Rawsthorne to use a life mask of Chopin to inform her series of portraits of her partner, the composer Alan Rawsthorne.[15] These masks inform the closed eyes of the central profile in *Three Studies of Isabel Rawsthorne*. Like Bacon, Rawsthorne had also painted Muriel Belcher, proprietor of the Colony Room. In *Portrait (Muriel Belcher)* (1953–4), she interpreted her sitter as a sculpture, based on the Naxian Sphinx (*c*.560 BCE), set on a table, and gave her a doubled presence in the form of a profile reflected in a mirror. The sculpture recalls Eliot's concept of art 'manipulating a continuous parallel between contemporaneity and antiquity'.[16] Bacon acknowledged Rawsthorne's vision of Belcher as Delphic guardian of the threshold of the Colony Room, in *Sphinx – Portrait of Muriel Belcher* (1979), a last memory painted on the occasion of Belcher's death. Such examples begin to unpack the reciprocal, intellectual dynamic between Bacon and Rawsthorne, demonstrating a relationship that was so much more than one between artist and muse. Bacon's last portrait of Rawsthorne, *Studies of Isabel Rawsthorne diptych* (1983), painted when she was 71 and he 74, tenderly references an operation to her eyes. This portrait reflects the fear that both artists felt for the loss of her sight, and captures the empathy of a fellow professional, collaborator and friend.

In Bacon's portraits of Rawsthorne and Moraes we can look beyond retrospectively imposed illustrative responses: a vanitas of addiction; a fallen beauty; the 'uninhibited exuberance until the onslaught of old age'.[17] Asked later in life whether she felt injured by Bacon's portraits, Moraes replied 'No, I don't feel at all wounded, I never did'.[18] When Bacon summoned their presence in his studio, it came with their thoughts, ideas and decades of conversations. As Moraes observed, the paintings are not simply 'somebody looking at something … they are somebody experiencing something while they paint'.[19]

Ghosts in the Glass: Filming Francis Bacon

John Maybury

Bare light bulbs cast harsh electric light on seated figures exuding shadows like souls seeping from bodies. The puissance of male flesh, an erotic knowledge of fingertips transferred into smears of paint combed by plastic or grained by the texture of scraps of corduroy. Zippers and fly-buttons. The hang and sag of Y-fronts, cotton yellowed and stained. The same erotic charge as muscle photography or clandestine encounters. An empire of signs and codifications. The rage of gestures, suppressed and oppressed, crushed under the weight of British stiff upper lips and polite society. The armour of suits and shirts and ties as containers for bags of flesh and blubber, blood and veins. Stubble and hairlines, Brylcreem and sweat. A lexicon of homoerotic hieroglyphs, tapping out a Morse code of secret knowledge. Polari dissolved in oil paint and turpentine. These figures are located on podia, in rooms, cages, bullrings, ritual sites from pagan pasts or distilled mass-media events. Actions represented by fragments of tripods, cameras, machines, chrome abstractions of Deco furniture, armatures and crucifixes, trapping figures in varicoloured arenas, void spaces, mindscapes. Against the grain of abstraction but aware of every incremental development taking place. And, at the centre of this kaleidoscopic array of devices, figurative portraits, likenesses of lovers, of friends and the self.

I want to frame this properly. Like many kids in early 1970s London and its suburbs, most of my experience was drawn from a patchwork of television and print media – comics, teen magazines, pop music papers and the underground press. From this grab-bag of sources, by my early teens I had constructed a homosexual family tree. Jean Genet and Jean Cocteau, William Burroughs and Andy Warhol, Pier Paolo Pasolini and Rainer Werner Fassbinder, David Hockney and Francis Bacon. Television introduced John Hurt as Quentin Crisp and Derek Jacobi in *I Claudius*. Glam Rock gave Marc Bolan and David Bowie. These makers and minds formed a matrix of queer identity that coalesced with the classical education my Jesuit teachers were forcing in, as they beat my cockney accent out. The priests were paving the way for an Oxbridge fast track, but glam and punk rock and TV deflected me towards art school. It was a liberation. I moved into a squat in Queens Gate in SW7; the art school was in Plaistow, E13. My BA was titled Expanded Fine Art, and I painted, printed, photographed, videoed and filmed. But my real teachers were not at the art school. The real teachers were in gay clubs and at punk gigs.

After a Siouxsie and the Banshees gig in 1977, I was chatting to a man about film. Would I be interested in working on a punk film he was planning? I said yes. His name was Derek Jarman, and the film was *Jubilee*.

Both Derek and punk introduced me to a world of artists and maverick designers, reprobates

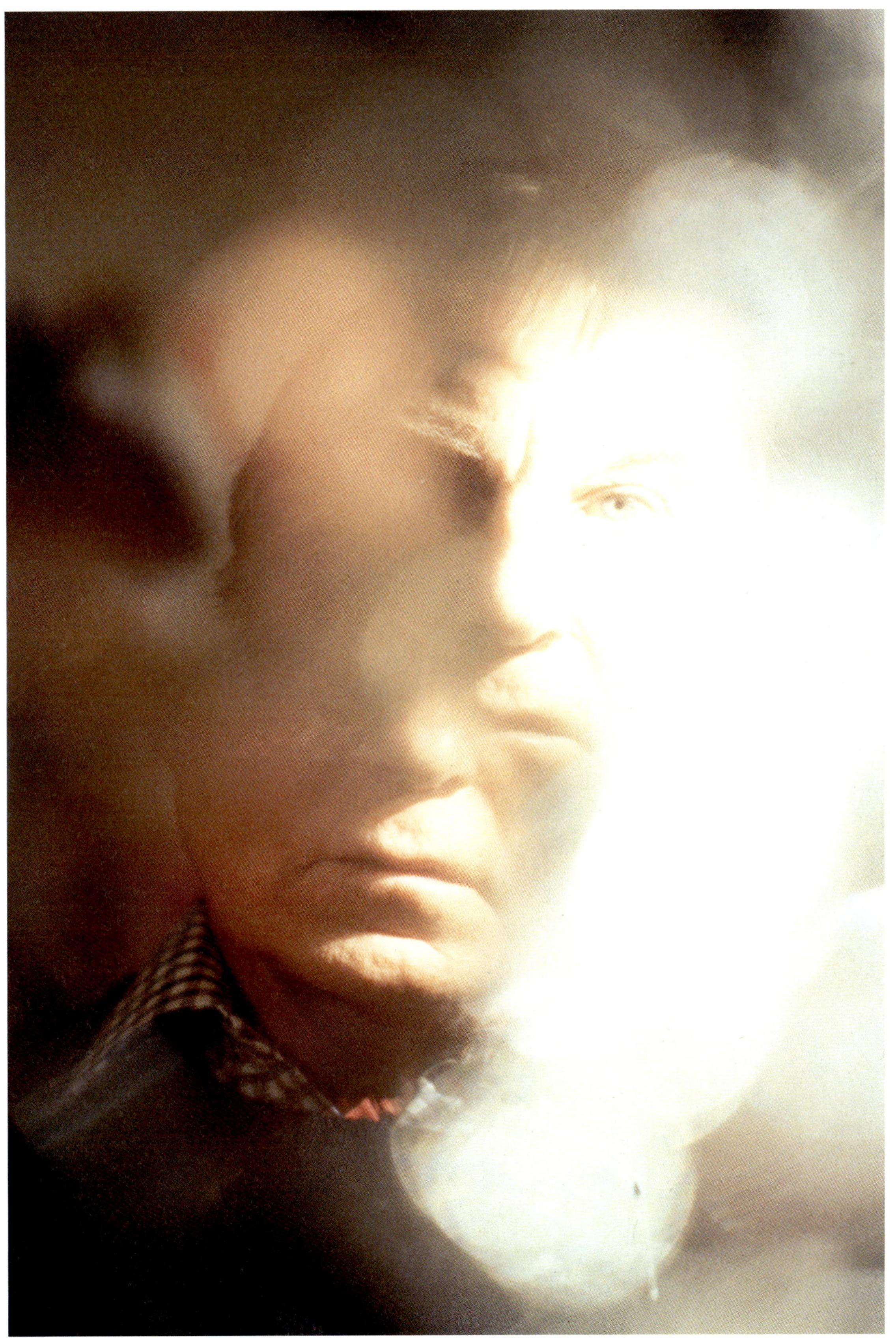

Fig. 1   Still of Derek Jacobi as Francis Bacon from *Love is the Devil: Study for a Portrait of Francis Bacon*   1998

and roués. Among these was Michael Wishart. Wishart was a figurative painter whose early success in the late 1950s was dissipated by a hedonistic lifestyle. In 1978 he took me to the Colony Room. Early on, Colony Room founder Muriel Belcher had made Bacon a member, allowing him to drink for free with the proviso that he used his connections to bring in the right people. Subsequently, a post-war proto-counterculture of artists, writers, journalists and other Soho flotsam and jetsam came together in the pokey, bilious-green room on the first floor. The roll-call would include Lucian Freud, Frank Auerbach, John Minton, Isabel Rawsthorne, Dennis Worth Miller, John Deakin, Henrietta Moraes, Nina Hamnett, Daniel Farson and George Melly, as well as countless others from Soho's clip-joints, theatres and film industry offices. The unifying qualities of membership being a sharp wit, a thick skin and a limitless capacity for drink. In all, it served as a refuge for outsiders in Britain's uptight post-war cultural drizzle. On my first visit, an afternoon in 1978, the nicotine-stained threadbare club was limping along. Muriel was propped on

Fig. 2 **David Cripps** *Daniel Farson* 1989
Gelatin silver print 183 × 256mm

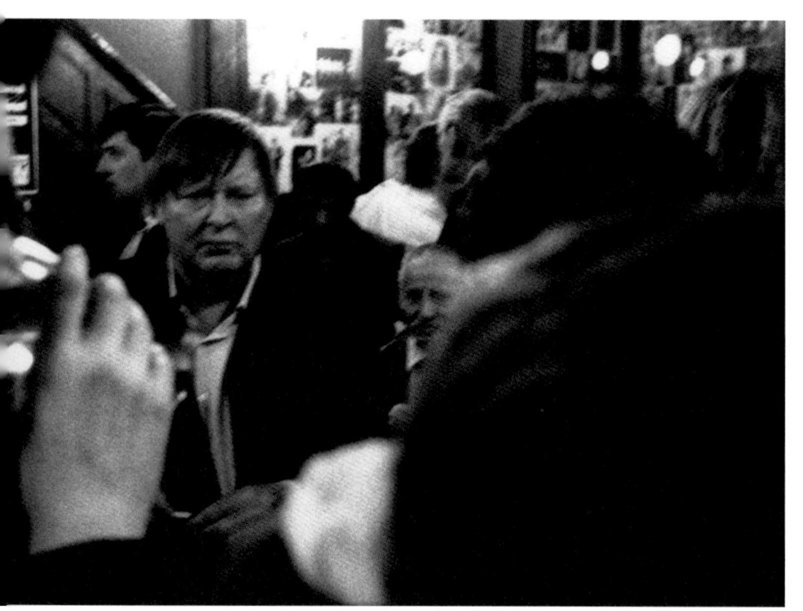

her stool drinking, and the few members there, like her, were not pleased to see Michael Wishart and what they assumed was his latest rent boy – me. After a couple of drinks and some particularly nasty banter between barman Ian Board and Wishart, I made my excuses and left.

In 1995, I was approached by George Faber of the BBC with whom I'd previously worked on my Tilda Swinton film, *Man to Man*. He had bought the rights to Daniel Farson's memoir, *The Gilded Gutter Life of Francis Bacon*, and was struggling with its development. In the intervening years, since my first Colony Room visit, I had pursued a career as an artist and experimental filmmaker, continued working on multiple projects with Derek Jarman, and even wound up winning some prizes at film festivals and MTV awards for my music videos. Although I had often seen Bacon on the streets of South Kensington back in my squatting days, and even up close at a party or two, I had never met the man. As they say, never meet your heroes. I told Faber I would love to take on the project.

A meeting was arranged with Daniel Farson (fig.2) in Soho's French House. Farson was an interesting man, a writer and journalist who had been a successful TV presenter and documentarian in the early 1960s. He was also a long-standing friend of Bacon, and the latter had given permission for the memoir to be published only after his death. The meeting began with great civility but soon, a few drinks in, descended into a glorified pub crawl, climaxing in my first return to the Colony Room since 1979. With Muriel now dead, the club was fronted by her ex-barman Ian Board, ably assisted by Michael Wojas. This would be the beginning of a most unorthodox period of alcohol-fuelled research. Farson was treated with disdain by many other Colony Room members. They had all heard his Bacon stories many times before and all felt that their stories were of far more value to me. I quicky came to understand a special kind of cruelty that was directed by one drunk to another, and the strange judgmentalism of ownership when it came to Bacon. But I could see that Farson was a sensitive and gentle soul, which made me strangely protective towards him. His book was a fantastic resource, full of anecdotes and gossip, very much embedded in the inaccessible private rooms of the 1950s and 1960s homosexual underworld.

The subsequent days and nights moving from the French House, to Wheelers, to the Colony Room, led to multiple introductions to a wide and varied cast of characters who would push forward to offer their stories of personal encounters with Bacon. The result became a perfect illustration of the Rashomon effect – wherein each person describes an event in a different and contradictory way that reflects their subjective interpretation and self-interested stance, rather than objective truth. The famous names – artists, actors, journal-ists – from the Colony Room were the main players, but the secondary roles were filled by ever-present observers of the action, offering these 'Rashomon' multiple perspectives.

Another significant resource was Robin Muir, curator of the exhibition *John Deakin Photographs* (1996) at the National Portrait Gallery. He gave me and my fledgling team – production designer Alan MacDonald, cinematographer John Mathieson and producer Chiara Menage – access to the chaotic John Deakin archive. This was assembled from Deakin's Condé Nast commissions and the huge body of work produced specifically for Bacon from the Hugh Lane Gallery. Deakin's images were wonderful. His intimacy with Bacon's circle of friends meant there was little or no artifice in his work. He rarely sought to flatter; in fact his photographs have an almost forensic quality, which obviously appealed to Bacon.

As I discovered, each biographer, each 'expert' and interviewer projects their own ideas onto their subject, and in that I am no different. While always guided by Farson's *Gilded Gutter Life*, I extended my research into the private spaces of sexual dynamics and the nuance of queer typologies, drawing on sado-masochistic literature and the gay underground press, the writer Jean Genet and the poet C.P. Cavafy, as much as from my own experiences. However, the language of Bacon's paintings would be at the centre of the film. Bacon's interest in Greek tragedy, and Aeschylus in particular, offered a key to the inner lives of his subjects, and a set of signifiers that gave clues to both their psychology and to his own. The frozen movement, a static trembling, of figures whose shadows bleed as though their life force were draining away. These are modern people pursued by the furies of a twentieth-century existential angst. Everything in Bacon's *oeuvre* resides in the shadow of the holocaust, of the nuclear bomb, of the Nuremberg trials and, ultimately, a brutal post-faith world.

Fig. 3   Still of Francis Bacon and Melvyn Bragg
from *The South Bank Show*   1988

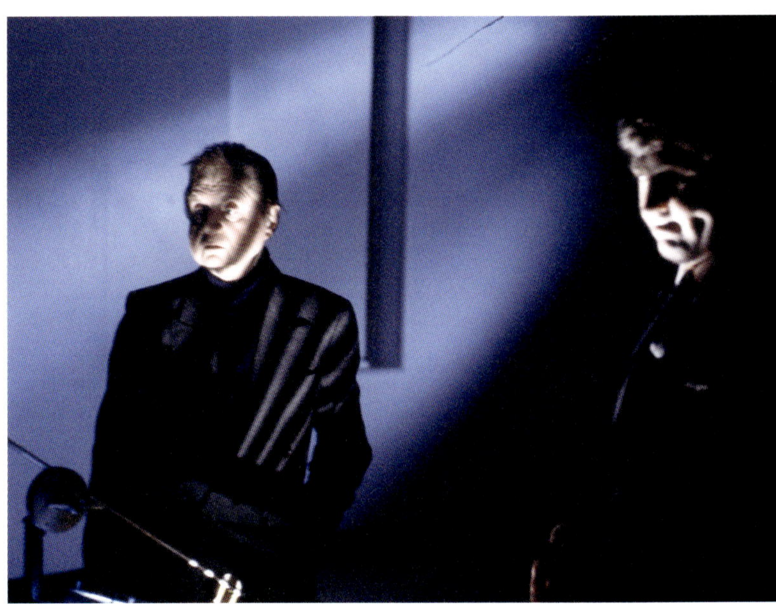

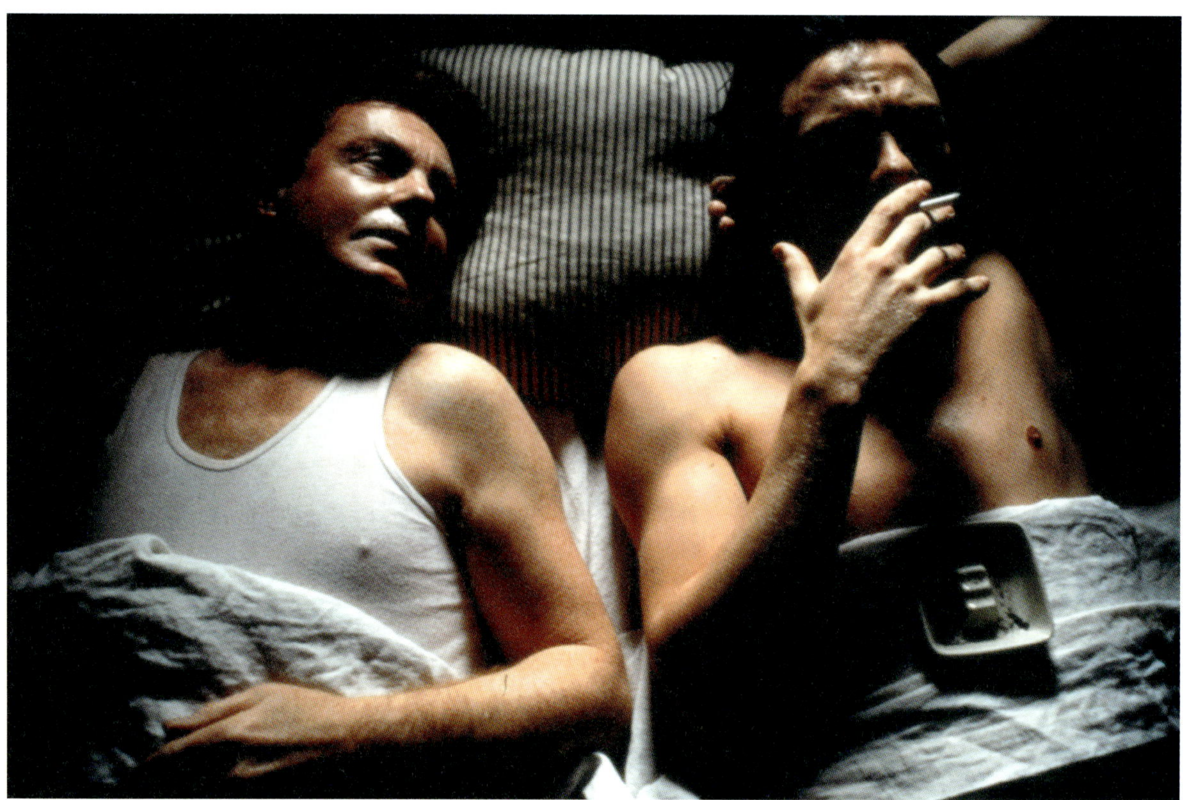

All this played out in my mind as I wrote. By the time *Love is the Devil: Study for a Portrait of Francis Bacon* had reached its seventh draft, we were ready to cast the film. When Derek Jacobi (fig.1) agreed to play Bacon, we immersed ourselves in archive material. Particularly useful was the Melvyn Bragg *South Bank Show* on Bacon from 1988 (fig.3), where Bacon and Bragg spent a day together talking, lunching and drinking, becoming increasingly drunk. As Bragg remembered:

> We met at 9 in the morning in his studio … After filming, we went round to the Italian restaurant where Francis took his meal of the day. He insisted we all drink the Bollinger he had lined up beside the sink and at the restaurant we drank rough red wine … This was an alcoholic waterfall. After the restaurant cleared, Francis and I pretended to have lunch and did the interview. We ate nothing but we drank on. We got very drunk. It showed. We were not a pretty sight and there was plenty to laugh at but what Francis said was true to the devil in him, and I kept it in.[1]

We found other incredible footage of Bacon in his studio swirling around a French film crew, sloshing a glass of milky Pernod at the camera. Jacobi built a portrait of Bacon that danced on the edge of the sharp intellect of the man and the caustic bitchiness of a shameless queen. Our carefully constructed set of the Colony Room, erected on a sound stage in east London, was a little too real. It was populated with extras, many of whom were original Colony Room members. Sandy Fawkes, a red-headed writer, possibly in her late seventies, had been swigging from her hip flask while waiting to film. When Jacobi

Fig. 5   Still of Tilda Swinton as Muriel Belcher and Derek Jacobi as Francis Bacon from
Love is the Devil: Study for a Portrait of Francis Bacon   1998

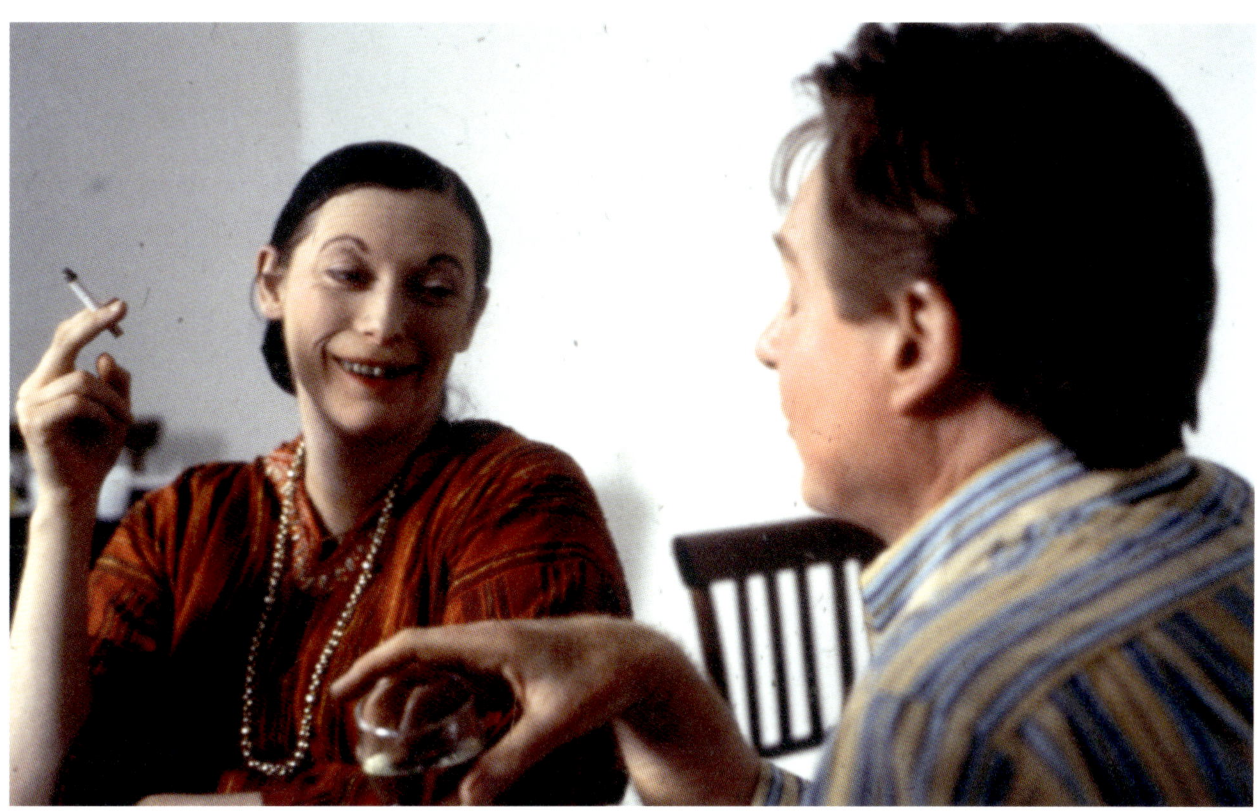

walked on set in his full Bacon costume, she burst into tears and hugged him saying, 'Francis! Francis! Where have you been? I've missed you so.' I had to take her aside and explain that it was in fact Derek and that this was a film.

For Daniel Craig, who was playing Bacon's lover George Dyer (fig.4), things were more difficult. While Dyer is a totemic figure in many of Bacon's greatest paintings, he remains a cipher. A person seemingly without agency, used by others for their own purposes. Bacon's friends dismissed him as rough trade. In some ways this enters a strange realm where the old queen language of hierarchy comes into play. Only the lover and the loved one can fully understand the power dynamics involved. Craig drew on this blank page notion, playing Dyer with a sweetness and fragility, as a presence rather than a fully

formed being. We had Deakin's photographs of Dyer and Bacon together, in which their intimacy reveals their chemistry. Farson liked Dyer and said that Bacon loved his honesty, his no-nonsense directness, his total lack of pretention. Bacon was unsentimental – he claimed to loathe sentiment – but there it is in the portraits of George Dyer, an alchemy of feelings transformed into paint. There it is again and again in each painting of Dyer, of John Edwards and of Peter Lacy, all lovers of his. The same can be said of many of the portraits of his friends – Isabel Rawsthorne and particularly Muriel Belcher.

Tilda Swinton took on the role of Muriel Belcher (fig.5). In this instance, the problem was a total lack of audio archive material. While Belcher is most famously quoted for her greeting 'Hello cunty!' and for calling Bacon 'Daughter' and he referring to her as 'Mother' (an insight in itself), the dearth of audio reference left the character open to free interpretation. Film and photographs of Belcher show an imperious but slight woman, either perched on her throne-like barstool in the club or moving through small, crowded rooms as if protected by some invisible force field.

The other actors – Anne Lambton as Isabel Rawsthorne, Adrian Scarborough as Dan Farson, Carl Johnson as John Deakin and Annabel Brooks as Henrietta Moraes – were able in some instances to talk to the actual people they were playing, though not all were forthcoming. To populate the film overall, the bars and pubs and restaurants in the screenplay were filled with friends and acquaintances from 1990s Soho and beyond, emulating Bacon's circle with my own. Tracey Emin, Sarah Lucas, Angus Fairhurst, Sue Tilley, Gary Hume, Princess Julia, Anita Pallenberg, Rifat Ozbek, Hamish Bowles ad infinitum filled the French House, the Colony Room set, Bethnal Green Town Hall and the Café Royal.

Just as mirrors are seen throughout Bacon's paintings, from shaving mirrors to huge interventions, distorted panels in landscapes or auditoria, so reflections are a central part of my film's cinematic language. The reflective glass that contains his images also protects them. The glass opens the paintings up like rooms, which the viewer subliminally enters. We become voyeurs and we see the shadow of ourselves caught in the act. This complicity with Bacon and his subjects was brought

home to me during the research period before the film was made. In 1996, the National Gallery exhibited masterpieces from the Doria Pamphilj collection. Velázquez's *Pope Innocent X* was hung opposite Bacon's Popes from 1951, 1961 and 1965. It was possible to see the Velázquez Pope reflected in the glass of Bacon's paintings, a circle Bacon himself was never able to complete. In *Love is the Devil*, we created Bacon's painterly effects by filming through glass lenses, clear glass ashtrays and outsized brandy balloons, and placed a distorted acrylic mirror behind bottles on shelves, and used celluloid and the play of light to emulate his images. My portraits of Bacon's friends, of naked lovers in the throes of lovemaking, of Bacon himself as portrayed by Jacobi, were distorted and manipulated by the language of cinema. Many people still claim to have seen Bacon's paintings in the film. They must have seen them in their mind's eye.

So, what was I filming? A study for a portrait of Francis Bacon? Yes, but also a portrait of a lost world, of a lost way of life, 'the twilight world of unhappy poofs', as expressed by one of the characters. This was a generation forced to live and love outside the law in the homophobic ruins of a post-Edwardian, post-two-world-wars iteration of empire, where a sneer or a slight, either written or verbal, could destroy a reputation. The fearlessness of emboldened alcoholics allowed to shout into the void in a small, nicotine-stained, green room: we are ghosts in the glass.

Picturing the Artist: Camera Portraits of Francis Bacon

Georgia Atienza

'I think one's sense of appearance is assaulted all the time by photography.'[1]

Repositioning Bacon into the role of sitter, the images that follow chart his biography through the lenses of key twentieth-century photographers and an artist-filmmaker. Fascinated by both his art and personality, they have created some of the most defining portraits of Bacon. These portraits, selected primarily from the National Portrait Gallery's Collection and the Francis Bacon MB Art Foundation, reflect on Bacon's working and living environments and his cultural context, as well as revealing aspects of his inner self. As an avid consumer of photographs, Bacon often drew from photographic material and commissioned photographs of his models, using them as reference points for his paintings.

The range of photographs presented throughout this publication reflects Bacon's vast iconography, which includes all kinds of photographic genres, from carefully composed set pieces to ad hoc street photography. During his formative years as a painter, Bacon was photographed in Berlin by Helmar Lerski (p.33), whose close-up and dramatically lit portrait brings into focus his youthful features. Francis Julian Gutmann, later Francis Goodman, made an arresting studio portrait of Bacon while the latter was in his twenties (p.12). Sam Hunter's photographs (pp.10 and 15), taken in Bacon's Cromwell Place studio, are the earliest images of Bacon's so-called 'working documents', the creative detritus that became an oft-cited feature of his studio. John Deakin's raw and direct portraits of Bacon, and of his subjects (fig.1 and pp.105, 122, 128, 136, 146 and 154), lay bare each sitter with an unequivocal intensity. Street photographer Harry Diamond

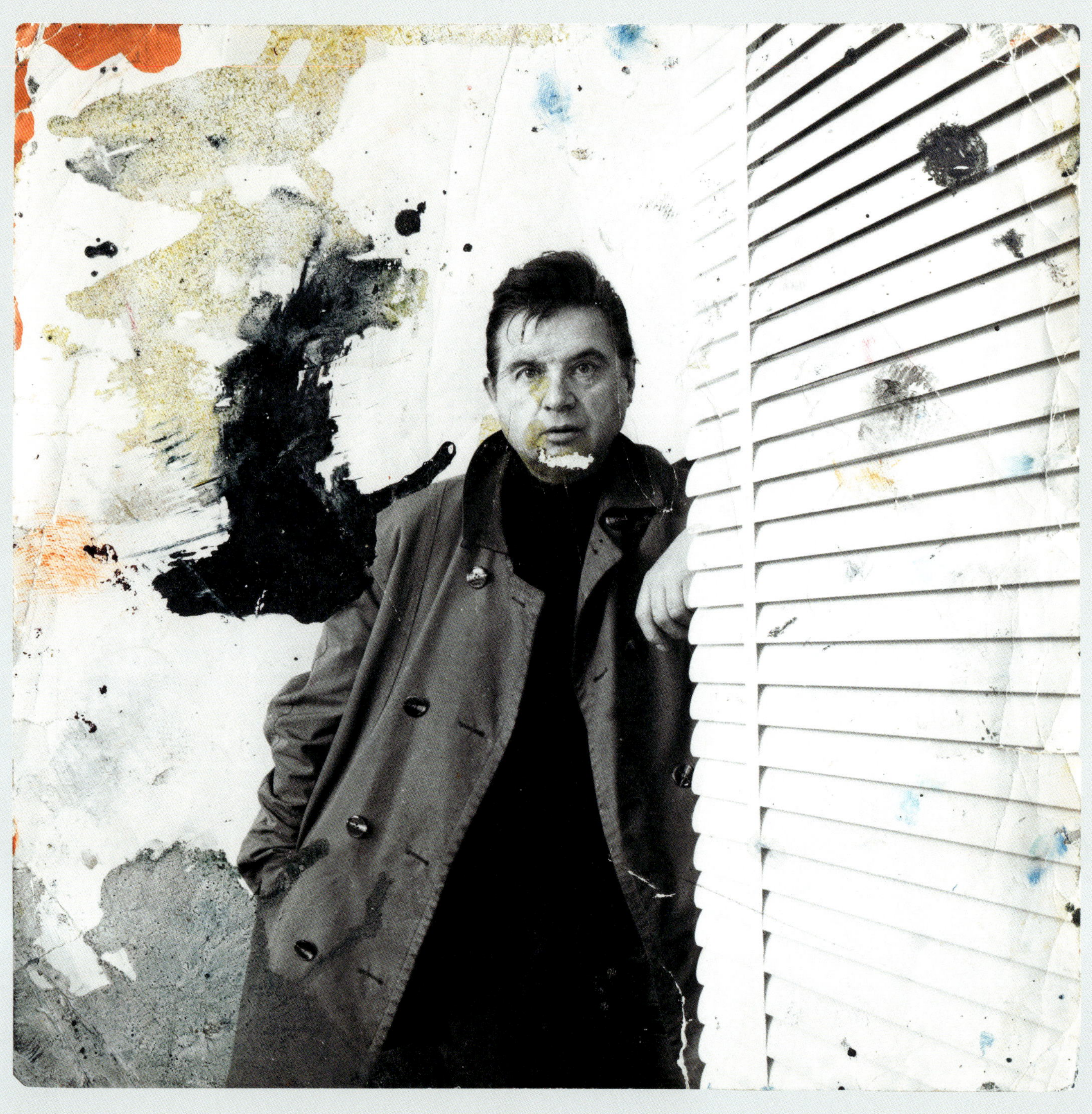

Fig.1   **John Deakin**   *Francis Bacon at Roland Gardens*   1967
Gelatin silver print   240 × 240mm

captured Bacon with his close friend Lucian Freud in
Soho (p.53).

Studied in greater depth is the portfolio by fashion
photographer Cecil Beaton who portrayed Bacon on a visit
to Reddish House (fig.2) and later made an intimate series of
photographs in his studio at Overstrand Mansions (see p.69).
Douglas Glass's compelling colour portrait shows the intense
48-year-old painter at the fore, with a glimpse into his studio
beyond (fig.3). Also included here are Irving Penn's enduring
image of the artist with Rembrandt's *Self-Portrait with Beret*
(fig.4), and Bill Brandt's celebrated study of Bacon in the
desolate London landscape (fig.5). Jorge Lewinski and
Guy Bourdin took inspiration from Bacon's own practice,
referencing his pictorial technique in their photographs
(figs 6 and 11). Mayotte Magnus used elements from the
Reece Mews studio to compose her portraits of Bacon (fig.8),
while Peter Stark's portrayals became sources of inspiration
for some of Bacon's self-portraits, and many of these
images were later found within the fabric of the studio (fig.9).
The artist Clare Shenstone made a series of photographs
of Bacon when he invited her to make a portrait of him
(fig.10). We see Neil Libbert's chance encounter with Bacon
on his eightieth birthday (fig.12). Expanding on the notion
of portraiture, Bacon's rich iconography also includes moving
image. In Peter Gidal's 16mm film *Heads* (1969), Bacon appears
head-on. Scrutinised in tight close-up, he seems at ease during
the three-minute exposure of his portrait (fig.7).

The breadth of images made of Bacon allow us to examine
the attraction and engagement between photographer and
sitter. Over the decades and in many different ways, these
portraits distil and communicate something incisive about
Bacon in a way that strengthens our understanding of the
artist. Bacon was captivated by photographs of himself and
he often used them as the basis for his self-portraits, as well
as arranging his own shots in photo booths. This wealth
of imagery contributed to his celebrity status in the public
imagination. Very much aware of the performative power
of the image, Bacon relished the prospect of sitting for
photographers, allowing them behind-the-scenes access,
and sometimes seeming to guide the process. As Bacon
grew in both artistic status and celebrity, so too did the desire
of many photographers to depict him and reveal something
of his persona.

Cecil Beaton

Bacon and Cecil Beaton forged a friendship during the 1950s, Beaton commenting that the two struck up a rapport from their first meeting. He described Bacon, 'with cherubic, apple-shiny cheeks', his 'hair bleached by the sun', and said that he was overcome by the painter's 'tremendous charm and understanding'.[2]

Beaton, a fashion and society photographer, first portrayed Bacon in 1951, while the painter stayed at Beaton's country retreat, Reddish House in Wiltshire. In this portrait, from their first sitting, a youthful Bacon poses against the richly decorated walls of Beaton's dressing room. In 1960, Beaton photographed him again, this time at Bacon's studio in Overstrand Mansions in Battersea. In his diary, Beaton noted of the studio that 'the floor was littered in a Dostoyevsky shambles of discarded paints, rags, newspapers and every sort of rubbish'.[3] In the 1960 series, Bacon appears relaxed in the studio (see p.69). Beaton recalled: 'His pose reminded me of a portrait of Degas. He curved his head sideways and looked at the canvas with a beautiful expression in his eyes.'[4] At the time, Bacon was preparing for a spring exhibition, his first at the Marlborough Fine Art Gallery in London. He had begun a portrait of Beaton in 1957, which took over two years to complete, and it is likely that the studio photographs were made during a later sitting for that portrait. After seeing Beaton's reaction to the painting, however, Bacon subsequently destroyed it.

Fig.2   **Cecil Beaton**   *Francis Bacon*   1951   Gelatin silver print   204 × 196mm

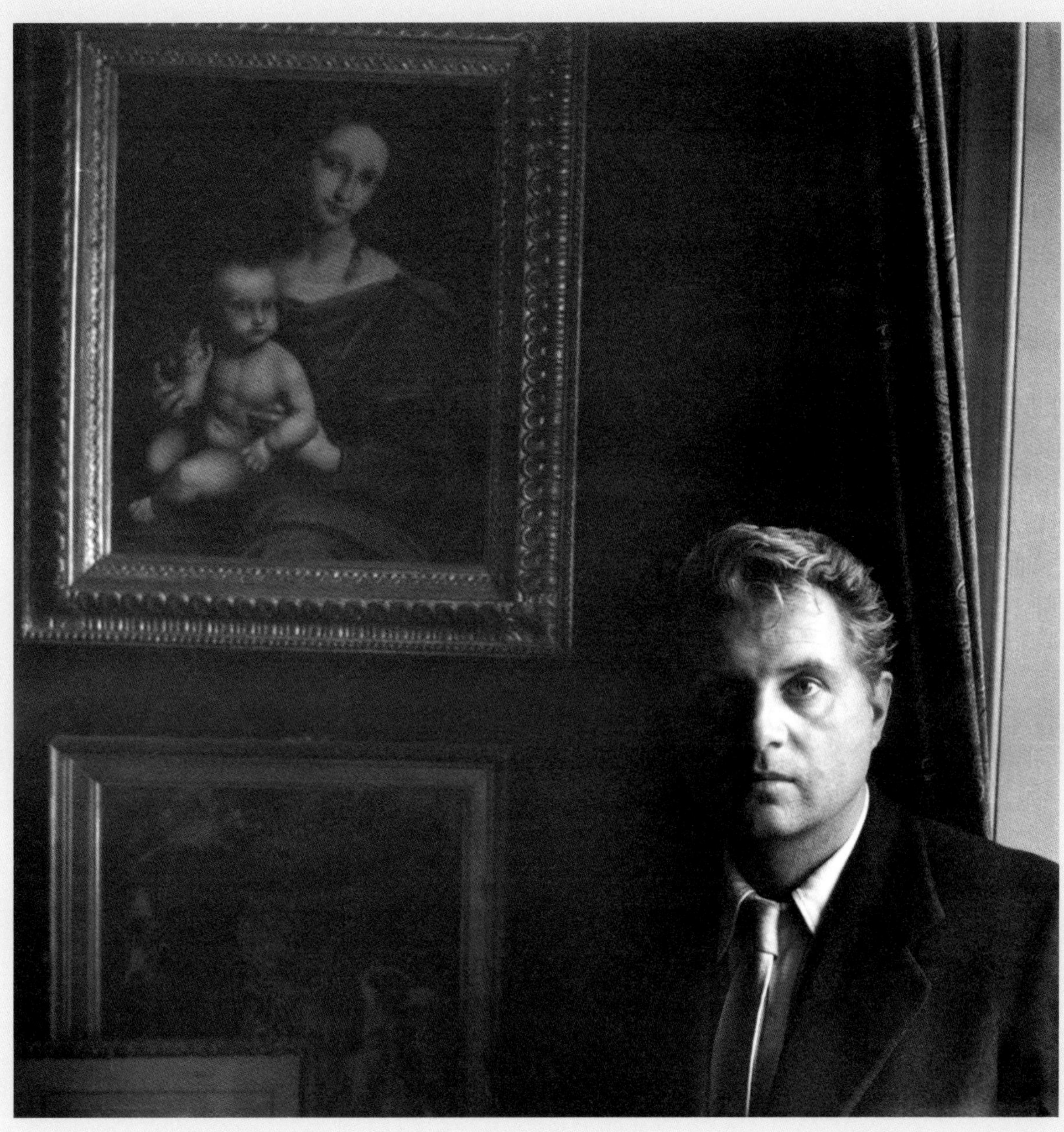

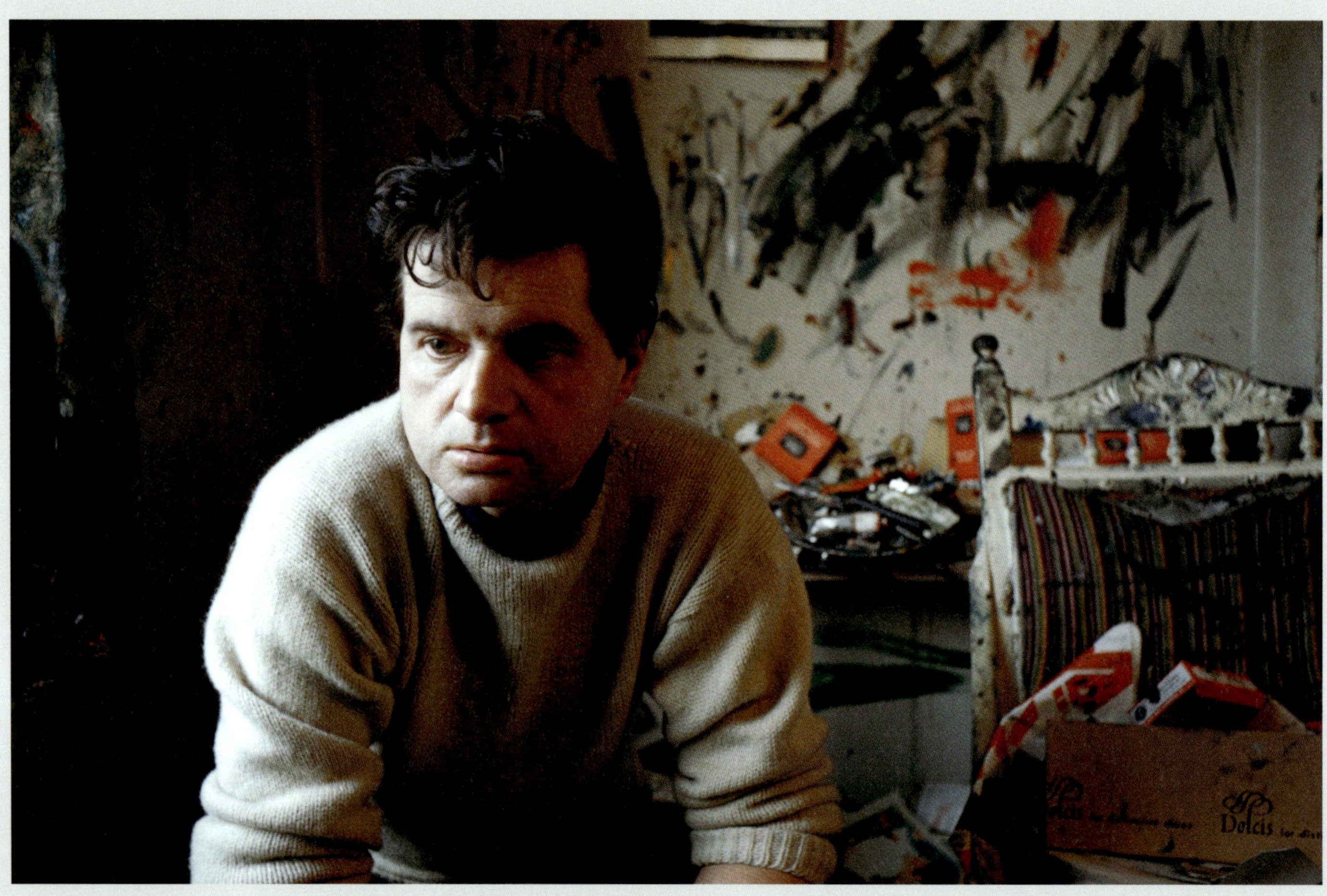

Douglas Glass

Douglas Glass photographed Bacon at 9 Overstrand Mansions,
his studio in Battersea, on two occasions, recording the
small room in which the painter worked. Describing Bacon
as 'the most disquieting of English living artists',[5] Glass's
portrait reveals the creative power of his sitter with unassuming
humanity. Encouraged by Augustus John, who advised him
to photograph 'people who matter',[6] Glass commented: 'I am
not interested in Photography as such: I'm more interested
in the subject.'[7]

Glass made his name as photographer of the 'Portrait Gallery',
a series he ran every week in the *Sunday Times* between 1949
and 1961. Specially photographed for this weekly feature,
Glass's portrait reveals a glimpse into Bacon's working quarters,
and we can discern in the background an array of materials
and splattered paint. In the article's accompanying text, Glass
describes the studio floor as being deep in ephemeral printed
matter, and the curtains as crusty from Bacon's habit of wiping
his paint-covered hands upon them. At the time, Bacon
inhabited Overstrand Mansions with the actor Paul Danquah
and his partner, Peter Pollock, who offered Bacon a space to
live and work. The year that this photograph was taken Bacon
had his first show in Paris, at the Galerie Rive Droite, and
was also busy preparing his forthcoming London exhibition
at the Hanover Gallery. Vigorously working on the Van Gogh
series (see cats 14 and 16), Bacon's palette shifted during this
period from dark monochrome tones to vibrant colours and
gestural brushstrokes.

Fig.4 **Irving Penn** *Francis Bacon* 1962 Platinum palladium print 321 × 324mm

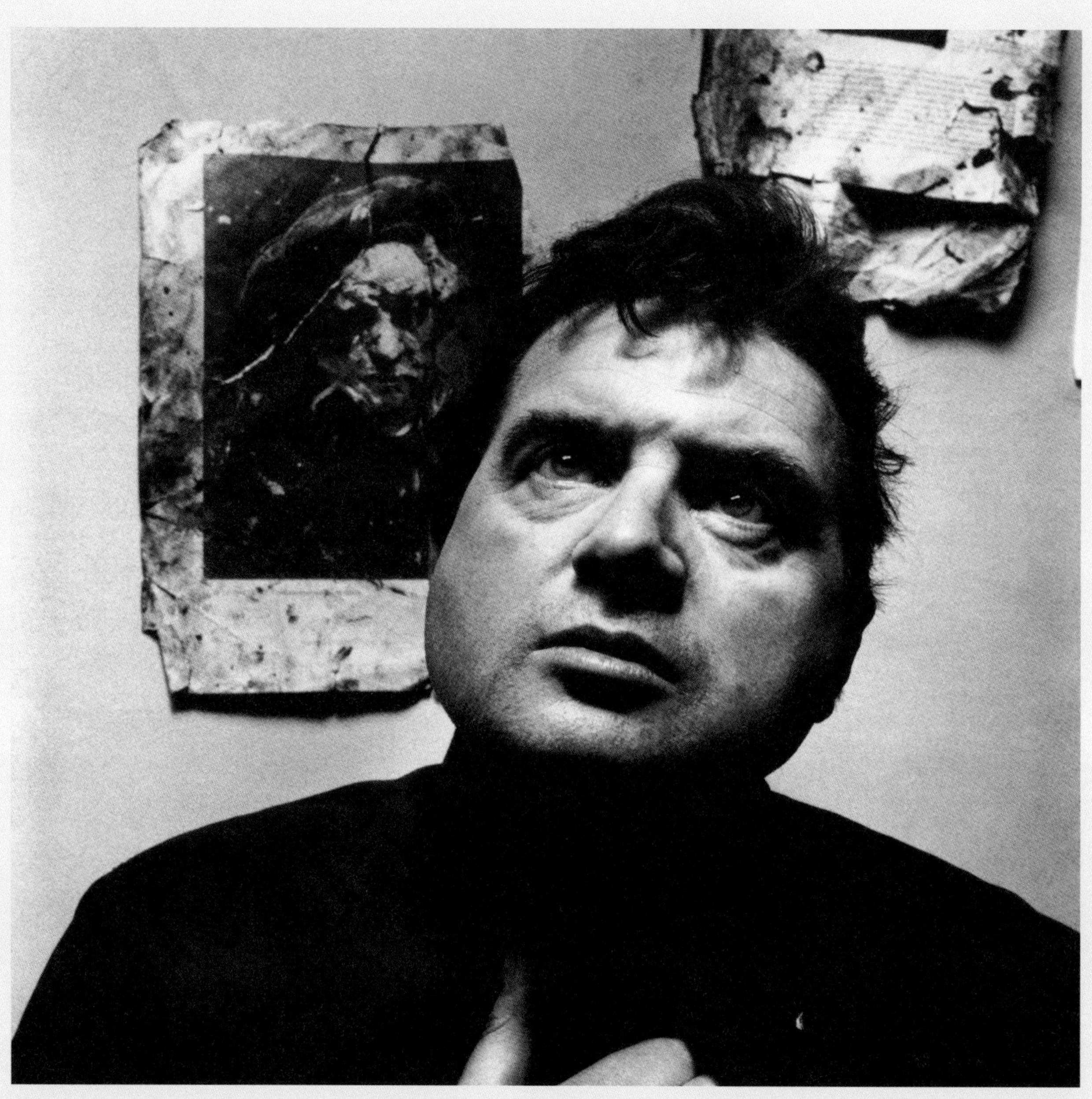

Irving Penn

This intimate image, made by the American photographer
Irving Penn, shows Bacon in his Reece Mews studio. Taken
from a low viewpoint, the painter gazes upward, appearing
almost reverent before the self-portrait of the Old Master
whose work acted as a major source of inspiration to him.
Much as Rembrandt documented the passage of time
through self-portraiture, Bacon also recorded the changes
in his appearance over a 36-year period, beginning in 1956
and ending with the unfinished portrait of 1991–2.[8] Numerous
fragments of Rembrandt's self-portraits, torn from books,
folded and splashed with paint, were found in Bacon's
studio. Bacon spoke in depth about this particular work by
Rembrandt, *Self-Portrait with Beret* (*c*.1659; p.18): 'Well, if you
think of the great Rembrandt self-portrait in Aix-en-Provence,
for instance, and if you analyse it, you will see that there are
hardly any sockets to the eyes, that it is almost completely
anti-illustrational. I think that the mystery of fact is conveyed
by an image being made out of non-rational marks.'[9]

In a second photograph from this sitting, Penn chose to make
a full-length depiction of Bacon, offering a glimpse into the
painter's own creative space. It was unusual for Penn to include
such a richly detailed environment, since the subjects of his
portraits from this period often filled the photographic frame.

Bacon owned a version of the bust-length photograph; his print
had extensive paint-markings and was possibly used as a source
for his self-portraits.

Bill Brandt

Modernist master Bill Brandt first photographed Bacon in
1951 for *Harper's Bazaar*. He photographed him again in 1963,
capturing the portrait opposite, which has become one
of the most celebrated images of the painter, even though
Bacon allegedly disliked the photograph. In a statement about
photography, Brandt commented: 'The good photographer
will produce a competent picture every time, whatever his
subject. But only when his subject makes an immediate and
direct appeal to his own interests will he produce a work of
distinction.'[10] This portrait of Bacon demonstrates Brandt's
unique vision as well as the characteristic high-contrast
printing style that he adopted during the 1960s.

Made at dusk in Primrose Hill, north London, Brandt used
a Hasselblad camera with a super wide-angle lens, which
allowed him to compose a cinematic scene. The film noir
atmosphere in the photograph is accentuated by Bacon's
signature black leather jacket. Portrayed in isolation on the
edge of the picture, with the far-reaching perspective and
distorted depth of field, it is with a sense of unease that
Bacon stands before the bleak landscape. When discussing
his photography Brandt explained: 'I found atmosphere to
be the spell that charged the commonplace with beauty ...
I only know it is a combination of elements, perhaps most
simply and yet most inadequately described in technical
terms of lighting and viewpoint, which reveals the subject
as familiar and yet strange.'[11] This photograph was made
just as portraiture was becoming an increasingly important
aspect of Bacon's *oeuvre*.

Fig.5   Bill Brandt   *Francis Bacon*   1963   Gelatin silver print   500 × 402mm

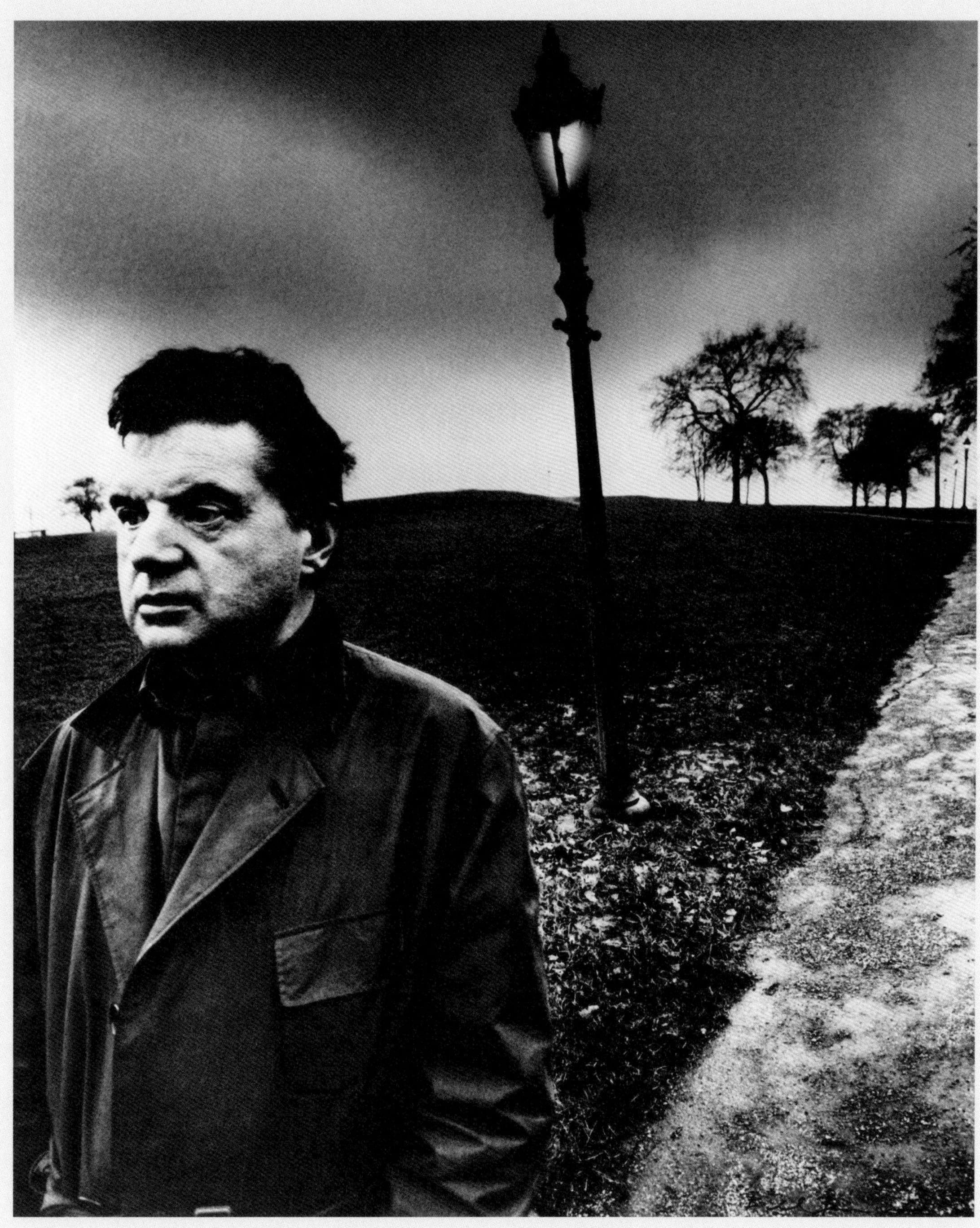

Jorge Lewinski

'Every time I photographed Bacon, I found him civil and helpful, a charming and fascinating conversationalist. But on one point he was always insistent: he would never be photographed with his paintings or at work. Painting is a solitary and all-absorbing activity; any outside interference would destroy his concentration.' [12]

Jorge Lewinski started to visit artists' studios in the early 1960s with the intention of making portraits that would reveal something of the inner world of each sitter. He built an impressive portfolio, offering a unique insight into twentieth-century British art, and photographed Bacon on several occasions. In this portrait, Lewinski depicts the painter from multiple viewpoints in double-exposure; Bacon's features are blurred and distorted, resembling his own painting style. Discussing his technique, Bacon commented, 'What I want to do is to distort the thing far beyond the appearance, but in the distortion to bring it back to a recording of the appearance.' [13] Bacon often used photographs as a source of inspiration, and Lewinski's portrait, with its shifting perspectives, may have helped in his preoccupation with self-examination and introspection. During the latter years of his life, Bacon worked intensely on numerous self-portraits, reflecting on his own mortality and the natural pattern of life.

Fig.6   **Jorge Lewinski**   *Francis Bacon*   1967   Gelatin silver print   360× 295mm

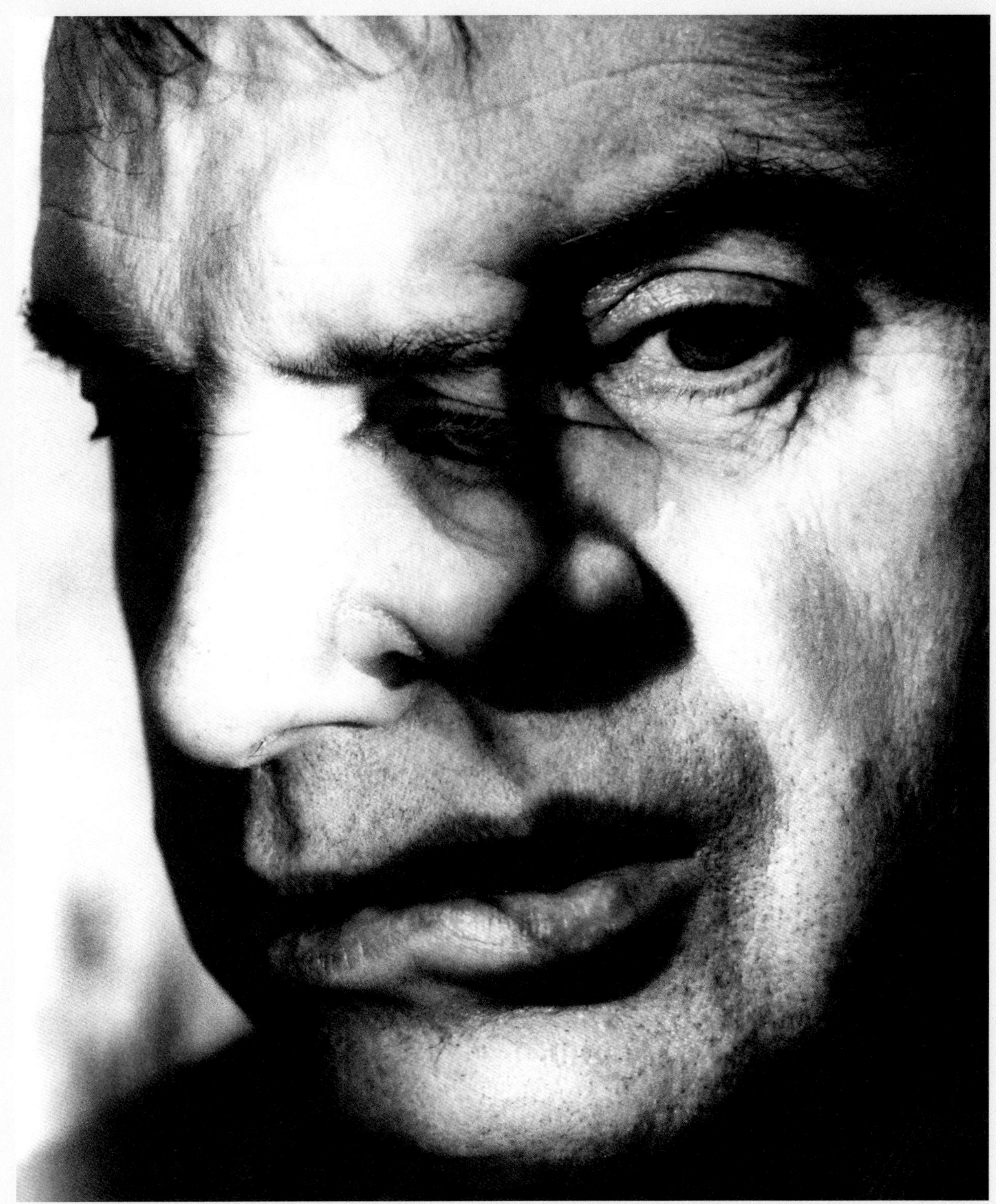

Peter Gidal

Peter Gidal is an acclaimed experimental filmmaker and writer whose films have featured in retrospectives at the Institute of Contemporary Arts, London, Centre Pompidou, Paris, and Anthology Film Archives, New York, amongst others. In 1969, he was studying at the Royal College of Art in London when he asked Francis Bacon to sit for a film portrait. The three-minute footage would become part of a group portrait entitled *Heads*, which features 31 sitters and was conceived as an homage to Andy Warhol, whom Gidal had met at The Factory in New York in 1967. Gidal's opportunity to include Bacon in his project came when the painter temporarily borrowed a studio at the Royal College of Art. Bacon responded with characteristic generosity, writing: 'I think your film sounds like a good idea. If it is any help to film me, please do so.'[14] In his studio, Bacon showed Gidal a painting of a lion he had recently begun and a book of animal photographs that he was using for reference. Gidal recalls: 'I placed him as I intended – standing, me standing opposite, and asked him to just stare into the 10:1 zoom lens for three minutes, with the instruction: "Don't do anything." (In other words, no talking, stay serious.)'[15]

As part of *Heads*, Bacon becomes absorbed into a 1960s cultural milieu with which he is not usually associated – including the artist Carolee Schneemann, as well as musicians Marianne Faithfull, Thelonious Monk and Charlie Watts. Gidal used a Second World War-issue Arriflex-S 16mm camera and each sitter appears in close-up for one minute. While some of the subjects betray nervousness or impatience, Bacon remained remarkably at ease throughout the full three minutes of filming. He had long been fascinated by cinema and the creative possibilities it presented, remarking to David Sylvester: 'I might make a film of all the images which have crowded into my brain.'[16]

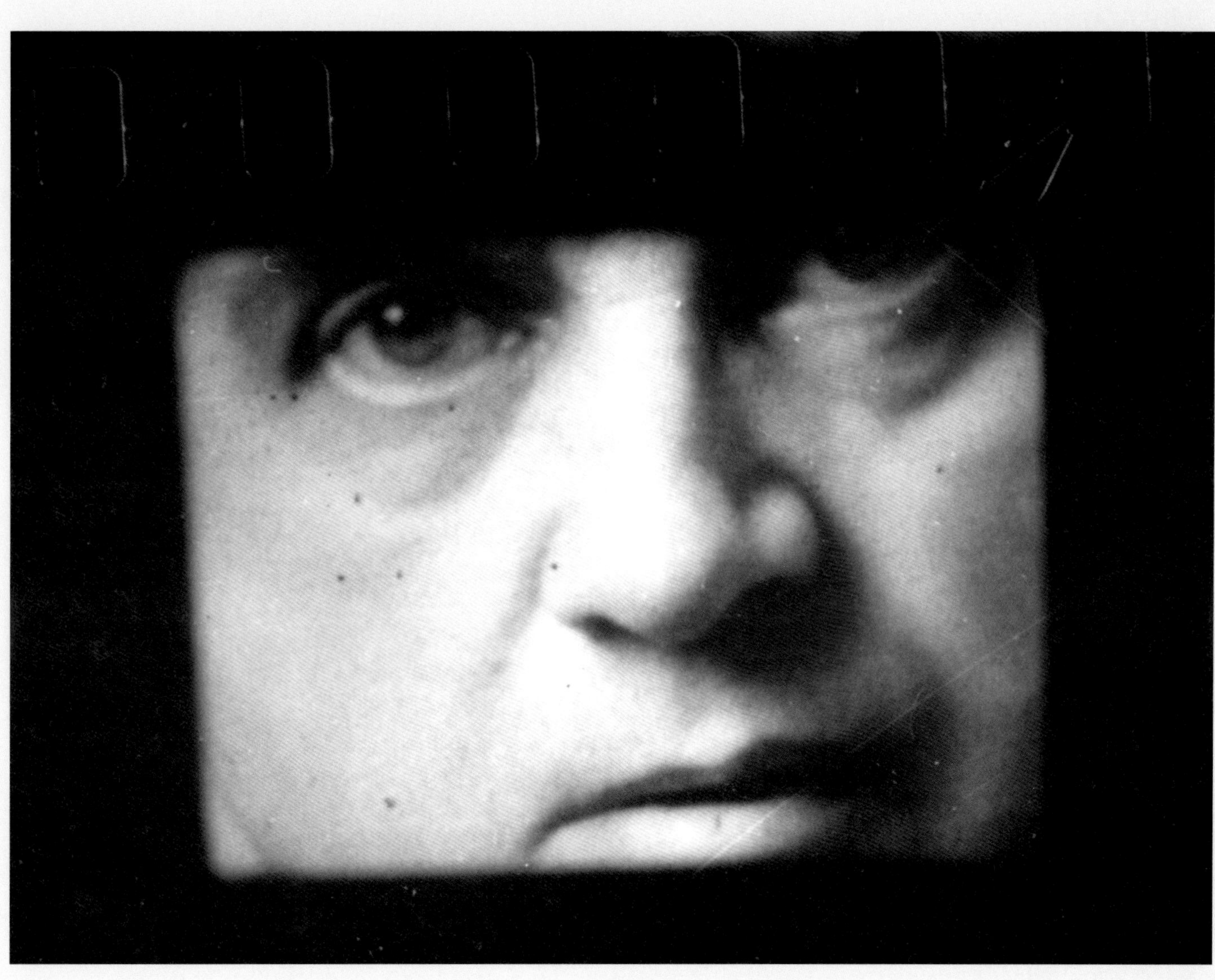

Fig.7 Peter Gidal *Francis Bacon* 1969 16mm film still

Mayotte Magnus

Mayotte Magnus visited Bacon's studio and home at 7 Reece
Mews on three occasions. It was always in the morning,
she explained, before his afternoon drinking sessions began.
Accompanied by her husband, the photographer Jorge
Lewinski, she remembered Bacon being extremely kind and
graceful, willing to pose and responding with good humour
to their demands. In the sitting-room-cum-bedroom there
was a large, cracked mirror. Bacon told them that someone
had thrown 'an ashtray at me and missed'.[17] Instantly both she
and Lewinski had the same idea: they wanted to photograph
Bacon and the mirror. The result is an image that offers
multiple angles of Bacon's persona and his surroundings.

Magnus remembers Bacon's studio as a space where
everything was seemingly in disarray; art books, paint,
brushes, photographs, canvases, newspaper cuttings and
other visual sources central to his art and way of working
were strewn across the floor. The sessions produced several
images, including one in which Bacon's easel is positioned
like a crucifix with Bacon behind it, his face dissected by
the wooden screw. During this period, Bacon painted a series
of 'black triptychs', an intense meditation on death in memory
of his partner George Dyer. He also worked intensively
on several self-portraits, completing ten in 1972, the highest
number for a single year in his career.[18]

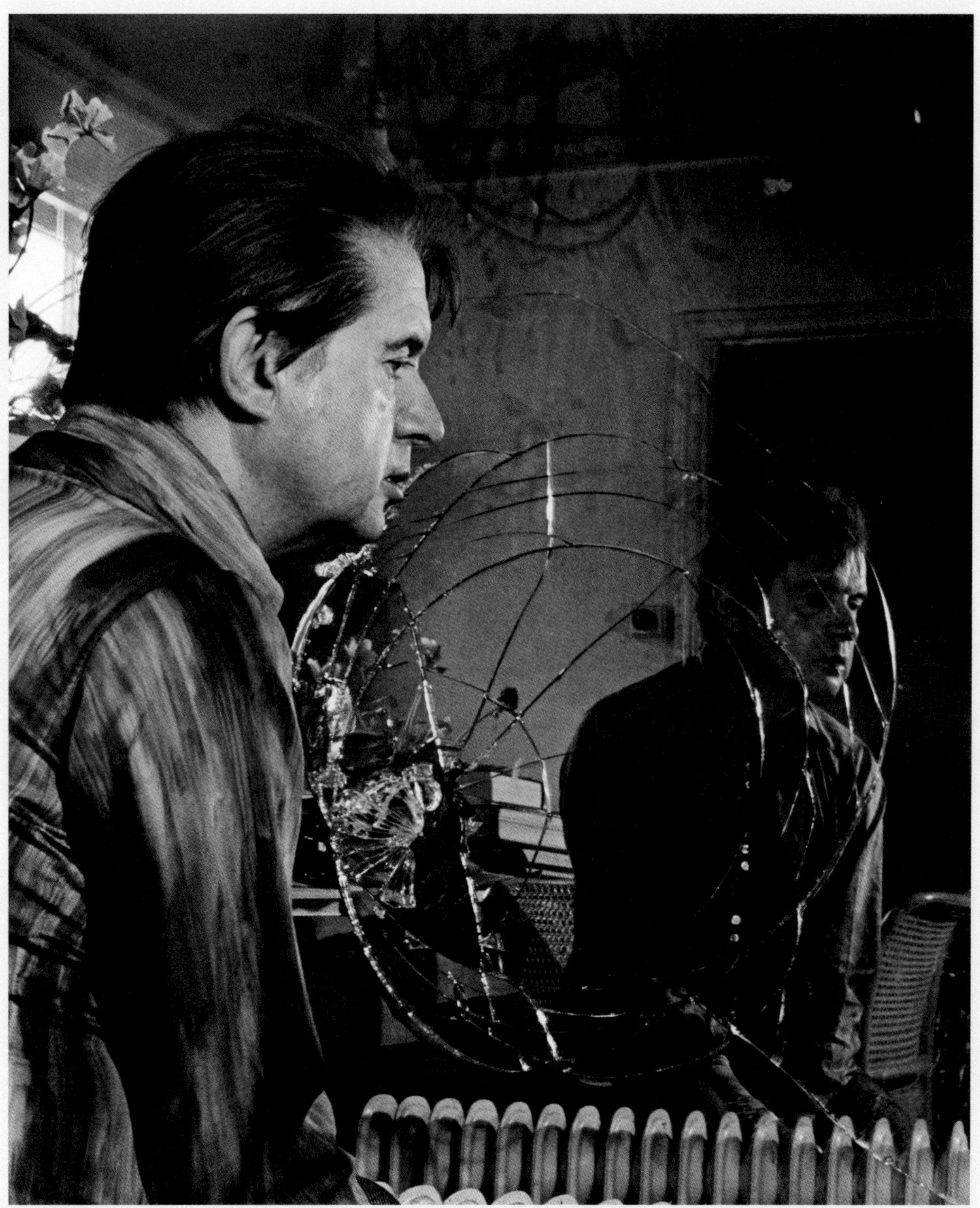

Fig.9   **Peter Stark**   *Francis Bacon*   1973–5   Cibachrome print   175 × 250mm

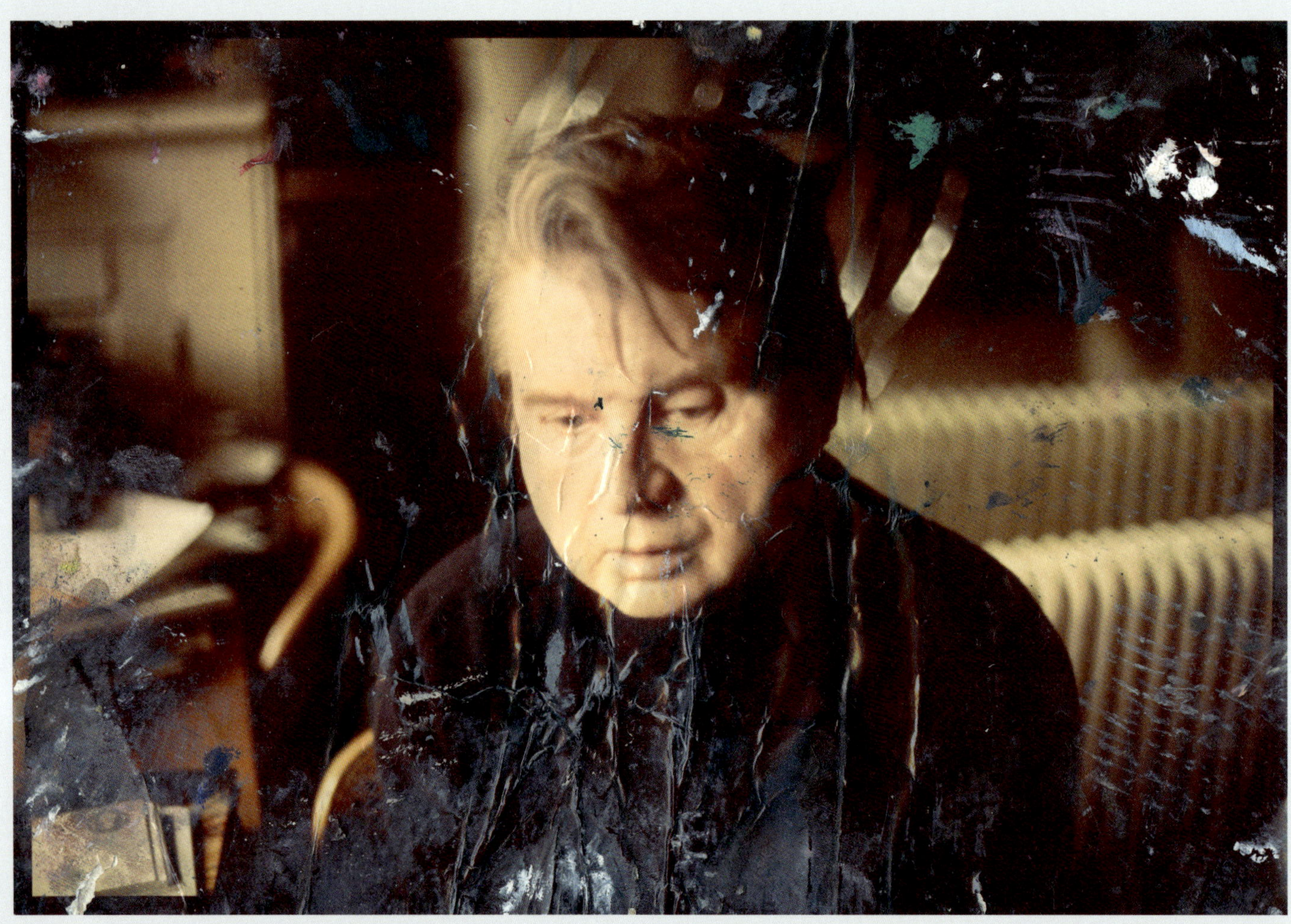

Peter Stark

Around 100 photographs by Peter Stark were found in Bacon's
studio after he died. Some of these prints were discovered
among layers of detritus and had been used as source material
for three of his self-portraits.[19] In 1961, Bacon moved to 7 Reece
Mews, a converted coach house, which provided the ideal
environment for him to work. 'For some reason, the moment
I saw this place I knew that I could work here. I am very
influenced by places – by the atmosphere of a room.'[20]

Bacon's biographers describe the significance of the setting:

*He maintained a small but essential difference between his studio
and the rooms where he cooked and slept. His studio he allowed to clog
with dog-eared books, yellowing newspapers, torn images, crumpled-up
boxes, empty cans. A mirror hung on the wall behind the easel,
in which he would sometimes glimpse himself as he worked. He flung
scabby paint, scraped dead from the easel, onto the floor and walls.
He rubbed dust from the studio into his paint to create texture and
modulate tone, as if the studio itself were a partner in his efforts.
The mess became a kind of mulch, nourishing his imagination, with
the art on the easel the only possible and momentary point of order.*[21]

Stark's intimate depictions of Bacon appearing pensive acquire
more significance with the additional creases and splodges
of paint from his work. A number show Bacon in his studio
with its notorious layers of artefacts (fig.9). Another captures
Bacon in the sitting room with portraits of George Dyer and
William Blake's plaster-cast mask in the background (p.9).
Stark also photographed Bacon in Soho, including at the
seafood restaurant Wheeler's with lifelong friend Muriel
Belcher, owner of the drinking club the Colony Room. Stark's
impressive body of work gives an insight into Bacon's life,
as well as serving as a sourcebook for his *oeuvre*.

Clare Shenstone

The artist Clare Shenstone met Francis Bacon in 1979 after he
had admired her degree show work at the Royal College of Art.
Bacon had been visiting to buy discounted wine from the Senior
Common Room, when he was drawn to a work by Shenstone
entitled *Janet*. Representing a woman's face, the piece was
moulded in relief in cloth with paint thinly applied. It was
likely to be the sculptural rendering of the subject's open
mouth and visible teeth that appealed to Bacon, who bought
the work and invited Shenstone to make his own portrait.

This photograph is part of a series taken towards the end of
a long sitting during which Shenstone had made numerous
drawings. Shenstone recalls: 'the extraordinary impact of my
first sitting ... He really did live in the present moment and
was utterly uncensored. As soon as I started drawing I felt
the intensity of his feelings [which were] constantly changing
and shifting both on his face and through his whole person ...
He would be warm and jolly one moment and aggressive
the next, then tearful the next.'[22] In this photograph, Bacon's
hands appear swollen – 'like the hands of an old pugilist'[23]
– a condition caused by prolonged contact with turpentine.
Shenstone was a regular visitor to Bacon's studio and produced
more than 100 portraits of the artist across a range of media,
including oil pastels and a remarkable cloth portrait relief,
which Bacon also acquired.

Fig.10   Clare Shenstone   *Francis Bacon*   1979   35mm colour transparency

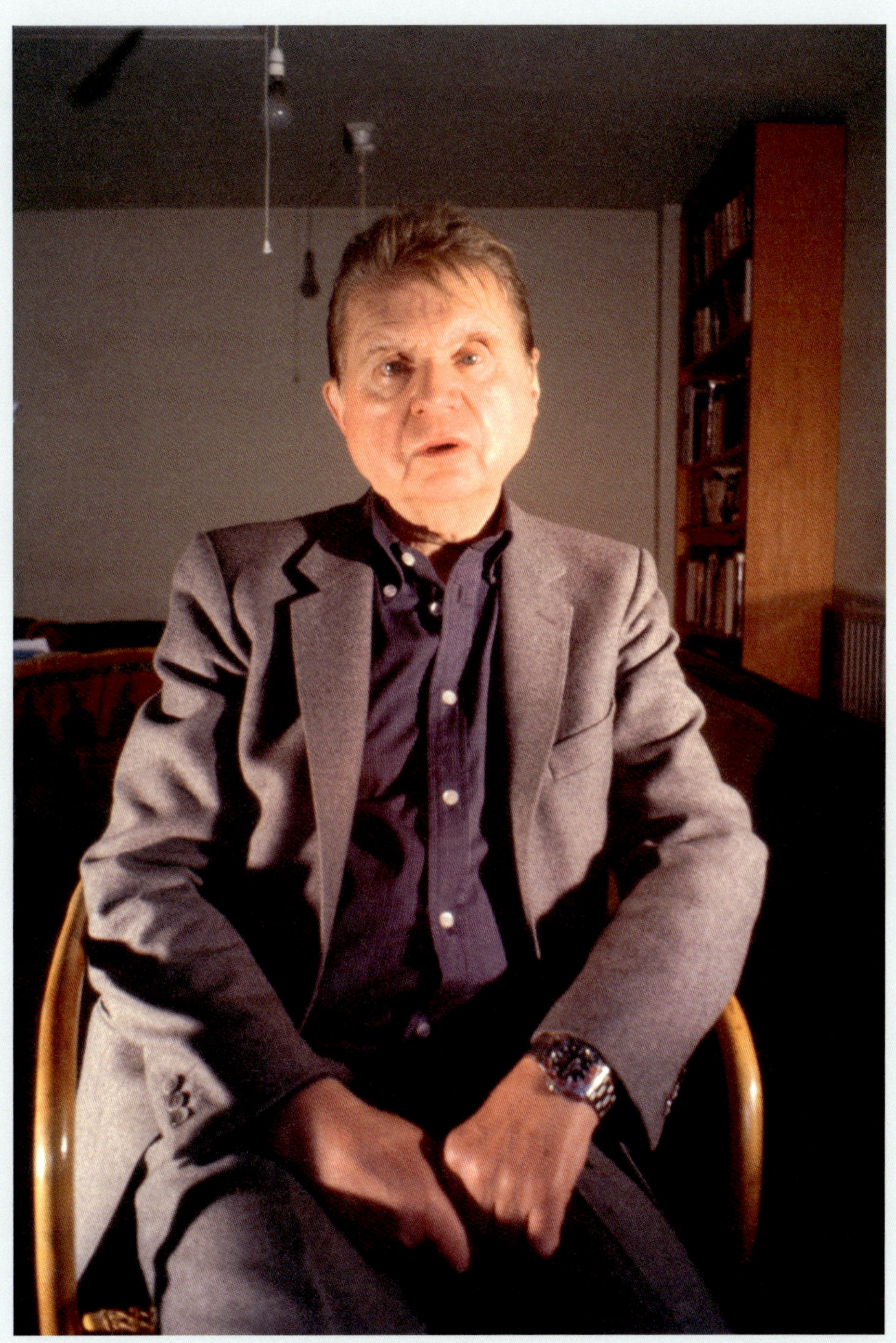

Fig.11 **Guy Bourdin** *Francis Bacon* 1986 (printed 2017) Chromogenic print 307 × 335mm

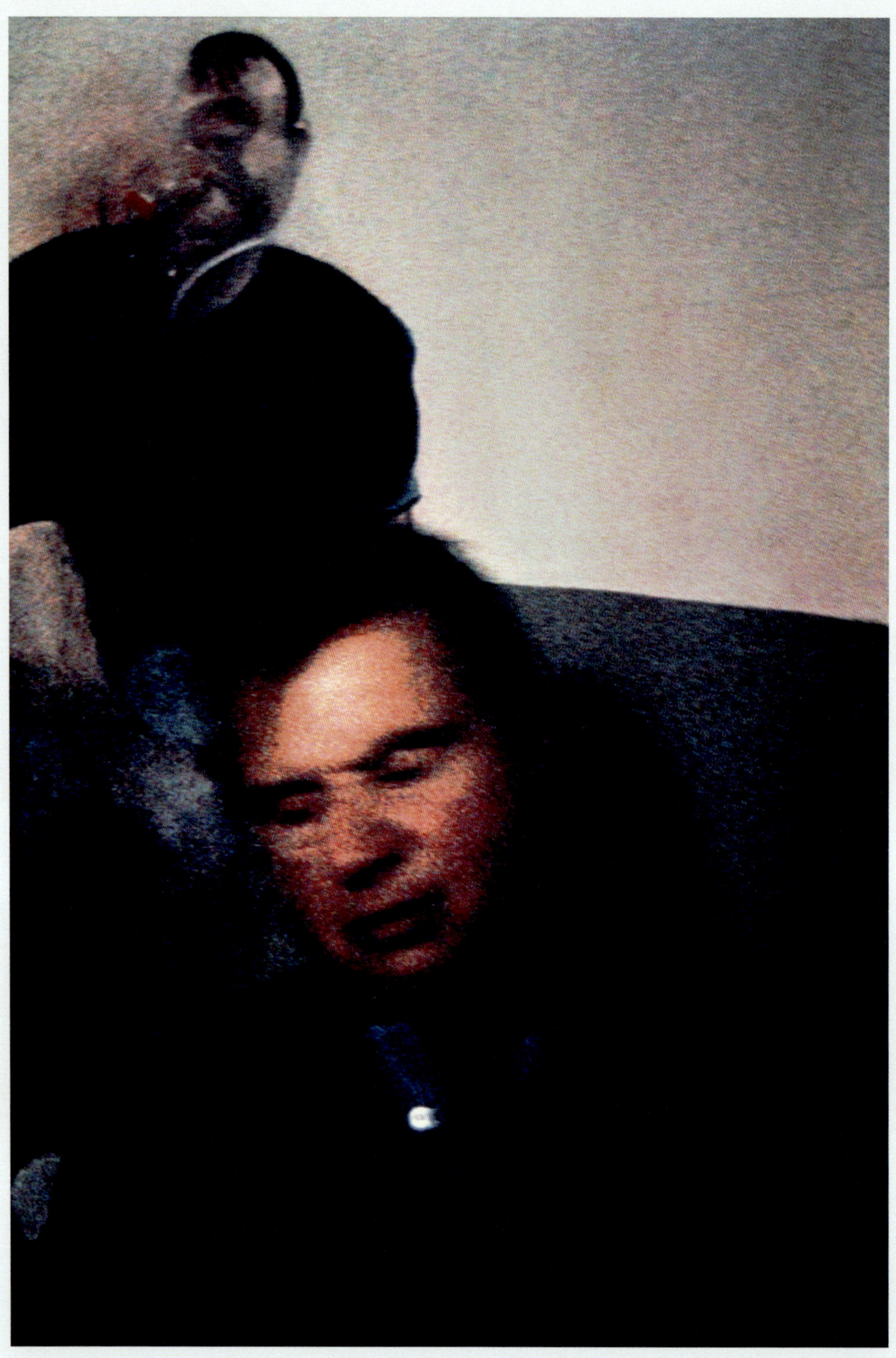

Guy Bourdin

French avant-garde fashion photographer Guy Bourdin was
fascinated by Bacon, sometimes referencing the painter's
imagery in his own works. In 1986 he was commissioned
by French *Vogue* to make this portrait. Using Polaroid film,
Bourdin recreated the swirling forms of Bacon's own paintings
as he posed in front of his work *Study for a Self-Portrait – Triptych*
(1985–6) at the Marlborough Gallery in London. Echoing
Bacon's assertion: 'I want a very ordered image, but I want it
to come about by chance,'[22] Bourdin explained, *'Je ne suis pas un
metteur en scène. Juste un ajusteur du hazard'* ('I am not a director.
Just an adjuster of chance').[24]

The photograph opposite exemplifies how, through the sitter's
movements, Bourdin was able to capture something unique
and expressive, while also alluding to Bacon's own self-portrait,
seen here emerging in the background. This photograph was
taken the year after Bacon's second retrospective at the Tate,
when the then-director Alan Bowness declared: 'No other artist
in our century has presented the human predicament with such
insight and feeling.'[25] During this period, with Bacon in his
seventies, his paintings showed a greater use of monochromatic
backgrounds, as well as the introduction of aerosol spray paint,
as seen in his self-portrait.

Neil Libbert

Portrait and press photographer Neil Libbert made this
photograph in the doorway of Bacon's Reece Mews studio
on the painter's eightieth birthday, 28 October 1989. In this
candid depiction of the artist, he captures an ordinary moment
of everyday life, as Bacon returns home with his shopping.
'I did happen to come upon him by chance,'[26] explained
Libbert, who was Bacon's neighbour.

Libbert spent more than 50 years working for national
newspapers, and had previously photographed Bacon several
times, including in and around Soho. At the time of this
photograph, Libbert was contracted to the *Observer* newspaper
and offered this image to them. It appeared on the front page
the next day. To mark Bacon's birthday, the Marlborough
Gallery organised a party and a celebratory exhibition, but
as Valerie Beston explained, Bacon did not attend the opening:
'He says he's not up for it.'[27] Soon after his birthday, Bacon
was diagnosed with cancer of the kidney. Despite successfully
undergoing surgery, his health was in slow decline.

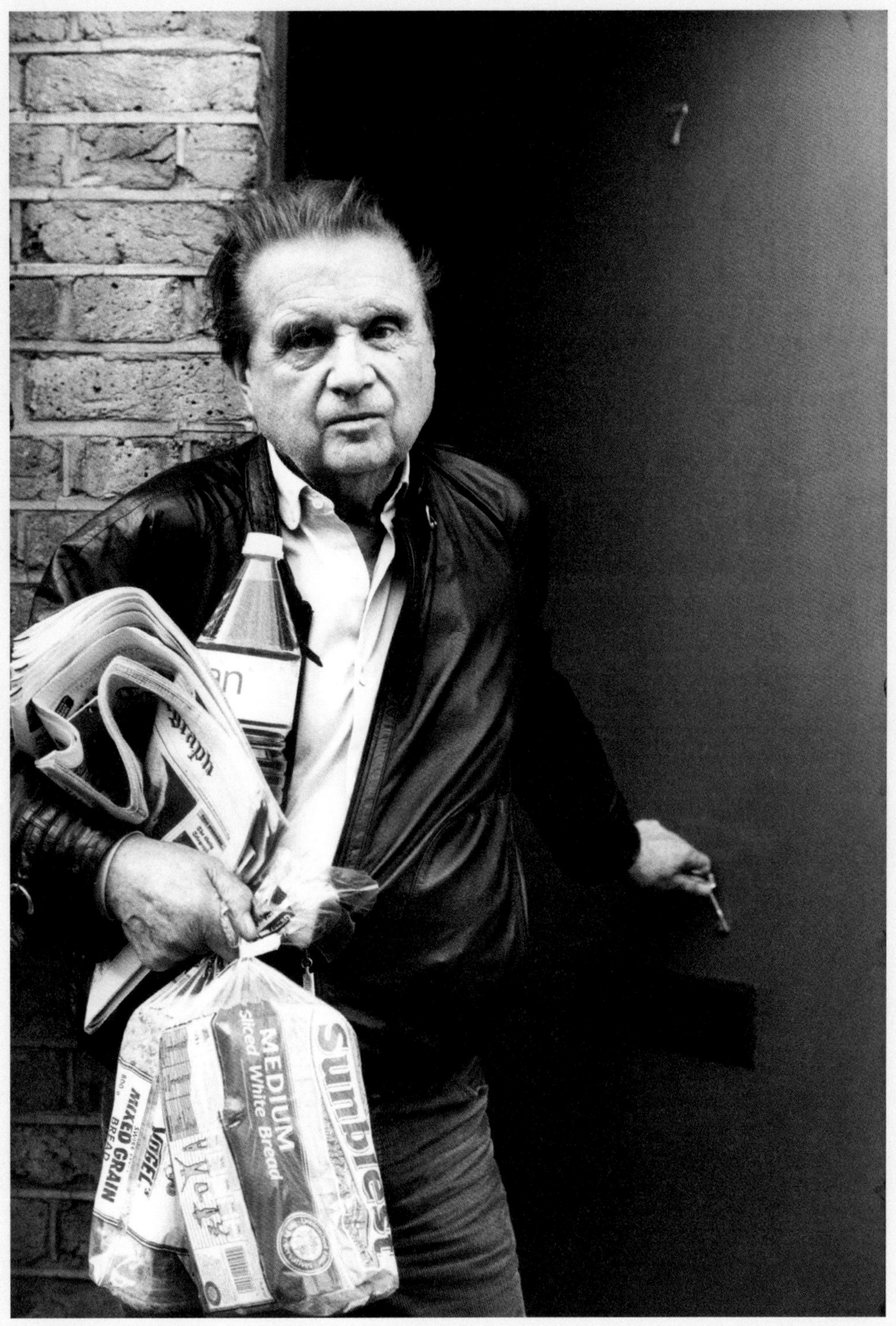

Fig.12 Neil Libbert *Francis Bacon* 1989 Gelatin silver print 343 × 231mm

Endnotes

Full details of the books cited in the notes are listed alphabetically by author in the bibliography (pp.210–1).

Francis Bacon: Human Presence

1 Sylvester, *Interviews with Francis Bacon*, 1980, p.105.
2 Ibid., p.18.
3 Ibid., p.63.
4 Domino, *Francis Bacon: Taking Reality by Surprise*, p.82.
5 Geldzahler, *Francis Bacon: Recent Paintings*, p.11.
6 Harrison, *In Camera*, p.8.
7 Sylvester, *Interviews with Francis Bacon*, 1980, p.122.
8 Interview with Hugh Davies quoted in Davies and Yard, *Francis Bacon*, p.11.
9 Stevens and Swan, *Francis Bacon: Revelations*, p.51.
10 Ibid., p.511.
11 Sylvester, *Interviews with Francis Bacon*, 1980, p.68.
12 Ibid., p.71.
13 Harrison, *In Camera*, p.55.
14 Sylvester, *Interviews with Francis Bacon*, 1980, p.82.
15 Gale and Stephens, *Francis Bacon*, p.26.
16 Sylvester, *Interviews with Francis Bacon*, 1980, p.48.
17 Stevens and Swan, *Francis Bacon: Revelations*, p.410.
18 Ibid.
19 Beaton, *The Restless Years*, p.101.
20 Ibid.
21 Stevens and Swan, *Francis Bacon: Revelations*, pp.464–5.
22 Sylvester, *Interviews with Francis Bacon*, 1980, p.38.
23 Ibid., p.41.
24 Peppiatt, *Francis Bacon: Studies for a Portrait*, p.167.
25 Sylvester, *Interviews with Francis Bacon*, 1980, p.58.
26 Bacon, Francis, 'Matthew Smith: A Painter's Tribute', in Rothenstein, *Matthew Smith*, p.12.
27 Sylvester, *Interviews with Francis Bacon*, 1980, p.81.
28 Dawson, *Francis Bacon in Dublin*, p.16.
29 Sylvester, *Interviews with Francis Bacon*, 1980, p.12.
30 Muir, *John Deakin: Photographs*, p.32.
31 Ibid., p.10.
32 Muir, *Gods and Monsters*, p.14.
33 Sylvester, *Interviews with Francis Bacon*, 1980, p.73.
34 Ibid., p.67.
35 Moraes, *Henrietta*, p.71.
36 Muir, *A Maverick Eye*, p.14.
37 Muir, *Gods and Monsters*, p.19.
38 Sylvester, *Interviews with Francis Bacon*, 1980, p.133.
39 Ibid, p.129.
40 Geldzahler, *Francis Bacon: Recent Paintings*, p.75.

The Portrait Emerges

p.23 Sylvester, *Interviews with Francis Bacon*, 1980, p.48.

Francis Bacon's Close-Up Heads: An Overlooked Source

This is an abridged version of the author's essay 'Bacon and Lerski: A Possible Dialogue' published in *Francis Bacon – New Studies: Centenary Essays* (2009), edited by Martin Harrison.

1 See Harrison, *In Camera*, and Mellor, David, 'Film, Fantasy, History in Francis Bacon', in Gale and Stephens, *Francis Bacon*, pp.50–63.
2 Correspondence between Lerski and the Museum of Modern Art is kept in the Lerski Archive, Museum Folkwang, Essen.
3 Eskildsen and Horak, *Helmar Lerski, Lichtbildner*, p.24.
4 Harrison, *In Camera*, p.26.
5 Mellor, 'Film, Fantasy, History in Francis Bacon', in Gale and Stephens, *Francis Bacon* p.51.
6 See Pipe, Francesca, 'Eric Allden's Diary', in Harrison (ed.), *Inside Francis Bacon*, p.43.
7 Known in German as *Verwandlungen durch Licht*. Although the series was not published as a book, exhibitions of it were held in Lerski's lifetime and, less frequently, after his death.
8 *Cavalcade*, vol.I, no.24, London, 27 August 1938, quoted in Ebner, *Metamorphosen des Gesichts*, p.102. The show was also noticed in the *Observer*, *News Chronicle* and *The Times*, as well as in the August 1938 issue of *Photography*.
9 The author is grateful to Martin Harrison for this information.
10 Sylvester, *Interviews with Francis Bacon*, 1980, pp.84, 134, 141.
11 Harrison, *In Camera*, pp.170–3.
12 The Lerski photographs are cat. nos 327–31. No.328 (*Chauffeur's Wife*) is illustrated in the Hayward catalogue. Material in the Barry Joule Archive suggests that Bacon's interest in Lerski continued in the 1980s: see Calvocoressi, Richard, 'Bacon and Lerski: A Possible Dialogue', in Harrison (ed.), *Francis Bacon – New Studies*, pp.54–5, 247–8, notes 23–5.
13 The 1979 triptych is illustrated in the 1980 edition of Sylvester's *Interviews with Francis Bacon*, at the beginning of interview no.6, p.144. This interview and no.7 were based on recordings made in March, August and September 1979. Since no.6 opens with Sylvester remarking that Bacon has been painting a lot of self-portraits, it is reasonable to assume that he saw the triptych at Marlborough Fine Art, Bacon's dealers, or in Bacon's studio before or during the first interview, i.e. March 1979. This was only a couple of months after the close of the Hayward exhibition. At the time, Sylvester was on the art panel of the Arts Council, which organised the *Neue Sachlichkeit* show.

Beyond Appearance

p.39 Sylvester, *Interviews with Francis Bacon*, 1980, p.120.
1 Ibid.
2 Russell, *Francis Bacon*, p.141.
3 Winner, Calvin, 'Portrait of Lisa', 2020, https://www.sainsburycentre.ac.uk/art-and-objects/rls-6-portrait-of-lisa/ [accessed October 2023].
4 Ibid.
5 Sylvester, *Looking Back at Francis Bacon*, pp.49–50.
6 Scott, Yvonne, 'Francis Bacon: "… to be an Egyptian"', in Harrison (ed.), *Bacon Review*, 1, p.26.

Queer Attachments to Francis Bacon

1 Cary Parkes, James, 'Small Portrait Studies by Francis Bacon', *Pink Paper*, 5 November 1993, p.17.
2 Ibid.
3 Ibid.
4 See for example, Ofield, Simon, 'Wrestling with Francis Bacon', *Oxford Art Journal*, vol.24, iss.1, 2001, pp.113–30; Hornsey, Richard, 'Francis Bacon and the Photobooth: Facing the Homosexual in Post-war Britain', *Visual Culture in Britain*, vol.8, iss.2, 2007, pp.83–103; and Janes, Dominic, 'Queer Juxtapositions in the Art of Francis Bacon and Lilliput Magazine', *Visual Culture in Britain*, vol.21, iss.3, 2020, pp.275–95.
5 Salter, *Art and Masculinity in Post-War Britain*, pp.53–77.
6 Edwards, Simon, 'Notes Towards Some Aspects of Gay Culture', *Lunch*, 1 February 1973, pp.23–5.
7 Cooper, Emmanuel, 'Good Art? Bad Art? Gay Art?', *Gay News*, 16 November 1978, pp.18–9.
8 Saslow, James M., 'The Ascent of the Gay Esthetic: Toward a Post-Pornographic Art', *Advocate*, 26 June 1980, pp.20–1, 27–9;

Cooper, Emmanuel, 'Art', *Gay Times*, July 1985, p.69; Saslow, 'Out of the Closet and into the Museum', *Advocate*, 1 September 1987, pp.52–4, 108–9.
9 Sanderson, Terry, 'Mediawatch', *Gay Times*, May 1988, pp.19–21; Various authors, 'Fighting censorship tooth and clause', *Sunday Times*, 3 April 1988, p.30.
10 'South Bank Show to air gay art', *Pink Paper*, 8 September 1988, p.5.

Lucian Freud & Francis Bacon: A Friendship of Two Halves

1 Freud was inspired by a scene in one of his childhood books, *Emil and the Detectives* by Erich Kästner (1929), where a town is covered with posters overnight.
2 Lucian Freud quoted in Gayford, Martin, 'Artist "mourns" missing work in photographs', *Daily Telegraph*, 22 June 2001, p.3.
3 Ibid.
4 See newspapers in National Portrait Gallery Collected Archives LMF/5/29.
5 Hoban, *Lucian Freud: Eyes Wide Open*, p.66.
6 Feaver, *The Lives of Lucian Freud: Youth*, p.367.
7 Interview with Sophie de Stempel in *Francis Bacon: First Impressions*, documentary, The Estate of Francis Bacon, 1 February 2022.
8 Letter held at the National Portrait Gallery, London. (Records associated with Lucian Freud and his family, part of accession 2024/01)
9 Feaver, *The Lives of Lucian Freud: Fame*, p.94.
10 Feaver, *Lucian Freud: Drawings*, p.14.
11 The only other painting of Bacon by Freud was started between 1956 and 1957, but was never finished.
12 Lucian Freud, 'In Conversation with M. Auping', in Howgate (ed.), *Lucian Freud: Portraits*, p.209.
13 Feaver, *The Lives of Lucian Freud: Youth*, p.371.

14 Interview with Sophie de Stempel in *Francis Bacon: First Impressions*, documentary, The Estate of Francis Bacon, 1 February 2022.
15 Freud is quoted as saying this to his friend Alice Weldon in Stevens and Swan, *Francis Bacon: Revelations*, p.579.
16 Held at the National Portrait Gallery Collected Archives, LMF/1/47/2.

Painting from the Masters

p.57 Stevens and Swan, *Francis Bacon: Revelations*, note 4, p.249.
1 Sylvester, *Interviews with Francis Bacon*, 1980, p.38.
2 Davies, *Francis Bacon: The Papal Portraits*, 2002, p.18.
3 Russell, *Francis Bacon*, p.91.
4 Ibid., p.92.
5 Sylvester, *Interviews with Francis Bacon*, 1980, p.66.

Corners of Filth & Fantasy: Bacon's Studios as Self-Expression

1 Johnson, *Roy de Maistre*, pp.20–2.
2 Zola, *Mes Haines*, p.25.
3 Ibid., p.347.
4 Van Gogh, Vincent, *The Letters*, https://vangoghletters.org/vg/letters/let249/letter.html [accessed 5 December 2023]
5 Ogden and Edwards, *7 Reece Mews*, p.13.
6 Beaton, *The Restless Years*, pp.100–2.
7 Ibid.
8 Kemp (ed.), *Leonardo on Painting*, pp.38–9.
9 Ibid.
10 Hall, *The Artist's Studio*, pp.10–ff.
11 Murger, *Bohemians of the Latin Quarter*, p.16.
12 Ibid, pp.40–3.
13 Daniels, Rebecca, 'Francis Bacon and Walter Sickert: "Images Which Unlock Other Images"',

Burlington Magazine, vol.151, no.1273, 2009, pp.224–30.
14 Penrose, *Picasso*, pp.412–3; Hall, *The World as Sculpture*, p.292.
15 Liberman, *The Artist in His Studio*, p.32.
16 Ogden and Edwards, *7 Reece Mews*, p.13.
17 Cappock, *Francis Bacon's Studio*, p.34.
18 Hall, *The World as Sculpture*, p.297.

Self-Portraits

p.75 Sylvester, *Interviews with Francis Bacon*, 1980, p.129.
1 Ibid.
2 Branczik, *Francis Bacon Self-Portrait*, p.28.
3 Ordovas (ed.), *Irrational Marks*, p.7.

Study from a Human Body: Francis Bacon & Medical Self-Portraiture

1 Davies, *Francis Bacon: The Papal Portraits*, 2001, p.64.
2 See also Harrison (ed.), *Inside Francis Bacon*.
3 Sylvester, *Interviews with Francis Bacon*, 1987, p.176.
4 Behr, Edward, 'Agony and the Artist', *Newsweek*, 24 January 1977, p.48.
5 I explore the implications of Bacon's eczema on his work in Pretorius, Sophie, 'A Pathological Painter: Francis Bacon and the control of suffering', in Harrison (ed.), *Inside Francis Bacon*, pp.184–9.
6 For a more detailed exploration of Bacon's revisions see Harrison and Pretorius, *Revisions: Francis Bacon in the Act of Painting*.
7 Harrison and Daniels, *Francis Bacon: Catalogue Raisonné*, p.1002.
8 For explicit use of red in the whites of eyes in Bacon's portraits of 1972, see Harrison and Daniels, *Francis Bacon: Catalogue Raisonné*, nos 72–04, 72–06, 72–08, 72–11, 72–23 and 72–13.

Friends & Lovers

p.103 Sylvester, *Interviews with Francis Bacon*, 1980, p.73.

Robert & Lisa Sainsbury

1 Benthall, Jonathan, 'An Interview with Sir Robert and Lady Sainsbury', *Anthropology Today*, vol.5, no.1, February 1989, p.2.
2 Peppiatt, *Francis Bacon in the 1950s*, p.155.
3 Ibid.
4 Stevens and Swan, *Francis Bacon: Revelations*, p.481.
5 Hooper (ed.), *Robert and Lisa Sainsbury Collection*, vol.1, cat.57, p.103.
6 Sylvester, *Trapping Appearance*, p.30.
7 Ibid.

Peter Lacy

1 Peppiatt, *Francis Bacon in the 1950s*, p.33, and Stevens and Swan, *Francis Bacon: Revelations*, p.358.
2 Peppiatt, *Francis Bacon in the 1950s*, p.40.
3 Stevens and Swan, *Francis Bacon: Revelations*, p.357.
4 Ibid., p.357.
5 Ibid., p.378.
6 Ibid., p.361.
7 Farson, *The Gilded Gutter Life of Francis Bacon*, p.139.

Muriel Belcher

1 Farson, *The Gilded Gutter Life of Francis Bacon*, pp.44–79.
2 Ibid., p.56.
3 Ibid., p.57.

Lucian Freud

1 Russell, *Lucian Freud*, p.7.
2 Feaver, *Freud at the Correr*, p.34.
3 Aronson, Stephen M. L., 'Sophisticated Lady', *Town & Country*, September 1993, p.147.

Isabel Rawsthorne

1 Jacobi, *Out of the Cage*, p.22.
2 Ibid., p.234.
3 *London–Paris: New Trends in Painting and Sculpture, An Exhibition of the Work of 16 Artists*, Institute of Contemporary Arts, New Burlington Galleries, 7 March – 4 April 1950.
4 See Jacobi, Carol, 'Picasso's Portraits of Isabel Rawsthorne', *Burlington*, vol.159, no.1374, September 2017.
5 Jacobi, *Out of the Cage*, pp.399–400.
6 Ibid., p.356.

Henrietta Moraes

1 Moraes, *Henrietta*, pp.72–3.
2 Ibid., p.71.
3 Ibid., p.72.
4 Ibid., p.73.

George Dyer

1 Lee Dyer interviewed in *Bacon's Arena*, documentary, BBC Four archive, 19 March 2005.
2 Terry Danziger-Miles quoted in Stevens and Swan, *Francis Bacon: Revelations*, p.506.
3 Quoted in Peppiatt *Francis Bacon: Anatomy of an Enigma*, p.259.
4 Stevens and Swan, *Francis Bacon: Revelations*, p.510.
5 Feaver, *The Lives of Lucian Freud: Youth*, p.583.
6 Stevens and Swan, *Francis Bacon: Revelations*, p.546.

John Edwards

1 Stevens and Swan, *Francis Bacon: Revelations*, p.619.

'I've decided to paint a few of my friends': Isabel Rawsthorne & Henrietta Moraes

1   Harrison, Martin, 'The Women in Bacon's Life', in Ordovas (ed.), *Bacon's Women*, pp.9, 16.
2   Hoare, Philip, 'Obituary: Henrietta Moraes', *Independent*, 16 January 1999; see also 'Isabel Rawsthorne: Obituary', *The Times*, 13 February 1992.
3   Ibid.
4   Maubert, Franck, 'Bacon: L'Ecorché solitaire', *Paris Match*, 14 May 1992, p.93.
5   Moraes, *Henrietta*, p.77; see also Jacobi, *Out of the Cage*.
6   Davies, Hugh, 'Interviewing Bacon, 1973', in Harrison (ed.), *Francis Bacon – New Studies*, p.96; *Alberto Giacometti, Sculpture, Paintings*, Arts Council Gallery, London, 4 June–9 July 1955; *Alberto Giacometti: Sculpture Paintings Drawings 1913–65*, Tate Gallery, London, 17 July – 30 August 1965.
7   Sylvester, *Looking Back at Francis Bacon*, pp.236–7.
8   Tate Gallery Report 1966–7, HMSO, London, 1967, p.18.
9   Withers, Jane and Anthony Fawcett, 'Carcasses and Crucifixes', *The Times*, 20 May 1985, p.10.
10 Davies, 'Interviewing Bacon, 1973', in Harrison (ed.), *Francis Bacon – New Studies*, p.97.
11 Ibid.
12 Moraes, *Henrietta*, p.77.
13 Davies, 'Interviewing Bacon, 1973', in Harrison (ed.), *Francis Bacon – New Studies*, p.95.
14 Ibid., pp.102, 111.
15 To view Rawsthorne's portraits and other paintings, see the film *Isabel Rawsthorne Rediscovered: The Poetry in Things*, Heni, 2022, https://www.youtube.com/watch?v=h6nNQ2-0P68&ab_channel=HENITalks [accessed 13 February 2024].
16 T.S. Eliot, 'Ulysses, Order, and Myth', *The Dial*, November 1923.
17 Farson, *The Gilded Gutter Life of Francis Bacon*, p.165.
18 Henrietta Moraes quoted in Parsey, Martha, *Model and Artist: Henrietta Moraes and Francis Bacon*, documentary, 1993.
19 Ibid.

Ghosts in the Glass: Filming Francis Bacon

1   Busfield, Steve, 'Melvyn Bragg and the South Bank Show: Five Moments to Savour', *Guardian*, 6 May 2009.

Picturing the Artist: Camera Portraits of Francis Bacon

1   Sylvester, *Interviews with Francis Bacon*, 1980, p.30.
2   Beaton, *The Restless Years*, p.101.
3   Ibid., p.102.
4   Ibid., p.103.
5   Glass, Douglas, 'Portrait Gallery', *Sunday Times*, 5 May 1957.
6   Mellor, *Reflected Glory*, p.11.
7   Ibid., p.5.
8   Ordovas (ed.), *Irrational Marks*, p.42.
9   Sylvester, *Interviews with Francis Bacon*, 1980, p.58.
10 Warburton (ed.), *Bill Brandt: Camera in London*, p.86.
11 Ibid., p.87.
12 Lewinski, *Portrait of the Artist*, p.21.
13 Sylvester, *Interviews with Francis Bacon*, 1980, p.40.
14 The author is grateful to Peter Gidal for this information.
15 Ibid.
16 The author is grateful to Mayotte Magnus for this information.
17 Harrison and Daniels, *Francis Bacon: Catalogue Raisonné*, p.998.
18 Ibid., p.1042.
19 Sylvester, *Interviews with Francis Bacon*, 2007, p.89.
20 Stevens and Swan, *Francis Bacon: Revelations*, p.465.
21 Sylvester, *Interviews with Francis Bacon*, 1980, p.56.
22 Charles Saumarez Smith quoted in *Clare Shenstone: Anima*, p.8.
23 The author is grateful to Clare Shenstone for this information.
24 Quoted in Pilto, Carrie, 'Guy Bourdin: Francis Bacon's *Painting 1946*', https://www.mbartfoundation.com/francis-bacon-the-artist/foundation-focus/guy-bourdin-francis-bacons-painting-1946-in-the-mirror-of-fashion-photography/ [accessed 4 November 2023].
25 Stevens and Swan, *Francis Bacon: Revelations*, p.638.
26 The author is grateful to Neil Libbert for this information.
27 Valerie Beston was an art dealer and administrator at Marlborough Gallery. During her 50-year tenure, she supported and nurtured the careers of many artists, most notably Francis Bacon. See Stevens and Swan, *Francis Bacon: Revelations*, p.674.

Bibliography

Ades, Dawn and Andrew Forge, *Francis Bacon* (Thames & Hudson, London, 1985)

Archimbaud, Michel, *Francis Bacon in Conversation with Michel Archimbaud* (Phaidon, London, 1993)

Arya, Rina, *Francis Bacon: Painting in a Godless World* (Lund Humphries, Farnham, 2012)

Beaton, Cecil, *The Restless Years: Diaries 1955–63* (Weidenfeld & Nicolson, London, 1976)

Borel, France and Milan Kundera, *Bacon: Portraits and Self-Portraits* (Thames & Hudson, New York, 1996)

Branczik, Alexander, *Francis Bacon Self-Portrait* (Sotheby's, London, 2007)

Calvocoressi, Richard and Martin Hammer, *Francis Bacon: Portraits and Heads* (National Galleries of Scotland, Edinburgh, 2005)

Calvocoressi, Richard and Martin Harrison, *Francis Bacon: Couplings* (Gagosian, London, 2019)

Calvocoressi, Richard, Dawn Ades and Michael Cary, *Francis Bacon: The First Pope* (Gagosian, London, 2022)

Calvocoressi, Richard, *Friends and Relations: Lucian Freud, Francis Bacon, Frank Auerbach, Michael Andrews* (Gagosian, London, 2023)

Cappock, Margarita, *Francis Bacon's Studio* (Merrell Publishers, London, 2005)

Cary, Michael (ed.), *Francis Bacon: Late Paintings* (Gagosian, New York, 2015)

Davies, Hugh and Sally Yard, *Francis Bacon* (Abbeville Press, New York, 1986)

Davies, Hugh, *Francis Bacon: The Papal Portraits of 1953* (Distributed Art Publishers, New York, 2001; Lund Humphries, London, 2002)

Dawson, Barbara, *Francis Bacon in Dublin* (Hugh Lane Municipal Gallery of Modern Art, Dublin, 2005)

Domino, Christophe, *Francis Bacon: Taking Reality by Surprise* (Thames & Hudson, London, 2010)

Ebner, Florian, *Metamorphosen des Gesichts: Die 'Verwandlungen durch Licht' von Helmar Lerski* (Steidl, Göttingen, 2002)

Eskildsen, Ute and Jan-Christopher Horak, *Helmar Lerski, Lichtbildner* (Museum Folkwang, Essen, 1982)

Farson, Daniel, *The Gilded Gutter Life of Francis Bacon* (Vintage, London, 1994)

Feaver, William, *Freud at the Correr: Fifty Years* (Museo Correr, Venice, 2005)

Feaver, William, *Lucian Freud: Drawings* (Blain|Southern, London, 2012)

Feaver, William, *The Lives of Lucian Freud: Youth 1922–1968* (Bloomsbury Publishing, London, 2019)

Feaver, William, *The Lives of Lucian Freud: Fame 1968–2011* (Bloomsbury Publishing, London, 2020)

Gale, Matthew and Chris Stephens (eds), *Francis Bacon* (Tate, London, 2008)

Gautier, Blaise and Maurice Eschapasse, *Francis Bacon* (Centre national d'art contemporain, Paris, 1972)

Geldzahler, Henry, *Francis Bacon: Recent Paintings 1968–1974* (Metropolitan Museum of Art, New York, 1975)

Gowing, Lawrence and Sam Hunter, *Francis Bacon* (Thames & Hudson, London, and Hirshhorn Museum and Sculpture Garden, Smithsonian Institution, Washington DC, 1989)

Günther, Katharina, *Francis Bacon: In the Mirror of Photography* (De Gruyter, Berlin, 2022)

Hall, James, *The World as Sculpture: The Changing Status of Sculpture from the Renaissance to the Present Day* (Chatto & Windus, London, 1999)

Hall, James, *The Artist's Studio: A Cultural History* (Thames & Hudson, London, 2022)

Hammer, Martin, *Bacon and Sutherland* (Yale University Press, New Haven and London, 2005)

Harrison, Martin, *In Camera: Francis Bacon, Photography, Film and the Practice of Painting* (The Estate of Francis Bacon Publishing/ Thames & Hudson, London, 2005)

Harrison, Martin (ed.), *Francis Bacon – New Studies: Centenary Essays* (Steidl, Göttingen, 2009)

Harrison, Martin and Rebecca Daniels, *Francis Bacon: Catalogue Raisonné*, 5 vols (The Estate of Francis Bacon Publishing, London, 2016)

Harrison, Martin (ed.), *Inside Francis Bacon: Francis Bacon Studies III* (The Estate of Francis Bacon Publishing, London, 2020)

Harrison, Martin (ed.), *Francis Bacon: Shadows, Francis Bacon Studies IV* (The Estate of Francis Bacon Publishing, London, 2021)

Harrison, Martin (ed.), *Bacon Review, 1* (The Estate of Francis Bacon Publishing, London, 2023)

Harrison, Martin and Sophie Pretorius, *Revisions: Francis Bacon in the Act of Painting* (The Estate of Francis Bacon Publishing, London, 2024)

Hoban, Phoebe, *Lucian Freud: Eyes Wide Open* (Amazon Publishing, Seattle, 2017)

Hooper, Steven (ed.), *Robert and Lisa Sainsbury Collection*, vol.I (Yale University Press, New Haven, 1997)

Howgate, Sarah (ed.), *Lucian Freud: Portraits* (National Portrait Gallery Publications, London, 2012)

Jacobi, Carol, *Out of the Cage: The Art of Isabel Rawsthorne* (EFB Publishing and Thames & Hudson, London, 2021)

Johnson, Heather, *Roy de Maistre: The English Years 1930–1968* (Craftsman House, Roseville, 1988)

Kemp, Martin (ed.), *Leonardo on Painting* (Yale University Press, New Haven, 1989)

Lewinski, Jorge, *Portrait of the Artist: 25 Years of British Art* (Carcanet Press, Manchester, 1987)

Liberman, Alexander, *The Artist in His Studio* (Penguin, London, 1960)

Mellor, David, *Reflected Glory: Photographs by Douglas Glass* (Rye Art Gallery/South East Arts Association, Rye, 1978)

Moraes, Henrietta, *Henrietta* (Penguin, London, 1994)

Muir, Robin, *John Deakin: Photographs* (Vendome Press, Palm Beach, 1997)

Muir, Robin, *A Maverick Eye: The Street Photography of John Deakin* (Thames & Hudson, London, 2002)

Muir, Robin, *Gods and Monsters: John Deakin's Portraits of British Artists* (Pallant House Gallery, Chichester, 2010)

Murger, Henry, *Bohemians of the Latin Quarter* (Vizetelly & Co., London, 1888)

Ogden, Perry and John Edwards, *7 Reece Mews: Francis Bacon's Studio* (Thames & Hudson, London, 2001)

Ordovas, Pilar (ed.), *Irrational Marks: Bacon and Rembrandt* (Ordovas, London and New York, 2011)

Ordovas, Pilar (ed.), *Bacon's Women,* (Ordovas, London and New York, 2018)

Penrose, Roland, *Picasso: His Life and Work* (Penguin, Harmondsworth, 1971)

Peppiatt, Michael, *Francis Bacon: Anatomy of an Enigma* (Weidenfeld & Nicolson, London, 1996; Constable, London, 2008)

Peppiatt, Michael, *Francis Bacon in the 1950s* (Yale University Press, New Haven, 2006)

Peppiatt, Michael, *Francis Bacon: Studies for a Portrait* (Thames & Hudson, London, 2021)

Peppiatt, Michael, *Francis Bacon: Man and Beast* (Royal Academy, London, 2022)

Rosenfield, John and Charles Saumarez Smith, *Clare Shenstone: Anima* (Kokon Inc., New York, 2005)

Rothenstein, John, *Matthew Smith: Paintings from 1909 to 1952* (Tate, London, 1953)

Rothenstein, John, *Francis Bacon* (Tate, London, 1962)

Rothenstein, John and Ronald Alley, *Francis Bacon* (Thames & Hudson, London, 1964)

Russell, Joanna, Brian Singer, Justin Perry and Anne Bacon, 'The materials and techniques used in the paintings of Francis Bacon (1909–1992)', *Studies in Conservation*, vol.57, no.4, 2012

Russell, John, *Francis Bacon* (Thames & Hudson, London, 1971)

Russell, John, *Lucian Freud* (The Arts Council, London, 1974)

Salter, Gregory, *Art and Masculinity in Post-War Britain: Reconstructing Home* (Routledge, London, 2020)

Seipel, Wilfried, Barbara Steffen and Christoph Vitali, *Francis Bacon and the Tradition of Art* (Skira, Milan, 2003)

Stevens, Mark and Annalyn Swan, *Francis Bacon: Revelations* (William Collins, London, 2021)

Sylvester, David, *Interviews with Francis Bacon 1962–1979* (Thames & Hudson, London, 1980; 1981; 1987)

Sylvester, David, *Francis Bacon: The Human Body* (Hayward Gallery, London, and University of California Press, Berkeley, 1998)

Sylvester, David, *Trapping Appearance* (Sainsbury Centre for Visual Arts, Norwich, 1996)

Sylvester, David, *Looking Back at Francis Bacon* (Thames & Hudson, London, 2022)

Van Alphen, Ernst, *Francis Bacon and the Loss of Self* (Reaktion Books, London, 1992)

Warburton, Nigel (ed.), *Bill Brandt: Camera in London* (Clio Press, London, 1993)

Zola, Émile, *Mes Haines; causeries littéraires et artistiques* (Achille Faure, Paris, 1866)

Exhibition Works

1   Arts Council Collection, Southbank Centre, London. © The Estate of Francis Bacon. All rights reserved, DACS / Artimage 2024. Photo: Prudence Cuming Associates Ltd

2   Museum of Contemporary Art Chicago. Gift of Joseph and Jory Shapiro, 1976.44. © The Estate of Francis Bacon. All rights reserved, DACS / Artimage 2024. Photo: Prudence Cuming Associates Ltd

3   Tate. Bequeathed by Simon Sainsbury 2006, accessioned 2008. © The Estate of Francis Bacon. All rights reserved, DACS / Artimage 2024. Photo: Prudence Cuming Associates Ltd

4   The Whitworth, The University of Manchester. © The Estate of Francis Bacon. All rights reserved, DACS / Artimage 2024. Photo: Prudence Cuming Associates Ltd

5   The Phillips Collection, Washington DC. © The Estate of Francis Bacon. All rights reserved, DACS / Artimage 2024. Photo: Prudence Cuming Associates Ltd

6   Collection Museum Boijmans Van Beuningen, Rotterdam. © The Estate of Francis Bacon. All rights reserved, DACS / Artimage 2024. Photo: Prudence Cuming Associates Ltd

7   Private Collection. © The Estate of Francis Bacon. All rights reserved, DACS / Artimage 2024. Photo: Prudence Cuming Associates Ltd

8   Tate. Purchased 1979. © The Estate of Francis Bacon. All rights reserved, DACS / Artimage 2024. Photo: Prudence Cuming Associates Ltd

9   Seattle Art Museum. Gift of the Friday Foundation in honour of Richard E. Lang and Jane Lang Davis, 2020.14.6. All rights reserved, DACS / Artimage 2024. Photo: Philipp Scholz Rittermann

10   Private Collection, UK. © The Estate of Francis Bacon. All rights reserved, DACS / Artimage 2024. Photo: Prudence Cuming Associates Ltd

11   c/o Cingilli Collection. © The Estate of Francis Bacon. All rights reserved, DACS / Artimage 2024. Photo: Sotheby's

12   San Francisco Museum of Modern Art. Gift of Helen and Charles Schwab in honour of Neal Benezra's leadership and dedication to SFMOMA. © The Estate of Francis Bacon. All rights reserved, DACS / Artimage 2024. Photo: Prudence Cuming Associates Ltd

13   Tate. Presented by the Contemporary Art Society 1958. © The Estate of Francis Bacon. All rights reserved, DACS 2024. Photo: Tate

14   Arts Council Collection, Southbank Centre, London. © The Estate of Francis Bacon. All rights reserved, DACS / Artimage 2024. Photo: Hugo Maertens

15   Private Collection. © The Estate of Francis Bacon. All rights reserved, DACS / Artimage 2024. Photo: Prudence Cuming Associates Ltd

16   Gothenburg Museum of Art, Sweden. © The Estate of Francis Bacon. All rights reserved, DACS / Artimage 2024. Photo: Prudence Cuming Associates Ltd

17   Private Collection. © The Estate of Francis Bacon. All rights reserved, DACS / Artimage 2024. Photo: Prudence Cuming Associates Ltd

18   Private Collection, Europe. © The Estate of Francis Bacon. All rights reserved, DACS / Artimage 2024. Photo: Elke Walford

19   Sainsbury Centre, University of East Anglia. © The Estate of Francis Bacon. All rights reserved, DACS / Artimage 2024. Photo: Prudence Cuming Associates Ltd

20   Private Collection ABG. © The Estate of Francis Bacon. All rights reserved, DACS / Artimage 2024

21   Amgueddfa Cymru – Museum Wales. © The Estate of Francis Bacon. All rights reserved, DACS / Artimage 2024. Photo: Prudence Cuming Associates Ltd

22   Ömer Koç Collection. © The Estate of Francis Bacon. All rights reserved, DACS / Artimage 2024. Photo: Prudence Cuming Associates Ltd

23   The Lewis Collection. © The Estate of Francis Bacon. All rights reserved, DACS / Artimage 2024. Photo: Todd-White Art Photography

24   Private Collection. © The Estate of Francis Bacon. All rights reserved, DACS / Artimage 2024. Photo: Prudence Cuming Associates Ltd

25   Private Collection. © The Estate of Francis Bacon. All rights reserved, DACS / Artimage 2024. Photo: Prudence Cuming Associates Ltd

26   The Lewis Collection. © The Estate of Francis Bacon. All rights reserved, DACS / Artimage 2024. Photo: Prudence Cuming Associates Ltd

27   Private Collection. Courtesy Skarstedt, NY. © The Estate of Francis Bacon. All rights reserved, DACS / Artimage 2024. Photo: Prudence Cuming Associates Ltd

28   Private Collection. © The Estate of Francis Bacon. All rights reserved, DACS / Artimage 2024. Photo: Prudence Cuming Associates Ltd

29   Städel Museum, Frankfurt am Main. On permanent loan from

Francis Bacon: Human Presence

Fig.1 Courtesy of the Sam Hunter
Estate & Archive and Francis
Bacon MB Art Foundation / MB
Art Collection. © The Estate of
Sam Hunter
Fig.2 Courtesy Francis Bacon MB
Art Foundation / MB Art
Collection.© Francis Julian
Gutmann
Fig.3 Galleria Doria Pamphij,
Rome, Italy. © Bridgeman Images
Fig.4 Courtesy of the Sam Hunter
Estate & Archive and Francis
Bacon MB Art Foundation /
MB Art Collection. © Sam
Hunter. Source clipping
© The Estate of Francis Bacon
2024. All rights reserved
Fig.5 National Portrait Gallery,
London, x135767. © National
Portrait Gallery, London
Fig.6 Previously held at the Kaiser
Friedrich Museum in Berlin,
destroyed by fire in May 1945.
© Bridgeman Images
Fig.7 Musée Granet, Aix-en-
Provence. © Claude
Almodovar / Musée Granet,
Aix-en-Provence
Fig.8 National Portrait Gallery,
London, x68941. © Luke Kelly
Fig.9 (exhibited work): Esther
Grether Family Collection.
© The Estate of Francis
Bacon. All rights reserved,
DACS / Artimage 2024.
Photo: Prudence Cuming
Associates Ltd

**Francis Bacon: Painting in
the Era of the Photograph**

Fig.1 Tate. Purchased 1950. © The
Estate of Francis Bacon. All rights
reserved, DACS 2024
Fig.2 Hugh Lane Gallery, Dublin.
© The Estate of Francis Bacon.
All rights reserved, DACS 2024.
Image © Hugh Lane Gallery,
Dublin
Fig.3 Courtesy of The Museum of
Modern Art, New York

**Francis Bacon's Close-Up Heads:
An Overlooked Source**

Fig.1 Courtesy Francis Bacon
MB Art Foundation / MB Art
Collection. © Estate Helmar
Lerski, Museum Folkwang, Essen,
2024.
Fig.2 Museum Folkwang, Essen.
© Estate Helmar Lerski, Museum
Folkwang, Essen, 2024
Fig.3 Museum Folkwang, Essen.
© Estate Helmar Lerski, Museum
Folkwang, Essen, 2024
Fig.4 Dyk Rudenski, *Gestologie und
Filmspielerei*, Hoboken-Presse,
Berlin, 1927
Fig.5 Museum Folkwang, Essen.
© Estate Helmar Lerski, Museum
Folkwang, Essen, 2024
Fig.6 The Metropolitan Museum of
Art, New York. Jacques and
Natasha Gelman Collection,
1998. © The Estate of Francis
Bacon. All rights reserved,
DACS / Artimage 2024. Photo:
Prudence Cuming Associates Ltd

**Queer Attachments
to Francis Bacon**

Fig.1 Hamburger Kunsthalle,
Hamburg. © The Estate of Francis
Bacon. © The Estate of Francis
Bacon. All rights reserved,
DACS / Artimage 2024. Photo:
Prudence Cuming Associates Ltd
Fig.2 Private Collection. © The
Estate of Francis Bacon. © The
Estate of Francis Bacon. All rights
reserved, DACS / Artimage 2024.
Photo: Prudence Cuming
Associates Ltd

**Lucian Freud & Francis Bacon:
A Friendship of Two Halves**

Fig.1 Private Collection. © The
Lucian Freud Archive. All Rights
Reserved 2024/Bridgeman Images
Fig.2 National Portrait Gallery,
London, x135768. © National
Portrait Gallery, London

Fig.3 © David Dawson. All rights
reserved 2024 / Bridgeman
Images
Fig.4 National Portrait Gallery,
London, LMF/1/47/2. © The
Lucian Freud Archive. All Rights
Reserved 2024

**Corners of Filth & Fantasy:
Bacon's Studios as
Self-Expression**

Fig.1 National Portrait Gallery,
London, x40009. © Cecil Beaton
Archive / Condé Nast
Fig.2 Private Collection. © The
Estate of Roy de Maistre. Photo
© 2024 Christie's Images Limited
Fig.3 Tate. Bequeathed by Lord
Amulree 1984. © Succession H.
Matisse / DACS 2024. Photo: Tate
Fig.4 Private Collection. © The
Estate of Francis Bacon. All rights
reserved, DACS / Artimage 2024.
Photo: Prudence Cuming
Associates Ltd
Fig.5 Rijksmuseum, Amsterdam.
© Rijksmuseum, Amsterdam

**Study from a Human Body:
Francis Bacon & Medical
Self-Portraiture**

Fig.1 National Gallery of Victoria,
Melbourne. © The Estate of
Francis Bacon. All rights reserved,
DACS / Artimage 2024. Photo:
Prudence Cuming Associates Ltd
Fig.2 Dublin City Gallery, The
Hugh Lane. © The Estate of
Francis Bacon. All rights reserved,
DACS 2024
Fig.3 Fondation Beyeler,
Riehen / Basel, Beyeler
Collection. © The Estate of
Francis Bacon. All rights reserved,
DACS 2024
Fig.4 Private Collection. © The
Estate of Francis Bacon. All rights
reserved, DACS 2024
Fig.5 Private Collection. © The
Estate of Francis Bacon. All rights
reserved, DACS 2024

Fig.6   Private Collection. © The Estate of Francis Bacon. All rights reserved, DACS 2024

Fig.7   Private Collection. © The Estate of Francis Bacon. All rights reserved, DACS 2024

Fig.8   The Estate of Francis Bacon. © The Estate of Francis Bacon. All rights reserved. DACS 2024

Friends & Lovers

p.106   Sainsbury Centre, University of East Anglia. Bequeathed by Lady Sainsbury, 2014. Photograph by Snowdon / Trunk Archive

p.112   Hugh Lane Gallery, Dublin. © The Estate of Francis Bacon. All rights reserved, DACS 2024. Image © Hugh Lane Gallery, Dublin. Photo: John Deakin

p.122   Hugh Lane Gallery, Dublin. © The Estate of Francis Bacon. All rights reserved, DACS 2024. Image © Hugh Lane Gallery, Dublin. Photo: John Deakin

p.128   Hugh Lane Gallery, Dublin. © The Estate of Francis Bacon. All rights reserved, DACS 2024. Image © Hugh Lane Gallery, Dublin. Photo: John Deakin

p.136   Hugh Lane Gallery, Dublin. © The Estate of Francis Bacon. All rights reserved, DACS 2024. Image © Hugh Lane Gallery, Dublin. Photo: John Deakin

p.146   Hugh Lane Gallery, Dublin. © The Estate of Francis Bacon. All rights reserved, DACS / Artimage 2024. Photo: John Deakin

p.154   Hugh Lane Gallery, Dublin. © The Estate of Francis Bacon. All rights reserved, DACS 2024. Image © Hugh Lane Gallery, Dublin. Photo: John Deakin

p.164   Hugh Lane Gallery, Dublin. © The Estate of Francis Bacon. All rights reserved, DACS 2024. Image © Hugh Lane Gallery, Dublin

'I've decided to paint a few of my friends': Isabel Rawsthorne & Henrietta Moraes

Fig.1   Private Collection. © The Estate of Francis Bacon. All rights reserved, DACS / Artimage 2024. Photo: Prudence Cuming Associates Ltd

Fig.2   Musée Granet-Aix-en-Provence. © The Estate of Alberto Giacometti. DACS 2024. Photo: Franck Legros / Alamy Stock

Fig.3   Private Collection. © The Estate of Francis Bacon. All rights reserved, DACS / Artimage 2024. Photo: Prudence Cuming Associates Ltd

Ghosts in the Glass: Filming Francis Bacon

Fig.1   The British Film Institute. © BFI / Courtesy of the BFI National Archive

Fig.2   National Portrait Gallery, London, x199729. © The Estate of David Cripps / DACS, 2024

Fig.3   ITV Archive. © ITV / Shutterstock

Fig.4   The British Film Institute. © BFI / Courtesy of the BFI National Archive

Fig.5   The British Film Institute. © BFI / Courtesy of the BFI National Archive

Picturing the Artist: Camera Portraits of Francis Bacon

Fig.1   Courtesy Francis Bacon MB Art Foundation / MB Art Collection. © The Estate of Francis Bacon. Photo: John Deakin

Fig.2   National Portrait Gallery, London, x40008. © Cecil Beaton Archive / Condé Nast

Fig.3   © J.C.C. Glass, 2024

Fig.4   National Portrait Gallery, London, P587. © 1963 Condé Nast Publications Inc.

Fig.5   National Portrait Gallery, London, x22403. © Bill Brandt Archive

Fig.6   National Portrait Gallery, London, x13707. © The Lewinski Archive at Chatsworth / Bridgeman Images

Fig.7   National Portrait Gallery, 6827. © Peter Gidal

Fig.8   National Portrait Gallery, London, x138805. © Mayotte Magnus / National Portrait Gallery, London

Fig.9   Courtesy Francis Bacon MB Art Foundation / MB Art Collection. © Peter Stark

Fig.10   Courtesy of the Artist. © Clare Shenstone

Fig.11   National Portrait Gallery, London, x199965. © The Guy Bourdin Estate 2024 / Courtesy of Louise Alexander Gallery

Fig.12   National Portrait Gallery, London, P760. © Neil Libbert

Contributors

Georgia Atienza is Assistant Curator, Photography, at the National Portrait Gallery, London. She has contributed to publications including *Taylor Wessing Photo Portrait Prize 2023* (2023), *Women at Work: 1900 to Now* (2023), *Yevonde: Life and Colour* (2023), *Love Stories: Art, Passion & Tragedy* (2020) and *Ida Kar: Bohemian Photographer* (2011).

Tanya Bentley is Curator, Contemporary, at the National Portrait Gallery, London. She has contributed to publications including *Herbert Smith Freehills Portrait Award 2024* (2024), *Icons & Identities* (2021), *Tacita Dean: Landscape, Portrait, Still Life* (2018) and *Gillian Wearing and Claude Cahun: Behind the mask, another mask* (2017). Her essay 'Lucian Freud's Sketchbooks' was published in *Burlington Contemporary Journal* in 2023.

Rosie Broadley is Head of Collections Displays (Victorian to Contemporary) and Senior Curator, 20th-Century Collections at the National Portrait Gallery, London. She has curated numerous displays and exhibitions including *Paul McCartney Photographs 1963–1964: Eyes of the Storm* (2023) and has contributed to publications including *BP Portrait Award 2018* (2018), *Suffrage and the Arts: Visual Culture, Politics and Enterprise* (2018) and *Laura Knight Portraits* (2013).

Richard Calvocoressi is a scholar and art historian. He has served as a curator at Tate, London, director of the Scottish National Gallery of Modern Art, Edinburgh, and director of the Henry Moore Foundation. In 2015, Calvocoressi joined Gagosian. His publications include *Lucian Freud on Paper* (2008), *Francis Bacon/Henry Moore: Flesh and Bone* (2013, with Martin Harrison), *Anselm Kiefer: Morgenthau Plan* (2013) and *Georg Baselitz* (2021).

James Hall is an art critic and historian, currently Research Professor at the University of Southampton. His books include *The World as Sculpture* (1999), *Michelangelo and the Reinvention of the Human Body* (2005), *The Sinister Side: How Left-Right Symbolism Shaped Western Art* (2008) and *The Artist's Studio: a Cultural History* (2022). *The Self-Portrait: A Cultural History* (2014) has been translated into five languages; an abridged version, *James Hall on the Self-Portrait* (2024), was issued as a 'timeless' text to mark Thames & Hudson's 75th anniversary. His essays have appeared in *Burlington Magazine*, *Oxford Art Journal*, *Simiolus* and *Times Literary Supplement*.

Martin Harrison is one of the foremost scholars of Francis Bacon, and the editor of *Francis Bacon: Catalogue Raisonné* (2016). His first publication on Bacon was *Points of Reference* (1999), while other titles include *In Camera: Francis Bacon* (2005) and *Francis Bacon: Incunabula* (2008). In 2009, he edited *Francis Bacon – New Studies: Centenary Essays*. He co-curated an exhibition of Bacon's work at Kunstsammlung Nordrhein-Westfalen, Dusseldorf, in 2006, and *Francis Bacon/Henry Moore: Flesh and Bone* at the Ashmolean Museum, Oxford, in 2013. He is editor of the series *Francis Bacon Studies* (2019 to date).

Carol Jacobi has taught, written and broadcast widely on 19th- and 20th-century art and is a Curator of British Art at Tate Britain. Recent displays include *Van Gogh and Britain* (2019), *Bill Brandt, Inside the Mirror* (2022) and *Alberto Giacometti and Isabel Rawsthorne, a conversation* (2022). She has lectured and published on Bacon, Rawsthorne, Giacometti and their circle for several decades, including the monograph *Out of the Cage: The Art of Isabel Rawsthorne* (2021), and essays for *Derain, Balthus, Giacometti, Une amitié artistique* (2017), *Francis Bacon: Paris, Monaco and the Cote d'Azur* (2016) and the award-winning *British Art in the Nuclear Age* (2014).

John Maybury is an award-winning British filmmaker. During the 1980s, he was a leading figure in the British underground film movement. In 1998, he produced his first full-length feature, *Love Is the Devil: Study for a Portrait of Francis Bacon*, a biopic of the artist's life, which achieved success at the Cannes Film Festival. In 2005, the *Independent on Sunday* included Maybury on their list of the 100 most influential LGBTQ+ people in Britain.

Sophie Pretorius is the archivist of The Estate of Francis Bacon collection. She has written and published numerous essays and articles on Bacon, and has transcribed all his surviving medical records. Pretorius has contributed essays to: *Wild Life: Francis Bacon and Peter Beard* (2021), *Francis Bacon: Shadows, Francis Bacon Studies IV* (2021) and *Inside Francis Bacon: Francis Bacon Studies III* (2020).

Gregory Salter is Associate Professor of History of Art at the University of Birmingham, who specialises in British art after 1945, with a focus on histories of gender, sexuality, migrations and the home. He has contributed essays to *Derek Boshier: Reinventor* (2023), *Lucian Freud: New Perspectives* (2022), *Postwar Modern: New Art in Britain 1945–65* (2022), *David Hockney: Moving Focus* (2021) and *All Too Human: Bacon, Freud and a Century of Painting Life* (2018). In 2019, Salter published *Art and Masculinity in Post-war Britain: Reconstructing Home*.

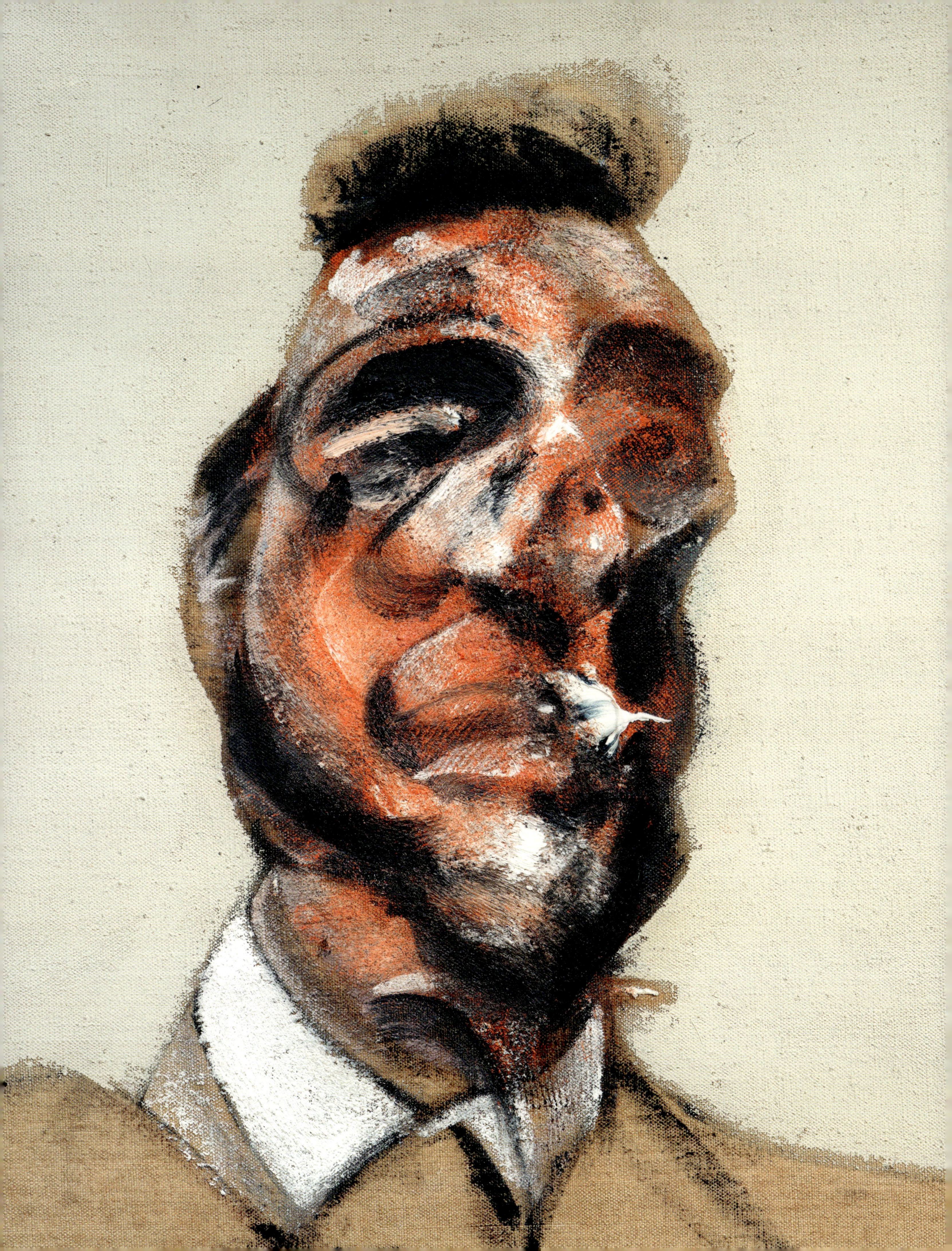

Amgueddfa Cymru – Museum Wales
Arts Council Collection, Southbank Centre, London
Cingilli Collection
The Estate of Francis Bacon
Fondation Beyeler, Riehen, Basel
Francis Bacon MB Art Foundation, Monaco
Peter Gidal
Gothenburg Museum of Art
Mr and Mrs Allan Green
Hugh Lane Gallery, Dublin
Lambrecht-Schadeberg Collection, Germany
Moderna Museet, Stockholm
Musée Granet, Aix-en-Provence
Museo Nacional Thyssen-Bornemisza, Madrid
Museum Boijmans Van Beuningen, Rotterdam
Museum of Contemporary Art, Chicago
Museum of Contemporary Art, Siegen
Museum of Modern Art, New York
National Portrait Gallery, London
Neue Nationalgalerie, Berlin
Ömer Koç Collection
The Phillips Collection, Washington
Private Collection, Europe
Private Collection, Courtesy Skarstedt, New York
Private Collection, New York
Private Collection, Switzerland
Private Collection, UK
Private Collection, USA
Dr Michael Reisen-Hall
Sainsbury Centre, University of East Anglia
San Francisco Museum of Modern Art
Seattle Art Museum
Städel Museum, Frankfurt
Tate
Whitworth Art Gallery, Manchester
YAGEO Foundation Collection, Taiwan

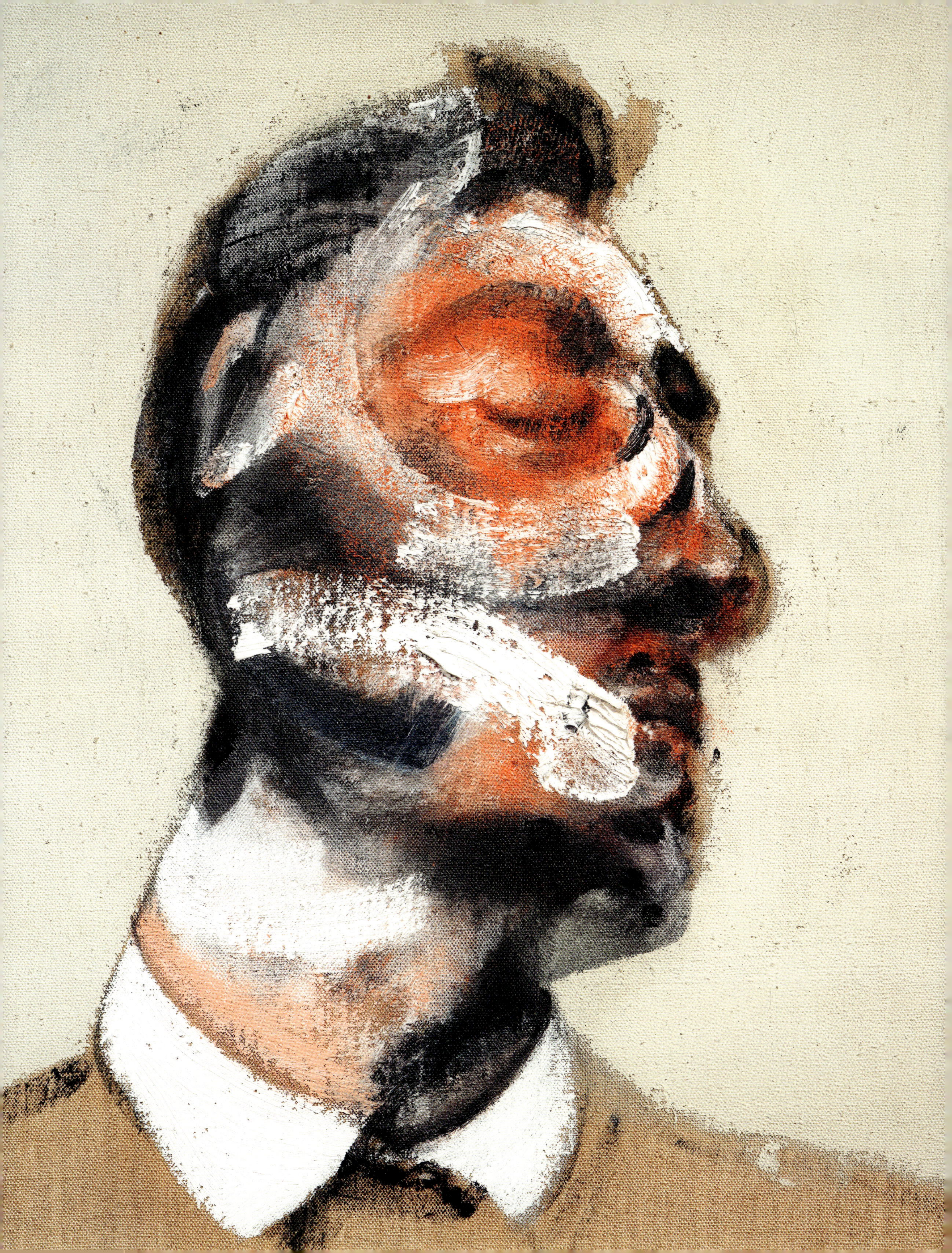

Director's Acknowledgements

It is with great pride that we are presenting the National Portrait Gallery's first, and long overdue, exhibition of Francis Bacon's work. Exhibiting the portraits of this remarkable artist has been a goal of the Gallery for many years, and I am thrilled to be doing so within our new, revitalised setting, following our reopening in the summer of 2023.

This achievement would not have been possible without the vision and hard work of Rosie Broadley, to whom I extend my sincere thanks and congratulations, nor without the invaluable support and generosity of Martin Harrison and The Estate of Francis Bacon, Hugh Lane Gallery in Dublin, the Francis Bacon MB Art Foundation in Monaco, and the exhibition's many lenders, both named and private. My thanks are also given to the Huo Family Foundation, who have supported the exhibition.

We are hugely indebted to those who supported us in locating and securing loans, and I am extremely grateful for the support of our touring partner, the Fondation Pierre Gianadda in Martigny, Switzerland, and in particular the late Léonard Gianadda, the Fondation's founding President.

In addition, I would like to acknowledge others who have significantly contributed to the exhibition's success. My thanks go to the internal project team for their hard work and dedication: Rosie Wilson, Director of Programmes and Partnerships; Eloise Stewart, Head of Exhibitions; Ulrike Wachsmann, Exhibitions Manager; Sarah Morris, Exhibitions Officer; Curators Tanya Bentley and Georgia Atienza for their dedicated curatorial support; Jude Simmons, Head of Design; Adriana Ferlauto, Senior Designer; and Andrea Easey, Interpretation Manager.

Many colleagues have contributed to the staging and success of the exhibition and its accompanying programme. I am grateful to Liz Smith, Director of Learning and Engagement, and all her team for their thoughtful and engaging Learning and Events Programme. I would like to thank our Development and Communications Teams led by Sarah Hilliam, Director of Development, and Denise Vogelsang, Director of Audiences and Communications, including Poppy Andrews, Senior Communications Manager, Sophie Colley, Digital Communications Manager, Chloe Jamieson, Corporate Development Manager, Georgia Perkins, Philanthropy Manager, Anna Pharoah, Senior Fundraising Manager, Eleanor Shakeshaft, Head of Individual Giving and Saoirse Walsh, Senior Marketing Manager. I am grateful to Melanie Pilbrow, Head of International Programmes, and Pauline Velge, International Partnerships Manager. The exhibition would also not have been possible without the expertise of the Art Handling and Conservation Teams, and the ongoing support of Chief Curator Alison Smith.

I would like to thank Anna Starling, Director of Commercial and Operations, Kara Green, Senior Publishing Manager, Priti Kothary, Production Manager, Tom Love, Project Editor, Jemma Jacobs, Publishing Assistant, Mark Lynch, Picture Library Manager, and Katie Anderson, Picture Researcher, for their collaboration and creativity in producing this catalogue. Its beautiful design is testament to the skill and care of Luke Hall, Izi Thexton and Jason Wolfe of Wolfe Hall, to whom I extend my sincere thanks.

I am grateful also to the writers who have contributed fascinating essays to this catalogue: Georgia Atienza, Tanya Bentley, Richard Calvocoressi, James Hall, Martin Harrison, Carol Jacobi, John Maybury, Sophie Pretorius and Gregory Salter.

**Dr Nicholas Cullinan OBE
Director, National Portrait Gallery**

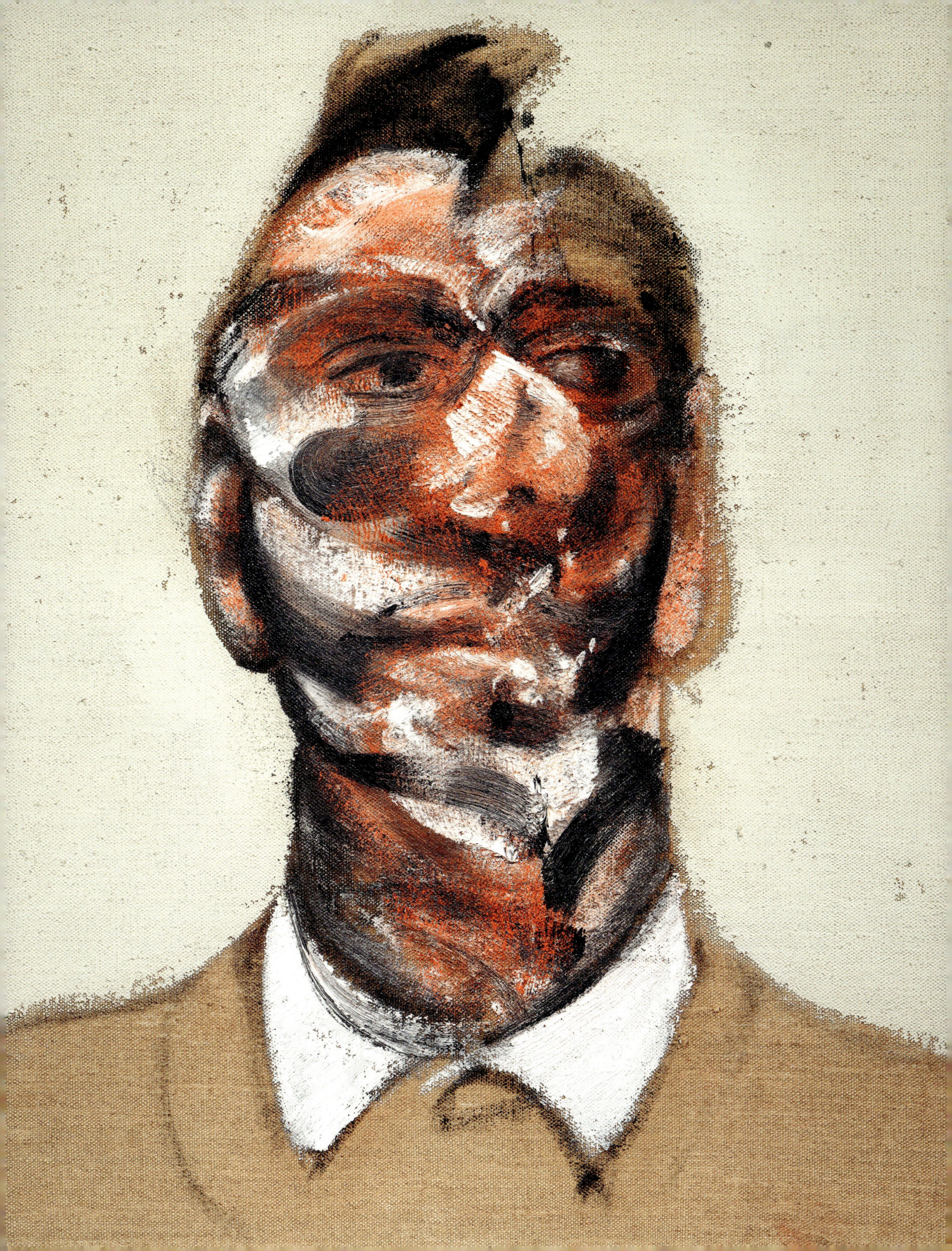

Curator's Acknowledgements

Any curator working on an exhibition of work by Francis Bacon must navigate the vast body of literature, written during his lifetime and after. An indispensable resource in my task has been the magisterial five-volume *Catalogue Raisonné*, published in 2016 and edited by Martin Harrison, through which the development of Bacon's portraiture can be mapped with clarity. I am hugely indebted to Harrison for his perceptive commentary on the artist's work through that publication, and in other works, including *In Camera*, the pioneering study of Bacon's uses of photography and film. I am delighted that he has also contributed to this publication on that very subject.

The starting point for all Bacon scholarship is the series of interviews he undertook with his friend, the critic David Sylvester, which remain startlingly immediate and relevant in thinking about his practice and motivations. In these, he spoke a great deal about the importance of figuration and portraiture, but very little about his sitters. In considering how portraiture manifests the complexities of Bacon's relationships and intimacies, I have found invaluable both Michael Peppiatt's accounts of his conversations with Bacon, and the artist's most recent biography, *Francis Bacon: Revelations*, by Mark Stevens and Annalyn Swan. Furthermore, recent scholarship on Bacon's sitters, particularly women, most notably Carol Jacobi's *Out of the Cage: The Art of Isabel Rawsthorne*, has ensured that the dialogue between Bacon and those who sat for him can now be far better represented. I am delighted that Jacobi has contributed to this publication with an essay on Bacon's women sitters.

The last major exhibition of Bacon's portraits, at the Scottish National Gallery of Modern Art in 2005, set the standard for exhibitions on this aspect of Bacon's *oeuvre*, and I am indebted to its curator, Richard Calvocoressi, for his advice in developing our exhibition in 2024. Catalogue essays by Calvocoressi and Martin Hammer for that show have been foundational texts in developing this exhibition, and Calvocoressi has contributed to this publication an essay on the influence of early film on Bacon's portraits.

I am enormously grateful to the support we have received from Elizabeth Beatty, Ben Harrison and Sophie Pretorius at The Estate of Francis Bacon, without whom this exhibition would not be possible, and I am so pleased that Pretorius has contributed an essay on Bacon's medical portraits to this publication. For *Francis Bacon: Human Presence* we have sought a variety of perspectives across a range of disciplines on his portraits, life and influence: in addition to those already mentioned, we have art historian Dr Gregory Salter writing on queer perspectives of Bacon, historian James Hall on the mythology of Bacon's studio, and filmmaker John Maybury on his experience of writing and directing the groundbreaking film about Bacon, *Love is the Devil*. These contributions enrich this publication hugely.

I am also indebted to my colleagues Tanya Bentley, Contemporary Curator, and Georgia Atienza, Assistant Curator, Photography, at the National Portrait Gallery, who have supported on research and in shaping this exhibition. Bentley has brought to the project not only her insight and eye for detail, but also the breadth of her research around Lucian Freud, one of Bacon's key sitters, gained as project curator for the Gallery's Lucian Freud Archive. She has provided an essay for this publication on Bacon and Freud's important personal and artistic relationship, in addition to individual biographies for each sitter. Atienza has selected important photographic portraits of Bacon from the Gallery's Collection and from the collections at Hugh Lane Gallery in Dublin and the Francis Bacon MB Art Foundation in Monaco, which provide a compelling visual biography. She has written about the portraits, the photographers and the circumstances of many of these portraits in this publication.

The exhibition also includes photographic representations of the sitters themselves – particularly those taken by John Deakin and held at the Hugh Lane Gallery as part of Francis Bacon's Studio Archive – which were crucial sources for many of Bacon's portraits. We are grateful for the time, flexibility and generosity of colleagues Barbara Dawson, Logan Sisley and AnneMarie Saliba, and the conservation team at the Hugh Lane Gallery, custodians of the extraordinary Francis Bacon's Studio, who lent so many unique works to the exhibition. We are incredibly grateful to Majid Boustany and Aurélie Valion of the Francis Bacon MB Art Foundation for their support, expertise, hospitality and generosity; their dedication to Bacon's legacy is inspiring. This exhibition would not be possible without the generosity of lenders, including international public and private collections, not least the Sainsbury Centre in Norwich, which has been particularly generous in lending many key works. Our utmost gratitude is expressed to those who helped us to secure loans, including The Estate of Francis Bacon, Richard Calvocoressi, Melanie Clore, Francis Outred, Per Skarstedt and colleagues at Christies, Sotheby's and Phillips.

I would like to extend particular gratitude to my colleagues in our Exhibitions Team, Ulrike Wachsmann and Sarah Morris, and to Rosie Wilson, for their untiring work and support on this project. Also to Jude Simmons and Adriana Ferlauto for their vision in designing the exhibition.

I extend my thanks to Andrea Easey,
Interpretation Manager, and to
colleagues in the Art Handling
Team, the Conservation Team led by
Stuart Ager, the Development Team
including Chloe Jamieson, Georgia
Perkins and Anna Pharoah, the
Communications Team led by Denise
Vogelsang, including Poppy Andrews,
Sophie Colley and Saoirse Walsh, and
to Ines Alves in the Digital Team and
Ed Simpson in the Retail Team. Also,
on the publication, I extend my thanks
to Katie Anderson in the Rights and
Images Team, and to my wonderful
colleagues in Publications, Tom Love
and Kara Green, for bringing this
catalogue together with such care, and
to the designers Wolfe Hall, who made
a book that showcases the vibrancy,
intensity and variety that characterises
Bacon's portraits.

This exhibition was initiated many
years ago by my colleague and
predecessor Paul Moorhouse, and
I am grateful for his early proposal,
and to Sarah Tinsley, former Director
of Programmes and Partnerships
at the National Portrait Gallery,
for her encouragement in reviving
this idea. I have also benefitted
greatly from the support, enthusiasm
and encouragement of the Gallery's
Director, Dr Nicholas Cullinan.

**Rosie Broadley, Senior Curator,
20th-Century Collections,
National Portrait Gallery**

Published in Great Britain by
National Portrait Gallery Publications
National Portrait Gallery
St Martin's Place
London WC2H 0HE

Published to accompany the
exhibition:

Francis Bacon: Human Presence

National Portrait Gallery, London
10 October 2024 – 19 January 2025

Fondation Pierre Gianadda,
Switzerland
14 February – 8 June 2025

This exhibition has been made
possible as a result of the Government
Indemnity Scheme. The National
Portrait Gallery, London, would
like to thank HM Government
for providing indemnity, and the
Department for Culture, Media
and Sport and Arts Council England
for arranging indemnity.

Every purchase supports the
National Portrait Gallery, London.
For a complete catalogue of current
publications, please visit our website
at www.npg.org.uk/publications

Hardback ISBN 978 1 85514 549 8
Paperback ISBN 978 1 85514 564 1

A catalogue record for this book
is available from the British Library.

10 9 8 7 6 5 4 3 2 1

Director of Commercial and Operations
   Anna Starling
Senior Publishing Manager
   Kara Green
Production Manager
   Priti Kothary
Project Editors
   Tom Love and
   Rosalind Furness
Copy Editor
   Lizzy Silverton, First Pages Ltd
Proofreader
   Patricia Burgess
Picture Rights Clearance
   Katherine Anderson
Publishing Assistant
   Jemma Jacobs

Designed by Wolfe Hall

Printed in the UK by Gomer Press
Origination by Dexter Premedia

Cover
Francis Bacon
Three Studies of Muriel Belcher, 1966
Oil on canvas, 355 × 305mm
Private Collection. © The Estate of
Francis Bacon. All rights reserved,
DACS / Artimage 2024. Photo:
Prudence Cuming Associates Ltd

p.2
Francis Bacon
Self-Portrait, 1973
Oil and dry transfer lettering
on canvas, 1980 × 1475mm
Private Collection. © The Estate of
Francis Bacon. All rights reserved,
DACS / Artimage 2024. Photo:
Prudence Cuming Associates Ltd

p.4
Irving Penn
Francis Bacon (detail), 1962
Platinum palladium print,
321 × 324mm
National Portrait Gallery, London
© 1963 Condé Nast Publications Inc.

p.6
Francis Bacon
*Study for Portrait II (after the Life
Mask of William Blake)*, 1955
Oil on canvas, 610 × 508mm
Tate. © The Estate of Francis Bacon.
All rights reserved, DACS / Artimage
2024. Photo: Prudence Cuming
Associates Ltd

p.9
Peter Stark
Francis Bacon, 1975
Gelatin silver print, 185 × 253mm
National Portrait Gallery, London
© Peter Stark

pp.217, 219 and 221
Francis Bacon
*Three Studies for Portrait of George Dyer
(on light ground)*, 1964
Oil on canvas, 356 × 305mm
Cingilli Collection. © The Estate of
Francis Bacon. All rights reserved,
DACS / Artimage 2024. Photo:
Prudence Cuming Associates Ltd

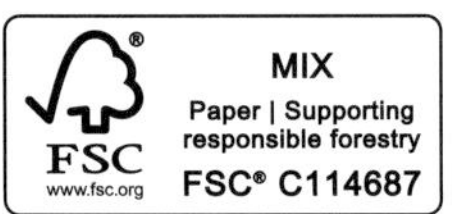

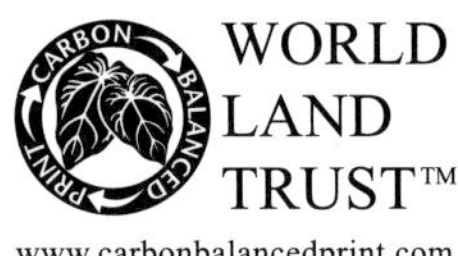